The Literature
of the Anglo-Saxons

1956

F

The Literature
of the Anglo-Saxons

By George K. Anderson

Princeton, New Jersey

Princeton University Press

1949

PRINTED IN THE UNITED STATES OF AMERICA
BY PRINCETON UNIVERSITY PRESS AT PRINCETON, NEW JERSEY

Preface

FOR all who desire to consider the literature written in England before the coming of William the Conqueror, there are always two questions of importance which must be answered satisfactorily. What has survived from those distant times? Where can one look beyond in order to know more than the general outlines of this literature? It has been my object in writing this book to put myself in a position to answer these two questions. In a brief compass, of course, the author of such a book can do no more; if he elects to serve as a sign-post, he can scarcely be expected to act as critic. For during the past fifty years enough has been accomplished in the study of Anglo-Saxon literature alone to make necessary a new Registry of Deeds, a new survey of attainment, insofar as it is possible to achieve our observations solely on the basis of what has been left to posterity by the insensate hand of circumstance.

In attempting such a survey I have avoided any direct treatment of linguistic matters as such, and have therefore referred the reader to the general bibliographies of the English language. I believe that it is high time to look at Old English literature not as a mere repository for the English language in its oldest historical state but as a storehouse, necessarily somewhat inaccessible, of the records, the thoughts and important deeds, of a clearly-defined, vital, and altogether basic period of English literature. Nor have I been interested here in studies of textual matters alone, except where such business may have bearing upon the significance of a given work of Old English literature when it is considered as a whole. Instead, I have tried to describe succinctly such Old English literature as has been left to us and to refer the reader who would know more to the appropriate sources of information, on the theory that literature must always speak for itself, directly to the intelligent reader, and can never be conveyed to him in its fullest implications when it has been predigested and pre-analyzed.

It is true that an account of Anglo-Saxon literature lends itself but poorly to an analysis of the history of ideas in the Old English era. I have endeavored, however, to take into consideration the entire canon of Anglo-Saxon writings, without undue emphasis upon the alleged major works of the period, partly on the assumption that these works have already been studied perhaps too much to do justice to Old English literature as a whole, and partly, no doubt, on the assumption that "all service ranks the same with God."

In following this long and rocky path I have incurred a debt of gratitude to many who have rendered me professional and scholarly aid for which all in my position should daily thank God. These stayers of my feeble sides are too many to name here; but I wish to convey herewith my special thanks to the officers and personnel of the Libraries of Harvard University, Brown University, Yale University, Princeton University, Cornell University, Columbia University, the Huntington Library and the Library of Congress. I have been encouraged greatly by the wise suggestions of Professor Charles W. Kennedy of Princeton University, whose help I appreciate deeply. To my wife, Ethel H. Anderson, whose aid and comfort to me in this task cannot be measured in words, I owe the greatest debt of all.

G. K. A.

Brown University
Providence, R.I.

Contents

Contents

MAPS

The Literature
of the Anglo-Saxons

I · The Anglo-Saxons

1. INVADERS OF BRITAIN

THE story of English literature may be said to begin with the conquest of Britain by Germanic[1] tribes, a conquest which began in the middle of the fifth century and which continued through the succeeding half-dozen generations. Little of the account of these Germanic invasions is anything but legendary; no historical event mentioned in the chronicles of Saxon England can be dated with assurance until the actual conquest was nearly complete. The fact of this Germanic conquest can be accepted, however, without a full knowledge of the details. It is from these fierce, virile bands of Germanic marauders that the Englishman has derived many of his habits of thought, much of his law and his social usage, the larger portion of his ethnic stock, and the entire framework of his language.[2] In spite of the later infusion of new blood, new racial increments, and foreign language-elements, the Englishman has changed surprisingly little in temperament and in philosophical outlook from his ancestors of a thousand years ago. His modern, greatly enlarged horizon has not disturbed the integrity of his racial origins; indeed, we have come to recognize a Germanic heritage in our artistic and moral standards which is often referred to as the Anglo-Saxon tradition.

Yet it is no easy matter to achieve an exact definition of this tradition. Perhaps such a definition might well be less illuminating than a series of diffuse statements. Assuming the existence of this tradition, moreover, one may still raise the question whether it stands as the honest issue of a legitimate national psychology which has become fixed with the passing of many centuries. Or is it instead a kind of lip-service to racial ideals which have long since become outmoded? An individual can hardly presume to judge; far better for him merely to point out the basic strands in the tapestry of Anglo-

Saxon culture and leave the student of English literature to trace for himself the recurrent appearances of those strands from the heroic epic of the eighth century to the immensely varied, sophisticated literature of the twentieth. Then will appear the loyalty to king and state, the love of action and adventure, the moral earnestness implicit in the conservative adherence to an established code of conduct, the grimness at need, the persevering and unimaginative plodding and muddling, the near-fatalistic acceptance of life as a somber fight that must be endured to the setting of the sun—all part and parcel of the English approach to living. Perhaps at certain periods of history these individual threads may be colored more brightly than at others. But the threads are always there for all who desire to see. The Anglo-Saxon bard and scribe have already begun the weaving of the tapestry and the fashioning of the design.

First, however, we must know something of the origins of this effective tapestry-maker and see something of what lay behind his design. His story begins in a dim half-light of history but reaches back into an outer darkness. He is called Saxon, or Anglo-Saxon;[3] and we know that his race is Germanic—a fact which goes to explain many of his physical and spiritual qualities. The particular invaders who participated in the Germanic conquest of Britain, known to us ever since the account of the Venerable Bede written more than twelve hundred years ago,[4] were the Angles, the Saxons, and the Jutes. No doubt there were other small Germanic tribes involved in this conquest somewhere along the road between 450 and 600. The probabilities are particularly strong that the Frisians played a part.[5] But, as is so often the case when one deals with this particular era, there is little definite proof on this point. One is therefore constrained to accept at face value the statement of Bede, which is, after all, much the best detailed account of importance to come down to us from a period near the time of the conquest itself. His statement will be considered at the appropriate time;[6] it is sufficient to remember that the Germanic invaders whom he mentions—the Angles, the Saxons, and the Jutes—constituted a little group of tribes living on the northwestern coast of what is now Germany, on the Danish peninsula, perhaps on the southern tip of what is now Sweden, who, made restless by the pressure of other savage tribes farther east during the course of that great upheaval of European civilizations known as the barbarian migrations, turned westward for new lands to occupy. Their home on the Continent had been along the sea-coast or not far inland, in a region low-lying, damp, swept by severe storms in winter and visited by an all too short and often inclement summer. Behind them was a wooded hinterland which yielded a modicum of arable land; before them was the almighty and ever-present sea. Their restless lives were spent in large measure beside the ocean or on its bosom; they were nomadic by nature, but their roving was chiefly sea-roving. From this wandering by the sea comes the fact that the Angles and Saxons and Jutes in the middle of the fifth century, like their Scandinavian cousins of a somewhat later date, are to be referred to the Viking Age.

They came, then, as Viking invaders of the eastern shores of Britain, which, with their low fenlands and estuaries, have always offered access to an enemy. But these Anglo-Saxons were not the first invaders, even within the short span of recorded history, although they were doubtless the most abiding. It is difficult for us to tell much about this Anglo-Saxon invasion. It is even more difficult to tell much about the advance of the Romans into Britain during the first century. It is impossible for us to gain any clear, detailed knowledge of what took place before the imperial Romans first set foot upon Britain. The much disputed arrival[7] of the Jutes in 449(?) under Hengest and Horsa—the ghostly advance-guard of the multitudes of Anglo-Saxons who pushed into Britain during the next hundred and fifty years—marked at least the third time in history that the foggy isles of Britain had been visited by a successful hostile force.

It is altogether probable, for that matter, that these islands had been invaded much more often than three times, especially since Britain yields evidence of the presence of Neolithic man. But one must be content with historical findings. At least thrice before the Jutes, a foreign people had come and vanquished those who had already settled in the British Isles. The short, dark-skinned Iberians had worked their will with the prehistoric inhabitants of Britain. Of that there is some archaeological evidence but nothing more.[8] (And what of the lost civilization or civilizations which left behind the monoliths of Stonehenge and the Butt of Lewis?) It is clear, moreover, that the Celtic tribes who came to be called the Gaels and Britons had submerged the Iberians, reducing them to the ignominy of bonded villagers whose duty it was to till the soil and tend the livestock of their masters. Next the Romans, from the arrival of their legions in 43 until their departure about 410, did much the same to the Britons, although in a more orderly and paternalistic fashion, as befitted the exponents of significant empire, until the migrating barbarians cracked the great Roman Empire wide open and then feasted upon the particles.

2. THE ROMAN OCCUPATION OF BRITAIN

RELUCTANTLY, for the subject is one of great fascination, we must dismiss the question of the pre-Celtic inhabitants of Britain. Nor did Celtic Britain before the Romans came contribute anything to the story of English literature.[9] Of the Roman occupation of Britain more is known. Nearly all of the written evidence of this occupation, however, is from Roman sources. But the soil of Britain yields much more impartial evidence. The islands of what we now call Great Britain had been fairly well known to Greek geographers;[10] and before them the Phoenician traders knew the land. The tin mines of Britain were famous in the days of the Roman republic; it was only a question of time before the expanding Roman organism would assimilate the whole region. Julius Caesar made some reconnoitering and not very successful expeditions into the island as early as 54 B.C.,[11] but nothing permanent resulted from this adventure. Nearly a century passed, during which Roman culture, through subjugated Gaul, began to permeate southern Britain, which was ruled during much of that time by the famous Cunobeline—Shakespeare's Cymbeline—who appears to have been a friend of Rome. But in 43 Cunobeline seems to have been dead, and the Romans began to push their policy of further colonial expansion, which had been encouraged by the Emperor Claudius. Several legions crossed to what is now the vicinity of Dover, advanced through what is now Kent, and thence up to the Thames. Within four years the Romans had pushed over the lowlands and midlands into the edges of the hills and woodlands of South Wales, modern Derbyshire, and the farther borders of Devonshire. Thenceforth the remains of Rome in Britain speak for themselves of the general success of Roman arms.

It is not for us to follow here the details of the Roman conquest; it suffices to observe that this Roman occupation did much for the island and indirectly had some effect upon the English language.[12] For the masters of the ancient world gave Britain many things it would have taken the Celtic inhabitants years to acquire. As a celebrated example, the Romans gave the island roads which have stood the weight of centuries. We can still trace the course of the Watling Street, the Ermin Street, or the Fosse Way.[13] These roads were mainly for military purposes and served as a means of rapid mobilization and transportation both on attack and on defense; likewise military were the usual fortifications of the Roman towns, and the great walls to the north built by Hadrian and Severus serve as mute reminders of the limits of Roman dominion in the island.[14] Something more intangible than roads and walls, however, was the Roman's important contribution to Britain—he brought law and a definite unity of government, the latter being something which the Celts have usually failed to achieve in centuries when left to themselves.

Not that the Roman did not work to the full the material resources of Britain. As a colonizer he could hardly have done otherwise. But it is questionable to what extent this Roman was suited to the island; how far, as a Mediterranean, could he be happy in northern surroundings? There is no way of knowing what the Roman population in Britain amounted to at any time during the Roman occupation, nor can one be certain as to the actual importance to the Roman government of Britain as a province. As has been said, the Romans worked the island for tin and some other metals,[15] although the British mines soon fell behind those of Spain in productivity and profit for the home government. Lead was also a useful asset of the British Isles, and there is reason to suppose that the mining and exporting of this metal constituted an imperial monopoly. Moreover, the predilections of imperial Rome for luxurious living could be gratified in remote Britain as well as in the mighty metropolis. The Roman baths and villas, which can still be traced in Britain, are excellent specimens; a careful study of the more elaborate of these—for example, those at Bath—will give a most vivid impression of the engineering skill and durability and of the eye for practical beauty which the Roman possessed. It is entirely reasonable to believe that this Roman, with his Italian love of gardens, practiced the art of landscape architecture to an unusual degree; it is unfortunate that archaeology in this case cannot present a clearer picture. Now gardening, mining, and soldiering all demand tools; these tools must, for the sake of usefulness, be made of iron; and therein lies another great contribution which the Roman made to Britain. For although the Celts possessed some knowledge of iron by the time the Romans appeared, it is undoubtedly true that the Romans brought with them a technical mastery of that metal which the Celts had never known.

The Romans probably never thought of Britain as anything more than one of the most remote of their many provinces; yet when the Christian religion began to sweep through the frame of the Roman Empire, the effect was felt even in far-off Britain. The seeds of Christianity were first sown in Britain during the Roman occupation. The name of the first Christian missionary to Britain and the year in which he came to the island will never be known; there are legends of all sorts, particularly those connecting Saint Paul or Joseph of Arimathea with the first conversion in the island. Doubtless there were missionaries from Gaul by the middle of the second century. Tertullian places the first Christians in Britain in the year 208; by 300 the number of Christians in the island had become sufficient to be worthy of note. Indeed, by 314 British bishops appear on the scene; and the first important martyrdom; that of Saint Alban, had taken place a few years before. Later in this century comes the influence of Saint Patrick of Ireland. All things considered, it is most likely that the Christianization of the Roman Britons was carried on by a number of individuals from different parts of the Christian world and over a considerable period of time. The conversion was probably never complete in this Roman-British era, but with the baptism of the Roman emperor Constantine on his death-bed (337), it had become at least official.

3. THE ANGLO-SAXON CONQUEST

IT MUST be remembered that the Romans came not much farther than the present-day boundary between England and Scotland; they did not penetrate into Cornwall or into the more remote mountain fastnesses of Wales; they did not seriously touch Ireland. They seemed content to occupy that part of Britain which is now England. Their activity against the inhabitants of regions lying beyond these frontiers gives every indication of having been strictly of a defensive nature; they did not, in other words, imbue those who dwelt in the extremities of Britain with any great sense of subjection to the Roman Empire. Nor was the Celtic character one to submit easily. Therefore, as the Roman hold upon Britain weakened, the pressure upon the Roman provincial government from un-Romanized Celts steadily increased. Besides, during the last century of the Roman occupation, the appearance of a special military official—the *comes littoris Saxonicae*, or guardian of the Saxon shore[16]—is ample testimony to the presence of Saxon marauders on the eastern coast of the island. For

many decades after the Romans had withdrawn the last of
their legions from Britain (ca. 410), the Romanized Britons
managed to fend off their aggressive and implacable neighbors
who were bearing down upon them—Irish, Scots, and Picts
from the west and north, in addition to Viking Anglo-Saxons
from the east and south—but eventually the crisis became
acute, and Vortigern, probably the best-known Roman-Briton
in that very dark and misty period, invited the help of some
Germanic warriors, headed by Hengest and Horsa.

The names of both of these Germanic chieftains signify
"horse," a fact which for some reason has caused some skepticism in regard to the historicity of their expedition.[17] *Hengest*
appears in the old poetry;[18] *Horsa* is otherwise unknown in
the legendary heroic tradition. Confusion and skepticism, for
that matter, attach themselves also to the old chronicles, not
only to the sober account of Bede but also to the narratives of
The Anglo-Saxon Chronicle[19] and of Gildas,[20] and particularly to the names of the successors of Hengest and Horsa;
but in spite of all this obscurity, there is no very impressive
reason for doubting the essential truth of the ancient story,
although at best it is easy enough for the careful historian to
doubt the essential truth of the statements regarding the entire
fifth century in Britain. Here, if at all, comes the mighty and
yet apparently legendary figure of King Arthur in its ques-
tionably historical frame. Yet Gildas, the only important
chronicler from a date nearly contemporary with Arthur,
makes no mention of him who became the traditional king of
the Knights of the Round Table.[21] Assuming the authenticity
of the Roman-Briton Ambrosius,[22] it may be conceded that the
Anglo-Saxon invasions received a temporary check at the Battle of Mount Badon (ca. 490). But there is no question about
the steady infiltration of Germanic tribes into the island. Their
way through eastern, southern, and central Britain lay straight
before them. The intangible momentum which had been acquired by all the Germanic nations during their migrations in
the fifth century carried the Anglo-Saxon tribes irresistibly
forward. As steadily and surely as a rising tide, the Angles

and Saxons and Jutes and Frisians[23] and Rugii[24] bit away at
the British coast-line. They gradually obtained temporary
footholds here and permanent settlements there, until the
whole area that had once been held by the Romans was occupied by the Germanic invaders. It would be interesting to
know, if it were possible, just which tribes and how many took
leading parts in the conquest. But the one fact that seems sure
—and the evidence here is at best only fragmentary—is that
the Jutes and West Saxons first set up rather important kingdoms in the south. Still, although the process of conquest was
slow and the details often completely obscured, the end was
none the less obvious. There may have been times when the
Germanic invaders were slowed down temporarily or even
beaten back. Of that there is little actual record.[25] But when
the curtain of darkness which had fallen upon Britain during
the fifth century is lifted about the year 580, it is at once apparent that the Roman Britons had succumbed to the Germanic tribes just as the Celtic Britons had yielded to the
Romans half a millennium before.

There is little doubt, moreover, about the fierceness of this
Germanic invader and the bloodiness of his conquest.[26] Here
was no friendly penetration of one people by their blood-
relatives. Nor was it only the more violent manifestation of
the instincts of a great nation for expansion and colonization.
As nearly as one people can exterminate another, the Anglo-
Saxons accomplished it against the Britons: those few who
escaped sword and spear were driven westward into Wales,
into Cornwall, into the north country beyond Hadrian's Wall
and even beyond the Firth of Forth. Or instead of death their
fate was captivity; they must live with their conquerors as the
conquered. The Anglo-Saxon incursions, indeed, never attained much above the dignity of piratical marauding; there
was little apparent system or order in the advance of these
Germanic tribes. Once the land was in their hands, however,
the Anglo-Saxons established themselves; it may even be
suggested that they muddled through, in traditional fashion,
to a settled sort of conquest.

And yet when all the brutality of this Anglo-Saxon conquest has been granted, one must also grant what may appear to be a contradiction. As it happens, the Germanic invaders found in Britain a civilization which, at least in externals, was superior to their own.[27] No doubt they took but little account of this in the heat of actual conquest. The ultimate impression made by this superior material civilization, however, is something else. Can it actually be said that the Anglo-Saxons were willing to accept the economic and social organization of the Roman-Briton much as they found it, provided that they could remain the masters? Probably not; the actual facts show that the Anglo-Saxons brought from the Continent their traditional customs and tribal governments. However, they had experienced, while still on the Continent, some contact with Roman culture, as certain Latin words found in their language will attest.[28] We must also remember still another tribute to the vitality of the Roman-British civilization. The invading Anglo-Saxons were heathens, but they proved before long to be remarkably susceptible to Christianity, as did their relatives on the Continent.[29] The details of their actual conversion make another story.[30] Undoubtedly their acceptance of the missionary efforts of Augustine and Aidan and Paulinus is but another sign of their spiritual inclination before a superior culture. Perhaps the Anglo-Saxons were not artistic by nature, but they were willing enough to put their Celtic subjects into the smithy to forge them splendid decorated swords and worshipful armor; and, having received their tribute, they could appreciate the beauty and cunning of the work and try to imitate it. The ivory-hilted swords of the Celts and their quaint enameled brooches may have survived to the present day largely in caves and subsoils, but it is inconceivable that the Anglo-Saxons should fail to notice them. To people whose gifts and mediums of exchange consisted chiefly of weapons and personal ornaments, these Celtic and Roman relics must have been of interest and even, perhaps, have suggested to the Anglo-Saxons some elaborations of their heavier, more massive workmanship in metals.[31] Such a statement, of course, is

ROMAN BRITAIN

ENGLAND IN THE AGE
OF ALFRED

(ca. 900)

to be taken only as an inference. Finally, the impressive efficiency of Roman law must have prompted the codification by the more far-seeing Anglo-Saxon kings of their traditional Germanic legal practices. Such codification must have taken place as early as 600, but it is proper to consider King Alfred (d.901) as the Justinian of the Anglo-Saxon kingdoms even though he was building upon a tradition which stretched back to centuries before his time. In short, while the Roman conquest of Britain was an imperialistic conquest, the Anglo-Saxon conquest of that same Britain became, in the long run, a spiritual and intellectual assimilation of the invader rather than the purely bloody, military conquest it started out to be.

4. SALIENT CHARACTERISTICS
OF THE EARLY ANGLO-SAXON SOCIETY
IN ENGLAND

At the same time, it must never be supposed that the Angle or the Saxon lost his identity. There were two possessions to which he clung tenaciously—his language and his individual conception of government, law, and society. There were also some moral characteristics which he was able to retain from the days of his conquest of Britain to the present. His psychology of living, however, can be better discussed in immediate association with his literature.[32] As for his language, it was a typical language of a young Germanic people—harsh, vigorous, muscular, consonantal, given little to sensuousness— aesthetically a poor thing. But it was his own, and, whatever the influence or importance of English literature before the Norman Conquest, one can safely assert that for practical purposes the Anglo-Saxon drove the Latin language into the monasteries and into the church assemblies. The common, everyday existence of the average man, we can be quite sure, was lived in the sound of the Old English vernacular to an extent far greater than is usually appreciated.

As the language of the Anglo-Saxon was peculiarly appropriate to his personality, so it was also with his idea of government. The kingship of his tribe was a position of great potential democracy: in times of peace the Anglo-Saxon king was not much more than a respected figure-head. To be sure, the king must be able to trace his ancestry back to Woden, king of the gods, although what we see of Anglo-Saxon genealogies indicates that that was no great feat. His succession, however, while hereditary, was subject to the approval of the council of elders, the *witan*, who represented the opinion of the tribe. In times of war, on the other hand, the Anglo-Saxon ruler was an absolute leader, a kind of Palladium, whose presence would inspire his warriors and whose death must be avenged by his people, to ultimate victory or to the death. This king-worship —for no better term can be used—was nevertheless not peculiar; it can be found in virtually every rude state of culture. The essential fact to emphasize here is, rather, the importance of the *witan*, who in their assembly, the famous *witenagemot*, appear in power to be not unlike the old Roman senators. But this parallel is probably inept; there is little of the Roman consul about any of the historical Germanic tribal kings. The chief of an American Indian nation would be a much better analogy.

The society of the Anglo-Saxon tribe was of the simplest. The basis of the tribe appears to have been patriarchal within historical times, although some dissenting scholars suspect that it was originally matriarchal.[33] In either case, however, the family was the living cell whence grew the tribe. Although it was the practice for all kings to trace their ancestry as far back as Woden, it was sufficient for others to remember that there were three well-defined branches of the people, derived ultimately from the three sons of the first man, Mannus, son of the god Tuisco, son of Woden. These three sons were Erminus, Inguo, and Instio, whence the threefold division of the Germanic peoples, first mentioned by Tacitus,[34] into Hermiones, Inguaeones, and Istaeuones. A similarly well-defined threefold branching of the Germanic languages has long been recognized by modern linguists; this branching indicates the separate existence of East, North, and West Germanic. All who could trace descent from Mannus were *eorlas* (earls); they comprised the ruling class of the historical Anglo-Saxon tribes. Those whose ancestry was not thus pure but who were basically Germanic would be recognized as *freomen* (freemen). A lower class of bonded peasants, descended partly from captives of the tribe, were known as *ceorlas* (churls). There is evidence to show that the older state of society among the Anglo-Saxon tribes recognized two groups only: the earls and the churls. The freemen, it is believed, were merely churls who, through rewards for meritorious services to their rulers or, rarely, from their own diligence and industry, were able to work their way out of their churlish bondage.

This fundamentally agricultural society was made to function through the unremitting labor of churls, who ploughed, hunted, fished and fowled, forged metals, and wove garments. The freemen were at first few in number. So it was that the churls went to make up an obscure proletariat, about whom we have little enough information, save as some earl or cleric might see fit to vouchsafe it. Nevertheless, the earl had the responsibility of protecting his own and his inferiors'. Fighting was his business if need be, and there was generally a need. Yet even here the churl was expected to take his onerous part; he had the privilege of fighting and dying beside his lord and earl.

In justice it must be insisted that the Anglo-Saxon, by the time he steps over the threshold of history, had a conception of society which transcended the individual. Every human being in his society had an intrinsic economic value which could be translated into monetary terms. If this particular human being should be damaged or removed from the scene through the willful act of another, the remover was liable to pay a price, to the full economic value of his victim. This was the celebrated *wergild*. From a study of the *wergilds* known to us, we can see that Anglo-Saxon society, even in its simplest outlines, admitted certain grades and classes, for an earl was worth far more *wergild* than a churl; certain families were worth more than other families; a male of whatever class was worth more than the corresponding female. For it was then an overwhelmingly male society. Women were necessary to the home, as household functionaries, marriageable commodities, biological accessories. They appear to have had hereditary legal rights. Only if she was a queen, however, or in later days a churchwoman, could the Anglo-Saxon female expect much social recognition in literature; and never could she, in real life, hold *sovereinetee* as did Chaucer's Wife of Bath. But she was respected. Germanic sexual folk-morality, praised both by Caesar and Tacitus,[35] is in sharp contrast to the practices of the later Roman Empire and the rather irregular customs of some of the early Celts.

Yet it would be unwise to urge any special moral values for the Anglo-Saxon which could not be urged for other tribesmen of different racial background at the same stage of ethnic development. After all, he was still an earthy tribesman— no more, no less—living by his agriculture, his hunting, fishing, and fowling; not until late, with the increase of freemen, does he manifest any great interest in commerce or attach any particular importance to trade. He knows the plough, the wagon, the usual domestic livestock. He is still and always the seafarer, for it is thus that he satisfies his nomadic cravings, which had been assuaged only partially by his settling down to an insular existence.

It is clear, therefore, that the Anglo-Saxon was his own master, and in spite of his obvious limitations he was not entirely an unseeing clod of barbarism. There was a grim vigor and vitality to his crudeness which can still assert themselves when we read his literature. He had, at the same time, an intuitive desire to avoid the sedulous aping of Roman civilization, which was intellectually removed from him by centuries of more advanced culture. Grant that the civilization of Rome, as illustrated by the Roman remnants in Britain, taught the Germanic invader a great deal, and grant further that he was quick to reach after those elements of that civilization which appealed to him. With these concessions it is best to stop. It cannot be shown that the Anglo-Saxon ever truly attained to that Roman culture.

5. FROM HENGEST AND HORSA TO
WILLIAM THE CONQUEROR

THE social history of the Old English period seems to have been remarkably static. Probably this sameness is due to the fact that we know so little about the period as a whole. But the political history of the island from about 500 to the time of the Norman Conquest in 1066 is, on the other hand, the story of a vivid and troubled but groping era. One must be thankful for such knowledge as we do possess, although, as it happens, we have never been overwhelmed by any excess of information concerning the doings of mankind during these centuries. Yet we know enough about the early Middle Ages to realize that this era can no longer be called the "Dark Ages." Have we in the twentieth century the right to call any previous human era "dark"? Still, the wonder persists that so much light managed to penetrate into Anglo-Saxon Britain, then close to the ends of the earth.

Then it was about four hundred winters and nine and forty from the incarnation of Our Lord. . . . The people of the Angles and the people of the Saxons were invited by the aforementioned king [Vortigern], and they came to Britain with three great ships; and in the eastern portion of this island took up a dwelling-place through this same king's commands, who had invited them hither, that they might fight for their native land. And they straightway fought against their adversaries, who had often before warred upon them from the north; and the Saxons took victory. Whereupon they sent messengers home and proclaimed the fertility of this land and the cowardice of the Britons.

And then straightway they sent a greater fleet of stronger warriors hither; and it was an invincible troop which they had joined together. And the Britons yielded and gave them dwelling among them, that they might fight for the peace and well-being of their land and struggle against their enemies;

and they granted the Saxons sustenance and favor for their fighting powers. They came from three folks of the strongest tribes of Germania, that of the Saxons and of the Angles and of the Jutes. From the Jutes are the origins of the men of Kent and the people of Wight, that is, the people who inhabit the Isle of Wight. From the Saxons, that is, those from the land called Old Saxony, come the men of Essex and Sussex and Wessex. And from the Angles come the East Anglians and Mid-Anglians and Mercians and all the tribe of the Northumbrians; this land is called Anglia among the Jutes and Saxons; it is said that from the time that they departed thence until today, that it remains waste.

Their first leaders and commanders were the two brothers Hengest and Horsa. They were sons of Wihtgils, whose father was called Witta, whose father was called Wihta; and the father of Wihta was called Woden. . . . Nor was there any delay before they came hither in great crowds, great bands of the people concerning whom we have been speaking. And the folk that came hither began to increase and multiply to such a point that they were a source of great terror to those land-dwellers who had invited and called them hither.[36]

There is further evidence, beyond the account from Bede's *Ecclesiastical History* just quoted, to indicate that the Germanic tribes named here as taking part in the conquest—the Angles, the Saxons, and the Jutes—had already developed into two nations, the Anglo-Saxon and the Jutish. Moreover, the Jutes, first in the order of conquerors, established the early kingdom of Kent, the boundaries of which were not greatly different from those of the present county of the same name. The setting up of this kingdom is in effect the sole contribution which the Jutes made to the origins of the English nation. The position of Kent as the most southerly of the Germanic kingdoms in Britain is largely responsible for its peculiar importance in early English history: it was here that the missionaries from Rome under Augustine landed (597) and instituted the systematic Christianization of the island. It happened that Kent was not only the first sizable Germanic kingdom of Britain in point of time, it was also the first to disappear as a political unit, for it was conquered by Ethelred of Mercia about 680. The Angles seem to have had an easier time in their conquest than did their colleagues. They made early an extensive settlement in Britain; their holdings in the island stretched at one time or another all the way from the Thames in the south to the Lowlands of Scotland in the North, with particular centers at Durham and at York. The section of Anglia north of the Humber was known as Northumbria; it consisted at first of two smaller units known as Bernicia and Deira. Bernicia was the more northerly of these two and ran from the Tees River north to the Firth of Forth; Deira ran south from the Tees to the Humber.

All the Germanic population north of the Thames, then, was of Anglian stock. The entire region, only rarely referred to as Anglia alone, extended from Northumbria in the northern half to Mercia and the eastern kingdom of East Anglia in the southern half. In a westerly direction the Anglian group of kingdoms had shifting boundaries. Northumbria, for example, seems never to have stretched beyond present-day Cumberland, Galloway, or Westmoreland until late—all three of these districts remained for a long time in the hands of Gaelic Celts (Scots); Mercia, on the other hand, pushed well past Chester to the shores of the Irish Sea. East Anglia was confined largely to the present counties of Norfolk, Suffolk, and Cambridgeshire.

To the south, the Saxons took over nearly all of the island except Wales and Cornwall. Most important in history was the kingdom of the West Saxons, or Wessex; but notice should be made of the East Saxons of Essex and of the South Saxons of Sussex. The Saxon domain extended from the Thames to the south and as far northwest as the valley of the Severn River, as far east as the western edges of Kent, and as far southwest as the Tamar River, the eastern boundary of Cornwall, which remained Celtic under the name of West Wales. There was much confusion about the frontiers of Wessex and Mercia, but in view of the almost continuous warfare between these two kingdoms during the seventh and eighth centuries, this confusion is only natural.[37] In Kent, as has been seen, and in the Isle of Wight lived the Jutes; but at least by the time of King Alfred of Wessex in the late ninth century, the Isle of Wight had come to be inhabited chiefly by West Saxons.

It is easy to see, therefore, that the political *mis-en-scène* of Anglo-Saxon Britain represents a nest of small kingdoms. There were for a time seven distinct units, which comprised the so-called Heptarchy (Northumbria, Mercia, Wessex, Essex, Sussex, East Anglia, and Kent). The first three of these played an important role in the history of the island; and the leadership, as will be observed, shifted from one to another of these three. The essential fact, however, is that this state of political culture among the kingdoms was not conducive to a national unity until several centuries after the coming of the Anglo-Saxons. There were too many highly individualistic rulers, who were far too close in tradition to the former isolated, self-sufficient kingship enjoyed on the Continent to be able to envisage an integrated English nation. All the evidence of early Old English literature points to a provincialism, even a parochialism, of outlook; there is in it nothing of breadth of vision or bigness of ambition. It is not until the middle of the tenth century that the West Saxon king Edgar becomes what may be called the first sovereign of a united England.

It might be well for the moment to lay aside the political spyglass and consider briefly the social factors which were responsible for this decentralization. The tribes which brought about the Anglo-Saxon conquest of Britain were built largely upon the old family organization or clan typical of the Germanic groups on the Continent. This point has been made before, but not the obvious fact that the Anglo-Saxon, like every one of his Germanic brothers and cousins, possessed a fierce pride in his antecedents, a pride which echoes again and again in his epic literature. He possessed also an abysmal ignorance of the world outside his little community, and this ignorance continued among his people as a whole until long after the

Norman Conquest. To such people, therefore, the concept of a national unity was of far less importance than the integrity of their local organization. As time went on, the smaller, less powerful kingdoms yielded to the larger and stronger. Essex, Sussex, Kent, and East Anglia were eventually swallowed up. Yet even when the Heptarchy had been well absorbed into the three major kingdoms of Northumbria, Mercia, and Wessex, the lack of a centralized force to develop the country at home and to strengthen her defenses against possible foreign aggression was all too painfully apparent.

Under such circumstances, the history of Anglo-Saxon England, or *Angelcynn* of the *Englisc*, as the land came to be named,[38] is in the period before the Norman Conquest a story of the rise and fall of kingdoms, with the final emergence of an ultimately unified realm. It is difficult to trace the exact sequence of events in the early years of this development. Kent was well established by the opening of the sixth century. But, once this first kingdom of Kent has been given its due, one observes that the supremacy among the various Anglo-Saxon kingdoms tended to travel from north to south. First Northumbria, the most northerly of the kingdoms, gained a political, social, and cultural ascendancy, which lasted from the year 588, when Ethelric of Bernicia combined his kingdom with that of Deira to form a Northumbrian whole, until 670, when Oswiu, last of the great Northumbrian kings, came to his appointed end.

The important event in this seventh century is the establishing of Christianity throughout the Anglo-Saxon kingdoms. Irish missionaries under the leadership of St. Columba had arrived in the north of England during the sixth century, and this mission received special impetus during the early seventh century through the remarkable efforts of Aidan. The mission from Rome under Augustine arrived in Kent in 597. These two missionary forces met in conflict in Northumbria, and the supremacy of the Roman mission was settled by the Council of Whitby (664). Actively associated with the spread of Christianity in Northumbria by Paulinus, during the inter-

vening years, were the able King Oswald and the saintly
Bishop Cuthbert (d.685). The death of King Oswiu, however, meant the decline of Northumbria, a decline which reduced the three great Anglo-Saxon kingdoms to political
parity, until the upward swing of the Mercians under Offa
(d.796). Partly because of the depredations of her restless,
warlike neighbors of Mercia, but even more because of the
activities of a new menace—the Viking Danes—Northumbria
was overrun in the eighth century, and the hegemony passed
for a short period southward into Mercia.

But one should pause briefly for a tribute to this impressive
Anglo-Saxon kingdom of Northumbria. Her greatness was
clearly due to her Christianization, to the fact that the Irish
missionaries of Lindisfarne had planted well, although they
did not eventually reap the harvest. Abbeys, churches, and
monasteries flourished, and the essential contribution of these
—learning. Therefore the collapse of this first important
Anglian kingdom did not occur without involving also the
general collapse of the highest state of culture which the British Isles were to know for nearly two hundred years. In a
period of general darkness and ignorance, seats of learning
like Jarrow, Durham, Wearmouth, and York shine forth as
beacons of enlightenment. There Aldhelm, Cuthbert, Bede,
and the half-legendary Caedmon labored and studied for
their allotted years, and their light has not yet been extin-
guished. One need but look upon the simple and impressive
"tomb" of Bede in the Galilee Chapel of rugged Durham
Cathedral to see symbolized the freshness and plain vigor of
the early Church in Britain. The *Lindisfarne Gospels* and the
Durham Ritual-Book[39] attest the artistic capabilities and
achievements of this former day. The first English scholars,
the first English historian, the first English translation of the
Gospels, the first English literary school, and the greatest
center of Anglo-Saxon Christendom had been the prized possessions of Old Northumbria. All this rich endowment, to be
sure, was not irretrievably lost. The scholars fled elsewhere;
much of the literature was to be rediscovered and disseminated

NORTH SEA

Edinburgh

LINDISFARNE I.

R. Clyde

R Tweed

BERNICIA

NORTHUMBRIA

STRATHCLYDE
(CELTIC)

Jarrow
Wearmouth
Durham

DEIRA

Whitby

ISLE OF MAN

R. Tees

R. Ouse

IRISH SEA

York

R. Aire

R. Humber

R. Mersey

Chester

R. Dee

R. Trent

Croyland

EAST
ANGLIA

R. Avon

R. Great Ouse

WALES
(CELTIC)

R. Severn

R. Wye

MERCIA

St. Albans

R. Thames

London

I. OF THANET

BRISTOL CHANNEL

WESSEX

R. Bourne

SUSSEX

Winchester

Canterbury

KENT

CORNWALL
(CELTIC)

R. Tamar

ISLE OF WIGHT

ENGLISH CHANNEL

THE HEPTARCHY

- - - - - Frontier of Anglo-Saxon Occupation

ENGLAND AFTER THE
DANISH CONQUEST

at a later date; some of the finest abbeys and churches were spared. We shall see that at least one monument of Northumbrian culture, Bede's *Ecclesiastical History of the English People*, was to be preserved for posterity. None the less, the destruction of Old Northumbria inspires in even the casual spectator the inevitable regrets that arise at all times from the contemplation of human endeavor largely wasted.

Unfortunately the Mercians, when the opportunity for leadership came to them, were unable to carry on the tradition of their Northumbrian predecessors. They had never been a cultured or enlightened people; one of their most celebrated kings, Penda, had been a most implacable enemy of Christianity and the chief instrument in the defeat and death of the "blessed" King Oswald of Northumbria. As has been said in later centuries of the Frisians, *Mercia non cantavit*, although we still have some religious writings which illustrate the painstaking efforts of sincere Mercian churchmen. A comparison of the *Lindisfarne Gospels* with the *Mercian Psalter* is sufficiently enlightening. Yet in fairness it should be remarked that even if the Mercians had possessed a Bede or a Caedmon, it is doubtful whether they would have had the opportunity to use such men. Mars and Minerva do not make a happy couple. The Danish menace which had engulfed the Northumbrians descended in turn upon the Mercians. Moreover, during the reign of Offa, the Mercians were being constantly threatened by the West Saxons.

Finally the West Saxons, under the leadership of Ecgbert, defeated the Mercians in 825 and assumed the hegemony. This triumph, however, was short-lived and hollow enough, for Wessex soon had to fight for existence against the Viking Danes. The chronicles of the early decades of the ninth century are terse accounts of the ever-encroaching spread of the Danes through the central eastern districts of Britain, into Essex, and finally into Wessex itself. For the remainder of the century the fight was on, tooth and nail. Danish marauders virtually surrounded Britain; they were harrying the mouth of the Thames, the Mercian frontiers, the ports along the Channel and around Cornwall into the Bristol Channel, even the coast of Ireland. Ecgbert of Wessex (d.839) gave these Vikings a partial check; his successor Ethelwulf (d.858) continued this successful resistance; but the pressure not only from the Danes but also from rebellious Britons in Wales and Cornwall grew ever greater. In 871 the West Saxon cause was at its lowest ebb. In the very midst of the crisis King Ethelred I died, and his brother Alfred succeeded him.

It was now that the Danes received their first real setback. In a fierce, random, guerilla-like warfare they were brought within eight years to a standstill. Yet this was accomplished by the West Saxons only after many reverses and discouragements. Indeed, the stanch figure of Alfred, who fully deserves the sobriquet "the Great," was the chief obstacle to complete Danish victory. Through his tireless and undeterred efforts the Danes were finally restrained, by the Treaty of Wedmore (878), to the region north of the line from London to Chester, approximately the renowned old Watling Street of Roman-British fame. This Danish concession was known for a long time thereafter as the Danelagh (the Danish occupation of which incidentally had considerable effect upon the later English language). In the Danelagh the Viking Danes lived amid comparative quiet for some time, although a later resurgence in the years following 892 caused Alfred great further anxiety.

Alfred emerged from his hard struggle as the greatest of all Anglo-Saxon kings, wise in politics, able in war, and, best of all, provident of the intellectual and social needs of his people. His immense services to the learning of his day must be reserved for a later chapter.[40] For the present it is necessary only to observe his most fortunate appearance in the panorama of early English history. Not only did he leave the foundations of a strong kingdom of Wessex, but he also accomplished more than anyone else before the Norman Conquest the revival of at least a share of the cultural splendor which had been Northumbria's some two centuries earlier. His own efforts, indistinct though they may sometimes ap-

pear now, toward the education of his people represent one of
the most definite and straightforward impulses ever expressed
by the enlightened ruler and sovereign of a fundamentally
backward people. Nor were all of his labors in this field of
peace purely theoretical. He attacked bravely the then formidable task of translating and adapting for the use of his
people the literary classics of his immediate age; he revised
the law-codes of Wessex; he stimulated the ancient chronicles
of his people; and he strove always for the literacy of Wessex,
a nation which he considered not so much Wessex as *Angelcynn*, England, for the *Englisc*.

The death of Alfred in 901 marked, therefore, the passing
of a figure never to be approached again in stature during the
Old English era. To be sure, his splendid personality could
not immediately be lost. Such a man always imparts a certain
momentum to his cause, a momentum which will carry it
through many a subsequent crisis. Moreover, Alfred's immediate successors were able enough, and his victory over the
Danes was maintained. Athelstan conquered (926) virtually
all of the Celtic tribes that had held sway in Wales since the
Roman conquest. Having achieved this much, the West Saxons turned northward. In the next twenty years they made
military and political penetrations into Mercia and even into
Northumbria. Gradually they won back the Danelagh, piece
by piece, although it was not until the death of Edgar (975)
that one could recognize a united England owing allegiance
to a single sovereign. At the same time, a remarkable religious
and scholastic revival came in this tenth century, in which
shines particularly the name of Dunstan, Archbishop of Canterbury.

This long, painful, groping achievement of what was probably an unappreciated ideal was to have but little duration.
As it had been in the days of King Ecgbert of Wessex, danger
straightway frowned upon this new England; and this time
the integrity of the recently unified realm was doomed to
early death. Perhaps it is only natural that history should
yield so many examples of a weak ruler opposed to a strong

enemy; perhaps such qualities as weakness and strength in this case are only relative. But Ethelred II (the Unready), who came to the throne in 979, was so ineffective that the usual consequences—usurping of power by unscrupulous earls and dissension among those earls—brought about a recurrence of the very evils against which Alfred had struggled a century before. Now a new generation of Danes descended upon the coasts of England, and now there was no Alfred to withstand them. Ethelred was cowardly and treacherous where Alfred had been courageous and firm; the inevitable sequel was the slow eclipse of the prestige of the Anglo-Saxon warrior in such a characteristic encounter as the Battle of Maldon (991). The Danish conquest was actually consummated when, in 1014, Swein captured the kingship of England. To such a man as the fiery Wulfstan,[41] the latter day of the English people had arrived.

There was a considerable difference, however, between the conquest of the Britons by the Anglo-Saxons on the one hand and the conquest of the Anglo-Saxons by the Danes on the other. The conquest of the Anglo-Saxons by a kindred people appears now as little more than a dynastic change. To be sure, there was much bloodshed, and an occasional massacre, the most notorious of which was committed by Ethelred (1003). There were pillagings and piracies, especially at Canterbury and along the Thames as far as London. But a study of England a few years after the accession of Swein—in 1020, for example—would reveal that the nation as a nation was no worse off than it had been for more than a half-century; the very least that can be said is that Swein and his successors were better rulers than the luckless Ethelred.[42] Thanks to the elastic nature of the English kingship even in those later days, a return to the West Saxon dynasty was always possible. The *witenagemot* in 1042 sanctioned the accession of Edward the Confessor, son of Ethelred the Unready. Since Edward was a saintly *fainéant*, the government was administered through the hands and minds of the most powerful of the king's thanes, the chief earls, of whom Earl Godwin was the most influential. A generation of political wranglings, disputed successions, and factional strife lay before England. Here appears the tragic figure of Harold, last of the Anglo-Saxon kings; at the end of the road lie the Battle of Hastings and the passing of the Old English period. Here, too, towers the person of William the Conqueror,[43] winning and ruling all England through "the splendor of God" and initiating a new age, more complex, more civilized, more rich in knowledge and thought than the age which had gone before. For unlike the Danish Conquest, the Norman Conquest of 1066 is in the nature of a national upheaval and marks the beginning of a new era in English history, the Middle English period. With that period we have here nothing to do. The Anglo-Saxon brought forth an individual kind of culture; most of that culture passed with the Battle of Hastings. It is rather for us now to see what the mind of this Anglo-Saxon produced in the six centuries during which he dominated the scene in England.[44]

NOTES TO CHAPTER ONE

1. For the many names that have at one time or another been applied to these peoples, and for the classification of these peoples, see in particular G. Schütte, *Our Forefathers—the Gothonic Peoples* (Cambridge, 1929-1933), I, 10ff. This book is invaluable for all kinds of information relating to the origins and history of the Germanic tribes. In spite of Schütte's choice of the term *Gothonic*, I prefer the term *Germanic*; and *Germanic*, still the most widespread and easily recognized of all the names given to the particular peoples of northern and central Europe, will be used throughout the present work.

2. To follow up the various aspects of English civilization implicit in this statement would be to call down upon oneself virtually the entire list of the multitudinous works upon England, English history, and the English language. A beginning is made in note 44 below. So far as the matter of the English language is concerned, however, the layman would do well to begin with A. C. Baugh, *The History of the English Language* (New York, 1935) and follow in detail the excellent bibliographical information contained therein. The essential lesson to be learned from any study of the nature of the English language is that,

in spite of its enormous amount of borrowing from other languages, particularly the French, English remains basically a Germanic language. The classical bibliography of English medieval history, C. Gross, *Sources and Literature of English History from the Earliest Times to about 1485* (rev. ed., London-New York, 1915), and of the English language, A. G. Kennedy, *A Bibliography of Writings on the English Language from the Beginnings of Printing to 1922* (Cambridge, Mass., 1927) are still indispensable.

3. The relative merits of the terms "Old English" and "Anglo-Saxon" are touched upon briefly later (see II, 1 below). I feel that both are admissible, are in frequent use, and for the sake of variety are best used interchangeably.

4. See the Old English version of Bede's *Historia Ecclesiastica Gentis Anglorum*, edited by T. Miller as volumes 95, 96, 110, and 111 of *Publications of the Early English Text Society, Original Series* (London, 1890-1891), Book I, Chapter 12, pp. 50-52. Good accounts of the Anglo-Saxon conquest, all drawing heavily upon Bede, are those in J. R. Green, *A History of the English People* (London, 1905-1908); C. W. C. Oman, *A History of England before the Norman Conquest* (London, 1904); J. H. Ramsay, *The Foundations of England* (London, 1898), i; H. M. Chadwick, *The Origin of the English Nation* (Cambridge, 1907); E. Wadstein, *On the Origin of the English* (Uppsala, 1927). Less effective though more ambitious is that by R. H. Hodgkin in *The History of the Anglo-Saxons* (Oxford, 1935); the most recent treatment, and a good one, is F. M. Stenton, *Anglo-Saxon England* (Oxford, 1943).

5. They are mentioned by Procopius (d.562) in his *Bello Gothico*, IV, 20; but see the works mentioned in note 4 above.

6. Bede's work is discussed later (see VII, 3 and VIII, 2 below).

7. The dispute concerns itself primarily with the date and locale of the invasion, for there is little reason to doubt the authenticity of Hengest and Horsa and their expedition. In addition to the treatment of this matter in the works cited in note 4 above, see also Nils Aberg, *The Anglo-Saxons in England* (Uppsala, 1926) and Carl Stephenson, *Medieval History: Europe from the Fourth to the Sixteenth Century* (New York, 1935). Alexander H. Krappe, however, in an article entitled "Les dieux jumeaux dans la religion germanique" in *Acta Philologica Scandinavica*, VI, 1-25, introduces Hengest and Horsa as legendary figures based on folklore. But, as some irreconcilables say of Shakespeare, if the leaders of this expedition were not Hengest and Horsa, they may have been two other men with the same names.

8. See especially R. B. Dixon, *The Racial History of Man* (New York, 1923), for a consideration of the early races in Europe; a consideration of the same material is H. F. Osborn, *Men of the Old*

Stone Age (New York, 1915). More recent than Osborn and more generally satisfactory is Norman Ault, *Life in Ancient Britain* (London, 1920).

9. The most impressive accounts of the Roman settlements in Britain, are those of F. Haverfield, particularly *The Romanization of Roman Britain* (London, 1905) and *The Roman Occupation of Britain* (Oxford, 1942); and those of R. G. Collingwood, especially *Roman Britain* (New York, 1932), which was elaborated into *Roman Britain and English Settlements* (Oxford, 1936). Useful also are B. C. A. Windle, *The Romans in Britain* (London, 1932) and John Ward, *The Roman Era in Britain* (London, 1911).

10. Herodotus mentions the "Tin Islands," about which, he adds, he knows nothing. But Aristotle in his *De Mundo* (Section VII) states: "Beyond the Pillars of Hercules the ocean flows round the earth, and in it are two very large islands called British: Albion and Ierne, lying beyond the Keltoi." Britain and Eire seem to be meant. Herodotus's "Tin Islands" have been interpreted as either Cornwall or the Scilly Isles.

11. Rice Holmes, *Ancient Britain and the Invasions of Julius Caesar* (Oxford, 1909).

12. Alois Pogatscher, *Zur Lautlehre der griechischen, lateinischen, und romanischen Lehnworte im altenglischen* (Strassburg, 1888).

13. Thomas Codrington, *Roman Roads in Britain* (London, 1903); also U. A. Forbes and A. C. Burmester, *Our Roman Highways* (London, 1904).

14. Paul Brown, *The Great Wall of Hadrian in Roman Times* (London, 1936).

15. J. W. Gough, *The Mines of Mendip* (Oxford, 1930).

16. Jessie Mothersole, *The Saxon Shore* (London, 1924).

17. See the article by Krappe mentioned in note 7 above.

18. See R. W. Chambers, *Beowulf* (Cambridge, 1932), in particular pp. 443-444.

19. See VIII, 3 below.

20. See VII, 1 below.

21. But see P. K. Johnstone, "The Victories of Arthur" in *Notes and Queries*, CLXVI, 381-382 and again CLXVII, 65; he is answered by H. Askew in CLXVI, 425-427. Askew has also an interesting article entitled "King Arthur's Last Battle" in *Antiquity*, v, 236-239; a preliminary to this is an article by Robert Birley, "The Battle of Mount Badon" in *Antiquity*, I, 459-463.

22. Probably the best single introduction to the figure of King Arthur in legend is to be found in J. D. Bruce, *The Evolution of Arthurian Romance* (Baltimore, 1932); but the older studies, John Rhys, *Studies in the Arthurian Legend* (Oxford, 1891) and Alfred

Nutt, *Celtic and Mediaeval Romance* (London, 1899) are still indispensable.

23. F. Kluge, "Geschichte der englischen Sprache" in Paul's *Grundriss der germanischen Philologie* (Strassburg, 1898), I, 928; but R. H. Hodgkin, in his *History of the Anglo-Saxons* (Oxford, 1935), I, 82 and 97, equates the "Frisians" with the Jutes. See also G. Schütte, *Our Forefathers: the Gothonic Peoples* (note 1 above), II, 285-286, for further references; also F. M. Stenton, *Anglo-Saxon England* (London, 1943).

24. For this and other sources of English place-names, see Eilert Ekwall, *The Oxford Dictionary of English Place-Names* (Oxford, 1936).

25. The chronicles of Gildas (see VII, 1 below), Nennius (see VII, 1 below), and Bede (see VII, 3 below) yield some clues.

26. But see R. V. Lennard, "The Character of the Anglo-Saxon Conquest" in *History*, XVIII, 204-215.

27. Every important writer on the period has had to wrestle with this question. In addition to the works already cited, the following give useful information bearing indirectly on the problem: Jan de Vries, *Die Welt der Germanen* (Leipzig, 1935); Amabel Williams-Ellis and F. J. Fisher, *A History of English Life Political and Social* (London, 1936), Vol. I; Nils Aberg, *The Anglo-Saxons in England* (Uppsala, 1926)—which is one of the best of the archaeological studies; Edward T. Leeds, *Early Anglo-Saxon and Celtic Archaeology* (London, 1936); H. St. L. B. Moss, *The Birth of the Middle Ages* (Oxford, 1935); J. E. Jolliffe, *Pre-Feudal England: the Jutes* (Oxford, 1933); Wilfrid Bonser, "Survivals of Paganism in Anglo-Saxon England" in *Transactions of the Birmingham Archaeological Society*, LVI, 37-70; F. P. Magoun, "On Some Survivals of Pagan Belief in Anglo-Saxon England" in *Harvard Theological Review*, XL, 33-46; S. J. Crawford, *The Anglo-Saxon Influence on Western Christendom* (Oxford, 1933); V. Gronbech, *The Culture of the Teutons*, translated by William Worster (Oxford, 1931); D. P. Capper, *The Vikings of Britain* (London, 1937); and D. Elizabeth Martin-Clarke, *Culture in Early Anglo-Saxon England* (Baltimore, 1947).

28. The monograph by Pogatscher (note 12 above) is probably the best treatment of this subject; but useful also are the monographs by A. Keiser, *The Influence of Christianity on the Vocabulary of Old English Poetry* (Urbana, 1919) and Roland G. Kent, *Language and Philology* (Boston, 1923), as well as the excellent study by R. E. Zachrisson, *Romans, Kelts, and Saxons in Ancient Britain* (Uppsala, 1927).

29. The appropriate pages in the first chapter of J. R. Green, *A*

Short History of the English People is the fullest earlier account in present-day scholarship. More specialized and much more detailed are W. Hunt, *The English Church from its Foundation to the Norman Conquest* (London, 1899) and A. J. Mason, *The Mission of Saint Augustine to England according to the Original Documents* (Cambridge, 1897).

30. See IV, 1 below; the work of Hunt cited in note 29 above affords a fascinating survey.

31. The studies of Aberg and Leeds have already been named in note 27 above; see in addition Reidar T. Christiansen, *The Vikings and the Viking Wars in Irish and Gaelic Tradition* (Oslo, 1931), as well as the three works by R. E. M. Wheeler: *London and the Saxons* (London, 1938); "The Paradox of Celtic Art" in *Antiquity*, VI, 292-300; and *Prehistoric and Roman Wales* (London, 1925).

32. See Chapter II *et seq.*

33. A. W. Aron, "Traces of Matriarchy in Germanic Hero-Lore" in *University of Wisconsin Studies in Language and Literature*, No. 9 (Madison, 1920).

34. Tacitus, *Germania*, section 2. A convenient edition is that in the Bohn Classical Library (London, 1911).

35. See note 34 above.

36. Bede's *Ecclesiastical History of the English People*, Book I, Chapter 12. For further references to this work, see VII, 3 and VIII, 2 below and note 4 above.

37. C. W. C. Oman, *England before the Norman Conquest* (London, 1904), Chapter XVI.

38. The word *Englisc* seems to be older than the word *England*; the Old English *Englisc* is the adjective applied first to the Angles. The earliest recorded use of the term *Englisc* in surviving Old English literature, however, is from the writings of King Alfred, but it is to be supposed that the word is probably much older than that. There is a comprehensive discussion of the matter in the NED under "English."

39. See X, 3 below.

40. See Chapter VIII below.

41. See X, 1 below.

42. F. M. Stenton, *The Danes in England* (Oxford, 1928) and *Anglo-Saxon England* (Oxford, 1943).

43. The most recent works are Phillips Russell, *William the Conqueror* (London, 1933) and M. Coryn, *The Acquirer, 1027-1087* (London, 1934). William has been the favorite of all the historians and chroniclers of the period.

44. In addition to the works already cited in the above notes, the following will be, in my opinion, most helpful for a true understanding of the Anglo-Saxon period and its life. This list is admittedly

selective and cannot, in the nature of things, be exhaustive. The *Cambridge Bibliography of English Literature* (Cambridge, 1941), the bibliographies in the *Annual* of *The Modern Humanities Research Association* (to be supplemented by the annual bibliographies published in the Supplementary Volume of *Publications of the Modern Language Association*) and the annual *Year's Studies in English*—these are the standard starting-places today for any detailed study of the life, language, and literature of the Old English period. For works on this period before 1922 there are two indispensable bibliographies: Arthur H. Heusinkveld and Edwin J. Bashe, *A Bibliographical Guide to Old English* (Iowa City, 1931), and W. L. Renwick and Harold Orton, *The Beginnings of English Literature* (London, 1939). Both the Heusinkveld-Bashe and Renwick-Orton bibliographies overlap to some extent the Annuals mentioned above.

In brief, the following items, made up in large measure of older studies, should combine with the works already listed in opening up to the beginner the field of Old English literature. The relative ages of these works are not necessarily to be taken as a reflection upon their merits; many a work written in the last century still holds its own against more recent competition. But, all things else being equal, the later work has the obvious advantage of drawing upon more recent studies in the field; and a great deal has been done in the study of Old English literature and civilization during the past thirty years.

1. General Origins of the Anglo-Saxons and the Vikings

Francis B. Gummere, *The Founders of England* (New York, 1930); H. M. Chadwick, *The Origin of the English Nation* (Cambridge, 1907); Donald A. McKenzie, *Teutonic Myth and Legend* (New York, 1936); T. E. Karsten, *Die Germanen* (Leipzig, 1928) —with French translation (Paris, 1931); T. D. Kendrick, *A History of the Vikings* (New York, 1930); Axel Olrik, *Viking Civilization* (London, 1931); Carl Clemen, *Altgermanische Religionsgeschichte* (Bonn, 1934); Frederic Seebohm, *Tribal Custom in Anglo-Saxon Law* (London, 1902) and *The English Village Community* (London, 1883); F. Liebermann, *The National Assembly in the Anglo-Saxon Period* (Halle, 1913); Georg Waitz, *Deutsche Verfassungsgeschichte* (Kiel, 1844); and J. H. Ramsay, *The Foundations of England* (London, 1898).

2. The Romans in Britain

Emil Hübner, "Das römische Heer in Britannien" in *Zeitschrift für celtische Philologie*, XVI, 513-584; James Curle, *A Roman Frontier-Post and its People* (Glasgow, 1911); W. T. Watkin, *Roman*

Cheshire (Liverpool, 1886) and *Roman Lancashire* (Liverpool, 1883)—of the long line of dreary county-histories in England, these two books are among the best; and H. F. Tozer, *A History of Ancient Geography* (Cambridge, 1897).

3. General Anthropological Situation

Henri d'Arbois de Jubainville, *Les premiers habitants de l'Europe* (Paris, 1877; 1889-1894); Joseph Deniker, *Les races et les peuples de la terre* (Paris, 1900).

4. Social History

H. M. Traill, *Social England* (London, 1910); Paul Vinogradoff, *English Society in the Eleventh Century* (Oxford, 1908); Aldo Ricci, "The Anglo-Saxon Eleventh-Century Crisis" in *Review of English Studies*, v, 1-11; J. W. Thompson, *The Middle Ages, 300-1500* (London-New York, 1931).

5. The Iron Age and Its Beginnings

Ludwig Beck, *Die Geschichte des Eisens* (Brunswick, 1884-1903).

6. County and Local Histories (suggestions only)

W. H. Dixon, *Fasti Eboracenses: Lives of the Archbishops of York* (London, 1863)—this, in spite of its title, is more interesting for local than for ecclesiastical history; John Tomlinson, *Doncaster from the Roman Occupation to the Present Time* (Doncaster 1887); T. R. Nash, *Collections for the History of Worcestershire* (London, 1781-1799, reprinted at Oxford, 1894-1895)—one of the best of the county histories; M. D. Harris, *Life in an Old English Town: a history of Coventry* (London, 1898); O. M. Edwards, *Wales* (London, 1902); W. A. Copinger, *The Manors of Suffolk* (London, 1905-1911) ; R. W. Eyton, *Antiquities of Shropshire* (London, 1854-1860); C. H. Hartshorne, *Historical Memorials of Northampton* (Northampton, 1848); C. J. Palmer, *A History of Great Yarmouth* (Great Yarmouth, 1856); George Norton, *Commentaries on the History, Constitution, and Chartered Franchises of the City of London* (London, 1829; 1869); G. L. Gomme, *The Governance of London* (London, 1907)—particularly good for Romanized London after the departure of the Romans; David Sinclair, *A History of Wigan* (Wigan, 1882); and J. A. Picton, *Memorials of Liverpool* (London, 1907).

The *Victoria County Histories*, still in course of publication, should obviously be consulted at all times; yet they are frequently less useful for particular matters than the older histories of the type just mentioned.

7. THE CELTIC WORLD, ESPECIALLY IRELAND

Henri Hubert, *The Rise of the Celts* (London, 1934); W. Krause, *Die Kelten und ihre geistige Haltung* (Königsberg, 1936); John Lanigan, *An Ecclesiastical History of Ireland to the Beginning of the Thirteenth Century* (Dublin, 1829); W. D. Killen, *The Ecclesiastical History of Ireland* (London, 1875); Alphons Bellesheim, *Die Geschichte der Katholischen Kirche in Irland* (Mainz, 1890-1891); J. Rhys, *Celtic Britain* (London, 1884).

8. TOWN-FORMATION

R. R. Tighe and J. E. Davis, *The Annals of Windsor* (London, 1858); F. W. Maitland, *Township and Borough* (Cambridge, 1898).

9. EARLY ENGLISH CHURCH HISTORY

Thomas Allison, *English Religious Life in the Eighth Century* (New York, 1929); E. L. Taunton, *The English Black Monks of Saint Benedict from the Coming of Saint Augustine to the Present Day* (London, 1898)—this work is much more important for the modern than for the medieval period; John Selden, *The History of Tithes* (London, 1618); H. O. Wakeman, *An Introduction to the History of the Church of England* (London, 1914); H. H. Milman, *A History of Latin Christianity* (London, 1854-1855)—still the classic treatment of this subject among English writings; A. S. Cook, "Theodore of Tarsus and Gislenus of Athens" in *Philological Quarterly*, II, 1-25—valuable for a discussion of the influence of the Christianization of England by Saint Basil (ca. 329-379); and W. F. Hook, *Lives of the Archbishops of Canterbury* (London, 1860-1876).

10. CONCEPTIONS OF REAL ESTATE

T. E. Scrutton, *Land in Fetters: or the history of the laws restraining the alienation and settlement of land in England* (Cambridge, 1886); Charles Sandys, *Consuetudines Kanciae: a history of gavelkind and other customs in Kent* (London, 1851); Paul Guilhiermoz, *Essai sur l'origine de la noblesse en France au moyen-âge* (Paris, 1902)—in the opening chapters there is a discussion of the significant analogy of real-estate laws in France at a time contemporaneous with the Old English period.

11. ARMY AND NAVY

C. W. C. Oman, *A History of the Art of War from the Fourth to the Fourteenth Century* (London, 1898); N. H. Nicolas, *A History of the Royal Navy* (London, 1847); G. Köhler, *Die Entwicklung des Kriegswesens von der Mitte des elften Jahrhunderts* (Breslau, 1893).

12. POLITICAL AND CONSTITUTIONAL LAW

Felix Liebermann, *Gesetze der Angelsachsen* (Halle, 1898)—the standard work on the subject; Felix Liebermann, *Über Pseudo-Cnuts Constitutiones de Foresta* (Halle, 1894); F. L. Attenborough, *The Laws of the Earliest English Kings* (Cambridge, 1922); Frederick Pollock and F. W. Maitland, *The History of English Law before the Time of Edward I* (Cambridge, 1898); F. W. Maitland, *The Constitutional History of England* (Cambridge, 1908); William Stubbs, *The Constitutional History of England* (London, 1874-1878)— which runs only to 1485; *The Cambridge Medieval History*—with all the virtues and all the vices of a great project undertaken by various hands; William Hunt and R. L. Poole, *The Political History of England* (London, 1905)—the first volume of this work, which is appropriate to the Old English period, is by Thomas Hodgkin. See also G. M. Young, *The Origin of the West Saxon Kingdom* (Oxford, 1934); J. N. L. Myers, "The Teutonic Settlement of Northern England" in *History*, xx, 250-262; C. H. Pearson, *A History of England during the Early and Middle Ages* (London, 1867)—an older work which overemphasizes the continuity of Roman constitutional law in England.

13. CANON AND MONASTIC LAW

William Dugdale, *Monasticon Anglicanum* (London, 1846); Emil Friedberg, *Corpus Juris Canonici* (Leipzig, 1879-1881); David Wilkins, *Concilia Magnae Britanniae et Hiberniae, A.D. 446-1718* (London, 1737).

14. SAINTS' LIVES AND BIOGRAPHIES
(See also Chapter X below)

Bibliotheca Hagiographica Latina Antiquae et Mediae Aetatis (ed. Socii Bollandiani; Brussels, 1898-1901); Jean Bolland *et al.*, *Acta Sanctorum* (Brussels, 1902); S. Baring-Gould, *Lives of the Saints* (London, 1897-1898)—still, in spite of its elementary nature, a standard work in English for the biographical material; John O'Hanlon, *Lives of the Irish Saints* (Dublin, 1875-1902).

15. MISCELLANEOUS MATERIAL PUBLISHED BY HISTORICAL SOCIETIES

See the publications of the Camden Society, the Canterbury and York Society, the Caxton Society, the Early English Text Society, the

English Historical Society, the Pipe Roll Society, the Roxburghe Club, the Scottish Text Society, the Irish Text Society, the Selden Society, the Surtees Society, and the Rolls Series.

16. Catalogues

The catalogues of the Bodleian Library, the University Library at Cambridge, the college libraries of Oxford and Cambridge, the cathedral libraries, and the Library of the British Museum (in particular the Cotton, Harley, Lansdowne, and Additional Manuscripts).

17. Costume, Food, and Drink

F. W. Fairholt, *Costume in England: a history of dress* (London, 1885); George Clinch, *English Costume* (London, 1909); F. W. Grube, "Cereal Foods of the Anglo-Saxons" in *Philological Quarterly*, XIII, 140-158; F. W. Grube, "Meat Foods of the Anglo-Saxons" in *Journal of English and Germanic Philology*, XXXIV, 511-529.

18. Fine Arts

G. Baldwin Brown, *The Arts in Early England* (London, 1903-1937)—a superb general account; Charles Cotton, *The Saxon Cathedral at Canterbury and the Saxon Saints Buried Therein* (Manchester, 1929); Francis Bond, *Gothic Architecture in England* (London, 1905); Francis Bond, *An Introduction to English Church Architecture* (London, 1913); G. T. Clark, *Medieval Military Architecture in England* (London, 1884); G. T. Files, *The Anglo-Saxon House* (Leipzig, 1893); George Petrie, *The Ecclesiastical Architecture of Ireland Anterior to the Anglo-Saxon Invasion: or an essay on the round towers of Ireland* (Dublin, 1845); J. H. Round, "English Castles" in *Quarterly Review*, no. 179, 27-57; J. H. Round, "The Castles of the Conquest" in *Archaeologica*, LVIII, 313-340; T. H. Turner and J. H. Parker, *Some Account of Domestic Architecture in England* (Oxford, 1851-1859); Robert Willis, *The Architectural History of Canterbury Cathedral* (London, 1845); A. W. Clapham, *English Romanesque Architecture before the Conquest* (Oxford, 1930).

19. General Archaeology

J. Y. Akerman, *Remains of Pagan Saxondom* (London, 1855); A. H. Allcroft, *The Earthwork of England* (London, 1908); J. R. Allen, *The Monumental History of the Early British Church to 1066* (London, 1889) and *Celtic Art in Pagan and Christian Times* (London, 1904); Joseph de Baye (translated by T. B. Harbottle), *The Industrial Arts of the Anglo-Saxons* (London, 1893); John Evans,

The *Ancient Bronze Implements, Weapons, and Ornaments of Great Britain* (London, 1881), and *The Ancient Stone Implements, Weapons, and Ornaments of Great Britain* (London, 1897); R. C. Hoare, *The Ancient History of Wiltshire* (London, 1821); George Stephens, *The Runic Monuments of Scandinavia and England*—the earliest substantial work on this subject, for which fuller references will be given at the point of discussion of runes and runic inscriptions (see V, 7 below); Charles Warne, *Ancient Dorset: the Celtic, Roman, Saxon, and Danish Activities* (Bournemouth, 1872); and Thomas Wright, *The Celt, the Roman, and the Saxon, Illustrated by Ancient Remains* (London, 1885).

20. Numismatics and Standards

Reginald A. Smith, "Early Anglo-Saxon Weights" in *Antiquaries' Journal* III, 122-129; J. Y. Akerman, *Roman-British Coins* (London, 1844); Jacob Dirks, "Les anglo-saxons et leurs petits deniers dits *sceattas*" in *Revue de la Numismatique Belge* (series V), II, 81-128, 269-320, 387-409, 521-541 (Brussels, 1870); John Evans, *The Coins of the Ancient Britons* (London, 1864)—there was a supplement to this, published in 1890; B. E. Hildebrand, *Angelsachsiska Mynt i Svenska Kongliga Myntkabinettet* (Stockholm, 1881); C. F. Keary and H. A. Grueber, *A Catalogue of English Coins in the British Museum: Anglo-Saxon Series* (London, 1887-1893)—the introduction to Volume I is especially helpful; John Lindsay, *A View of the Coinage of the Heptarchy* (Cork, 1842); C. L. Stainer, "Oxford Silver Pennies" in *Publications of the Oxford Historical Society* (Oxford, 1904), 925-1272.

21. Geography and Local Nomenclature

C. H. Pearson, *Historical Maps of England during the First Thirteen Centuries* (London, 1870); J. J. Egli, *Nomina Geographica* (Leipzig, 1893); Edmund Hogan, *Onomasticon Goedelicum Locorum et Tribuum Hiberniae et Scotiae: an index, with identifications, to the Gaelic names of places and tribes* (London, 1910); H. J. Mackinder, *Britain and the British Seas* (London, 1902); J. J. Egli, *Geschichte der geographischen Namenkunde* (Leipzig, 1886); P. W. Joyce, *The Origin and History of Irish Names of Places* (Dublin, 1913); Heinrich Leo (translated by B. Williams), *A Treatise on the Local Nomenclature of the Anglo-Saxons* (London, 1852); C. W. Bardsley, *English Surnames: their sources and signification* (London, 1903-1906), and *A Dictionary of English and Welsh Surnames* (London, 1901); and Ernest Weekley, *The Romance of Names* (New York, 1914).

22. HERALDRY

W. A. Shaw, *The Knights of England* (London, 1906); Charles Boutell, *A Manual of Heraldry* (London, 1913).

23. PALEOGRAPHY IN GENERAL

Thomas Astle, *The Origin and Progress of Writing* (London, 1876); Falconer Madan, *Books in Manuscript: a short introduction to their study and use* (London, 1893); Cesare Paoli (translated by Karl Lohmeyer), *Programma scolastico di paleografia latina e di diplomatica* (Florence, 1883-1901)—this work is considered the most comprehensive treatment of the subject; Maurice Prou, *Manuel de paléographie, suivi d'un dictionnaire des abreviations* (Paris, 1910); E. M. Thompson, *Handbook of Greek and Latin Paleography* (Oxford, 1912); E. A. Lowe, *Codices Latini Antiquores: a paleographical guide to Latin manuscripts prior to the ninth century* (Oxford, 1935); and especially W. Keller, "Angelsächsische Palaeographie," volume 43 of *Palaestra* (Berlin, 1906).

24. LANGUAGE

See first the bibliography by Kennedy cited in note 2 above. The standard dictionaries are J. R. Clark Hall, *A Concise Anglo-Saxon Dictionary* (3rd ed., Cambridge, 1931) and the more compendious and older Bosworth-Toller Dictionary (London, 1882). Staple grammars of Old English are E. Sievers (translated by A. S. Cook), *An Old English Grammar* (3rd ed., Boston, 1903); K. D. Bülbring, *Altenglisches Elementarbuch* (Heidelberg, 1902); Joseph and Elizabeth Wright, *Old English Grammar* (rev. ed., Oxford, 1914); and the Wrights' *An Elementary Old English Grammar* (Oxford, 1923). There are many Anglo-Saxon readers and anthologies, however, which contain excellent introductions to the language; the best of these are James W. Bright, *An Anglo-Saxon Reader* (New York, 1891; 1935); George T. Flom, *An Old English Grammar and Reader* (rev. ed., New York, 1930); Marjorie Anderson and Blanche C. Williams, *Old English Handbook* (Boston, 1935); G. P. Krapp and A. G. Kennedy, *An Anglo-Saxon Reader* (New York, 1927; 1929); Henry Sweet, *An Anglo-Saxon Reader* (Oxford, 1887); Samuel Moore and Thomas A. Knott, *The Elements of Old English* (Ann Arbor, 1919; 1940); Alfred J. Wyatt, *An Anglo-Saxon Reader* (Cambridge, 1925)—an anthology only; Samuel Moore, *Historical Outlines of English Phonology and Morphology* (Ann Arbor, 1925).

For etymology, the best work is unquestionably Ferdinand Holthausen, *Altenglisches etymologisches Wörterbuch* (Heidelberg,

1934), which in most respects supersedes the Clark Hall and Bosworth-Toller dictionaries mentioned in the preceding paragraph.

Most histories of the English language are obliged to treat Old English at some length. See A. C. Baugh, *The History of the English Language* (New York, 1935), Chapters III and IV, with bibliographies, or some of the following: Albert H. Marckwardt, *Introduction to the English Language* (New York, 1942); Oliver F. Emerson, *History of the English Language* (New York, 1922); Otto Jespersen, *Growth and Structure of the English Language* (New York, 1929); Stuart Robertson, *The Development of Modern English* (New York, 1934); Mary S. Serjeantson, *A History of Foreign Words in English* (London, 1935); Henry C. Wyld, *A Short History of English* (New York, 1929) and *The Historical Study of the Mother Tongue* (New York, 1906); and Logan P. Smith, *The English Language* (London-New York, 1912). Karl Luick's monumental *Historische Grammatik der englischen Sprache* (Leipzig, 1921) remains incomplete as to its original design.

II · A Foreword to the Literature
of the Anglo-Saxons

━━━━━◀▬▶━━━━━

1. "ANGLO-SAXON" OR "OLD ENGLISH"?

THERE has been the usual amount of academic quarreling over the name which should be given to the literature produced in England before the Norman Conquest.[1] The two terms in common use are (1) *Old English*, which is currently much in favor, and (2) *Anglo-Saxon*, which has existed from the beginnings of scholarship dealing with the period. If there is any choice to be made between these two terms—and I am not persuaded that such a choice is necessary—it should be made in favor of *Old English*, even at the risk of causing confusion in the minds of those who think of anything before the twentieth century in England as "Old English." The reasons for this preference are based usually upon one or the other of the following considerations:

I. The people who produced the literature in England before the Norman Conquest were some of them Angles, some Saxons, some Jutes or Frisians or something else. At the same time, most of the written remains which have descended to posterity belong to a time when these people were at least beginning to get a glimmering conception of an English whole.[2] We have seen that *Angelcynn* was the term King Alfred used in referring to his kingdom, although it was, strictly speaking, Saxon; *Englisc gewrit* was to be the product of his literary and educational labors. It matters little that Alfred's successor Athelstan spoke of himself only as king of the Angles and the Saxons. It matters little that to the Celts of Britain these Germanic invaders remained only Saxons, or Sassenachs. The greatest king of the Old English period attained a prophetic note in his use of the term *Englisc*; it is for succeeding generations to honor the soundness of that proph-

ecy. There is, in other words, both an historical and a senti-
mental basis for the preferred use of the term "Old English."

II. A more convincing fact in favor of "Old English" over
"Anglo-Saxon" is the language spoken by the Englishman
before the Norman Conquest. Here a brief digression is indicated. English, the language which has become a well-nigh
universal language today, belongs to the Anglo-Frisian
branch of the West Germanic languages. It is most closely
related to Frisian, which is still spoken in the most northerly
parts of Holland, and to the "Plattdeutsch" or Low German
dialects of northern Germany. It is of course unnecessary to
observe that English, as a Germanic language, is therefore a
member of the Indo-European family of languages.

Before the Norman Conquest and for a century or so later,
English remained in a highly inflected state, even more so
than Modern German. It possessed a variety of dialects, most
of which appeared to some extent in the written literature.
However, its vocabulary showed much less than in Modern
English the aptitude for borrowing from foreign languages,
for in the main the native elements in the language were kept
strikingly pure. Its grammar, when compared with that of
Modern English, was reasonably complicated; its syntax
less so.

Prior to 1100 four major dialects are recognizable in the
language: the Northumbrian, Mercian, West Saxon, and
Kentish. These are the ancestors of the four major Middle
English dialects (1100-1500)—Northern, Midland, Southern, and Kentish respectively. Northumbrian and Mercian
are obviously Anglian in origin; West Saxon is the dialect of
the most important Saxon nation in England; Kentish is the
dialect of the early kingdom of Kent founded by the Jutes.
The great majority of surviving manuscripts in the Anglo-
Saxon period come from a West Saxon dialect, usually mixed
with elements from other dialects.

Inflectional endings are the distinctive marks of *Old English*; a sloughing off of these characterizes the course of *Middle English*. Nevertheless some of these inflectional endings

have persisted to this day. It is clear, at any rate, that there is a linguistic basis for the use of the term "Old English" as applied to the literature written before the Norman Conquest; "Old English" confirms the organic unity of the writings as an essential part of English literature as a whole. This organic unity is manifest throughout the traditional threefold division of English into Old, Middle, and Modern—the Old English (500-1100) being the period in which the language shows full inflections; the Middle English (1100-1500), the period of weakening and disappearing inflectional endings; the Modern English (1500 to the present), the period of loss of inflections, with a few exceptions.

All such reasons aside, however, there is still no imperative need for making a choice between the two terms "Old English" or "Anglo-Saxon." Both are clear enough, and the use of both makes for variety. In the minds of many competent scholars in the field, the two terms are interchangeable; the greater accuracy and comprehensiveness of "Old English" are balanced by the fact that it is rather confusing to the uninitiated, while "Anglo-Saxon" has behind it the weight of a long tradition and possesses distinctive value.

2. SOME AXIOMS OF OLD ENGLISH LITERATURE

OLD English literature, or Anglo-Saxon literature, is, whatever its name, a literature of great potentialities as well as one of glaring weaknesses, reflecting, as does all significant literature, the temper of the age which produced it but also transcending in its loftier moments the confines of its immediate era and touching, if only briefly and fitfully, the universal. It is, even at its best, what we should call unsophisticated literature—at times even a little primitive—and like every unsophisticated literature, it is too often limited by its environment. It is somber, oftentimes groping and misty, often cold, and usually devoid of a towering imagination. It is precisely the sort of literature that one could expect from a people who lived in a damp climate, in raw sea-driving winds, with

more than a happy share of foggy, overcast days in which sun-
light too often shone feebly or was lost altogether. This literature, in all its forms, is inclined to speak but little of the all
too brief northern summer; instead, it is cast in the mood of
autumn and winter, to which spring comes but slowly if at all.

Further criticism of this literature must be deferred to a
later chapter,[3] after all the material has been examined. Yet
there are certain indubitable facts which every reader of Old
English literature should bear in mind before he reads a line
of Anglo-Saxon writings. One fact is the somberness just mentioned, which pervades all of the literature and which appears
to be a fundamental psychological ingredient in the composition of the Anglo-Saxon. For he is serious-minded; even
when he shows humor, it is likely to be a grim humor.

Another fact, already cited, is that this literature is the
naïve utterance of a people not too long emerged from a
tribal state, with a relatively narrow intellectual outlook.
Again, the civilization which produced Old English literature
was primarily agricultural and only secondarily mercantile.
To the average Anglo-Saxon, life was a bitter struggle against
climate, hostile foes, and primitive living conditions (or so
the modern age would see them). It was a struggle in which
the strong man only could survive.

Such were undoubtedly the physical and spiritual circumstances under which the Anglo-Saxon lived when he first came
to Britain. But most essential to remember of all facts pertaining to Old English literature is the fact of Christianity. The
first significant date in the history of the Anglo-Saxons in
Britain is the date of the arrival of Christianity in Kent in 597,
because from this mission of Augustine developed an organization and an integration of the scattered efforts of earlier
Christian missionaries in Britain, as well as the establishment
of a powerful centralized church in the island. Now the presence of Christianity meant to the early Anglo-Saxons in
Britain the presence as well of literacy and learning; it is apparent, then, that virtually all of the written literature of the
Anglo-Saxons dates from Christian times. The priest, who

was more often than not himself an Anglo-Saxon, was the great preserver of Old English literature; he was, of course, dedicated to the service of God and His Church, but he admired the pagan literature composed by the Anglo-Saxons in former days and saw to it that much of that pagan literature was kept somehow for the future. Most of it, no doubt, was modified and softened by clerical scribes in the interests of their Christianity. At the same time, the Church produced an even greater amount of literature for its own purposes. In short, one must reckon with a pagan Old English literature as well as with a Christian Old English literature; the warrior and the priest both sang their songs, told their stories, and gave counsel in those dim and shadowy times. It was the priest, however, who must be thanked for the survival of both pagan and clerical Old English writings. He brought to England not only the forms and spirit of Catholic Christianity; he brought also a knowledge of the Latin language fuller than anything the Anglo-Saxon had known of that language on the Continent; he brought also a knowledge of a moderate amount of Latin literature. He even acquainted some of the Anglo-Saxons with Greek. Through his scriptural and classical traditions he imparted to the wild, rhapsodic pagan literature a certain sense of order and discipline, a certain stylish turn of phrase, perhaps a certain freeing of the poetic imagination, for he introduced occasionally legends of the south and of the Orient which, however incongruous they may appear in Viking dress, aided in the gradual warming, fructifying process that Old English literature was to undergo.

It was, therefore, a supreme service which the Christian priest rendered the Anglo-Saxon world. And yet to the modern reader it is inevitably the pagan elements in Old English literature which make it most attractive. The story of strong men championing the cause of their people is always moving; to the sophisticated reader, moreover, there is always something of a paradoxical fascination in the contemplation of the primitive or near-primitive. Then, too, the mysteriousness of pagan Anglo-Saxon times, the struggle of the hardy Vikings against their natural and human foes, the spectacle of the ruthless survival of the fittest—these have in them raw drama which cannot fail to exert a special romantic appeal. One may well feel that the Anglo-Saxon warrior, with his grim and fatalistic philosophy of life, strikes a kindred chord in the breasts of the violent twentieth century, whereas the patient teacher, the cleric, lingers in his chapel and monastery, which can be only a chapel and a monastery. Perhaps we have no right to judge Old English literature thus in advance. Whether the pagan or the Christian side of these writings is of greater significance may be a matter of opinion. The calm dignity and fervent faith of a Bede afford a complete contrast to the tumultuous carnage of *The Battle of Brunanburh*; no doubt this dignity and this faith are in the long run more important. But there is little else to refute the thesis that those features of Old English literature which are most comprehensible to a present-day layman are those which pertain most clearly to the pagan sphere.

There is, for example, the Old English heroic epic, the characteristic expression of a people in the hero-worshipping stage of their tribal civilization—what the ethnologists call their Heroic Age. Side by side with this epic stands the Old English elegiac lay, which is mainly lyrical, although but a small handful of surviving Anglo-Saxon poems are pure lyrics. As a final representative of Old English pagan literature there is the scattered residuum of folklore, such as the charms, most of the riddles, and a great deal of the proverbial, sententious ("gnomic") verse and prose. As it happens, this pagan literature is virtually all poetry, not only in form but also in intent and often in achievement; it exhibits, in other words, the childlike love of sound, rhythm, and fancy that is habitually associated with an untutored people. So tenacious is this pagan tradition that the poetry written by the clerics who undertook the education of the mind and the salvation of the soul of these pagan Anglo-Saxons was suffused with the light which the pagan bards had first set aglow. There is, for instance, a Christian epic which clothed Biblical story in the garments of the old heroic epic and expressed its imaginative turns in the same phraseology and the same measure as did the bard, or *scop*, of older times. Perhaps it is no exaggeration to say that not until the neo-classical standards of the eighteenth century dominated English verse was there again such a rigid mold for formal poetry in English literature as there was before the Norman Conquest. Finally, Anglo-Saxon writers produced a large body of miscellaneous Christian prose, which derived largely from the classical models of church fathers and Ciceronian rhetoricians, from Roman and Greek philosophers, grammarians, and scientists, yet not to the complete exclusion of earlier traits of writing employed by those to whom Cicero and Virgil, even the Vulgate Bible itself, would not be recognized names.

It is our misfortune, perhaps, that we shall never be in a position to follow along the path of Old English literature in an orderly chronological progress. For one thing, the detailed sequence of political and social events during the period before the Norman Conquest is still none too clear, nor is it ever likely to be much clearer. We may often consider ourselves fortunate in having the main outlines before us. Moreover, the individual authors, with the exception of Bede, Alfred, Aelfric, Cynewulf, and a few others, are neither influential enough as authors nor definite enough as personalities to deserve chronological treatment. Finally, it is difficult to see any thought-progression during the centuries from 700 to 1000. When the subject-matter of Old English literature did not pertain to a dim and unreal heroic past, it was prone to deal with moral sentiments perilously approaching platitudes or spiritual matters of a religious hue. Since the early Church is an institution of growing material power but of limited intellectual and spiritual horizons, the static content of Old English literature is easy to explain. But not even the church, with its power to make men conform and the urgency with which it preached a new life to come, could quench the essential masculine vigor, moral integrity, and undaunted courage which are among the most prized of Anglo-Saxon resources in life. Far better, then, to depart from a purely historical plan and to consider Old English literature according to its obvious types—the epic, pagan or Christian; non-dramatic poetry of various kinds, such as the elegiac lyric, the personal lyric, the riddles and charms, the gnomic or homiletic verse; and in conclusion the considerable variety of prose composition.

3. A NOTE ON ANGLO-SAXON POETIC STYLE

IT HAS been observed of Anglo-Saxon poetry that it is cast in a stylistic and formalistic mold as rigid as that of any period in the history of English literature. The *scop* and his audience obviously believed that any occasion calling for poetic utterance was no ordinary occasion, and the language and style to be used could not be any ordinary language or style. The bard had therefore amassed a storehouse, or "word-hoard," of poetic words and phrases which could hardly have been the possessions of the ordinary individual. The *scop*, in fact, was inclined to "let the welkin ring," with all that such a rotund cliché implies. Hence the staple use of compound words, particularly those which in their composition and phraseology had some metaphorical value—the *kenning*.[4] "Whale-road," "gannet's bath," "playground of the winds" could represent *sea*; "light of battle," "leavings of the files" could represent *sword*; "peace-weaver," "dwelling-ornament" could represent *woman*. Nor did the *scop* believe that the hammering home of a poetic concept was in any way inartistic—rather, he sought repetition by the lavish use of synonyms and the playing in and out of appositional words and phrases, sometimes to the ruin of normal word-order but always with the effect of emphasis.

The universal metrical form observed by Germanic bards is but another tribute to the importance and well established conservatism of the *scop*'s traditional technique. The Anglo-Saxon poet, like his other Germanic colleagues, was obliged to use an irregular line, divisible into two half-lines, or hem-

istichs, and habitually given four main stresses to the line—
two to the half-line. In a few passages here and there more
than four main stresses will be noted, but such lines are
classed as hypermetric and anomalous. As long as the four
main stresses are accounted for, it is immaterial how many
unaccented syllables are in the line. The chips can fall where
they may, but there is an undeniable tendency to make com-
pact the final foot in each half-line.

Sievers, in his great work on Germanic metrics,[5] pointed
out that the metrical pattern of each half-line falls usually
into one of five basic types. These he designated as follows:
Type A— / x | / x; Type B— x / | x /; Type C— x / | / x;
Type D— / | / x x (with a subdivision possible according to
whether the inevitable secondary accent in the second foot
came on the *first* or the *second* of the two unaccented sylla-
bles); and Type E— / x x | /. Extra unaccented syllables are
admissible in the first foot of Types A, B, and C but only
very rarely in Types D and E. In general the second foot in
each type is not to be extended in any appreciable degree, although syncope and elision are allowable.

These five types are demonstrably true of the vast majority
of half-lines in Old English verse; but that the poet ever arranged these half-lines in some deliberate design is not at all
apparent, and the net impression received by one who scans
any large number of verses in Old English poetry is one of
accident rather than of plan. It is worth noting, however, that
three of the five types (A, D, and E) are trochaic in quality;
only one (B) is clearly iambic; and the remaining one (C) is
half-iambic and half-trochaic. The rapid, aggressive, urgent
qualities imparted to the half-line by the dominance of trochaic types seem to be entirely characteristic of the Germanic
temperament, to which action is more important than introspection. A scanned passage from *Beowulf*, with a free-verse
Modern English translation, will serve as an illustration.[6]

In spite of the elastic patterns in Old English verse (for
seldom are Sievers's five types used for any extensive number
of lines without many variations), the four main stresses in

the line are nevertheless a general requirement. So, too, is the alliteration or, as it has been sometimes called, the *initial-rime*. This alliteration is found under the main stresses. The third of the four stressed syllables (that is, the first stressed syllable in the second half-line) gives the key to the alliteration in any given line. Stressed syllable 3 alliterates with stressed syllable 1; sometimes also with stressed syllable 2; almost never with stressed syllable 4. The alliteration is customarily a matter of identical consonants; sometimes there is vowel-alliteration. Consonants must, of course, have the same phonetic value in order to alliterate;[7] but a vowel can theoretically alliterate with any other vowel.[8] When allowed free play, the stresses will clearly fall upon the important words in the line—upon nouns, verbs, adjectives, and occasionally pronouns and adverbs; it is apparent that the alliteration is not only a metrical device but also to some extent a syntactical design, since it calls attention to and emphasizes those words which should be emphasized. *End-rime*, which is virtually universal in Modern English prosody, is extremely rare in Old English; when it does take place, it is usually between two half-lines in the same full metrical line—in other words, it constitutes for the most part internal rime.[9]

A specialized type of poetic diction and freedom of word-order; a considerable license in syntax; repetitious elements introduced for the sake of emphasis; a rough but consistent tetrametrical plan; and alliteration—these are the earmarks of Germanic verse in general and of Anglo-Saxon verse in particular. As is the case with all such formalistic poetry, the devices frequently get in the way of the poetic spirit, and technique often supplants essential poetry.[10] The exigencies of alliteration, much more formidable than those of simple end-rime, require that the poet use words which alliterate, whether or not the alliterating words are the best that could be used. The repetitiousness clogs the syntax, to say nothing of the metrical movement, of the verses and gives a curious cloudiness or muddiness to many lines of the poetry. The kennings, though often bold and striking bits of imaginative expression, are all too often vague and inadequate as images; and the general effect rendered is frequently that of great poetic naïveté. But such was the plan of the *scop*, for better or for worse, and he adhered to it, even transmitting some of this technique to the prose-writers, for when Aelfric or Wulfstan seek an oratorical flight, they often assume an appreciable amount of alliteration and repetition. Has any English writer, however, particularly one with poetic inclinations, avoided completely this tendency toward alliteration? It would seem to be a basal characteristic of English literature. Indeed, some of our contemporary twentieth-century poets have sought freshness in these Old English metrical devices, thereby assuming a debt to the past which goes to make all English literature kin.[11]

NOTES TO CHAPTER TWO

1. Some of this disputing has found its way into print. In the years from 1928 to 1932 in particular there was much intellectual probing of the limits of the term "Anglo-Saxon." There were short notes and articles by Kemp Malone in *American Speech*, II, 147, 192, and 243; in *Review of English Studies*, III, 455-456; and in *Modern Language Notes*, XLV, 178-179; by Edward G. Fletcher in *American Speech*, II, 367 and IV, 346; by E. E. Ericson in *American Speech*, VI, 311-312; once more by Kemp Malone in *Anglia*, LV, 4-7. Much the best synthesis of the whole problem, however, is the article by Kemp Malone, " 'Anglo-Saxon': a semantic study" in *Review of English Studies*, V, 173-185. A serious objection to the use of "Anglo-Saxon" in reference to the period before the Norman Conquest, implied below in the pages of the present work, is that it suggests something not English, or at least *pre-English*; and logically this implication is completely unacceptable. On the other hand, usage frequently transcends logic.

2. Speaking from the point of view of politics and political organization, one can hardly detect such a concept before the time of the West Saxon ascendancy in the ninth century. See G. M. Young, *The Origin of the West Saxon Kingdom* (Oxford, 1934) and especially C. M. Grieve, "English Ascendancy in British Literature" in *New Criterion*, X, 593-613, for the germ of the idea. But Bede, writing in the eighth century, thinks of the "gens Anglorum" in his *Ecclesiastical History* as covering the whole island. The matter is difficult to ascertain; as a last resort, see F. Liebermann, "Vorstufen zur staatlichen Einheit Britanniens bis 1066" in *Englische Studien*, LX, 94-118.

3. Particularly Chapter XIV.

4. For a brief bibliography of the *kenning*, see Chapter IV, note 17.

5. But while Sievers's theory is a most valuable pioneer work in the field, it has been considerably modified by recent scholars. Nevertheless, see E. Sievers, "Zur Rhythmik des germanischen Alliterationsversen" in *Paul und Braune's Beiträge*, x, 209, 314, and 451-545, reprinted in New York in 1909; also his noted *Altgermanische Metrik* (Halle, 1893), especially pp. 29-34, for the Anglo-Saxon contribution. There have been several important studies following Sievers, notably M. Kaluza, *Der altenglische Vers* (Berlin, 1894); J. Schipper, *Grundriss der englischen Metrik* (Vienna-Leipzig, 1895), translated into English under the title *History of English Versification from the Earliest Times to the Present Day* (London, 1911); J. W. Rankin, "Rhythm and Rime before the Norman Conquest" in *Publications of the Modern Language Association*, xxxvi, 401-428; J. Routh, "Anglo-Saxon Meter" in *Modern Philology*, xxi, 429-434; W. W. Greg, "The 'Five Types' in Anglo-Saxon Verse" in *Modern Language Review*, xx, 12-17—something of a protest against Sievers's classifications; E. W. Scripture, "Die Grundgesetze des altenglischen Stabreimverses" in *Anglia*, lii, 69-75—which argues against the division of Old English verse into half-lines and maintains that the alliterating groups have a rhythm independent of any line-division; P. F. Baum, "The Character of Anglo-Saxon Verse" in *Modern Philology*, xxviii, 143-156—which represents the only metrical pattern in Old English poetry to be the two stresses to the half-line, with light syllables variously placed, a view typifying the older opinion; S. O. Andrew, *The Old English Alliterative Measure* (Croydon, 1931); and P. F. Baum, "The Meter of the Beowulf" in *Modern Philology*, xlvi, 73-91 and 145-162.

The first important modification of Sievers's theory came from Andreas Heusler—see his *Deutsche Versgeschichte, mit Einschluss des altenglischen und altnordischen Stabreimverses*, published as volume 8 of Paul's *Grundriss der germanischen Philologie* (Berlin-Leipzig, 1885-1929). While following the nomenclature of Sievers's classification, Heusler calls attention to the prominence in Old English verse of anacrusis, which gives frequently the value of the freely run-on line, or enjambement. (For the special matter of enjambement in Old English verse, see Kemp Malone, "Plurilinear Units in Old English Poetry" in *Review of English Studies*, xix, 201-204.) Heusler's ideas were supplemented by W. E. Leonard, "Four Footnotes to Papers on Germanic Metrics" in *Studies in English Philology: a miscellany in honor of Frederick Klaeber* (Minneapolis, 1929), 1-13. Leonard developed the importance of the musical rest in the line.

Something of a revolution has been achieved by John C. Pope in *The Rhythm of Beowulf* (New Haven, 1942), which is not only the most complete of contemporary studies but also has developed a new theory. Pope, too, keeps the traditional nomenclature but throws into special relief the lines of verse beginning with an unaccented syllable or syllables, discusses the possibilities of Heusler's theory of anacrusis here, and decides upon the necessity for a rest before these unaccented initial syllables, or, in other words, an initial rest, *which is the occasion for the sounding of the harp in some kind of accompanying beat or chord.* The great virtue of Pope's theory is that it restores to the picture the harp, the "glee-wood" or "game-wood," which is often referred to in Old English verse but which is thought to have become extinct by the time the Beowulf Poet, let us say, actually composed his poem. As Pope points out, such a radical change in the method of delivery as the laying aside of the harp is contrary to the traditional practice under any circumstance. This is to say, then, that these verses may well have been delivered as a recitative with harp accompaniment rather than as a direct oral recitation without benefit of musical adornment. It might be observed that both Leonard and Pope prefer the musical type of notation in their scansion.

6. The passage chosen comprises lines 710 to 727 inclusive of *Beowulf.* The metrical type of each half-line is marked in the margins by the appropriate letter. For the sake of simplicity, the older prosodic marks are employed.

A (with anacrusis)	Ðā cōm of mōre under misthleoþum	C
A	Grendel gongan Godes yrre baer	E
A	mynte se mānscaþa manna cynnes	A
A	sumne besyrwan in sele þām hēan.	B
A	Wōd under wolcnum tō þaes þe hē wīnreced	C
A	goldsele gumena gearwost wisse	A
A	fǣttum fāhne. Ne waes þaet forma sīþ	B
D (with anacrusis)	þaet hē Hrōþgāres hām gesōhte	A

C næfre hē on aldordagum   ǣr nē sīþþan   A

A heardran hǣle,   healþegnas fand!   E

A Cōm þā tō recede   rinc sīþian   D

A drēamum bedǣled.   Duru sōna' onarn   E

E fȳrbendum faest,   syþþan hē hire folmum æthrān   B

A (with   on¦brǣd þā bealohȳdig,   þā hē gebolgen waes,   B
anacrusis)

A recedes mūþan.   Raþe aefter þon   E

B on fāgne flōr   fēond treddode   D

A ēode yrremōd;   him of ēagum stōd   B

A ligge gelīcost   lēoht unfǣger.   A

(The predominance of A-types in this passage is due chiefly to the fact that the lines present a swift-moving narrative.)

A free-verse translation follows:

Then from the moorland   under cover of mists
Grendel came stalking;   God's wrath he bore.
He intended, that arch-foe,   to entrap
Some human sleeping   within the high hall.
He moved under the clouds   until the wine-hall,
Gold-covered work of man,   appeared before him,
Gilded and shining.   That was not the first time
That he had sought   the house of Hrothgar;
But never in the days of his life   before or since
Was he to find harder luck   or braver hall-thanes!
So came to the building   the monster advancing,
The hall silent and desolate.   The door came away,
Though fast with forged bands,   when he put his fist upon it;
With evil intent he ripped away—   for he was raging—
The mouth of the building.   Quickly thereafter

Along the bright floor   the fiend stepped his way
Irefully moving;   from his eyes arose
A hideous light   most like to flame.

7. Except that the velar *g* and velar *k* (gold, corn) may alliterate with the palatal ʒ and palatal *c* (as in the first line of *Beowulf*, for example).

8. But many believe that this so-called vowel-alliteration is a species of consonant-alliteration. The physical effort of beginning a word with a vowel-sound is, to state it crudely, the equivalent of a consonant; this consonant would be a *glottal stop*. In effect, then, words beginning with a vowel cannot mechanically be uttered without some function of the tongue; this movement of the tongue and accompanying movement of the glottis, in the opinion of many, is enough to establish a consonantal rather than a vocalic sound. Such a point of view, of course, automatically destroys the possibility of any kind of initial vowel in pronunciation.

9. See especially the article by J. W. Rankin mentioned in note 5 above.

10. A. C. Bartlett, *The Larger Rhetorical Patterns in Anglo-Saxon Poetry* (New York, 1935)—a very helpful study.

11. Individual works treating Old English literature alone, without particular reference to Middle English literature as well, are almost non-existent. The two best examples to date have been Stopford A. Brooke, *The History of Early English Literature* (London-New York, 1892), which has good, though dated, Victorian criticism of the literature, and the same author's *English Literature from the Beginning to the Norman Conquest* (London-New York, 1898), which has some good translations of Old English poetry, although better and more complete translations are available elsewhere. For the rest, the student of the period will find the first seven chapters of the *Cambridge History of English Literature*, Vol. I, very useful. Especially good for a foreigner's viewpoint is J. J. Jusserand, *A Literary History of the English People* (London, 1905), I, 1-222; the same, however, cannot be said for either E. Legouis, *A Short History of English Literature* (Oxford, 1934), 1-15, or E. Legouis and L. A. Cazamian, *A History of English Literature* (London, 1926), 3-54. A reliable study, now somewhat out of fashion, is B. Ten Brink, *Early English Literature*, translated by H. M. Kennedy (London, 1883). The treatments of the subject in P. G. Thomas, *English Literature before Chaucer* (London, 1924), and Allen R. Benham, *English Literature from Widsith to the Death of Chaucer* (New Haven, 1916), are adequate, but from the very scope of their material they are obliged to treat Old English literature in rather cursory fashion. Benham's book has copious illustrations of text, so much so as to be at times a virtual

anthology. The most recent effort to replace Stopford Brooke is Elizabeth E. Wardale, *Chapters on Old English Literature* (London, 1935). It is my opinion that Miss Wardale's book is conservative and acceptable enough as to scholarship but lacks a proper appreciation of the vigor of Old English literature and life.

There are several readers and books of selections; these will be referred to in the notes of this work where they may be of use. The same procedure is followed in the case of translations, but a helpful item to be recognized early is R. K. Gordon, *Anglo-Saxon Poetry* (No. 794 of the Everyman Library), which gives literal but effective prose translations of all the important pieces of Old English verse.

In one special department of Old English literature, there is an excellent treatment by C. W. Kennedy in his *Early English Poetry* (New York, 1943). See also W. Thomas, *L'épopée anglo-saxonne* (Paris, 1924), and the following articles on individual phases of the poetry: E. D. Hanscom, "The Feeling for Nature in Old English Poetry" in *Journal of English and Germanic Philology*, v, 439-463; W. E. Mead, "Color in Old English Poetry" in *Publications of the Modern Language Association*, xiv, 169-206; A. R. Skemp, "The Transformation of Scriptural Story, Motive, and Conception in Anglo-Saxon Poetry" in *Modern Philology*, iv, 423-470; and H. C. Wyld, "Diction and Imagery in Anglo-Saxon Poetry" in *Essays and Studies*, xi, 49-91. Other items will be mentioned below in due course.

The two fullest bibliographies of Old English literature, that of Heusinkveld and Bashe and of Renwick and Orton, as well as the *Cambridge Bibliography*, have been cited in Chapter I, note 44 above.

III · The Old English Heroic Epic Poems

1. THE PROBABLE GENESIS OF THE EPIC

ALTHOUGH it is likely that the epic literature of the Germanic peoples was of great extent, both in amount and in geographical distribution, it is still difficult to ascertain the relative importance of the Old English heroic epic within this great framework. The Gothic nations, for instance, have left us nothing of this kind of work in writing; yet there are enough allusions in the poems of other Germanic nations to Gothic heroes and their feats for us to postulate the existence of Gothic epic cycles in the third, fourth, and possibly fifth centuries.[1] These Gothic legends, however, probably existed only in oral form. The Scandinavian and the German peoples have left behind a large crop of heroic materials; most of it is of comparatively late date, certainly none before the seventh century (which is already a good two hundred years after the historical Heroic Age of the Germanic tribes), and some as late as the fifteenth century. On the other hand, there is surviving Old English heroic literature from a probable date of composition earlier than that of any other similarly surviving epic poems among the Germanic nations. Yet there is no epic poem, dating from these ancient heroic centuries, in which an Anglo-Saxon is the protagonist; and, as a matter of fact, there is left only one specimen of the Old English heroic epic which can be called complete. The preservation of that specimen has been, as so often, something in the nature of pure chance.

There are two possible reasons for this curious state of affairs. First, all the Old English epic literature of native origin might have been stamped out between the upper millstone of the Danes and the lower millstone of the Church. It is not inconceivable that the Danes were guilty of this vandalism; they comported themselves for generations as destructive marauders on large stretches of Anglo-Saxon coastal and inland regions. The Church, however, was inclined, at least among its individual members, to look with leniency on these old pagan stories. Since all surviving Old English literature was written down in Christian times, one is justified in regarding the Church as a kind of haphazard protector of the Old English epic remains.

Perhaps, on the other hand, the fact of the Danish invasions and the ultimate conquest of England by the Danes may have had something to do with the presence in surviving Old English legendry of Norse heroes like Beowulf and Hnaef. But a still easier explanation of the absence of any definitely Anglo-Saxon hero is that those factors which go to make up the Heroic Age of the Anglo-Saxon tribes—that childhood period through which all peoples seem to pass, in which hero-worship is the underlying psychological motif[2]—obtained while the Anglo-Saxons were still on the Continent rather than after their migration to the British Isles. On the Continent these Anglo-Saxon tribes were, so far as we can surmise, illiterate; their epics were transmitted by oral tradition only. An epic in the process of oral transmission would be passed about from tribe to tribe, even from nation to nation, by itinerant bards; national boundaries, therefore, tended to be subordinated to ethnical boundaries. Moreover, this store of epic material could later be drawn upon by all kinds of writers for various purposes. We shall see in *Beowulf* a passage explaining the genesis of the heroic epic in its simplest form; we can observe in *Widsith* evidences of the universality of this epic material; and we shall find example after example among the Caedmonian and Cynewulfian poems of how the older bardic epic tradition was adapted to Christian story and doctrine.

But every surviving heroic epic poem from the period before the Norman Conquest was written down decades and even generations after the original composition (probably oral) of the whole poem or parts thereof. This generalization may appear to be sweeping; but, so far as we can tell, there is no extant manuscript of Old English poetry which is the original author's own copy. Rather, the manuscript represents the effort of a later individual to fix an older poem in writing for the benefit of posterity. We must, in other words, distinguish between the originator(s) of *Beowulf* or *Widsith*, or parts thereof, and the single writer who put the poems down in their present form at a later date, the single individual to whom we refer as the Beowulf Poet or the Widsith Poet. Such a distinction, of course, takes no account of later scribes who copied a finished poem and may even have altered it in the copying.

To repeat, it is obvious that those poems in Old English literature which can be called heroic epic poems—*Widsith*, *Beowulf*, *The Fight at Finnsburg*, the *Waldere Fragments* —are not Anglo-Saxon so much as they are Danish or Low German, although they may have been written in the Old English language. The first-named of these poems ranges in its allusions far and wide over almost the entire Germanic world. Figures like Beowulf and Hrothgar and Garulf and Theodric do not have a habitation on English soil. Instead, these characters are identifiable as Continental Germanic; and the locales of the poems, it has been shown repeatedly, are Low German or Scandinavian. We should consider these survivors of the Old English epic, therefore, as having been composed on the basis of old legends common to several Germanic tribes, recited by the bard or *scop*[3] perhaps even before the Anglo-Saxon conquest of Britain, transmitted as usual by oral tradition, brought to England either by Viking Anglo-Saxons or Viking Danes or individual bards, and elaborated there— still by oral tradition. In England, with the advent of a literary culture under the auspices of the Church, and with the development of that stage of civilization which looks back with affectionate idealization upon the glorious deeds of a bygone past, these poems were finally reduced to writing, subject to the philosophical comment or religious editing natural to their eventual redactor.[4]

Such a process may seem fanciful and might justifiably be

so considered, were it not possible to fit the theory of it into certain otherwise embarrassing facts. Of course there is no satisfactory proof that the theory can be made to cover every individual example of the folk-epic among the Germanic peoples; and it certainly has no application to such definitely "literary" imitations as *The Battle of Maldon* (III, 4). But by this theory we can account for the obvious passage of time between the deed celebrated and the version of that deed which has come down to us—often a matter of centuries. We can thus account for the episodic, repetitious structure of these old epics. We can explain the apparent inconsistencies and the incongruous blend of pagan and Christian elements by the theory of protracted oral transmission. For then the accretions of the original story, the digressions and modifications, all brought about by the natural tendency of successive bards to add to a good thing, become self-evident, and so do the presence of Scandinavian and German heroes in Anglo-Saxon epics.

2. *WIDSITH*

THE poem *Widsith*[5] is a case in point; no piece of poetic antiquity has in recent years received a more thorough and scholarly treatment. The critical judgments of all this scholarship have varied in wide degree. There is reasonably general unanimity, however, that at least one portion of the poem is the oldest surviving piece of English verse. As to structure, there is further general agreement that the poem is a concretion of several ancient fragments. But the scholars are not in accord as to the order, the date, or the interrelationship of these several fragments. The name of the poem, which signifies literally "far journey" and by extension "far traveler," may or may not be the actual name of the chief figure, who speaks throughout the poem in the first person.

Earlier students considered the work autobiographical; later scholars, however, have virtually abandoned this point of view. It is certainly a man who calls himself "Widsith" who "unlocks his word-hoard" and proceeds to tell of the many kings and nations he visited during his career as a wandering *scop*. He dwells for some time on certain events associated with individual kings—kings who have definite historicity and at the same time are figures of prominence in the songs of Germanic legendry. Such a person as "Widsith" is doubtless representative of a very well known type in early Germanic society—the bard errant, whose progress from one Germanic people to another spread in its train countless contributions to the ever-growing body of Germanic heroic story. But, so far as the poem *Widsith* is concerned, no one man could have seen all the individuals mentioned in the long Catalogues of Kings, or *thulas*,[6] which take up some forty lines of the total of 143 in the text of the poem. On the other hand, the opening part and the latter portion of the poem, which tell of "Widsith's" last journey and are garnished with details of his manner of life as a wandering bard, make plausible enough autobiography. It is now usually conceded that the autobiographical "prologue" and "epilogue" are of a date later than that of the various legendary episodes contained in the body of the poem. The *thulas* are for the antiquarian the most interesting features of the work; they serve as valuable indices of allusion to Germanic kings and tribes of the Heroic Age; and in many of these allusions they throw light upon other Germanic heroic poems—*Beowulf* and *The Fight at Finnsburg*, to name two Anglo-Saxon examples. The real problem raised by the relation of the bard to the Catalogues of Kings is the fact that some of the kings visited by the *scop* belong historically to the fourth century, such as the Goth Eormanric; and some to the sixth, such as the Lombard Aelfwine (Alboin). This fact alone kills the autobiographical reality of the poem. If the episodes, for example those of Eormanric or of Aelfwine, are legendary from the standpoint of the mysterious "Widsith"—an assumption which appears to be inevitable—then we have one or more obvious interpolations; but if so, which interpolation was made first, and what is the relation between interpolations?

One is gradually forced, therefore, to regard the poem

Widsith in its existing version as a poem of composite structure. The first Catalogue of Kings is of great antiquity, probably antedating the migration of the Anglo-Saxons to Britain,
at any rate from early in the sixth century. It is consequently
the oldest extant piece of English poetry. The remaining pair
of *thulas* and the diffused legendary material are probably a
little later in date. The "autobiographical" portions are more
recent still. Yet even if this sixth century date for the first
thula be granted, it must also be granted that the traditions
represented by the Catalogues of Kings belong to the late
fourth, the fifth, and the early sixth centuries. On the other
hand, as just noted, the prologue and most likely the epilogue
as well seem to belong to the period of the flourishing of Old
English bardic poetry—to the latter part of the seventh and
the first half of the eighth centuries. Particularly do the closing lines of the poem—

> So the minstrels of men go wandering
> Over many a land as fate decrees,
> Speaking their needs, uttering thanks;
> Ever meeting, to south or to north,
> A man wise in song, generous in giving,
> Who wishes to raise up his fame before the warriors,
> To perform earlship, *until it all passes,*
> *Light and life together.*[7]
> Still he gains glory, and holds under the heavens
> A lofty honor that will not pass away.
>
> [135-143]

—suggest the more sophisticated bard of the time of *Beowulf*,
of the Christian epics, of the elegiac poems—in brief, of the
eighth and ninth centuries.[8] It is therefore easy to suppose that
Widsith, as we have it, was put into shape by a single author—
the Widsith Poet—who incorporated the old Catalogues of
Kings and some legends into a personal lay of imaginative
character with a moral purpose—to point out how good kings
are supported by their subjects. The poet wrote, let us say, in
the late seventh century, and his work was subsequently
copied, perhaps with a few additions or interpolations until it

came to be included in *The Exeter Book*[9] during the latter
years of the tenth century. When we hypothesize in this manner and weigh carefully the net achievement of the poem, the
author becomes almost a real person. Yet there is an undeniable flavor of archaism about *Widsith* which no other Old
English poem possesses in similar degree. No doubt some of
this archaism lies in the appearance, during one of the Catalogues of Kings, of the names of such people as the Medes
and the Persians, the Hebrews and the Egyptians, the Israel-
ites themselves beside such a shadowy figure of Germanic
mythology as Wade. Whether the inclusion of these particular names is due to interpolation by a later scribe or to blunders
by a copyist or to inept imagination on the part of the Widsith
Poet,[10] the poem comes close to being a massive example of
what Poe called "a sort of runic rhyme."

The whole problem of *Widsith*, when posed thus abruptly
before the layman, is bewildering and exasperating; no doubt
the casual reader will be wise enough to ignore the full academic implications of the matter. But *Widsith* as a whole is
extremely interesting and even essential to the student of the
Old English period, not only because it antedates, at least in
part, any other surviving work in Old English literature, but
also because it serves as a valuable reference-work in the field
of Germanic saga-material, incomplete as its references necessarily must be. There are allusions to most of the known Germanic tribes of the Continent and to many tribes and kings
that are still very obscure. The possibility that each and every
one of these kings and tribes may well have been the subject
of some heroic epic or epic-cycle, now unfortunately lost, is to
the scholar a tantalizing business. Specifically, for example,
there are references in *Widsith* to epic figures found in other
extant Old English epics; the poem, therefore, hints at the
not unlikely possibility that many other Old English epic
poems were once in existence, poems which dealt with other
Old English figures named in *Widsith* but now lost in obliv-
ion. The allusion to Offa, for instance, is sufficiently detailed
to conjure up at once the outlines of a full-blown epic. We

know, from the appearance of his story in *Beowulf*, far more about the deeds of Breca of the Brondings than the terse reference in *Widsith* vouchsafes; how many more such stories were thus in circulation?

No doubt very many; but there is little likelihood that we shall ever know much more about this matter than we know now. The very survival of *Widsith* is in a way a kind of double accident. Its material evidently happened to interest some Old English cleric-poet whose antiquarian inclinations were strong enough to permit him to overlook the pagan origins of the poem. Moreover, the poem, along with all other extant pieces of Old English literature, managed to survive the ravages of time and the malice of men. Neither the destruction of the monasteries by Henry VIII in the sixteenth century nor the depredations of Cromwell in the seventeenth —by both of which careers of unnecessary damage an untold number of manuscripts were lost to posterity—happened to bring *Widsith* to naught. For, as we have seen, the manuscript of *Widsith* by good fortune came to be embedded in the large collection of Old English poetry known as *The Exeter Book*.

3. *BEOWULF*

UNQUESTIONABLY the most important monument of Old English epic literature, however, is the poem *Beowulf*.[11] Its importance lies not alone in the fact that it embodies in characteristic fashion the ideals of the Germanic warrior; it is also the only example in Old English poetry of a heroic epic in what seems to be a complete state. It is in addition a happy hunting-ground for the linguist, the scholar, and the critic. In *Beowulf*, we are beyond the first stage of the heroic folk-epic, the individual lay concerning an epic feat by an individual hero—no good illustration of which can be found in Old English literature—and have come to the second stage, the concatenation of more than one feat by a single hero, covering in fact the essential achievements of the hero's entire career. In these manifold deeds of the hero are portrayed the ideals of the Geatish people—ideals which may properly be considered the ideals of the Germanic hero no matter what his tribal origins.

> ... I ruled this people
> For fifty winters; there was no folk-king
> Among any one of the neighboring tribes
> Who dared approach me in hostile war-clash,
> Or oppress me with threats of terror.
> I awaited my destiny on earth;
> I held well my own,
> Nor did I seek intrigue, nor did I swear
> Many oaths wrongfully. For all this,
> Though sick with mortal wounds, I rejoice;
> And so the Ruler of mankind need not charge me
> With the murder of kinsmen, when my life
> Departs from my body. . . .   [2732-2743]

And on the other side of the coin *Beowulf* depicts the loyalty of warrior to chieftain; of freeman, earl, and churl to their king—a whole-souled devotion to which the Anglo-Saxon was ready to dedicate his life. "Death is better for every earl than a life of shame!" cried young Wiglaf at his lord Beowulf's passing (2890-2891).

Beowulf, to the reader who first meets it, is a rather confusing succession of incidents, although a closer acquaintance with the work will reveal that the confusion is more apparent than real and that the author knew well where he was going. In spite of the admitted multiplicity of these incidents, however, the poem falls into two general parts: that having to do with the adventures of Beowulf the Geat at the Danish court of King Hrothgar, and that dealing with the mighty struggle between Beowulf and the fire-dragon at home in Geatland. Into the first part stalk two great mortal enemies of Beowulf, Grendel and Grendel's mother. There is also detailed reference in this section to a previous feat by Beowulf, the swimming-race with Breca. In the second part, during the narrative of Beowulf and the fire-dragon, there come many shreds of other stories—allusions, often of some length, to incidents in the wars between the Geats and the Swedes or between the Danes and the Heathobards, and to isolated figures of Germanic legendry who stride majestically through a few lines.

Beowulf the hero stands forth as a man of dignity and polish, in the sense that he knows to perfection the complicated etiquette expected of a champion. There is a suggestion that as a youth he was considered slow and lazy (2183-2189); but it is further apparent that as a child of seven winters he was, according to the custom of Germanic princes, taken from the keeping of his father and brought up by some one else—in this case, by his grandfather Hrethel, then King of the Geats. His training must, in the long run, have been successful; but in the "slowness" of Beowulf as a youth we see illustrated that common theme of folklore: the unpromising stripling who makes good, the "male Cinderella." As a young man in his twenties, however, Beowulf has physical attributes which are nothing short of overpowering; he is a fabulous swimmer and diver, for one thing. Nothing could be more appropriate than to find a maritime colossus as the hero of the only complete surviving epic in Old English literature. For even if Beowulf is not himself Anglo-Saxon, he has the attributes of a seafaring man, for which the English have always been famous. As examples, there is first of all his swimming-contest with Breca, a feat of epic proportions; there is next his even more remarkable accomplishment of covering the sea-stretches from the mouth of the Rhine to his home in Geatland (presumably in the Baltic), with thirty coats-of-mail on his back (2361-2362). The whole Breca episode should be read with one eye upon the muscularity and grim vigor of the text, as in

> Then we two together were swimming in the sea
> Five nights space, till the flood drove us asunder,
> Boiling waves and coldest of tempests,
> Lowering night, and the northern wind
> Whirled about hostile and grim—savage were the waves!
> As for the sea-fishes, their rage was aroused;
> But to me among my foes my body-corslet

> Hard and hand-linked rendered good help;
> The woven war-sark lay on my breast
> Adorned with gold. Down to the sea-bottom
> My savage foemen drew me; held me fast
> In their grim grasp; still it was granted
> That I reached the monster with point of sword,
> The valiant war-bill; and the bitter onset of battle
> Carried off the sea-beast through the work of my hand.
>   [544-558]

or again in

> Indeed they knew well my mighty strength;
> They themselves had seen it, when I came from battle,
> All bloody from my foes, where I killed five,
> Made havoc of the race of etins, and in the waves
> Slew nicors at night. Sore anguish I suffered;
> I avenged the insult to the Weders . . .
> I ground my enemies to pieces.   [418-424]

Combined with the sinewy indefatigability of Beowulf in the water is his superb lung-capacity. He can dive into the mere after Grendel's mother and follow down into the inky depths for a day before he can perceive the bottom of the sea (1495-1496). A similar feat is implied in a passage from the Breca Episode. Here, after describing in some detail the rigors of the northern sea and the terrors that were his because of the presence of various sea-creatures, Beowulf goes on to say:

> So my bitter enemies again and again
> Pressed hard upon me. I served them well
> With my precious sword, as was most fitting.
> Not for them the joy of feasting
> Or of unspeakable deeds, not for them to partake of me
> As they sat about their banquet near the bottom of the sea;
> But in the morning time, wounded by my weapon
> They floated upward along the salt sea's edge
> Put to sleep by the sword. . . .   [559-567]

Finally, Beowulf possesses at least by reputation the strength of thirty men in his hand-grip (377-381); it is sufficient, at any rate, to tear out the arm of the monster Grendel (815ff.).

Indeed, Beowulf relies upon this grip to the exclusion of the sword in fighting Grendel; and that unfortunate monster, "the shepherd of crimes,"

> Knew that he never had met in this world,
> In the four quarters of the whole wide earth
> In any other man a mightier hand-grip. [750-753]

These physical attributes, then, are Beowulf's peculiar contribution to the epic tradition of great strength and prowess. They are comparable to Roland's mighty blasts on the horn, to the weight-throwing gift of Ajax, to Cuchulain's marvelous dexterity and eyesight. But these are, after all, physical attributes only. In addition to qualities of bodily strength there are in Beowulf moral virtues of more than passing worth: there is nobility and gravity and an unshaken courage. Yet this courage is translatable chiefly into terms of action. It is more physical than moral. It is sober and sure but never brilliant; there is little in it of hot impetuosity. Even if one discounts the usual amount of conventional boasting in which Beowulf, as any good epic hero, indulges before a combat, there still remains an aura of confidence about him which is extraordinary. Neither the grim ferocity of the "mighty merewife," Grendel's mother, nor the flames pouring from the head of the fire-dragon dissuade Beowulf from his advance into danger. If there is any appreciable flaw in his character—any tragic defect of body or spirit which brings about his downfall, such as Achilles or Siegfried or Roland suffered—it is a superabundance of this valor and a resulting overconfidence which prompts him to sally forth against the fire-drake with inadequate protection at a too advanced age.

There is more than enough of platitude and of Christian admonition in the poem. The bloodiest and crudest of primitive battle-narratives will jostle against the most approved rules of conduct, either practical or spiritual. There are some, incidentally, who believe that the poem was intended, in its present form, as a book of conduct for kings and princes to follow; but this point of view, while attractive, need not be accepted.[12] In many passages Fate (*Wyrd*) and her warriors, both the doomed and the undoomed, wrestle with the Christian God for supremacy. Such inconsistencies, however, are easily enough understood when we remember that *Beowulf* as we have it today has a story many features of which belong to the pagan Germanic world of the sixth century or earlier and a form which belongs to Christian England of the eighth century as regards language and of the early eleventh century as regards manuscript.

The Beowulf Manuscript is the second of the four chief repositories of Old English poetry to be mentioned thus far, the first being, of course, *The Exeter Book*. One of the most prized items in the possession of the British Museum, the manuscript is designated as Cotton Vitellius A XV. Its survival, again, was a matter of fortuitous circumstances; as usual with all remaining Anglo-Saxon pieces, the Beowulf Manuscript somehow managed to escape the destruction which overtook so many of the literary monuments of ancient England when the monasteries were abolished in 1536. Sir Robert Cotton (1571-1631), the distinguished antiquarian, got possession of the manuscript, whose official classification-title preserves his name and the name of the Roman emperor under whose bust it lay in the Cottonian Library. When this famous library was destroyed by fire in 1731, the Beowulf Manuscript once more escaped, although it was somewhat scorched around the edges.

Beowulf is the next to last of the nine items in Cotton Vitellius A XV. The poem opens with the account of the coming and passing of Scyld Scefing, a Danish king whose name and whose story suggest at once that he is of mythological origin ("Shield, the son of Sheaf"). The opening section of approximately fifty lines has nothing to do with the story of Beowulf the Geat, although it introduces the name "Beowulf" as the name of Scyld Scefing's son. The origin of this name "Beowulf," which may be broken down into "Bee" and "Wolf," has been the subject of endless and not very fruitful debate.[13] The presence of "Bee" suggests that the original Beowulf was a culture-divinity of some sort, and that the divine qualities of this god, along with his name, were transferred to some mortal hero; the net result of such a transference would undoubtedly be the protagonist of an epic poem. Such an origin for the hero of our Old English epic is plausible enough, but it should be remembered that animal-names are universal among the Germanic peoples, "Wolf" in particular being extremely common, both as a simple name and as a part of a compound name, such as Cynewulf, Aethel-wulf, and others. Whatever mythological or folkloristic connections there may once have been among such animal-names and the names of heroes are no longer clear.

Nevertheless, this opening Prologue to *Beowulf*, while it evokes the dim shadows of forgotten deities, also establishes the poem as an epic of the Danes. It relates the name "Beo-wulf," borne by an early king in the Danish royal line, to the Geatish hero who plays the title-role in our epic poem, and implies therefore a close connection between Dane and Geat. More than that, the Prologue furnishes a fine touch of atmos-phere to a poem about the epic past. Scyld Scefing was of mysterious birth; he was found destitute, but he rose to become a great ruler—another male Cinderella. When he died, he departed into the bosom of the sea, as told in magnificent alliterative lines; like Arthur in Tennyson's *Idylls of the King*, he moved "from the great deep to the great deep."

Then, after a certain amount of genealogical information, the Beowulf Poet introduces us to Scyld Scefing's descendant Hrothgar, King of the Danes, and to his marvelous mead-hall Heorot, greater than any other building of its kind. It had been Hrothgar's own edifice, and so he proceeded to glorify it by holding feasts in it and dispensing gifts to his deserving subjects—the sure way for a Germanic king to recommend himself to his people.

Meanwhile the sounds of minstrelsy come from the hall, and the bard sings forth praise to the Creator. The sound of revelry enrages the envious Grendel, a supernatural monster of uncertain physical aspect, whom the Christian Beowulf Poet regards as the descendant of Cain. Grendel proceeds to harry the hall apace, taking off the Danes in batches until Heorot has been rendered useless. With the characteristic grim, humorous understatement[14] of the Anglo-Saxon, the poet observes:

> Then it was easy to find him who elsewhere
> Sought for himself a more spacious couch . . .
> [138-139]

Hrothgar is at his wit's end and prays to his heathen shrines; the poet, ever the Christian, reminds us that such efforts are all futile, and that Hrothgar is merely shoving his soul into Hell by such actions. In fact, nothing can be done about the matter, and years pass, until Beowulf the Geat, who has heard, while at home across the sea, of the depredations of the diabolical champion, arrives to offer his aid to the harassed King Hrothgar, who had befriended Beowulf's father in former times. There is a picturesque account of the voyage of the Geats from Geatland and of their reception by the punctilious coast-guard in the land of the Danes. Particularly striking are the formal behavior and grave politeness of all people concerned, and the tendency toward the set speech, which has long been pointed out[15] as a prime characteristic of the true heroic epic. Shortly after the arrival of Beowulf at Hrothgar's court, he is taunted by the malcontent Unferth; and a digression tells the story of Beowulf's victory in a gruelling swimming contest with Breca of the Brondings.

Then night comes and with it Grendel. In a grippingly recounted conflict, Beowulf tears out the arm of Grendel; and the monster flees, mortally wounded. The passage is in many ways the most primitive and savage bit of poetry in all Old English literature.

> Then from the moorland under cover of mists
> Grendel came stalking; God's wrath he bore.
> He intended, that arch-foe, to entrap
> Some human sleeping within the high hall.

He moved under the clouds until the wine-hall,
Gold-covered work of man, appeared before him,
Gilded and shining. That was not the first time
That he had sought the home of Hrothgar;
But never in the days of his life before or since
Was he to find harder luck or braver hall-thanes!
So came to the building the monster advancing,
The hall silent and desolate. The door came away,
Though fast with forged bands, when he put his fist upon it;
With evil intent he ripped away—for he was raging—
The mouth of the building. Quickly thereafter
Along the bright floor the fiend stepped his way
Irefully moving; from his eyes arose
A hideous light most like to flame.
He saw in the building many a warrior,
A band of kinsmen sleeping together,
A troop of brave young fighters.—
Then he laughed aloud;
He meant, that dire champion, ere day should come,
To sever in each one of them
Life from body, for upon him had come
A lust for feasting. But it was not yet fated
That he should devour any more of mankind
After that night. Stouthearted, the kinsman of Hygelac
Looked on to see how the mighty foe
Would comport himself under a sudden onset.
Nor did the monster think to delay,
But he quickly seized in his first attack
A sleeping warrior, tore him ruthlessly,
Bit into the bone-joints, gulped the blood from the veins,
Swallowing huge continuous morsels; forthwith
He had consumed the whole dead warrior,
Even his feet and hands. Nearer he came;
On the couch he seized with his fist
The strong-hearted warrior. Beowulf returned the grasp
With hostile purpose, propping himself up on his arm.
Straightway he discovered, that shepherd of crimes,
Knew that he never had met in this world
In the four quarters of the whole wide earth,
In any other man a mightier hand-grip.

In heart he was terrified, astounded in mind;
But no better could he escape for that . . .
It was a great wonder that the wine-hall
Stood against these mighty fighters,
That it did not fall down to the ground,
That fair earth-dwelling; but it was fast
Within and without clamped by iron bands,
The cunning work of the smith. Then from the sill
Broke many a mead-bench—so I have heard—
Adorned with gold, while the two foes struggled . . .
          . . . Up rose a roar
Passing loud; in the hearts of the North-Danes
Stood a grisly fear, yea, in each one of them,
When they heard from the wall the yells, ·
God's adversary crying out a lay of terror,
Victoryless song, the captive of Hell
Bemoaning his wounds. Beowulf held him fast,
He who was the greatest man of strength
In that day of this life.   [710-790]

If we count the story of the swimming-contest with Breca
as the first feat of Beowulf celebrated in the poem, we may
designate the fight with Grendel as the second. The Breca
Episode is, to be sure, much shorter, much less detailed than
the stories of the fights with Grendel or with Grendel's
mother. It has been aptly termed by Klaeber the "Breca Inter-
mezzo."[16] For the rest, it is rather impracticable to summarize
further in detail the two remaining chief incidents in Beowulf's
career—the struggle with Grendel's dam and the fatal encounter with the fire-dragon—since the fight with Grendel
will illustrate sufficiently the vigor and the forthrightness of
the poet's best narrative manner. After the monster Grendel
has been disposed of, the Danes and their guests, the Geats,
turn to a joyous celebration. This celebration, an occasion
which brings the traditional epic banquet, oratory of com-
mendation, and presentation of suitable gifts to a triumphant
warrior, offers us a view behind the scenes, at least as far as
the epic poet and his craft are concerned. It is rather fortunate
that the long and rather static passages following the flight of

Grendel have been preserved, for they tell us much, if we read between the lines, about the genesis of the heroic epic and about the audience that gave its attention to epic literature.

The more one reads and studies *Beowulf*, the more one is impressed by the design of the Beowulf Poet, in spite of the fact that his gift for digressive incidents is remarkable. There are forward pointings and backward glances sufficient to demonstrate that the poet was not indulging in an amateurish crazy-quilt of incident. Besides, the admittedly episodic structure illustrates in the main the individual epic lay, the narrative unit which serves as the individual tile in the mosaic which is the full narrative poem. For that reason it would be well to enumerate the major lays which present themselves in *Beowulf*. It will be noted that the subject-matter of these lays is often very remote from the Beowulf story. But, to stick at first to the lays in *Beowulf* having reference to the Geats and the Danes, there is, for example, the brief account of Beowulf's conduct in the battle fatal to his king Hygelac (2354-2379). This incident is alluded to more than once in the poem. It is at least one event mentioned in *Beowulf* which seems to be historically authentic. Again, there is the lay of the death of Ongentheow, king of the Swedes, in the first of the Geatish-Swedish wars (2472-2509). This is an elemental passage with a singularly romantic turn. The Swedes, under Ongentheow, had been at first victorious over the Geats; but when the tide of battle turned, the old Swedish king is brought to bay and killed by a rather obscure young Geatish warrior, Eofor. As a reward for this decisive blow the Geatish king, Hygelac, gives Eofor his only daughter in marriage. There are still other allusions to the Geatish-Swedish wars and to the feud between the Danes and Heathobards, as well as to the famous Finnsburg conflict (1060-1159).

But some of these lays, on the other hand, are extraneous and didactic in purpose. There is the rather chance allusion to the "unapproachable queen" Thryth, or Modthryth,[17] a figure reminiscent of Atalanta, Brunhild, and others (1931-1962). This originally evil person is described as a contrast and foil to a sympathic character, Queen Hygd of the Geats. Similarly, there are two references to a tyrannical King Heremod, a more or less legendary ruler in Danish tradition, who is everything that a king should not be; he is thrown into sharp contrast with Beowulf and with the great North Germanic hero Siegmund (901-915). All these allusions are, in effect, individual epic lays, which, if expanded and linked to other lays about the same character, would produce an heroic epic of full dimensions. The appearance of these lays, digressive and instrusive as they are, indicates that the Beowulf Poet was well versed in Germanic legendry and could use his materials for whatever purpose he saw fit. It is impossible to say whether he is following closely some current epic material on the subject of these miscellaneous lays or whether he is improvising. We can be sure, however, that there was plenty of actual copying of manuscripts either in whole or in part; in other words, the material was there to be used by other poets.

In many ways one of the most interesting passages in *Beowulf*, so far as the student of the beginnings of literature is concerned, occurs after Beowulf has killed Grendel. The interest lies not in the aesthetics of the passage—for it happens to be a rather arid stretch—but in the implications of the technique of early Germanic minstrelsy. It is essential to bear in mind that such information as we can gather from this passage concerning the genesis of the epic is inferred and not explicitly stated. The entire troop, Geats and Danes together, follows the track of the "gloryless one" where he crawled off to his den to die. In their minds was much more than the casual rejoicing that comes from the defeat of a commonplace enemy. For twelve winters they had been decimated by the ravages of a monstrous foe of anthropoid nature, a foe whom no sword could vanquish and who was as remorseless as he was invincible.

> There came all the old retainers,
> Likewise many a stripling, back from their joyous journey,
> Brave men riding their steeds from the mere,
> Warriors on their white horses. *There was Beowulf's*

Glorious deed recounted; many a one repeated
That south or north by the two seas
No other man over the spacious earth,
Under the expanse of heaven, lived better
Among shield-holders, more worthy of a kingdom.
Nor, indeed, did they reproach in any way
Gracious Hrothgar, for he was a good king!
At times the brave in battle let leap
Their light-colored steeds, let them race
Wherever the earth-paths seemed fair,
Known for excellence. *At times a thane of the king,*
A man laden with stories of glorious deeds,
Mindful of lays, who remembered of ancient sagas
A countless number, framed a new story
Founded upon fact. Skilfully did he relate
The adventure of Beowulf, and successfully uttered
A tale which was apt, varying it with words . . . [853-874]

The reader of Old English poetry will soon recognize what
the poet meant by the last half-line of the passage just quoted;
it is an indication of the inevitable repetitiousness of Old English poetic style. This interpretation of the phrase *founded
upon fact* is only one of many; literally, the passage must be
translated "a word found another rightly bound." The suggestion has been made by Bugge[18] and by Rieger[19] that
"bound" refers directly to the alliterative devices of Germanic
poetry. At any rate, it is evident that this man, the "thane of
the king," is the local *scop* or bard attached to Hrothgar's
circle. There can be little doubt that we are to understand that
this *scop* produced on the spot an individual lay on the subject
of Beowulf's victory over Grendel, a lay which he follows up
immediately with another on the subject of Siegmund, hero
of the Norse *Volsungasaga.* It is true that this passage is
crudely written and is in some ways extremely obscure. Possibly the language is used in a rather technical sense or as
scop's jargon. Perhaps it has been inaccurately copied by the
scribe of the Beowulf Manuscript. The difficult lines may
refer to the making of alliterative verse.[20] They may refer to
a blending even in the original lay of fact and fancy. But in

any case there is here the account of the creating of epic material in its simplest form. The word *ʒidd* occurs in this passage; it is best translated "lay," for it seems to be a song or chant expressed with due regard to set form and structure. The word *sith* appears also; it is best translated as "adventure" or "journey." A combination, then, of lyrical praise and narrative action, "skillfully varied" with words—this is an excellent though naïve definition of the Germanic epic, with its strange contrasts of violent deeds and calm, repetitious harangues.

Equally striking is the passage in *Beowulf* describing the lair of Grendel and his dam (1357-1377). In these twenty lines lives one of the earliest pieces of landscape poetry in English literature. Hrothgar is speaking:

> I have heard land-dwellers, my people,
> And hall-counselors say that they have seen
> Two such mighty march-steppers holding the moors,
> Frightful and alien spirits. One of them was—
> So far as they could clearly perceive—
> In woman's shape; the other creature
> Trod paths of exile in likeness of a man
> And yet he was larger than any other man.
> Him in days of yore the dwellers on earth
> Named Grendel; they did not know his father,
> Nor whether any mysterious spirits
> Had been born of them in times long past.
> They dwell in a hidden land, the retreat of wolves,
> Wind-swept headlands, terrible fen-defiles,
> Where the mountain-stream rushes down
> Under the mists of the headlands, a flood
> Under the earth. It is not far hence
> In mile-measure that the mere is found;
> Over it hang frosty groves, and trees
> Firm by the roots lean over the water.
> There dire wonders can be seen every night,
> A fire on the flood. No wise man lives
> Among the sons of men, who knows the bottom
> Of that dark pool. Although the heath-stepper
> Pursued by hounds, the hart with antlers trim,
> Seeks that grove, put to flight from afar—

Sooner he will give up his life on the bank
Than plunge within to protect his head;
It is not a good place! From that pool arise
Welling surges and vapors dark to the clouds,
Till the very air grows murky
And the heavens weep.

The resemblance of the landscape in these lines to that of the
approach to the underworld found in the classical epics, notably to the scene in Book VI of Virgil's *Aeneid*, has been
frequently discussed.[21] There is no reason whatsoever why the
Beowulf Poet should not have known Virgil's epic and used it
as an inspiration for secondary details; but the actual scene is
described elsewhere in Germanic legends where there is no
need to assume Virgilian influence. It is not inconceivable that
the mountain-vistas of Norway might be even more influential
than Virgil, if the author of these lines was familiar with
them; or he may have had in mind the Lake Country of
northwestern England. The reader can decide for himself.

Two other sections of *Beowulf* serve as introductions to
another type of Old English literature to be discussed later—
elegiac verse. The first of these is the implied lament of a
father for a son who has been hanged (2444-2462):

So it is a sorrowful thing
For an old fellow to endure, that his son
Though young should ride on the gallows;
Then he will make a lay, a mournful song,
When his son hangs, a sport for the ravens,
And he himself cannot help him,
Old and wise as he is, nor aid him at all.
Always he is reminded on every morning
Of his son's journey elsewhere. In his halls
He cares not to await another heir,
When that one has, through the constraint of deeds,
Tasted of death. Sorrowful in heart
He gazes upon the couch of his son,
On the wine-hall desolate, on the wind-swept beds
Deprived of sound. The horsemen sleep,

Heroes in their graves; there is no song of the harp,
Nor joy in the home, as there was of yore.

The second is the excellent piece of lyric poetry uttered by the
last survivor of the race of men guarding the gold-hoard—
that sinister gold-hoard of which the fire-dragon eventually
becomes a jealous custodian (2247-2266):

"Hold thou now, O earth—since heroes cannot—
The possessions of earls! Lo, good men
Found them once in thee; war-death
With wicked life-bale has carried off
All the men of my nation. All have given up
This life, the hall-mirth of men.
I have no one to bear the sword
Or polish the plated chalice, the precious drinking-cup;
My veterans have departed elsewhere.
The hard helmet of fairly wrought gold
Must fall from its plating; the cleanser sleeps,
Who should polish the battle-mask. Likewise the byrnie,
Which at battle endured the bite of iron
Over the crashing of shields, decays with the warrior.
Nor can the ringed coat-of-mail travel afar
After its war-chief, by the side of a hero.
There is no joy in the harp, no mirth in the gleewood;
Nor does the good hawk swing through the hall,
Nor the swift steed stamp in the courtyard.
Baleful death has sent forth many mortals on their way!"
Thus, mournful in mind, the man alone
Lamented his sorrow for all the others,
Moved about unhappily day and night
Till the surge of death touched his heart.

These two passages should be considered along with the
rather magnificent harangue of the garrulous, somewhat Polonius-like Hrothgar, as he makes his banquet-speech celebrat-
ing Beowulf's victory over Grendel but warning him of the
inevitable end of man:

It is a wonder to tell how mighty God
Dispenses wisdom to mankind; through His generous heart

He gives out land and earlship;
He is the Ruler of all. Sometimes He lets
The thoughts of noble men pass to things of love;
He gives him at home joy of the earth,
To hold the fortress of men;
He makes subject to him so many parts of the world,
Of the spacious kingdom, that the foolish man
Cannot imagine the end of prosperity.
He dwells in good fortune; sickness or old age
Do not in any way afflict him,
Nor is evil care grievous in his heart,
Nor does sword-hatred anywhere show itself;
But the whole world moves at his very will;
He cannot imagine a worse life—till within him
A deal of pride waxes and flourishes;
Then the guardian spirit sleeps,
The keeper of the soul. That sleep is too deep,
Bound fast by responsibilities;
The slayer very near, who shoots in malice from the bow;
Then he is hit under his guard
With a bitter arrow in his vitals—
Himself he cannot protect—
With the crooked counsel of the devil.
It seems to him too little,
What he has for a long time held.
Angrily he covets; he no longer bestows
Plated treasures in pomp; he forgets
And neglects the destiny which God gave him,
The Ruler of glory, his share of riches.
In the end it comes to pass, that his transient body
Droops and falls fated; another succeeds him,
Who deals out his treasures unstintingly,
Heirlooms of his ancestors, and takes no heed.
    Protect thyself from this wickedness,
Beloved Beowulf, best of men, and choose for thyself
The better wisdom of the ages; take no heed
Of overweening pride, famous warrior!
Now the fame of thy strength will be for a time;
But soon it shall be that sickness or the sword
Will separate thee from thy strength,

> Or the embrace of fire, or the surging flood,
> Or the bite of daggers, or the flight of the spear,
> Or dire old age; or the brightness of thine eyes
> Will fail and grow dark. It shall be presently,
> O prince, that death will overwhelm thee.... [1724-1768]

The essential significance of these four preceding paragraphs, when taken together, will be revealed later (V, 1). It should be observed, however, that the Beowulf Poet, on the evidence of these passages alone, must have been a man of considerable literary background for his time. As I have remarked before, the description of Grendel's cave contains some Virgilian echoes; the elegiac passages demonstrate that the Beowulf Poet was steeped in the poetic traditions of his own people. Moreover, there emanates from Hrothgar's homily a strong Biblical and scriptural atmosphere; it can be shown that many phrases in *Beowulf* exhibit the influence of the Vulgate Bible.[22] We are probably justified in assuming this threefold literary material—classical, Biblical, and native—to have been the stock-in-trade of the English writers of the period before the Norman Conquest.

One macabre but highly typical detail of Old English battle-poetry shows again how definitely the Beowulf Poet was drawn to the bardic tradition of his people. This detail recurs several times in the epics of the Anglo-Saxon and the Norse. In *Beowulf* it is illustrated in the brief glimpse of a battlefield given us through the speech of young Wiglaf, Beowulf's companion at need in his mortal combat with the fire-drake. The youth is prophesying dire events for the Geats, now that their king, Beowulf, lies dead:

> ... Now the war-leader has laid aside laughter,
> Mirth and revelry. Therefore shall many a spear
> Lie cold in the morning, enwrapped by the hand,
> Brandished in the fist; no longer will the harp-sound
> Arouse the warriors. But the black raven
> Eager for the doomed man will chatter much,
> Will tell the eagle how he sped at the feast
> When he with the wolves pillaged the corpses.
>   [3020-3027]

But the name of the Beowulf Poet, the *scop*—or the priest —who shaped so worthily the 3,182 lines of the poem *Beowulf*, and the names of the two scribes[23] who have given us our existing manuscript-version are alike unknown. In pondering this mystery of the Beowulf Poet, we should bear one fact in mind—the civilization portrayed in *Beowulf* is not necessarily the civilization in which the Beowulf Poet actually lived. In fact, it could not be, for Beowulf the Geat moves in a setting fundamentally heathen, epic, and heroically exaggerated, whereas the Beowulf Poet breathed a Christian atmosphere. The question of the authorship of *Beowulf*, whether single or multiple, has raged since Thorkelin's first edition of the poem in 1815.[24] Much has been made of the historicity of the characters and of the possibility that some of the events of the poem have a basis in fact. None of the questions of authorship, however, seems to depend upon whether or not this event or that one is actually true. It might be one individual, "laden with stories of glorious deeds," who composed the poem which we have before us; it could just conceivably be more than one, the first being the *scop* who celebrated some single event mentioned in the poem. The same question, of course, can be raised concerning any heroic epic unless, as with the *Aeneid* or *Paradise Lost*, we recognize the unmistakable fact of single authorship of a "literary" epic. But all epics are in that sense "literary," and the inevitability of a single author for any completed poem is clear whenever the matter has been carefully considered.

Gregory of Tours, a contemporary chronicler,[25] has given authority to that last, fatal battle in which Hygelac engaged; according to him, it took place about 520. Obviously this makes that event stand out apart from other events in the work; it affords a convenient *terminus a quo* for certain parts of the story. At the same time, there is no longer any reason to accept this particular battle as the only historical happening in *Beowulf*. It is simply that it is an event which held great authority for the earlier editors of the poem. Since the mid-nineteenth century days of Grundtvig, the first to identify the

Gregory of Tours allusion to Hygelac's death as the tale told in *Beowulf*, other chronicles have received attention, so that it is now possible to infer a reasonably satisfactory account of the Danish tribes during the time covered by the action of the poem.[26]

One man, however, could put into place the individual lays into which the structure of *Beowulf* can be broken down, and he could do it better than several. As in *Widsith*, there are portions of *Beowulf* which belong to pagan legendry and are dateless. There are also parts of the poem which have relation of a vague sort to history. Now it is unlikely that any poem so Scandinavian in sympathy would be written in England before the Danish invasions had at least begun. Hrothgar and his people are Danes and so need no further discussion as Norsemen. The identity of the Geats, however, is still obscure; they are scarcely the Jutes of Jutland, but more likely the Old Norse Gautar, a tribe inhabiting the southern tip of what is now Sweden. At any rate they were Scandinavian. A poem so thoroughly Norse in subject-matter as *Beowulf* would probably not be well received in Anglo-Saxon territory during the actual progress of the Danish invasions, which began in the eighth century and reached peaks in the late ninth and late tenth centuries. It will be remembered that the Danes overran Northumbria and Mercia; their influence both in language and in literature showed itself first in the northern sections of England. Yet the manuscript of *Beowulf* is written in a dialect generally West Saxon, with a considerable degree of Anglian admixture.

It is likely, then, that the *manuscript* of the poem is the work of West Saxon Christians writing at a time when Danish influence was strong even in the south of England—in other words, about the time of the Danish Conquest (1014). This date checks well with the scribal evidence. But the date of *original composition* is another matter. The poetic forms and devices, to say nothing of the language, indicate that *Beowulf* was written in the heyday of bardic poetry in England—the eighth century. Most scholars assign the poem a date near

725, though some are willing to venture a date either half a century earlier or more than a century later. This, therefore, would be the time of the flourishing of the Beowulf Poet, who might be of Danish ancestry, living in Anglia and writing his poem in an Anglian dialect—probably Mercian, possibly Northumbrian. These details, however, can be only speculation. We are agreed that he was a cleric, a scholar beyond the average for his time, and a poet of high order.

The period from the *terminus a quo* in 520 to 725—a span of two centuries—is not at all excessive for the slow growth of an heroic epic; in that time the patchwork structure, while still too obvious, will nevertheless have taken on more settled lines, perhaps a rude pattern. It will only remain then for a gifted synthesizer to come along, as the Beowulf Poet came. The very early dates of the authentic historical events in *Beowulf* are of little importance in reference to the completed literary form; they only go to show the manifest fact that the saga has all its vital roots in the Germanic Heroic Age, at a time when the tribes which gave it birth were still on the Continent. If one takes the period from about 725 to about 1000, both the Beowulf Poet and the final scribes belong to the era of Christianity in England, and the blend of paganism and Christianity in *Beowulf* has been consummated.

And so, to summarize, one may grant the pagan qualities of the original story; one may further assume that one or more bards contributed descriptive details, didactic passages, elegiac lays, some historical or legendary digressions, until eventually a more gifted individual, known as the Beowulf Poet, put the accumulated epic and lyric material down into his individualized concept, much as we have it now. This Beowulf Poet may have composed the major part of the poem as it now exists—perhaps all of it—or he may only have transcribed the poem as he knew it from a predecessor or predecessors. But he is responsible for *Beowulf* as we understand it, and he composed it some time in the eighth or ninth century. The poem came to be incorporated in the Beowulf Manuscript—Cotton Vitellius A XV—near the year 1000. Whether or not the scribes who compiled Cotton Vitellius A XV made important alterations in the poem composed by the Beowulf Poet cannot be shown; but it is not likely that much was changed. Beyond this one cannot go in a survey of this kind; but it can be insisted that a theory of single authorship of a piece is much more practical than a theory of multiple authorship.[27]

Needless to say, parallels to certain features of the Beowulf story appear in other Germanic literature. The conception of the fire-drake guarding a treasure is established in Germanic folklore; and in *Beowulf* itself there is reference to a combat between the hero Siegmund and just such a dragon. This may or may not be the same story as the one later attributed to Siegfried, son of Siegmund. It is sufficient to note that it affords a parallel. Then again, the deeds which Beowulf performed at the court of Hrothgar, when he rescued the Danish ruler and his people from the desolation wrought by Grendel and his dam, were evidently referred to other Germanic heroes, especially in the Norse sagas of the thirteenth century. The *Gretissaga* tells of a male and a female monster, of men disappearing at night from a particular house; and the hero Grettir grapples with this gigantic female troll, cutting off her arm. There is even a cave underneath a waterfall, which the hero must reach by diving, and a magic sword hanging on the wall of the cave. The episodes here are strikingly similar to those in *Beowulf*. The same reminiscences of these particular happenings appear in the *Thorsteinsaga* (*Vikinssonar*), the *Hrolfssaga*, and the *Ormssaga* (*Orms thattr Storolfssonar*).[28]

A comparison of *Beowulf* with the superb Homeric poems is naturally highly disadvantageous to the Old English epic;[29] but as a head-piece to English literature, *Beowulf* deserves a most honored position. The weakness of the poem lies in its architectonics, but too much has been made of its alleged laxity of structure. Perhaps the episodes are not always too well proportioned; yet when it is recalled that the entire work is a typical stringing together of separate epic materials, such a state of affairs is not surprising. On the other hand, Beowulf the hero, who is endowed with an undeniably strong personality, serves excellently as an integrating influence. Besides, it is impossible to deny that the poem has power, a massive strength, and a more than adequate amount of poetic atmosphere. In spite of its digressions, it tells its story well. Best of all, it touches the universal situation of danger to be faced and odds to be overcome, both outward terrors and inward fears, life for a people opposed to death for an individual. In these respects alone *Beowulf* has elements of true greatness. Yet it is a mistake to insist, as many scholars in the Old English period have done, that this poem is the only significant achievement of Old English literature. There are, as it happens, too many other pieces which can vie with it. But *Beowulf* admittedly has one point of preeminence.

> So the people of the Geats lamented
> The death of their lord, did his hearth-companions;
> They said that he was among the kings of this world
> The mildest of men and the most gentle,
> Kindest to the people and most eager for praise.
>
> [3178-3182]

With this touching and simple little tribute the poem ends. Indeed, the hero himself has passed from the world more than two hundred lines before, to reappear only as a corpse on the funeral-pyre. The somber pomp of his obsequies has subsided. There is no reason to suppose that any more lines followed. Beowulf has departed to seek "the judgment of the righteous." He leaves no heir behind, probably not even a widow. If we are right in these suppositions, then *Beowulf* stands apart as the only complete heroic epic surviving from Old English literature—complete in its narrative and complete in its portrayal of a mighty man of deeds.

4. OTHER SURVIVING OLD ENGLISH EPIC PIECES

As HAS been remarked, the profusion of separate epic materials in *Beowulf* suggests the former existence of many other epics of the kind which this poem represents most favorably. To repeat, however, there is nothing that has come down to us comparable to *Beowulf* in scope or in essential unity; instead, a few mere flints and shards of epic narrative. There are one or two authentic fragments and two late imitations, all of which should be mentioned briefly at this point. The fragments, insofar as can be judged by their styles and contexts, are undoubtedly portions of epics of considerable length— whether or not the entire poems, of which these fragments are parts, were longer and more ambitious than *Beowulf* will never be known. The imitations, on the other hand, are shorter lays; although one of them lacks a beginning and a conclusion, there is no reason to consider it seriously incomplete.

First of all there is the arresting fragment known as *The Fight at Finnsburg*, or the *Finnsburg Fragment*.[30] The story of this sterling piece is clearly a well known Germanic legend —well known, because there is in *Beowulf* a sequel to the events told in the *Finnsburg Fragment*, known as the Finnsburg Episode, and because some of the names of warriors associated with the story appear in *Widsith*. In its essentials, the epic is a striking example of the Germanic heroic poem. But only forty lines are left us, in *The Fight at Finnsburg*, of this account of a battle between the Danes under Hnaef and the Frisians, together with their allies, under Finn Folcwalding. Associated with the Frisians are the mysterious people called the *Eotan*, who are usually taken to be the Jutes.[31] Whether the Jutes are here synonymous with the Frisians, or whether they are the same tribe as the one mentioned by Bede, which invaded England under Hengest and Horsa—only this time serving in a group under Finn—is not precisely clear. For our purposes, however, it is immaterial, because *The Fight at Finnsburg*, as well as the Finnsburg Episode in *Beowulf*, is told from the Danish point of view. In short, here is another bit of Old English epic material with a distinctly Scandinavian origin.

The Fight at Finnsburg gives us rather impressionistically the spectacle of the beleaguered Danes withstanding the attack of the Frisians. The antecedents of the conflict are very hazy; but it seems that a band of Danes, under Hnaef, had been visiting the home of Finn, whose wife Hildeburh was a Danish princess and sister to Hnaef. For some reason, probably because of a long-standing feud between the two peoples, a feud which Hildeburh's marriage to Finn had presumably been intended to heal, hostilities break out through the "bad faith" of the Eotan (Jutes or Frisians)—whatever that may mean. The Danes are attacked in the hall. That is as much as *The Fight at Finnsburg* tells. The rest of the story we can gather from the Finnsburg Episode in *Beowulf*, although many of the details are still dark. Evidently the Danes lost Hnaef, and the Frisians lost Finn's son; and thus Hildeburh

> . . . . . . on the pyre of Hnaef
> Entrusted her own son to the flames;
> Let them burn his body, when she laid him on the fire,
> By the shoulder of his uncle.
> [BEOWULF, 1114-1117]

for she,

> . . . . . . Hildeburh, had no need to praise
> The faith of the Eotan; guiltless she
> Was bereft of her loved ones at the shield-play
> Of son and brother. . . .
> [BEOWULF, 1071-1074]

Apparently the Frisians themselves were so weakened that they were obliged to enter into a truce with the Danes; and the two peoples, glowering at each other, were forced to stay together in Frisia for the whole winter. The next year, however, saw a journey of revenge on the part of the Danes under Hengest (who might just conceivably be the Hengest of Hengest and Horsa),[32] the killing of Finn, and the return of the grieving Hildeburh to her people.

Our acquaintance with *The Fight at Finnsburg* is even more fortuitous than our acquaintance with some other pieces of Old English literature. It was found by George Hickes (1642-1715), a celebrated divine and antiquarian, as a part of the binding of a group of Old English homilies in the Lam-

beth Library; and it was subsequently lost. Fortunately, however, Hickes had made a transcription, which he published in
1705; this is the only extant version.[33]

On the basis of subject-matter and language, the same general date can be given to this fragment as was given to *Beowulf*. The Christian elements found in *Beowulf*, however,
are missing. But it should be borne in mind that this poem,
like *Beowulf*, is fundamentally Scandinavian. Moreover, its
forty lines are taken up exclusively with a battle-scene; consequently the lack of Christian didacticism is not significant.
The proper attitude would be to regard the author of *The
Fight at Finnsburg* as an individual of the same time and probably of the same general locale as the Beowulf Poet. In fact,
although it is reckless to generalize from a mere forty lines
beside the more than three thousand of *Beowulf*, it is not
foolish to suggest that the Finnsburg Poet was fully as gifted
as the Beowulf Poet—perhaps more so. The fragment man-
ages, in its all too short course, to convey magnificently an atmosphere of strife and mysterious turmoil; the romanticist
would find in it much of the quality of old, unhappy, far-off
things; and the battles long ago would be conceded by even
the most cerebral of antiquarians. The piece opens in the middle of a line; the Danes have evidently been disturbed by
some unexplained light or fire.

> Then spoke up Hnaef, the king young in war:
> "That is not day dawning in the east, nor is it a dragon in
> flight;
> Nor here in this hall are the gables afire.
> But now carry on! The birds of prey sing;
> The gray-coated one howls; the war-wood dins out;
> Shield answers shaft. Now the moon is shining,
> Wandering under the clouds; now arise deeds of woe
> Which will bring to fulfillment the struggle of the people."
> [2-9]

There follows an incident of a young, impetuous warrior beside an old veteran—a striking glimpse of youth beside age in
time of stress. Then the young man

...... Garulf fell,
First of all earls among earth-dwellers,
The son of Guthlaf; about him many a good man;
The corpses of the valiant. The raven wandered,
Swart and seal-brown. The gleam of the swords
Shone as if all Finnsburg were afire.   [31-36]

And so they fought for five days and held the door to the
hall, probably even brother against brother or father against
son. Then the fragment breaks off with mention of a wounded
Dane who dropped out of the fight, saying that his armor was
broken. Was he the agent of treachery and disaster, the ful-
fillment of tragedy? As Klaeber puts it, the rest is silence, but
we know the fatal outcome of the story from the episode in
Beowulf.

Much less satisfactory is the state of knowledge about the
two short epic fragments joined together under the name of
Waldere.[34] They appear to be pieces of a poem which must
have been of considerable length. They were discovered at
Copenhagen in 1860 by Werlauff; how they came there is
unknown, unless Thorkelin, the Danish scholar who first
edited *Beowulf*, was responsible. After basting together the
two fragments, scholars were agreed that they came from an
Old English version, presumably of the eighth or early ninth
century, of the epic legend of Walter of Aquitaine, or Walter
of Spain, a narrative subsidiary to the great Volsung-Nibe-
lungen sagas of Germany and Scandinavia. This, in brief, is
the significance of the *Waldere* fragments—they confirm the
fact that the circulation of legendary epic material throughout
the Germanic world was widespread. As it is, no one could
make much sense out of the existing Old English fragments
without a thorough knowledge of the Continental and Norse
versions of the story as a whole. Probably the best version of
the legend is that given in Latin by Ekkehard of St. Gall,
who died in 973.

The leading characters are Hildegund, a Burgundian princess; Walter; and Hagen, a warrior of the Franks. These

three are hostages of Attila, the famous king of the Huns—a character who represents one of the prime examples of a historical figure waxing legendary. Hagen goes to join his king Gunther; Walter and Hildegund are lovers, and escape from Attila, taking with them a great store of treasure. Gunther the covetous persuades Hagen to rob Walter and Hildegund; they beset the lovers in a narrow mountain-pass; Walter offers battle against Hagen and his eleven companions. All the Franks except Hagen and Gunther are slain on the first day of fighting; on the second, these two attack Walter. Gunther loses a leg, Hagen an eye, and Walter his right hand; and the combat closes.

There is no indication from the existing Old English fragments how closely this Old English version follows the story as told by Ekkehard. The first fragment is evidently part of a speech by Hildegund urging on her lover Walter; the second opens with a speech, apparently by Gunther, and continues with the defiant reply of Walter. Neither fragment is at all interesting except from the standpoint of the antiquarian; and it is virtually impossible to concede the author of these pieces any merit as a writer. The love-element in the story is most unusual for Old English literature in general and is virtually unheard of in the true heroic epic; its presence here suggests that the Old English poet had derived his material part and parcel from some more sophisticated Continental writer, for it is generally agreed that love-stories at this period in the history of western literature come from the Continent.

No mention of the Old English heroic epic would be complete without some consideration of the two fine specimens of late vintage known as *The Battle of Brunanburh* and *The Battle of Maldon*. Perhaps "late vintage" is a misleading phrase. The point is that while both of these poems belong to a period some two centuries after the Beowulf Poet was composing, they still make use of some of the old style and phraseology of epic poems like *Beowulf*. But the subject-matter of both poems has to do with definite historical events; there are no digressions and no introductions of legendary material from another age or another people. Both are strongly Anglo-Saxon in feeling. Barring natural epic hyperbole there are no supernatural elements—no trolls or giants or water-nixies or fire-dragons. The didacticism is kept down to a minimum. Consequently the poems sound almost modern.

On the whole we may call them imitations of the older epic, since they follow the style and vocabulary of the earlier poems even down to the actual repetition of phrase. And yet there is no doubt whatsoever about the earliest possible dates of these two poems. They were probably written very soon after the battles which they celebrate. We know that those battles took place in the tenth century, not in the eighth—at a time actually more noted for its prose than for its poetry. The effect of *The Battle of Brunanburh* and *The Battle of Maldon*, taken together, is almost as striking as that of the earlier heroic epic poetry; moreover, these two poems demonstrate that one of the two important traditions of Old English life and literature—the warrior tradition—was far from silent as late as the tenth century. It should be remembered that this tenth century was, in its first half, the period of Wessex triumphant, when the successors of King Alfred were winning back the Danelagh and achieving a united England. For this half of the century, *The Battle of Brunanburh* stands as a wild kind of national ode. The second half of the century, on the other hand, saw the gradual decay of West Saxon power and the twilight days of King Ethelred the Unready; these days *The Battle of Maldon* celebrates in heroic, tragic tones.

The first of these poems, *The Battle of Brunanburh*,[35] tells of the victory of King Athelstan of Wessex over a coalition of Norsemen and Scots in 937.

> . . . . Nor had there been a greater slaughter
> In this island ever yet,
> More people felled before this
> By the edge of the sword, as the books tell us—
> The old wise men—since the time
> When Angles and Saxons came hither from the east,
> Sought Britain over the broad-spreading sea,

> Haughty war-smiths overcame the Britons,
> Valiant earls got for themselves a home.   [65-73]

This work of a little more than seventy lines is found in most of the manuscripts of *The Anglo-Saxon Chronicle* (VIII, 3) as the entry for the year 937.

The second poem, *The Battle of Maldon*,[36] recounts the victory of the Danes under the famous Olaf Tryggvason (956-1000), one of the most illustrious of the Viking leaders and later king of Norway. The events of the poem took place in 991, during the slow but steady weakening of Saxon rule through the remorseless encroachment of the Danes. In a sense, then, the fate of the gallant Byrhtnoth and his army is symbolic of the fall of most of what Alfred the Great and his immediate successors had worked for—the rule of a united England by an Englishman. The melancholy story is told here with the fidelity and power of observation of a keen eye-witness; and the poem must have been written soon after the actual combat.

Both poems are clear and convincing testimony to the vitality of the Old English battle-epic tradition; the authentic ring sounds out years after the Beowulf Poet, Caedmon, and Cynewulf have been laid to rest. The last significant specimen of this kind of poetry surviving from a time before the Norman Conquest, *The Battle of Maldon* utters a stirring statement of the theme so dear to the Old English thane—loyalty to one's king and leader, even unto death. In both poems, too, as in the older pagan epics and in the Christian epics soon to be discussed, there is the same rejoicing in the clash of conflict. "Shield answered shaft"; the birds and beasts of prey—"the swart raven," "the eagle eager for carrion," "the gray-coated one, the wolf from the field"—all enter to claim what is due them; "the slaughtered fell to earth." In both *The Battle of Maldon* and *The Battle of Brunanburh* is the blend of pagan and Christian which characterizes *Beowulf*. So in *The Battle of Brunanburh*

> Fated they fell; the field was slippery
> With the blood of men, when the sun

Up in the morning-time, that glorious star,
Glided over the earth, God's bright torch,
The eternal Lord's, until the noble creation
Sank to rest. . . .   [12-17]

and in *The Battle of Maldon*

Then he speedily struck at the other,
So that the byrnie broke; he was wounded in the breast
Through the linked mail; at his heart stood
The venomous point. Byrhtnoth was all the happier;
He laughed, that brave warrior, said thanks to the Lord
For the day's work which God had given him.   [143-148]

But it is not all muscular, grisly carnage. There is a deathless
valor about these men; in their dire emergency, distinctions
between earl and churl vanish away; and Dunnere, the aged
churl, calls out above the tumult, while the others listen in
dismay at the death of their leader, Byrhtnoth:

He must not waver, who thinks to avenge
His lord among the people,
Nor can he love his own life!   [258-259]

Nor is there a more courageous text to buttress the ideals of
the Anglo-Saxon warrior than

Mind shall be the harder, heart the keener,
Courage the greater, as our strength grows less!
I am an old man; I will not go hence
But beside my beloved lord I will lay myself down.
                                   [312-319]

It is thus the poem ends; and from our superior vantage-
point of history we know that the brave English forces were
annihilated before the Viking Danes got possession of the
field. Be that as it may, the warrior of this battle in 991 had,
at least in this poem, the same will to combat as his brother-
in-arms in *Beowulf*. It is not necessary to assume that this
manifestation of courage is mere poetic idealism. Nor is it
necessary to regard it as some concession to popular tradition.
On the contrary, it seems fair to suppose that even in the days
of decaying national leadership, under the shield of the luck-

less Ethelred, the relation of the warrior to his chieftain is of the same fixed quality it had been during the Heroic Age. And therefore we must consider this loyalty to an able and brave leader an essential part of the Anglo-Saxon tradition.

Note, however, that it is not so much a nationalistic, and therefore a rather remote and generalized, concept of leadership that inspires the warriors in *The Battle of Maldon* as it is the immediate presence of a valiant personal leader. If the king of England, Ethelred, failed him, the Anglo-Saxon warrior still felt reverent devotion to courageous Byrhtnoth, the old and experienced fighter.

> Then the son of Aelfric urged them on,
> A warrior young in winters,
> Aelfwine spoke in stout-hearted words:
> 'Remember the times when we spoke over our mead,
> When we raised up boasts along the benches,
> Heroes in the hall, eager for a hard fight;
> Now let us see who is brave.
> I will make known to all my lineage;
> I am of worthy descent among the Mercians;
> My ancestor was named Ealhelm,
> A wise prince, prospering in this world.
> The thanes of my people can never reproach me
> That I was willing to leave this troop,
> To seek my native land, now that my leader lies
> Hewn to pieces in the battle.
> For me no sorrow could be greater,
> He was at once my kinsman and my lord.'   [209-224]

It is precisely this spirit which breathes through the vast and unwieldy bulk of Old English epic poetry. When "the heathen rascals" finally put an end to Byrhtnoth's life,

> Then went forth the haughty thanes,
> Uncowardly men surged eagerly ahead;
> They were all desirous of one of these twain:
> To give up their lives or avenge their dear lord.
>   [205-208]

Yet it is not alone in defeat that this Anglo-Saxon warrior lifts his spirit to grandeur, although the courage to pluck honor from disaster is a jewel amid bitterness. It is fully as easy to perceive the fierce, savage exultation which follows a great victory, as in *The Battle of Brunanburh*:

Now Athelstan the king, lord of earls,
Ring-giver to the warriors . . .
Struck forth life-long glory with the edges of swords
Near Brunanburh; they clove the shield-wall,
Hewed the heathen bucklers with the leavings of hammers.
[1-5]

Whatever the outcome of the fight, however, victory and life or defeat and death, undoubtedly the relation of the war-leader to his *comitatus* is one of the most important themes in Old English literature and life, as all these poems have borne witness. Of course there were other themes—one of them, the religious motif, of vital significance. We can only wish, nevertheless, that we might have more literature to publish the experiences of the churl. With his obscure toiling and inarticulate emotions, he is potentially the material of an effective literature of the proletariat. But he has no spokesman. So also does the Anglo-Saxon woman call for an interpreter. The time for her champion, however, never arrived. Much as we may miss the presence of humble folk in general and of women in particular—the necessary ingredients of a modern literature —their absence in Old English times can awaken no surprise. For the earl and the churchman are dominant, and in their august presences there is little room for either a churl or a woman. The churchman we shall turn to next. As for the earl, fighting, by which the destinies of his people were decided, was very much his own business, and he gloried in it. For he was the defender of his community against terrors from without; he was the man of action in all the emergencies which an active, practical people could envisage. His leader was a walking, breathing symbol of life as those people saw it. No wonder, then, that the prestige of the fighter never departed during the Old English period. But broaden the stage a trifle. Consider the Germanic world and its long, adventurous development. Can it be fairly maintained that the glory of the warrior has ever been lost there?

NOTES TO CHAPTER THREE

1. Since there is no first-hand material to go by, the matter remains anchored in speculation, but see Hermann Schneider, *Germanische Heldensage* (Berlin-Leipzig, 1928), Vol. I, 211ff.

2. Probably the best introduction to the epic—its origins, psychological and emotional, and its characteristics—among the Indo-European peoples is still H. M. Chadwick, *The Heroic Age* (Cambridge, 1926). Much discussion of the figure of the epic hero, however, has taken place during the past few years. Among older works should be enumerated Francis B. Gummere, *The Beginnings of Poetry* (New York-London, 1901), especially pp. 182ff., 222ff., and 434ff.; W. P. Ker, *Epic and Romance* (London-New York, 1898; 1908); and *The Dark Ages* (Edinburgh-London, 1904). For the development of epic narrative method, no work is better than Walter M. Hart, "Ballad and Epic" in *Harvard Studies and Notes in Philology and Literature*, XI (Boston, 1907). More recent studies which may add little in fact but give fresh interpretations of familiar material are H. V. Routh, *God, Man, and Epic Poetry: a study in comparative. literature* (Cambridge, 1927); H. M. Chadwick and N. K. Chadwick, *The Growth of Literature* (Cambridge, 1932); Lord Raglan, *The Hero: a study in tradition, myth, and drama* (London, 1936); and Rhys Carpenter, *Folktale, Fiction, and Saga in the Homeric Epics* (Berkeley, 1946).

3. The bard of Old English epic poetry—a particularly national name for an ancient and honorable general profession. See L. F. Anderson, *The Anglo-Saxon Scop* (Toronto, 1903).

4. In general, this means the insertion of Christian doctrine, dogma, or moral teaching into the pagan material. As will be seen, such insertions are practically universal in Old English literature.

5. In addition to the discussion of *Widsith* in the works on the epic noted above (see notes 1 and 2), there are other works to be considered in treating this extremely interesting piece of literary antiquity. The definitive edition of the poem is Kemp Malone, *Widsith* (London, 1936), which contains also an invaluable introduction and bibliography. Malone's labors in the preparation of this edition were the

source of a number of short articles on detailed matters of the text and the allusions therein. Perhaps the most general in appeal of these short articles is "Widsith and the Critic" in *English Literary History*, V, 49-66. The best of recent foreign treatments is, in my opinion, K. F. Sunden, *Den fornengelska dikten Widsith* (Göteborg, 1929); of the older editions, R. W. Chambers, *Widsith* (Cambridge, 1912) remains a thoroughly satisfactory performance. The relation of *Widsith* to the Gothic epic tradition is treated specifically in Caroline A. Brady, *The Eormanric of the Widsith* (Berkeley, 1937). W. A. French, "Widsith and the Scop" in *Publications of the Modern Language Association*, LX, 623-630, argues that the poet was an unemployed *scop* selling himself to a new patron.

6. Kemp Malone, *Widsith* (see note 5 above), I.

7. The italics are mine.

8. See in particular Chapter V below.

9. There are four manuscripts which contain the greater bulk of Old English poetry. These are 1) the Beowulf Manuscript (Cotton Vitellius A XV); 2) the Junius Manuscript; 3) *The Exeter Book*; and 4) *The Vercelli Book*. These four manuscripts are being systematically edited and published in definitive editions by the Columbia University Press; and the Junius Manuscript, *The Exeter Book*, and *The Vercelli Book* have already been so treated in respect to their text. The Junius Manuscript, edited by G. P. Krapp, appeared in 1931; *The Vercelli Book*, edited also by Krapp, was published in 1932; and *The Exeter Book*, edited by G. P. Krapp and E. V. K. Dobbie, was issued in 1936. The Beowulf Manuscript volume has yet to be done; in the meantime the best edition is that published by J. Zupitza as volume 77 of *Publications of the Early English Text Society, Original Series* (London, 1882). There is a very comprehensive study of the Beowulf Manuscript by Max Förster, published most inaccessibly in *Berichte über die Verhandlungen der sächsischen Akademie der Wissenschaften*, LXXI, No. 4 (Leipzig, 1919). There is another edition of the Junius Manuscript by I. Gollancz, *The Caedmon Manuscript of Anglo-Saxon Biblical Poetry* (Oxford, 1927). There is also another edition of *The Exeter Book*, published in two volumes: the first edited by R. W. Chambers, Max Förster, and Robin Flower (Bradford, 1933); the second by W. S. Mackie (London, 1934). *The Vercelli Book* will be mentioned again later; it has been the subject of a useful article by Stephen J. Herben, "*The Vercelli Book*: a new hypothesis" in *Speculum*, X, 91-94.

10. Scholars writing on their pet subjects are prone to idealize the accomplishments of the authors of that which they are studying. Thus it is no surprise to observe that most of the *Widsith* specialists seem unwilling to admit that the Widsith Poet could have had an inept kind

of imagination. I agree, however, that the inclusion of these Biblical names in the *thulas* seems to be due to interpolation.

11. It would be manifestly impracticable to attempt here a complete list of the multitude of works written about *Beowulf* since it first appeared. As to editions of the poem, there is little difficulty. The magnificent edition by F. Klaeber, *Beowulf* (New York, 1922; 1936) contains also *The Fight at Finnsburg, Deor's Lament,* the *Waldere* Fragments, and *Widsith,* the last-named in abbreviated form. For detailed information bibliographical, historical, and textual it is head and shoulders above its predecessors. Its nearest rival would be A. J. Wyatt and R. W. Chambers, *Beowulf* (Cambridge, 1914). Other editions, noted in their day, were those of W. J. Sedgefield (1910); F. Holthausen (1905-1929); and Moritz Heyne (1863), which, as recast by L. L. Schücking (1908), has been revived in the last few years. Klaeber's edition, however, makes unnecessary any further list of works here. But I recommend in particular the following selected items, and it is understood that works dealing with purely textual or linguistic matters are not included.

TRANSLATIONS: The best translation in verse is probably Charles W. Kennedy, *Beowulf: the Oldest English Epic* (New York, 1940); but other good ones, which are even closer to the original, are those of William E. Leonard (1923) and Francis B. Gummere (1909). See also A. Strong's (London, 1925). Gummere's translation, in *The Oldest English Epic* (New York, 1909), is still probably the most celebrated of all, since it was incorporated into Charles W. Eliot's *Harvard Classics.* The best prose translation is that of Chauncey B. Tinker (New York, 1920; 1910); others are by John Earle (Oxford, 1892) and George K. Anderson (in *The Literature of England,* Vol. 1; Chicago, 1936); less successful are those of Clarence G. Child (Boston, 1904) and J. R. Clark Hall (London, 1901). But apparently translating *Beowulf* has been something of a pastime for many.

AUTHOR: James R. Hulbert, "A Note on the Psychology of the Beowulf Poet" in the *Klaeber Miscellany* (Minneapolis, 1929); Arthur E. Du Bois, "The Unity of *Beowulf*" in *Publications of the Modern Language Association,* XLIX, 374-406; George Bond, "Links between *Beowulf* and Mercian History" in *Studies in Philology,* XL, 481-493; and B. J. Timmer, "Beowulf, the Poem and the Past" in *Neophilologus,* XXXII, 122-126.

FOLKLORE AND LEGEND: Karl Müllenhoff, "Der Mythus von Beowulf" in *Zeitschrift für deutsches Altertum,* VII, 419-441; Gregor Sarrazin, "Neue Beowulf-Studien" in *Englische Studien,* XXIII, 221-267; XXXV, 19-27; and XLII, 1-37; Friedrich Panzer, *Studien zur germanischen Sagengeschichte* (Munich, 1910); S. J.

Crawford, "Grendel's Descent from Cain" in *Modern Language Review*, XXIII, 206-208; Heinz Dehmer, "Die Grendelkämpfe Beowulfs im Lichte moderner Märchenforschung" in *Germanisch-Romanische Monatsschrift*, XVI, 202-218; Gustav Hübener, "*Beowulf* und nordische Dämonenaustreibung" in *Englische Studien*, LXII, 293-327; Elias Wadstein, "The Beowulf Poem as an English National Epic" in *Acta Philologica Scandinavica*, VIII, 273-291; J. R. Tolkien, *Beowulf: the monsters and the critics* (Oxford, 1937), Hilda M. Ransome, *The Sacred Bee in Ancient Times and Folklore* (London, 1937); Kemp Malone, "Young Beowulf" in *Journal of English and Germanic Philology*, XXXVI, 21-23; and "Hrethric" in *Publications of the Modern Language Association*, XLII, 268-313; H. B. Woolf, "The Name of Beowulf" in *Englische Studien*, LXXII, 7-9; and Stephen J. Herben, "Beowulf, Hrothgar, and Grendel" in *Archiv*, CLXXIII, 24-30; Kemp Malone, "Beowulf" in *English Studies*, XXIX, 161-172.

LITERARY AND CRITICAL STUDIES: K. Müllenhof, "Die innere Geschichte des Beowulfs" in *Haupt's Zeitschrift für deutsches Altertum*, XIV, 193-244—containing this author's famous, though now generally suspect, "lay-theory"; Alois Brandl, "Hercules und Beowulf" in *Sitzungsberichte der preussischen Akademie der Wissenschaft*, 161-167; F. A. Blackburn, "The Christian Coloring in 'Beowulf'" in *Publications of the Modern Language Association*, XII, 205-225; Sister Mary Angelica O'Neill, *Elegiac Elements in Beowulf* (Washington, 1932); C. C. Batchelor, "The Style of *Beowulf*" in *Speculum*, XII, 330-342; Joan Blomfield, "The Style and Structure of *Beowulf*" in *Review of English Studies*, XIV, 396-403; Franklin Cooley, "Early Danish Criticism of *Beowulf*" in *ELH*, VII, 45-67; and H. B. Woolf, "On the Characterization in Beowulf" in *ELH*, XV, 85-92.

ORIGINS AND ANALOGUES: E. Wessen, "Die nordiska folkstammarna i *Beowulf*" in *Kungl. Vitterhets Historie och Antikvitets Akademiens Handlingar*, XXXVI, 2; M. Deutschbein, "Beowulf der Gautenkönig" in *Festschrift für Lorenz Morsbach* (Halle, 1913); W. W. Lawrence, "*Beowulf* and the Saga of Samson the Fair" in the *Klaeber Miscellany* (Minneapolis, 1929), 172-181; Kemp Malone, "The Identity of the Geatas" in *Acta Philologica Scandinavica*, IV, 84-90; T. B. Haber, *A Comparative Study of the Beowulf and the Aeneid* (Princeton, 1931); Walter A. Berendsohn, *Zur Vorgeschichte des Beowulfs* (Copenhagen, 1935); Ritchie Girvan, *Beowulf and the Seventh Century* (London, 1935); Stephen J. Herben, "Heorot" in *Publications of the Modern Language Association*, L, 933-945; Kemp Malone, "Healfdene" in *Englische Stu-*

dien, LXX, 74-76; F. Olivero, *Introduzione al Beowulf* (Turin, 1934)—the leading southern European treatment of the poem, which is followed by an Italian translation; Kemp Malone, "The Burning of Heorot" in *Review of English Studies,* XII, 462-463; Kemp Malone, "Swerting" in *Germania Review,* XIV, 235-257; and George Bond, "Links between *Beowulf* and Mercian History" (see AUTHOR above).

SCENERY AND DESCRIPTIVE ELEMENTS: Roberta D. Cornelius, "Palus Inamabilis" in *Speculum,* II, 321-325; W. J. Sedgefield, "The Scenery in *Beowulf*" in *Journal of English and Germanic Philology,* XXXV, 161-169; W. S. Mackie, "The Demon's Home in *Beowulf*" in *Journal of English and Germanic Philology,* XXXVII, 455-461; W. W. Lawrence, "Grendel's Lair" in *Journal of English and Germanic Philology,* XXXVIII, 477-480—see also Lawrence's earlier articles in *Publications of the Modern Language Association,* XXVII, 208-245; and XXXIII, 547-583.

WEAPONS AND ARMOR: The opening essay of Knut Stjerna, *Essays on Questions Connected with the Old English Poem of Beowulf,* translated by John H. Clark Hall (Coventry, 1912) is particularly good. See also Hjalmar Falk, "Altnordische Waffenkunde" in *Videnskapsselskapets Skrifter: II. Hist.-Filos.-Klasse,* no. 6 (Kristiania, 1914); Hans Lehmann, "Brunne und Helm im angelsächsischen Beowulfliede," in *Germania,* XXXI, 486-497; Julia D. Adams, *Swords of the Vikings* (London, 1929).

GENERAL STUDIES: In addition to the shorter pieces cited above, see in particular W. W. Lawrence, *Beowulf and the Epic Tradition* (Cambridge, Mass., 1928) and R. W. Chambers, *Beowulf* (Cambridge, 1914; 1932). Both of these books, and particularly that by Chambers, must be considered indispensable for the more advanced study of *Beowulf.*

12. For the special conception of *Beowulf* as a conduct-book for kings and princes, see L. L. Schücking, "Das Königsideal in *Beowulf*" in *Bulletin of the Modern Humanities Research Association,* III, 143-154.

13. Attention should be called again to Hilda W. Ransome, *The Sacred Bee in Ancient Times and Folklore* (London-Boston, 1937); also to Erik Bjorkman, *Studien über die Eigennamen im Beowulf* (Halle, 1920) and "Beow, Beaw, und Beowulf" in *Englische Studien,* LII, 145-193.

14. F. Bracher, "Understatement in Old English Poetry" in *Publications of the Modern Language Association,* LII, 915-934.

15. H. M. Chadwick, *The Heroic Age* (Cambridge, 1926), 320. The whole of Chapter XV in this work is an admirably clear and detailed exposition of the characteristics of the epic and its importance

as a manifestation of the Heroic Age, and might well be read first in the book.

16. F. Klaeber, *Beowulf* (New York, 1922; 1936), 144ff. This is without question the best short, comprehensive treatment of the subject.

17. The manuscript gives the two words *mod þryþo*, "the mind of Thryth." But this has proved unsatisfactory from the viewpoint of the grammarians, since the genitive ending here should be *-e*; and the tendency now is to consider the two words as one—Modthryth, the name of the queen. See S. Stefanovic, "Zur Offa-Thryþo Episode im *Beowulf*" in *Englische Studien*, LXIX, 15-31. Klaeber has accepted the Modthryth form in the later edition of his *Beowulf* (1936). See also Edith Rickert, "The Old English Offa-saga" in *Modern Philology*, II, 29-76, 321-376.

18. Sophus Bugge in *Zeitschrift für deutsche Philologie*, IV, 192-224.

19. Max Rieger in *Zeitschrift für deutsche Philologie*, III, 381-416.

20. S. O. Andrew, *The Old English Alliterative Measure* (Croydon, 1931).

21. In addition to the items noted under SCENERY AND DESCRIPTION in note 11 above, see *Herrig's Archiv*, CXXVI, 341ff. and W. W. Lawrence's article on Grendel's mere in *Publications of the Modern Language Association*, XXVII, 208-245. The analogues of this scene are, moreover, at least as much Scandinavian (i.e. from the *Gretissaga* materials) as Biblical or Virgilian. A similar passage in one of the *Blickling Homilies* (see X, 2 below) is very striking; probably the Beowulf Poet and the author of the homily were working from the same source. See Lawrence's article just cited, as well as those of G. Sarrazin in *Englische Studien*, XLII, 4ff. and *Anglia*, XXXVI, 185-187; A. S. Cook in *Modern Language Notes*, XVII, 209ff. and XXII, 146ff.; and Carleton Brown, "*Beowulf* and the *Blickling Homilies* and Some Textual Notes" in *Publications of the Modern Language Association*, LIII, 905-916, which ties a section from *The Battle of Maldon* (note 36 below) into the picture.

For the general matter of Virgilian influence, see the work of T. B. Haber in the section on ORIGINS AND ANALOGUES, note 11 above; and F. Klaeber, "Aeneis und Beowulf" in *Archiv*, CXXVI, 40-48, 339-359.

22. F. Klaeber, "Die christlichen Elemente im *Beowulf*" in *Anglia*, XXXV, 111-136, 249-270, 453-482; and XXXVI, 169-199.

23. There are two known scribes to the text of *Beowulf* in the Beowulf Manuscript. Scribe A begins the poem and carries through to line 1939, or about sixty per cent of the entire text; Scribe B, who is considered contemporary with Scribe A, begins with the last word of line

1939 and completes the poem as we have it. See Charles Davidson, "Differences between the Scribes of 'Beowulf' " in *Modern Language Notes*, v, 85-89. There is a brief comment on Davidson's article by Charles F. McClumpha in *Modern Language Notes*, v, 245-246, and a reply by Davidson in the same volume, 378-379.

24. *Beowulf*, first mentioned by Wanley in his *Antiquae literaturae septentrionalis* in 1705, did not receive careful editorial treatment until nearly a century later. Thorkelin, the Danish scholar, made transcripts of the manuscript in 1787 and a complete edition in 1815.

25. St. Gregory of Tours (ca. 540-594) was the author of a *Historia Francorum* in ten books—his major work, as well as an account of the miracles of Christ in seven books.

26. This account is given admirably, with full bibliography, in Klaeber's *Beowulf* (see note 11 above), xxix ff.

27. Beside the comprehensive treatment of the problem in the introduction to Klaeber's *Beowulf* (see note 11 above) and the exhaustive bibliography listed there, one should pay special heed to L. L. Schücking, "Wann entstand der *Beowulf*? Glossen, Zweifel, und Fragen" in *Beiträge zur Geschichte der deutschen Sprache und Literatur*, XLII, 347-410.

28. The *Gretissaga* is given in English translation in Eirikr Magnusson and William Morris, *The Story of Grettir the Strong* (London, 1901); there is also one in the Everyman Library (No. 699) by George A. Hight. The standard edition is that of R. C. Boer, *Grettis Saga Asmundarsonar* (Halle, 1900). The *Thorsteinsaga* is most easily accessible in Gwyn Jones, *Four Icelandic Sagas* (Princeton, 1935). The *Hrolfssaga* is found in the edition by Finnur Jonsson, *Hrolfs Saga Kraka* (Copenhagen, 1904), and a translation by Stella M. Mills (Oxford, 1933). The *Ormssaga* was edited by G. Vigfusson and C. R. Unger in the *Flateyjarbok*, I, 521-533 (Christiania, 1860). Covering all in reference to *Beowulf* is R. W. Chambers, *Beowulf: an Introduction* (Cambridge, 1932), 48-68 and 129-195.

29. But see James R. Hulbert, "*Beowulf* and the Classical Epic" in *Modern Philology*, XLIV, 65-75.

30. The best edition is that included in F. Klaeber, *Beowulf* (see note 11 above), 219ff. The Finnsburg Episode in *Beowulf* has been the subject of much investigation, for which see W. J. Sedgefield, "The Finn Episode in *Beowulf*" in *Modern Language Review*, XXVIII, 480-482; Kemp Malone, "The Finn Episode in *Beowulf*" in *Journal of English and Germanic Philology*, XXV, 157-172; R. W. Chambers, *Beowulf: an Introduction* (Cambridge, 1932), 245-289; W. W. Lawrence, "*Beowulf* and the Tragedy of Finnsburg" in *Publications of the Modern Language Association*, XXX, 372-431; R. A. Williams, *The Finn Episode in Beowulf* (Cambridge, 1924);

and Arthur G. Brodeur, *The Climax of the Finn Episode* (Berkeley, 1943) and "Design and Motive in the Finn Episode" in *University of California Publications in English*, XIV, 1-42. The fullest bibliographies concerning *The Fight at Finnsburg* are primarily that in Klaeber's edition and secondarily that in Chambers's study. Of particular recent interest are the following: H. F. Scott-Thomas, "The Fight at Finnsburg: Guthlaf and the Son of Guthlaf" in *Journal of English and Germanic Philology*, XXX, 498-505; F. Klaeber, "Garulf, Guþlaf's Sohn, im Finnsburg-Fragment" in *Archiv*, CLXII, 116-117; and A. C. Bowman, "The Heroes of the Fight at Finnsburh" in *Acta Philologica Scandinavica*, X, 130-144.

31. Consider R. W. Chambers, *Beowulf* (Cambridge, 1932), 333-345 and 262, n.3.

32. See H. M. Chadwick, *The Origin of the English Nation* (Cambridge, 1924), 49; W. Meyer, *Beiträge zur Geschichte der Eroberung Englands durch die Angelsachsen* (Halle, 1912); also Harry M. Ayres, "The Tragedy of Hengest in *Beowulf*" in *Journal of English and Germanic Philology*, XVI, 282-285. Two excellent studies are A. G. Van Hamel, "Hengest and his Namesake" in the *Klaeber Miscellany* (Minneapolis, 1929), 159ff. and N. G. Aurner, *Hengest: a Study in Early English Hero Legend* (Iowa City, 1921).

33. Printed in Klaeber's *Beowulf* (see note 11 above), 233ff.

34. Probably the definitive edition is that by F. Norman, *Waldere* (London, 1934). An autotype edition was put out by F. Holthausen at Göteborg in 1899. There is also an excellent edition by Holthausen in his *Beowulf nebst dem Finnsburg-Bruchstück* (Heidelberg, 1905-1913). The edition by Bruce Dickins in his *Runic and Heroic Poems of the Old Teutonic Peoples* (Cambridge, 1915) contains a good prose translation along with the usual introduction and notes. See also F. Klaeber, "Zu den Waldhere-Bruchstücken" in *Anglia*, XXXIX, 121-127. But for the legend of Walter of Spain as a whole and for an accumulation of material treating of the Germanic epic in general, the reader is referred to the translations in H. M. Smyser and F. P. Magoun, *Survivals in Old Norwegian of Medieval English, French, and German Literature, together with the Latin Versions of the Heroic Legend of Walter of Aquitaine* in *Connecticut College Publications* (New London, 1948); and Alexander H. Krappé, "The Legend of Walter and Hildegund" in *Journal of English and Germanic Philology*, XXII, 75-88.

35. See Alastair Campbell, *The Battle of Brunanburh* (London, 1938). Most of the discussion of this poem has centered about its uncertain locale. Its text is not so much of a problem, since it is intimately bound up with *The Anglo-Saxon Chronicle* (see Chapter VIII, note 7 below). Once the poem has been read, however, the work to be

consulted would be J. H. Cockburn, *The Battle of Brunanburh and its Period Elucidated by Place-Names* (London, 1931). Various articles contributing to the discussion are O. G. S. Crawford, "The Battle of Brunanburh" in *Antiquity*, VIII, 338-339; A. H. Smith, "The Site of the Battle of Brunanburh" in *London Mediaeval Studies*, edited by R. W. Chambers, F. Norman, A. H. Smith (London, 1937), Vol. I, part I, pp. 56-59; W. S. Angus, "The Battlefield of Brunanburh" in *Antiquity*, XI, 283-293; W. E. Varah, "The Battlefield of Brunanburh" in *Notes and Queries*, CLXXIII, 434-436; and J. W. Fawcett, "The Battlefield of Brunanburh" in *Notes and Queries*, CLXXIV, 412.

36. The best edition is that of E. V. Gordon, *The Battle of Maldon* (London, 1937) and the best historical discussion of the circumstances of the battle is E. D. Laborde, *Byrhtnoth and Maldon* (London, 1936), although the piece is generally printed, like *The Battle of Brunanburh*, in all the readers and anthologies of Anglo-Saxon literature (see Chapter I, note 44, section 24 above). The single manuscript in which the poem survived (Cotton Otho A XII) was destroyed in the fire at the Cottonian Library in 1731. But a few years before (1726), Thomas Hearne had published a copy of it in his *History of Glastonbury*. An older edition by W. J. Sedgefield, *The Battle of Maldon* (Boston, 1904), is still extremely useful. Two special articles, the nature of which is obvious from their titles, are Bertha S. Philpott, "The Battle of Maldon: some Danish affinities" in *Modern Language Review*, XXIV, 172-198 and Margaret Ashdown, *English and Norse Documents Relating to the Reign of Ethelred the Unready* (Cambridge-New York, 1930), which is a very valuable historical monograph.

IV · The Old English Christian Epic

1. THE CHRISTIANIZATION OF ANGLO-SAXON ENGLAND

IT IS now time to look away from the heroic epic, as well as from its later descendants like *The Battle of Brunanburh* and *The Battle of Maldon*, and to consider what effect a force philosophically the antithesis of militarism exerted upon the story of arms and the man. It was the function of the priest to bring to the life of Anglo-Saxon England what we choose to call civilization, to soften and to humanize the character of the Germanic tribesman and to bring him, however slowly and painfully, to a world of knowledge and culture. The actual process of the nominal Christianization of the Anglo-Saxon kingdoms is not difficult to follow in outline; but the true impact of this Christianization upon the literature of the period is something else.

In this process, two distinct currents of Christian teaching are discernible; these two currents eventually flowed together, and the earlier and feebler was absorbed by the later and stronger. After the passing of Saint Patrick of Ireland (ca. 430), Irish missionaries came to northern England and southern Scotland and established various centers of Christian culture in those virtual wildernesses. The most famous of these missionaries was Saint Columba, or Columbkill (Columba of the Churches) (521-597); and the seat of his endeavors was the island of Iona, off the coast of southwest Scotland, where he founded the monastery of Hii. There is no denying the historical importance of these Irish efforts; but, whatever their achievement, they were sporadic and unsystematic. In the year of Columba's death (597), Augustine, a subordinate of Pope Gregory the Great, brought a Christian mission from

Rome to the people of Kent—the opening wedge of the great Italian mission which was eventually to conquer the whole Anglo-Saxon world.

The story is told[1] that Gregory saw some Saxon slaves in the marketplace of Rome, was struck by their fair appearance, and when told their identity and whence they came, made asseveration, not without the help of some atrocious puns upon the names of these slaves' nation and ruler, that "it was fitting that the praise of God our Creator be sung in those distant parts." The tale is told with gravity and simplicity by the Venerable Bede. There is no reason to disbelieve it. When Gregory became Pope, he proceeded at once to institute the mission. It can hardly be said that the immediate effect of Augustine's preaching upon Ethelbert, king of Kent, was startling; and it appears that Eadbald, son of Ethelbert, showed a distressing tendency to lapse into heathendom. Such an act must have been particularly disturbing to his mother Queen Bertha, who as a Christian Frankish princess had actually brought some priests with her to Kent when she married Ethelbert. Nevertheless, Augustine had gained his foothold and had achieved the conversion of a Kentish king—where it had been done once it could obviously be done again.

The mission then moved northward under the leadership of one Paulinus, who arrived in Northumbria in 601 and was made Bishop of York in 625. For a time the same wavering state of affairs attended the introduction of the faith into this northerly section as had attended it in Kent. Paulinus, however, continued his unremitting efforts, and his first marked success came with the conversion of Edwin, king of Deira (southern Northumbria) in 627. The story of this conversion, told most eloquently by Bede,[2] is the peak of achievement in Old English prose (VIII, 2). Even more important in the career of Paulinus, however, was the conversion of Oswald, who came to the throne of a united Northumbria in 634, and under whose secular and spiritual guidance Christianity flourished to such an extent that Oswald himself was canonized after his death in battle (642).

It was Oswald who was largely responsible for the emergence of Aidan (d.651) as founder of the Northumbrian church. Aidan had spent his earlier life in the monastery of Iona and had caught the eye of Oswald, who, when he wished to found a missionary movement in Northumbria, turned to the brothers at Hii. The career of Aidan will always be associated with the island of Lindisfarne, off the coast of Northumbria. Here he poured out his energies preaching the faith, helping to establish churches, and fostering learning wherever the soil was fertile. As a reward he became Bishop of Lindisfarne. The Venerable Bede was to speak later of Aidan as "the blessed Aidan," who toiled for the glory of God and became the bright star among early Christian teachers in Northumbria.

One deterrent to the spread of the faith at this particular time in the north was the friction between the Irish missionaries still scattered about in that north country and their fellow-workers under Paulinus. The issue finally resolved itself into the question whether the Irish churchmen could maintain their independence of forms and teachings or whether they must defer to the forms and teachings of the missionaries from Rome. In the meantime the Saxons began to come under the influence of their more brilliant northern neighbors. The Mercians, on the other hand, held out for the older paganism during a considerable period. Indeed, the fierce and warlike Penda of Mercia, who ruled from 625 to 655, stood out as the chief obstruction in the way of a complete conversion of England. But the death of this prickly thorn in the flesh of Anglo-Saxon Christianity put a terminus to one difficulty; and the other, the problem of the Irish missionaries, was also settled within a decade. In 664 all the Christian kingdoms of England were incorporated into the Roman Church by the Council of Whitby. Here the organization of the English church was perfected; the synod severed the Anglo-Saxon Christians from even nominal adherence to Celtic Christianity, and much of the work of Aidan was undone. The naming of Theodore of Tarsus as Archbishop of Canterbury and the presence of his capable subordinate, Abbot Hadrian, were the final details in the establishing throughout England of one medieval church. For nearly nine hundred years thereafter the nation was to be under the spiritual guidance of one of the most powerful institutions that man has thus far evolved. It is perhaps superfluous to add that the Council of Whitby antedates anything of any literary significance whatever that may appear in English literature, unless it be portions of *Widsith*.[3]

The actual spiritual state of the Anglo-Saxon pagan thus converted almost within a human lifetime to an entirely different concept of religion would be an interesting study if we could only see it clearly. Perhaps the most striking thing about this conversion was its comparative rapidity. Travel and communication in this virtual wilderness of seventh century Britain must have been extremely difficult; it is a glowing tribute to the Christian missionary that he overcame the hardships thus beyond his power to control and proceeded successfully to his task. To be sure, the beautiful passage in Bede's account of the conversion of King Edwin of Northumbria,[4] already referred to, indicates that the Anglo-Saxon pagan grasped the hope offered by Christianity as infinitely better than anything in his originally somber concept of life. ". . . So this life of man appears for a short space, but of what went before or what is to follow, we know nothing. Therefore, if this new doctrine contains something more certain, it seems justly to deserve to be followed." This naïve expectation is undoubtedly responsible for much of the speed of the conversion.

The word "naïve" is used here advisedly. It would not be correct to accept too unreservedly the consistent statements of the Old English churchmen and the often fervid rhapsodies of the Old English poets as entirely representative of the attitude of the Anglo-Saxon himself. For one thing, the literature itself is the product of Christian writers. Again, once the forms of Christianity—its doctrine, its organized machinery, its ritual, its missionary zeal—had been received by the

Anglo-Saxon earl, churl, and freeman, it is still possible to wonder how thoroughly these people had absorbed the Christian spirit. There are a great many circumstances under which the essential paganism of the Germanic tribesman asserts itself. What of the obvious survivals of folklore, found in England even at the present time? What is the derivation of the word *Easter*? What of the Yule log, the mistletoe, the names of the days of the week? What of the numerous charms and incantations, to be examined later, or the curious lore concerning flora and fauna? Better still, of course, we see the pagan spirit surviving in the unquenchable fatalism which permeates most of Old English literature, whether the subject-matter be Christian or pagan, on every appropriate occasion, sometimes on inappropriate ones. To be sure, there is a superfluity of moralizing in this literature, but some of the sententiousness is a matter of the original Germanic temperament, pagan as well as Christian. Indeed, it is unnecessary to call attention here to the universal tendency of unsophisticated peoples toward apothegm, precept, and proverb—the accumulated store of wisdom which has been generated by centuries of bitter experience.

For example, a poem more non-Christian than *The Wanderer* (V, 1) it would be difficult to imagine; and yet the didactic, or "gnomic" element bulks large even when one ignores the clearly intrusive last lines of the poem. To assert that Christianity stimulated these wise saws and modern instances is the most obvious of truisms. Moral earnestness and persuasive preaching would be the most elementary of essentials in the equipment of the priest. On the other hand, the aforementioned folkways, charms, leechdoms, and what-not must have been the property of the everyday inhabitant of England; the folk-games and the folk-plays of uncertain history belonged, together with the occasional balladry which we can but surmise,[5] to the people as a whole. Here there is a far cry from Paul and the followers of Peter. Nor was even the literature which was the peculiar product of the Church entirely free from a secularizing and almost a popular debasement. For instance, one famous attempt of the Church to focus attention upon the important Church holidays—the beginnings of the drama, which seem to date from some time in the Old English period—evidently resulted later in a type of entertainment with universal popular appeal. However, the story of how the English folk took their early-born drama and turned it to their own uses must be told in another book.[6]

It is only fair to remark, as has often been observed, that "Anglo-Saxon literature is not the direct expression of the pagan age."[7] Certainly it is not; but there are nevertheless plenty of indirect reflections which bespeak the pagan, and nowhere more than in the clash of religious philosophies apparent to any careful reader of Old English poetry. Dismiss for the moment the professional churchman and let the subconscious mind of the Anglo-Saxon speak for itself. Between the blind forces of Wyrd, the pagan goddess of destiny, and the conception of an all-wise, all-knowing, provident Father of man, there is a gulf difficult if not impossible to bridge. This fact has provided the fuel for countless sermons since the Sermon on the Mount. Sincere and honest theologians have satisfied themselves at various times in Christian history that the gulf has been bridged. Yet it is altogether evident that the gulf has not been bridged satisfactorily for any thinking man; still more, then, should there be doubt whether the Anglo-Saxon of the period before the Norman Conquest performed this difficult task. For the Anglo-Saxon tribesman, this bridge would mean a passing from one antithesis to the other. What a surprising, even grotesque contrast there is between Beowulf or Caedmon's Christ on the one hand and the philosophy of the Sermon on the Mount on the other! It becomes completely pertinent to raise the question whether the Englishman has ever fully attained Christianity—outside the church and the cloister.

2. GENERAL NOTES ON THE CHRISTIAN EPIC

THE Christian epic nevertheless constitutes an important part of Old English literature. When one considers the total-

ity of Church control over all Old English literature, for
reasons that have already been pointed out, it is not in any
way anomalous that there should have been such a thing as an
heroic epic based on Christian story-materials, which is an apt
enough definition of the term "Christian epic." That is to say,
the Old English bard, equipped with all the poetic subjects,
styles, and techniques of the *scop* of the Heroic Age, applied
his profession to the great field of Biblical narrative. Therefore, in the earliest surviving examples of the Christian epic
in England, in the poems ascribed to Caedmon and his followers, there is the same antique fashion to be found that
there was in *Beowulf*. The characters, for all their occasionally
colorful striding about, are rather vague and shadowy, as in
Beowulf. The style, as in the heroic epic, is repetitious and
childlike both in outlook and in expression. The entire performance is stark, massive, and altogether ingenuous. Material which a Milton could forge into titanic lines stands forth
baldly in bare monologue. The massiveness is all too often
likely to degenerate into prolixity, even a kind of eloquent
garrulity. Nor is there any real saving leaven of humor. The
poems of the Cynewulfian cycle (IV, 4) are, however, more
sophisticated, although they adhere strictly to the external
mold of the earlier poems. It is evident that this Cynewulfian
cycle is of later date than that of Caedmon. In the passage of
something more than a half-century, the churchly tradition
has advanced the Anglo-Saxon considerably along the road
to a greater knowledge and imitation of classical literature; at
least the poems of Cynewulf and his group are more Virgilian
than their predecessors. They are vigorous, straightforward,
from a literary point of view more artistic achievements; one
is more likely here than in the Caedmonian poems to be aware
of a conscious designer at work in his art. There is a further
point of interest concerning the poems of the Cynewulfian
cycle. In four of them (*Christ, Elene, Juliana, The Fates of
the Apostles*) the author, presumably Cynewulf, has signed
his name in runic letters;[8] sometimes these runic letters are
grouped in scattered words of the text; more often they are

not runic letters alone but rather representations of words, and the resulting esoteric quality of the passages in which these runic letters occur is often most baffling. Nevertheless, these are signatures which should probably be accepted as bona fide signatures; and however little they may advance us in the quest for Cynewulf's identity, they succeed in dissipating the clouds of anonymity which have clustered about the authors of all the works heretofore described. It is possible that a realization of this fact may be a psychological reason for our considering Cynewulf's poems as more sophisticated. It seems fairer, however, to insist upon the likelihood that Cynewulf took himself seriously as a poet and strove more obviously to perfect himself in his art, although the Beowulf Poet doubtless did likewise in more unobtrusive fashion. The results of Cynewulf's efforts we shall examine briefly in a moment. At least we are right in believing that Cynewulf brings us to the "historical" stage of English poetry, where we can see something of an individual author of more than one work, beyond a name and a theory.

3. THE CAEDMONIAN CYCLE

A SIMILAR identity and even greater biographical detail have been argued in the case of Caedmon. If one accepts him as a real person, then he is the first known English poet with a name. And if Caedmon is the first English poet with some sort of identity, it is the Venerable Bede (VII, 3), the saintly abbot at Jarrow, who is chiefly responsible. As with the story of Hengest and Horsa, Bede is our sole authority. But in the matter of Caedmon, the story is also recognized as something of a motif in folklore—the humble man who receives poetic inspiration from on high—and Bede's narrative becomes at once suspect as history, which is not necessarily true of his chronicle of Hengest and Horsa.[9]

This still charming account by Bede tells us that there was a cowherd in the employ of Hild, abbess of Whitby (d. 680). He was unable to partake of the minstrelsy of the banquet, as an educated man should: "when there was adjudged a cause for rejoicing, and they all were to sing in turn to the harp, when he saw the harp approaching him, then he arose for shame from the feast, and went home to his house." On one occasion, after he had thus quitted the feast, a man appeared to him in a vision and "hailed him and greeted him and named him by name," begging the cowherd Caedmon to sing him something. In spite of Caedmon's protestations of inability, he was able to sing a hymn to Creation. To repeat, this story is the common one of the divine inspiration of a humble, inarticulate person to make songs in praise of a god or a godlike idea. There is a most interesting parallel relating to the Greek poet Hesiod, and to students of Germanic literature an equally striking instance in the case of the Icelander Hallbiorn. The acceptance of Caedmon's authenticity is largely dependent upon what one thinks of Bede as a sober historian.

By no stretch of the truth can it be said that a single line of the poems which Bede attributed to Caedmon—insofar as these poems exist in survival—was indubitably written by Caedmon. The one poem actually quoted by Bede, and known to us as *Caedmon's Hymn*[10]—

> Now let us praise the guardian of Heaven,
> The might of the Lord and his divine purpose,
> The work of the Father of glory, as He,
> The eternal Ruler, established each wondrous beginning.
> He first created for the children of men
> Heaven as a roof, did the holy Creator;
> Then the Guardian of mankind, the eternal Ruler,
> Later formed the universe,
> The almighty Lord built the earth for men.

—is apparently a translation of the Latin verses mentioned by Bede. This translation existed in a Northumbrian dialect— and is for that reason a great rarity for the linguist—and later in a West Saxon version; but whether or not the Northumbrian version represents Caedmon's own composition is extremely doubtful.

As for the Caedmon "Canon," which Bede proceeds to give in his story, there exist in Anglo-Saxon literature poems on the topics mentioned by Bede; there are even poems on those identical topics which we have referred specifically to the Caedmonian cycle. What is known of these poems, however, indicates that it would be impossible for one man to have written all these poems as we have them. There are far too many irregularities of grammar, phonology, and dialect. But here is Bede's statement for what it is worth:

"He [Caedmon] sang first of the creation of the world and the beginning of mankind, and all the story of Genesis, that is the first book of Moses, and again of the Exodus of the people of Israel from the land of Egypt and of the entrance into the promised land, and of many other tales of holy writ . . . and of Christ's incarnation, and of His passion, and of His ascent into Heaven; and of the coming of the Holy Ghost, and the teachings of the apostles; and of the day of future judgment and of the terror of punishment full of torment, and of the sweetness of the heavenly kingdom he wrote many a lay; and also he wrought many others concerning divine benefits and judgments."

If Caedmon the poet accomplished all this on the scale, let us say, of *Beowulf*, he was one of the most prolific of English poets. Truly, then, the day following Caedmon's vision, when he went before the wise men of the abbey and demonstrated his newly acquired divine inspiration, would have been an historic day in the development of English poetry. But no such ambitious canon as that defined by Bede actually survives. There are some poems, it is true, dealing with the subjects of Bede's catalogue and showing certain stylistic resemblances which warrant inclusion in a cycle that even the most cautious of present-day scholars can refer to as the Caedmonian cycle. It is impossible to tell how widespread these poems were; they were certainly the creation of poets well versed in both the heroic epic technique and tradition as well as in Christian story.

Only one manuscript of these poems survives. It was discovered by Archbishop Ussher in the seventeenth century and edited by Junius (François Dujon) of Leyden in 1655, and has always been known since as the Junius Manuscript,[11] now the property of the University of Oxford. It dates, apparently, from the tenth century. Thus its problem is akin to that of the Beowulf Manuscript, for while scholars agree on the relatively late date of the manuscript itself, they are equally agreed that the language of the manuscript points to a date of composition somewhere in the early eighth century. The Junius Manuscript comprises the poems, written in the style and manner of the heroic epic, of *Genesis*, *Exodus*, and *Daniel*, with which must be associated *Azarias*, from *The Exeter Book*;[12] in addition there is a group of stories in somewhat later handwriting entitled *Christ and Satan*, which includes the Fall of the Angels, the Harrowing of Hell, the Resurrection, the Ascension, the Pentecost, the Last Judgment, and the Temptation.[13] The list of these works corresponds roughly to the statement of Bede about Caedmon's work; but, as pointed out, scholars have seen in these poems such a surprising amount of variations and discrepancies as to language, vocabulary, and personality that the theory attributing the entire list of works to the pen of one man, at least in the form in which they have survived, rapidly becomes untenable. A striking example of such deviations within the group of poems will be mentioned in a moment. It is altogether possible, however, to believe that there was such a man as Caedmon, that he was of humble birth but developed a poetic talent, that he actually composed poems on Biblical subjects, as Bede has said, and that he founded a kind of literary school. This last point, which is of much significance, is clearly implied by Bede himself. "And his songs and his lays were so winsome to hear that his teachers themselves learned and wrote from his mouth." On such grounds we are free to speak of Caedmon as an author.

Nothing, however, will indicate better the rapid development of the tradition of the Christian epic in Old English, its multiple authorship, its tendency to circulate outside strictly English boundaries, than the case of the poem *Genesis*. This poem was long regarded as a unit and the work presumably

of Caedmon or some immediate disciple. But embedded in
the poem is a passage of some six hundred lines and more
which an adequate knowledge of Anglo-Saxon linguistics
must mark apart from the rest of the poem. This passage,
always known since the recognition of its peculiarities as *Genesis B*, is a good century later in composition than the remainder (*Genesis A*); that is, *Genesis B* belongs to the ninth
century and *Genesis A* to the eighth. As long ago as 1875
Sievers pointed out the essential discrepancies in meter, vocabulary, and style between the two parts of the poem;[14] indeed, he observed that *Genesis B* was different in these respects from other poems in Old English and ventured the
theory that it was a translation from a Low German (Old
Saxon) poem.[15] In 1894 parts of such a German poem were
actually discovered in the Vatican Library. No very good explanation of how a portion of this poem came to be interpolated in an Old English Christian epic has ever been made.
However, there are obviously enough close relationships between Old English and Old Low German; there are both
linguistic and ethnic strands equally close; and it is a known
fact that Anglo-Saxon scholars and clerics received their education frequently on the Continent and traveled there extensively.[16] A vague explanation of the problem in *Genesis* is
therefore easy. It happens that *Genesis B* is on the subject of
Paradise Lost; and striking resemblances, to be pointed out
in a moment, between the Caedmonian poem and Milton's
epic occur at this point. No other work in the Caedmonian
cycle shows so vividly and romantically the heterogeneous
nature of the cycle; but the diversity of language and the
mixture of dialects hold in some slight degree throughout,
and in consequence the theory of a multiplicity of authors in
the Caedmonian cycle is virtually inescapable.

These Caedmonian poems have been defined as bardic
epics with characters taken from Biblical story. If the heroic
epics were delivered at the court of tribal or national kings, in
the presence of their *comitatus*, the Caedmonian poems were
more probably delivered in a religious gathering, although

the secular aristocracy may also have been present. We are assuredly correct in regarding this Christian epic as fully as "aristocratic" in its origins as the heroic epic, except that it is a priestly aristocracy rather than a social or political one which gave it birth. The tradition of the Anglo-Saxon *scop*, the alliterative tetrametrical type of verse with marked caesura after the second irregular foot, the copious use of appositives, the rude imagery based on the kenning,[17] the repetitious "varying of words,"[18] the characteristic understatement, or litotes—all are present in the Caedmonian cycle as they were in *Beowulf*. Where the kenning in *Beowulf* was usually a compound word ("whale-road," "gannet's-bath" for *sea*; "hammer-leavings," "battle-light" for *sword*), in the Caedmonian poems they were more likely to be phrases ("foundations of the people" for the *comitatus*), and so in the Caedmonian poems there were possibly fewer actual kennings and more rhetorical figures, such as the hendiadys of "vapor and darkness" for *vaporous darkness*. Of course the Latin poetic influences are discernible in both the Caedmonian poems and *Beowulf*; actually they seem less in the Caedmonian poems than elsewhere. Christ replaces Beowulf as the hero, for example; or it may be Moses. Yet the substitution entails no apparent difference in character; Christ is spoken of as "the bold warrior" or "the mighty leader," and his physical prowess is entirely comparable to that of Beowulf. The apostles are but little different from the thanes who accompany Beowulf on his adventures. There is one feature, however, much better developed in the Caedmonian poems than in *Beowulf*, and that is the landscape.

> May the glory of worldly craft and all works,
> May the heavens and angels bless Thee, gracious Father!
> And the clear waters which by just command
> Abide in glory above the heavens, they honor Thee;
> And all creatures, the stars radiant in the sky,
> Keeping their course, the sun and moon. . . .
> The stars of heaven, the dew and precious rain,
> May they glorify thee! May souls praise Thee,

Almighty God! Let burning flame and bright summer
Praise the Saviour, night together with day. . . .
And let the frost and snow, the bitter winter storm,
And the paths of the clouds praise Thee on high,
Mighty Lord! And the flash of lightning, gleaming and swift,
Let it praise Thee! All the sheets of earth,
The hills and plains and lofty mountains,
The salt waves, the flood and rush of the surf,
The gushing of springs, they praise Thee,
Eternal Lord, rigtheous God.   [DANIEL, 362-385]

Or again,

They pressed on northwards; they knew that southwards
Lay the land of the Sun Folk, and burnt hills,
People blackened by the heat of the sun.
There holy God guarded his folk against the mighty heat;
He threw over the burning sky a canopy. . . .
The heavenly sign arose every evening, the other wonder
Marvelous after sunset, the flaming pillar,
It failed not to shine with its fire o'er the warriors. . . .
Shields gleamed; shadows shrank away. . . .
The new night-guardian hovered by need over the band,
Lest ever the terror of the desert, the gray heath,
Should in a tempest put their souls to flight
In sudden fear.   [EXODUS, 68ff.]

These nature-settings may be construed as interpretations of
the northern English moorlands or the jagged hill-country
of the Cheviots, of Skiddaw and the Langdale Pikes, or the
cliffs and ledges of the Northumbrian coast. The descriptive
note sounds again and again in this Christian epic. It seems,
indeed, to be a true contribution of the priest to Old English
literature, the quickening of a half-glimmering appreciation
of nature, prompted in part by the tradition of Virgil and applied by men of poetic instincts who have awakened to the
expression of a feeling for the wonders of nature about them.
Only in the descriptions of the approach to Grendel's mere or
the brief reference to the voyage of the Geats to Hrothgar's
land in *Beowulf* are there comparable passages in the surviv-

ing Old English heroic epic. No doubt it is unfair to generalize complacently about this lack in the heroic epic. The substance of an epic, however, need not preclude descriptive material, as the Homeric poems gloriously attest. Perhaps such material may have existed in the heroic epic more fully than we now realize, but there is not enough left to justify such a guess.

Moreover, there is in the Caedmonian cycle, as usually in the Christian epic, a softer temperament at work—there is pity mixed with grimness. Satan is an arch-fiend, of course; but some of the tragedy of his fall is apparent to the author of *Genesis B*. The pursuing hosts of Pharaoh are doomed; they are scourged for their persecution of the chosen people, but in their doom they are praised as brave. Throughout the Caedmonian poems there is a superior type of imagination on display, cramped as it undoubtedly is by the requirements of the strictly alliterative poetic form. Not without reason has the probably erroneous suggestion been advanced that Milton may possibly have owed something to the Junius Manuscript when he came to write *Paradise Lost*.[19] He probably was acquainted with Junius while the latter was librarian to the Earl of Arundel. This suggestion raises fascinating speculation on which little light can now be thrown; but the monologues of Satan in *Genesis B*, to be quoted in a moment, parallel in spirit, if not in actual phraseology, the great monologues in Books I and IX of *Paradise Lost*. With this statement of a possible obligation, however, it is better to stop, for there is a vast abyss between the poetic standards and accomplishments of a half-legendary Northumbrian cowherd, even if divinely inspired, and those of the mighty poet who was to come a thousand years later.

Not that there are no impressive, even powerful passages in the Caedmonian poems. Some indication of their many virtues has already been made and is indeed apparent from the lines out of *Daniel* quoted above. Such purple patches could well be multiplied, but a few must suffice here. There is the terse battle-scene attendant upon the taking of Sodom and Gomorrah by the Elamites in *Genesis A*:

Then came together fierce bands of slaughter;
Javelins rang aloud; the swart bird dewy-feathered,
Sang among the shafts of spears, eager for carrion.
The warriors hastened in mighty troops, brave in heart,
Until the helmet-bearing heroes had come together in a host
From south and north. There was grim war-play;
The exchange of deadly spears, the turmoil of battle,
Loud clamor of the fight. Men drew forth
Their ring-adorned swords, mighty of edge,
From out their sheaths. There was fighting enow
For earls and those who never had known
Much of battle. Treacherous were the Northmen
To the people of the south; the men of Sodom and Gomorrah
Were bereft in that battle of their dear gold-giver,
Their comrade in arms. So they fled from the field
To save their lives, though beaten down by warriors;
Behind them lay dead the sons of kings,
Their eager companions, put to sleep by the sword.
[1982-2003]

And then the somber soliloquies of Satan in *Genesis B*:

'Why should I struggle?' said he. 'I have no need
Of a master; I can work with my own hands
As many wonders; I have full powers
To prepare a goodlier throne
And a higher in the heavens. Why should I yield
To his favor, or bow before him in such homage?
I can be God as well as he.
Strong comrades stand beside me, who will not fail me,
Brave-hearted heroes in the strife;
They have chosen me for master—
Hardy warriors!—with such one can bethink himself
Of strategy; with such henchmen he can well succeed.
They are keen in friendship to me,
Loyal in their heart and soul;
I can be their master and rule in this kingdom.
So it seems not right to me,
That I should needs flatter God
For aught of benefits; I will no longer be his servant!'
[278-291]

... 'Alas! had I but the strength of my hands,
And could gain freedom for one hour,
Even for a winter's hour, then with this host I—
But around me lie iron bonds; the chain and fetter are on me.
I am powerless; the hard bonds of Hell have grappled me
   close.'   [368-374]

The foregoing passages seem to be the germs of the speeches
of Satan in *Paradise Lost*:

All is not lost—the unconquerable will,
And study of revenge, immortal hate,
And courage never to submit or yield:
And what is else not to be overcome.
That glory never shall his wrath or might
Extort from me. To bow and sue for grace
With suppliant knee, and deify his power
Who, from the terror of this arm, so late
Doubted his empire—that were low indeed;
That were an ignominy and shame beneath
This downfall; since by fate the strength of Gods,
And this empyreal substance, cannot fail;
Since, through experience of this great event,
In arms not worse, in foresight much advanced,
We may with more successful hope resolve
To wage by force or guile eternal war,
Irreconcilable to our grand Foe,
Who now triumphs, and in th' excess of joy
Sole reigning holds the tyranny of Heaven.
                                     [1, 106-124]

or

If I could joy in aught—sweet interchange
Of hill and valley, rivers, woods, and plains,
Now land, now sea, and shores with forest crowned,
Rocks, dens, and caves! But I in none of these
Find place of refuge; and the more I see
Pleasures about me, so much more I feel
Torment within me, as from the hateful siege

Of contraries; all good to me becomes
Bane, and in Heaven much worse would be my state.
But neither here seek I, nor in Heaven,
To dwell, unless by mastering Heaven's Supreme:
Nor hope to be myself less miserable
By what I seek, but others to make such
As I, though thereby worse to me redound.

[IX, 115-128]

Even the casual observer, however, will see in this juxtaposition of the Caedmonian and Miltonic passages the essential differences between the simplicity of the one and the sophistication of the other, between the physical, sinewy type of mentality in Caedmon and the elaborate psychology and rich *décor* in Milton's great epic. This physicalness of the Anglo-Saxon of the eighth century receives perhaps its most vigorous expression in the passage from *Exodus* describing the destruction of Pharaoh's army:

Panic came upon the folk; the terror of the flood
Beset their sad hearts. The abyss menaced them with death,
The mountainous waters were mingled with blood;
The sea spewed forth gore. There was a clamor of the waves,
And the water was full of weapons. There rose a deadly
    haze.
The Egyptians were hurled back; they fled in fear;
They encountered sudden horror; panic-stricken they
    yearned
To seek their homes; less blithe were their boasts.
A horrid rush of water darkened over them; none returned;
For Wyrd blocked the road behind them with water.
Where once the paths lay before them, the sea now raged;
The warriors were engulfed. Up rose the waves
And a tempest high in the heavens; the mightiest of out-
    cries.
The foemen screamed aloud in doomed voices;
So the very air grew murky; blood stained the water.
The shielding walls were pulled down;
The greatest of drownings scourged the sky ...
Drowning in truth for the doomed host,

When the surge of breakers, the cold ocean,
Naked messenger of woe, hostile wanderer that o'er-
    whelmed foes,
Returned to its everlasting foundations, as its wont,
With its reckless salt waves.
The blue sky was shot with blood;
And the bursting sea ended with terror of death
The journey of the travelers, as the true Lord
By the hand of Moses unloosed its fury.   [447-481]

Enough has been quoted already to indicate the poetic possibilities in the poems of the Caedmonian cycle. There is no
need, however, to foster any illusions about the poems as literary achievements. It is hardly just to dismiss them as childish effusions, as certain critics would have them;[20] neither is it
proper to hail them as untutored literary art at its highest.
The truth as usual lies halfway between these two extremes.
The work of the Caedmonian school is uneven, and the same
can be said of nearly all Old English poetry. The positive
virtues of this literature, which will be summed up in Chapter
XIV, are amply represented here. It has raw, unpolished
strength which is only a trifle mannered and self-conscious; it
has also an imaginative force which represents a real advance
over the purely heroic epic. On the other hand, the homiletic
tendency of the Germanic writer in general and of the Old
English churchman in particular cannot be avoided; and
passages of dreary moralizing and prolix didacticism follow
hard upon the heels of passages of authentic poetry.

4. CYNEWULF AND THE SIGNED POEMS

CYNEWULF, the chronological and perhaps the literary successor to Caedmon and his school, is not superior as an essential poet to any of his predecessors; but he is a man much
more deliberate and conscious as an artist, and his ear is much
more delicately attuned to the tonal qualities of his rough
Anglo-Saxon language. It seems probable that Cynewulf's
education was much more extensive than that of the shadowy

Caedmon, whatever the facts about the latter's life. The Cynewulfian poems certainly exhibit a much more obvious impress of the monastic churchman. But while one can assert with some degree of confidence that Cynewulf actually wrote this or that poem, the personality of the author is only a little less vague than that of Caedmon. There are some lines at the close of *Elene*, one of the poems bearing the Cynewulf signature, which scholars have professed to regard as autobiographical. In these lines the poet speaks of himself as formerly unregenerate and unhappy; when God's ministers taught him, he was no longer young, but since that time he had been able to compose poetry—on religious themes, needless to say —and had come into a state of blessedness which had no longer any thought for the joys of youth or of worldly riches.

Cynewulf appears to have been a man from the north of England,[21] but whether a Northumbrian or a Mercian is uncertain. The general tendency has been to follow Sievers's theory that he was a Northumbrian,[22] a theory which was based chiefly upon the Northumbrian texture of his meter and assonance; but scholars are free to concede that such a belief is based almost equally upon the altogether negative point that our state of knowledge concerning the Mercian dialects is still far from satisfactory. Yet all except the very earliest critics like Grimm[23] accept the fact that he was Anglian and not Saxon. The usual assumption is that his life fell somewhere between 750 and 825. His "signature" is now *Kynewulf* (or Cynewulf), now *Kynwulf* (or Cynwulf).[24] Certain recorded Anglo-Saxon proper names with the first element of this compound have the form *Cyni-*, but they are considered to be early. The linguistic development of this compositional element is chronologically from the *Cyni-* to the *Cyne-* forms; the weakening of *-i* to *-e* is believed to have taken place in Anglia about 750. The syncopated form *Cynwulf*, however, is clearly of the ninth century.

Unfortunately one cannot satisfactorily connect the Cynewulf signatures or the poems which contain them to any historical character named Cynewulf known in this period, but it happens that there are two or three possibilities.[25] In fact, the name is not at all unusual. It can be shown on both linguistic and historical grounds that the poet was not Cenwulf, Abbot of Peterborough (d. 1006) and Bishop of Worcester; but he may well have been Bishop Cynewulf of Lindisfarne, who died about 782.[26] There is also the possibility that he was the man named Cynwulf who appears in the records of a synod at Clovesho in 803 and was a priest in the diocese of Dunwich.[27] The date is right, and the form of the name would be possible for that date; Dunwich was the seat of a considerable school, at which Cynewulf could have acquired his undoubted knowledge of theology, could have come under the hardly less certain influence of Aldhelm (VII, 2), and could have received his strong, articulate feeling for the ocean. The striking fact is that this element—the glory and wonder of the sea—must be reckoned with in any attempt to fix Cynewulf's dwelling or identity. Even more than the Beowulf Poet he is the true sea-poet of the age.

Essentially it matters very little whom we select as the real Cynewulf. Certain qualities in his poems are their own excuse for being. This love of the sea is one, and perhaps it is the most poetically appealing. Religiousness is another; there could be no possible doubt that he was a cleric, and all his poetic purpose is the poetic purpose of a churchman who is fired with a zeal to propagate the faith. Along with his religious inclinations and poetic feelings, he is something of a mystic and an ascetic. Perhaps it is proper to regard this trinity of mysticism, asceticism, and poetic insight as a typical combination in the literature of the medieval Church.

The historical significance of Cynewulf, then, as the first English author to sign his name is clear enough, as are the variant forms of that signature and their probable dates. The four poems bearing the signature (*Juliana*, *Elene*, *Christ*, and *The Fates of the Apostles*) survive in separate manuscripts— *Christ* and *Juliana* are in *The Exeter Book*; *Elene* and *The Fates of the Apostles* are in *The Vercelli Book*. Although the dates of 750-825 are acceptable enough for Cynewulf himself and for the language of these poems, the two collections (*The Exeter Book* and *The Vercelli Book*) comprise, of course, pieces of various dates. Moreover, in both collections are many other poems closely resembling in subject-matter, idiom, and style the four signed poems. In this miscellaneous group should be included a notable set of *Riddles* (V, 4) found in *The Exeter Book*; some of these were for a long time attributed to Cynewulf, although modern scholarship has rejected the ascription. These various Cynewulfian poems will be considered in the next section (IV, 5).

Because of the existence of these miscellaneous pieces resembling Cynewulf's signed poems, some scholars have suggested a very extensive achievement by Cynewulf himself; others more cautious have expressed themselves as believing in a Cynewulfian cycle. In other words, the situation is similar to that which obtains in the case of the poems of Caedmon and his school. More definite ascriptions can be made to Cynewulf than to Caedmon, it is true; nevertheless, it is better not to assign any but the four signed poems to the master of the school and therefore to recognize the presence of a Cynewulfian cycle.

For purposes of summary, then, it must be repeated that in addition to these four poems with signature, the cycle comprises *Andreas*, *Guthlac A* and *Guthlac B* (an apparently separate poem following line 791 of *Guthlac A*). Like *Juliana* and *Elene*, *Andreas* and the *Guthlac* poems are saints' lives, which constitute an extremely common and important type of medieval literature. Further in the list are *The Phoenix*, the impressive *Dream of the Rood*, and the *Physiologus* (or *Bestiary*)—all at one time or another attributed to Cynewulf and certainly showing what may be called a Cynewulfian influence. As will be apparent, however, from even a cursory reading of these various poems, it is not wise to proclaim one or another of them as specifically or predominantly the handiwork of some immediate follower of Cynewulf. That Cynewulf set a tradition for various disciples and imitators cannot be denied. The rugged sea-faring strength, even the tang of the sea, can be detected in nearly all of these poems in the Cynewulfian cycle. Even to a greater extent does the ascetic atmosphere cling to them all. But granted that Cynewulf had influence; so did Caedmon, and behind Caedmon lies the great pagan heroic epic tradition. When the turmoil of critical discussion has subsided, certain facts remain, and it is important to keep them in mind throughout the reading and study of the Anglo-Saxon Christian epic poetry. Caedmon may have been the pioneer of the Biblical epic in English literature; Cynewulf contributed the mysticism and the conscious art. Unquestionably, however, there was already in Caedmon's time a well-developed storehouse of epithet, kenning, stock phrase, and bardic formulas which any poet of pretensions was supposed to have at his beck and call. For all we know, there were other poets of pretensions beside Caedmon and Cynewulf.

Let us concern ourselves for the moment with the four works bearing the Cynewulf signature. *Juliana* and *Elene* have the author's name as *Kynewulf*, a form which cannot be found in records before 740-750. *Christ* and *The Fates of the Apostles* give it as *Kynwulf*, a form close to the year 800.[28] The older two, *Juliana* and *Elene*, are both lives of saints, and of female saints at that—something sufficient to deserve comment. The appearance of women in the heroic epic was never very striking; they were royal personages who passed the ceremonial cup in the banquet-hall and then, having graced the assemblage with their presences, discreetly retired, or else they were obscure like the old woman who uttered her lamentation in *Beowulf* (3150) and then was lost from sight. In fact, the negative—or negligible—role played by women in the heroic epic was one of its hallmarks, for this epic was the product of an ultra-masculine society and was intended for an ultra-masculine audience; and in the presence of such an audience women were mainly important for their queenly status or for their pictorial attributes. Something of this tradition seems to have been carried over into the Caedmonian cycle, although the primitive Biblical narrative either precluded women or, as in the case of Eve, painted them from the early Christian standpoint as unworthy vessels that had wrought the ruin of man. On the other hand, the history of the early Christian Church was strewn with female martyrs. A levelling of the sexes in Christian hagiology was inevitable, for medieval Christianity was a sexless religion. But such a levelling was something new to Old English literature. Once it was accepted, it boded well for the future of womankind. There is nothing in the Old English period, however, comparable to the cult of the Virgin which swept over Europe in the latter part of the eleventh century and gave a powerful impetus to the chivalric movement. Still, the admission, grudging though it might be at times, that women could attain to the kingdom of God earned for women a respect which, at least in literature, had never been accorded to them since the days of ancient Greece and republican Rome.

As for *Juliana* and *Elene*, judged as literary creations, they are not particularly distinguished, unless the colorful speech of the devil in *Juliana* be worthy of mention. But then devils have always been most interesting in literature, usually far more so than their holy antagonists:

> 'Now I hear—thanks to thy utterance
> That I perforce shall be driven by thy enmity
> To reveal my mind as thou hast commanded me,
> To suffer affliction. My plight is full dire,
> My calamity measureless! I must suffer
> And endure all things at thy decree,
> Disclose sinful deeds, dark deeds,
> All I ever contrived. Oft I took away sight,
> Blinded countless men with evil thoughts,
> Covered with a helmet of mist the light of the eyes,
> Or with a poisonous breath and dark attack;
> And the feet of some with evil snares
> I have broken to pieces; some I sent to burn
> In the embrace of fire, so that their footsteps
> No longer were seen. And some I mauled
> So that their bone-frames spurted forth blood,
> So that suddenly they relinquished life
> In the jets from their veins. Some in seafaring

Were whelmed on their way by the waters
In the vast ocean-flood through the work of my craft,
Down into the fierce eddies. Some I gave to the cross,
And they in anguish high on the gallows
Yielded their lives. Some I have led by counsel,
Brought into strife, so that suddenly
They awoke old grudges while drunk with beer;
I proffered them enmity from their goblets,
So that they in the wine-hall
By the bite of swords let slip their souls
Doomed from the body, embracing grisly wounds.
Some I found without God's token,
Needless, unblessed; those I boldly
Struck with my skillful hands and killed by many deaths.
I could not tell, though I sat for a long summer's day,
All the miseries which, early or late,
I wrought in my wickedness. . . .'   [461-497]

Characteristic is the passage from *Elene* including the signature; it forms part of the supposedly autobiographical section already referred to above:

In comfort to my old age, a glorious gift
The mighty King measured out for me and poured into my
     mind,
Revealed to me brightness, making it more spacious,
Unbound my bone-frame, unloosed the constraint of my
     breast,
Unlocked the art of song, of which I have gladly partaken,
Yea, joyously in this world . . .
. . . Ever until then the man
Had been beaten down by sorrow-surges; a smouldering
     torch(C),[29]
Though he in the mead-hall had received treasures,
Apple-shaped gold. The bow(Y)[30] lamented,
The companion in need(N)[31] endured close-pressing sor-
     row;
Cruel secret thoughts, though for him the horse(E)[32]
Measured the mile-paths, coursed proudly ahead
Superb in his trappings. Hope(W)[33] has departed,
And pleasure, as the years pass; youth has fled away,

And pride of old. Ours(U)[34] was of yore
The splendor of youth. Now are former days
Passed forth in due procession;
Joy of life has vanished, even as the flood(L)[35] glides
    away,
Even as moving waters. Wealth(F)[36] for every man
Is fleeting under the heavens, the adornments of the earth
Depart under the clouds, most like to wind,
When it rises up loud before the warriors,
Whirling about among the clouds, howling forth
And then in turn growing still once more
Confined in its narrow prison,
Oppressed by might. . . .   [1247-1277]

The saint's life is likely to be at best rather drab narrative;
besides, it receives more extensive treatment in the English
vernacular after the Norman Conquest rather than before.
The accounts of martyrdoms have, of course, the melancholy
sensationalism which has always attended the story of unjust
persecutions fostered for propagandistic ends; they have the
gory morbidity of something like Foxe's *Book of Martyrs*,
with all its sadistic possibilities, but they are not appealing to
a modern reader, who would be much more likely to appreciate the stark grisliness of Beowulf than all the many syn-
thetic woes of obstinate Christianized maidens like Juliana.
Elene, on the other hand, might have as subtitle "The Quest
of the True Cross," and therefore merits consideration along
with *The Dream of the Rood*. The immediate comparison of
the two would hardly be fair to either, however, because *The
Dream of the Rood* is primarily lyrical—much of it attaining
a high degree of emotional intensity—whereas *Elene* is fundamentally narrative. The best parts of *Elene* are not the
passages recounting the finding of the Cross so much as they
are those describing the sea-voyages of Helena.

The other two poems signed by Cynewulf, *Christ* and *The
Fates of the Apostles*, might be called epics in a general sense,
but they differ from the poems of the Caedmonian cycle and
from both *Elene* and *Juliana* in being more "literary" and

more devoted to the elaborate figure of speech. They are also far more lyrical; indeed, the lyric element often threatens to clog the narrative completely. Thus,

> Now it is indeed much as if we on the sea-flood
> Over the icy water were voyaging in ships,
> Over the broad sea in our sea-steeds,
> Our flood-wood. The eddies are perilous,
> The waves illimitable, that we sport on here
> Throughout this changeful world; wind-swept billows
> Over a deep channel. The wayfaring was hard
> Before we had come to land
> Over the fierce ridges; then help came to us,
> And to the harbor of salvation led us,
> God's spiritual Son, and gave us grace
> That we might learn while aboard the ship
> Where we should moor our sea-steeds,
> Our old horses of the waves, fast at anchor.
>
> [CHRIST, 850-863]

The heroic epic was generally content with kennings or at most extended metaphors. The most elaborate of these occurs in *Beowulf* (1368ff.), where the mere of Grendel is described as so forbidding that a stag pursued by hounds would rather give up his life on the shore than plunge in. As is obvious from the lines of *Christ* just quoted, the Cynewulfian imagination observes the sea vividly and effects a reasonably successful figure of speech. Consider again:

> Then suddenly the mighty Day
> Of the sovereign Lord shall seize at midnight
> All the earth-dwellers in its power,
> All fair creatures, as often as a wicked harmer,
> A stealthy thief, who moves in darkness,
> On a black night surprises
> Careless men wrapped in their sleep,
> And falls wickedly upon men ill prepared.
>
> [CHRIST, 867-874]

where the metaphor is presented in its most characteristic form, in structure not unlike the Homeric simile, with its combination of detail and aptness.

Christ also contains a brief passage which is neither narrative nor lyrical, but dramatic—a short dialogue between Mary and Joseph. This passage, and the implications of dramatic composition[37] which it offers, will be mentioned again later in Chapter VI. [38,39] It is still a question whether or not, in dealing with *Christ*, one is confronted with a single poem or three separate poems joined together by the central figure of the Deity. At any rate, the poem has three easily recognized parts, treating respectively the Nativity, the Ascension, and the Day of Judgment. The first part, on the Advent, is based upon the ecclesiastical Antiphons for that particular feast-day; the second part is traceable to a sermon by Pope Gregory the Great; and the third part, as with any discussion of the Day of Doom, is founded upon many sources any one of which, working on the poet's imagination, could have produced the final result.

Viewing *Christ* as a whole, then, and comparing it with the Caedmonian *Christ and Satan*,[40] one is impelled to the conclusion that Cynewulf's poem is not so much a direct narrative of the events treated in *Christ and Satan* as it is a lyrical and dramatic handling of the story of Christ and a prophecy of Doomsday. As for *The Fates of the Apostles*, it is a brief piece, for long associated with *Andreas* (IV, 5); it contains no remarkable lines and merely gives a list of the Apostles with a brief account of their fortunes.

5. MISCELLANEOUS CAEDMONIAN AND CYNEWULFIAN POEMS

THAT the remaining religious epics of Old English literature should reveal the influence of either Caedmon or Cynewulf might well be assumed. Enough has been said of the differences between the two cycles of the Old English Christian epic to indicate how their respective influences would exhibit themselves. The remaining poems of this type are scattered through the four important manuscripts of Anglo-Saxon poetry.[41] All are at least of the eighth century and most of them seem to be of later date. They have been the subject of continual argument on the questions of their origins and authorship; and the general findings of the scholars are pretty well agreed on one point. The great majority of these poems are Cynewulfian rather than Caedmonian. It is naturally rather futile to attempt to establish a claim of authorship by one or the other of these two early names in English literary history, particularly when the men to whom these names are attached happen to be so shadowy. Yet it cannot be unduly emphasized that all Old English poetry has come down to posterity through the workings of a lucky destiny; it must be repeated that there may have been other poets of importance beside Caedmon and Cynewulf, and therefore possibly other schools of poetry. For that speculation there is no longer any satisfactory answer; but whoever the authors of these miscellaneous pieces may have been, there were among them men of much talent.

As a first illustration we may take *Judith*, an epic on a Biblical subject, only the closing sections of which have survived. This fragment exists in the Beowulf Manuscript (Cotton Vitellius A XV) and follows immediately after the close of *Beowulf*. The date of the piece is as usual highly uncertain. *Judith* shows resemblances to both the Caedmonian and the Cynewulfian cycles and also to *The Battle of Brunanburh*; it is customary to date it most conservatively anywhere between 850 and 940. Certain critics have been willing to admit the insecure possibility that it is the work of Cynewulf himself.[42] It is a narrative poem of great energy and fiery story-telling and is devoid of the superfluity of homiletic elements which often mar its companion *Beowulf*. Since it appears to be of at least the latter half of the ninth century—in other words, contemporary with King Alfred the Great—some have seen in it a kind of allegory of the Danish invasions, with the hostile Assyrians in the role of the Danes and the Hebrews representing the Anglo-Saxons. There is never any possibility of disproving such an interpretation of the poem, although it must be observed that allegory is a sophisticated type of composition. On the other hand, there is little possibility of proving the point, either.

Whatever the facts, the poem remains anonymous, although to me it suggests the story-teller Caedmon rather than the more complex poet Cynewulf. There is no doubt, however, that *Judith* seems in date to be beyond the temporal grasp of either individual and is much more likely to be the work of an independent writer who was familiar not only with the Caedmonian and Cynewulfian traditions but also with the whole heroic epic tradition behind them. In this epic, the primitive, forthright, and savage heroine of the Apocrypha appears as a Christian champion of virginal purity; and although her career is necessarily curtailed in this fragment, she remains the most interesting of Anglo-Saxon epic heroines —indeed, the only one who can be called a heroine in the tribal or national sense. She is virtually a warrior and therefore has transcended the limitations of her sex, to take her place beside the bravest of the king's thanes. This position of Judith is almost sufficient argument in itself in favor of a later date for the poem; Christianity has by this time so saturated the literary tradition that the old heathen's biased subordination of women has been overlooked.

Andreas, in *The Vercelli Book*,[43] like the *Guthlac* poems of *The Exeter Book*, brings us back to the saint's life. The story of the saint who became the patron saint of Scotland has an ultimately Greek source, known in English simply as *The Acts of Andrew and Matthias*,[44] but the immediate source was probably a Latin version of the Greek original. The *Guthlac* poems[45] were evidently based upon the oral tradition which accrued to the figure of St. Guthlac of Croyland, Lincolnshire (d.714); but the second of these, known as *Guthlac B*, may be built upon a Latin life of the saint (VII, 6). All three poems are in the manner of Cynewulf and should be included in the Cynewulfian cycles; as a matter of fact, they were for a long time attributed to Cynewulf himself in spite of the absence of the runic signature. They have significant sea-passages which betray the influence of the hypothetical, obscure churchman of Dunwich or Lindisfarne. They are rhetorical at the sacrifice of narrative action, and as usual they make capital of all the stylistic paraphernalia of the older heroic epic. Interesting parallels between these poems and the older works spring up almost at first glance. To the careful and discerning reader, however, these three poems seem somewhat artificial in their imitation of the heroic style; bardic formulas stunt their artistic growth. The opening of *Andreas* shows in arresting fashion the not too congruous blend of paganism and Christianity, beginning as it does in the manner of *Beowulf*:

> Lo! we have heard from days of yore
> Of twelve glorious heroes, thanes of the Lord,
> Under the stars. Their glory failed not in fight
> When battle-standards clashed together. . . .
> They were famous throughout the world,
> Bold folk-leaders and active in war,
> Courageous battlers, when on the field of combat
> Hand and shield defended the helmet. . . .   [1-8]

Here is a type of device all too common in the lesser Christian epics. It results in the tendency to clothe moralistic, antimilitaristic Christian leaders in all the trappings of Viking warriors, and it endows the spiritual with an ultra-physical being. The "twelve warriors" of the above passage are the Twelve Apostles, and references to their powers on the "slaughter-place" are frequent. Christ has some of the pomp and panoply of an Oriental potentate; he is referred to constantly in *Andreas* as the "mighty Prince." One notable kenning describes him as "the glory of kings"; another, as "the guardian of the princes." In this poem arises also the pervading aroma of the Church militant; the spirit of the Crusader is to suffer martyrdom; he does not linger long in patience. There is a nervous pace about the narrative and an almost jerky continuity. But, once more, the truly noteworthy passages in *Andreas* are those where the motif of the sea appears; this motif recurs throughout the poem and is expressed often

in terms which are easily recognized by the reader of *Beowulf*,
for we have the same terse kennings, although they are often
arranged a little too consciously to be altogether effective:

> . . . Thy angel can perform that with ease.
> From Heaven he knows the stretch of oceans,
> The salt sea-streams, and the swan-road,
> The surging of breakers and the terror of deep waters,
> The waves pouring over the world.   [194-198]

At one point in the story God and his two angels appear—

> They, the earls, were in dress like unto sailors,
> Seafarers, when they toss on the cold water.
>
> [250-252]

—a descriptive touch which the reader of the late Greek
romances will remember, but which is a newcomer to Old
English literature. And occasionally there comes a sharper,
more incisive detail:

> Then the whale-ocean was troubled and confused;
> The swordfish sported, darting through the deep,
> The gray gull wheeled about, greedy for carrion;
> The candle of the sky darkened; the wind rose;
> The waves dashed; the floods raged fiercely;
> The rigging creaked; the sails were soaked. [369-375]

Guthlac A has little to recommend it to anyone other than
the antiquarian and student of Old English language and
poetry; but *Guthlac B* shows marked resemblances to the four
signed poems of Cynewulf, and may well be from the hand of
that author. *Guthlac B* opens with a brief account of the fall
of man and then proceeds to make clear that some have always
been trying to do God's will in spite of all dangers and hardships. Of such as these was Guthlac. The story of his life then
follows. The narrative of the holy man's sickness and death is
a more elaborate literary effort than that other death-bed scene
in Old English literature—the passing of Caedmon as related
in Bede's *Ecclesiastical History*,[46] and it therefore naturally
misses the note of simple pathos sounded by that fine prose-

writer, but it is effective none the less. It is a long and painful illness which Guthlac suffers toward the end, but he takes comfort in enjoining his servant to live a good life and to be prepared for death,

> When body and limbs and the spirit of life
> Shall part their union in the wrench of death.
>   [1176-1178][47]

Finally Guthlac sinks down and bows his head to experience the bitter hug of mortality:

> So did the holy man's breath mount up
> The livelong day till evening.
> Then the glorious splendor
> Sought its setting; the black northern sky
> Lowered dark under the clouds. The world was wrapped
> In mist, was covered with darkness;
> Night came rushing down over the world,
> Over the jewels of the land.   [1276-1282]

This foreboding setting of the sun is not described elsewhere in Old English literature with such stark effect. It gives ample conviction to the statement that the author of a Cynewulfian poem must know the sky as well as the sea. But the somber scene is not permitted to remain:

> Then came the most radiant of lights
> In holiness from the heavens, shining clearly,
> Glowing over the town-dwellings.   [1282-1284]

The conclusion of *Guthlac B* is missing in the text, but there is no reason to suppose that there was more to the narrative itself. Gerould[48] is of the opinion that the missing lines comprised a runic signature of Cynewulf's name; and, in view of the strongly Cynewulfian flavor of the whole poem, such may very likely be the case.

To the modern reader, however, *The Dream of the Rood* (in *The Vercelli Book*) would probably have greatest appeal, for nowhere else in Old English literature, except in Bede's *Ecclesiastical History*, do we find the same combination of

lyrical freshness, tenderness, and simple religious feeling. The
poem has its charm for the layman as well as for the confirmed
medievalist. Such is hardly the case with many even greater
poems produced under the immediate inspiration of the medieval Church. The intimate subjective quality of *The Dream
of the Rood*, however, a quality which is so prominent and
withal so unusual for the age, has much to do with the excellence of the work. The poem unfolds itself in the form of a
vision—the most remarkable example in Old English literature of a type that was to become famous in Middle English
literature.[49] But the human being describing the vision occu-
pies a position entirely secondary to the glorious cross which
he saw in the vision, for the cross itself speaks:

> Then, as I lay there long,
> I gazed sadly upon the Saviour's cross,
> Until I heard it speaking,
> Heard the fairest of crosses utter these words:
> 'It was long ago (I remember it still),
> I was hewn down at the edge of the forest,
> Cut off from my trunk. Strong foes seized me there,
> Wrought me there as a spectacle,
> Bade me raise aloft their sinful men;
> There men bore me on their shoulders,
> Set me down on a hill and made me fast—
> There were enemies enow!
> Then I beheld the Lord of Mankind;
> Bravely and willingly He hastened to ascend me.
> I dared not bow or break against the Lord's word,
> When I felt the earth tremble;
> I could have crushed His foes,
> But I stood firm.
>   'Then the young hero, God Almighty, unclothed
>   Himself,
> Strong and unflinching; bravely He ascended the high cross
> In the sight of the multitude;
> He wished to redeem mankind.
> When the hero embraced me, I quivered,
> Yet I dared not bow to earth,

Or fall to the ground; I must stand fast.
As a rood I had been raised; I lifted up the brave King,
Lord of Heaven; to stoop I did not dare.

    'They drove me through with dark nails;
The malicious wounds may still be seen;
And still I dared not harm them,
They reviled us both; I was all drenched with blood,
Poured from the Man's side; then He yielded up his spirit.

    'Many cruel deeds have I seen on that hill;
There I saw the Lord of Hosts
Stretched out in agony; clouds and darkness
Had come to cover the body of the Ruler;
Lowering shades under the heavens
Overcame the gleaming daylight.
All creation wept, mourning the fate of the King;
Christ was on the rood.

    'Yet good men came in haste from afar
To the presence of this one Man.
Then they took Almighty God,
Lifted Him from His grievous torment;
Warriors left me behind,
Steeped in blood and wounded with nails.
They laid Him down, the limb-weary man;
They stood at His head; they gazed upon the Lord of
    Heaven,
And He rested Him there a while
After the mighty ordeal. They wrought for Him a tomb,
Even in the sight of His slayers;
They carved it out of bright stone,
They placed therein the King of Victories.
They sang for Him a lay of sorrow,
Wretched in the eventide.
Then wearily they turned them homewards
From the presence of the glorious Prince.
There He rested with a small troop.

    'Still we crosses stood weeping in our places
For a goodly time; warriors raised their voices;
The body grew cold, fair house of the soul.
Then they felled us all to earth;
That was a dreadful fate!

They buried us in a deep pit, but the thanes of Christ
Sought me and found me and decked me with gold and
    silver.
            'Now you have heard, my beloved hero,
The deeds of sorrow and anguish which I have borne.
Now the time has come,
When men far over the earth,
And all this worshipful creation will honor me,
Will humble themselves before my emblem.
On me the Son of God suffered a while;
Therefore I now tower
In glory under the heavens, and I can heal
The soul of every man in awe of me—
I, once a hated instrument of torture
To mankind, can now reveal a way of life
True for all mankind.
Lo! the Prince of Glory has honored me,
Above all trees of the forest,
The Guardian of the heavenly kingdom,
Even as He, the Almighty God, exalted
His mother Mary above all womankind.'   [24-94]

Where we have such a poetic accomplishment we naturally
turn to find the author, but he eludes us. The poem, as many
of those in *The Vercelli Book*, seems to have been composed
in the latter half of the eighth century. There is a curious relationship between this work and a piece of antiquity, a relationship which is not easy to explain satisfactorily. An old stone
relic, the Ruthwell Cross from Dumfriesshire, Scotland, dated
near 700,[50] presents in a few lines a rather impressionistic picture of the Crucifixion, told in the first person and obviously
from the point of view of the Cross itself. The parallelism
with a few lines of *The Dream of the Rood* is so close that the
entire inscription of the Ruthwell Cross, which is very short,
can be quoted here.

        God Almighty prepared Himself
        To ascend upon the gallows,
        Brave in the presence of men.
        To bow . . .[51]

I did not dare to hold
The mighty King, the Lord of Heaven.
Men reviled us both together;
I was drenched with blood
Poured from . . .[51]
Christ was on the rood.
But good men came in haste from afar
To the presence of this one Man—I beheld all that.
Sorely was I oppressed with sorrows,
Brought low . . .[51]
Wounded with nails.
They laid Him down limb-weary,
They stood at His head,
They looked into Heaven.

At the bottom of the inscription comes the statement "Caedmon made me," which implies ostensibly that Caedmon was
the author of the writing. The supposed date of the Ruthwell
Cross makes such a statement entirely possible. So, to some
extent, does the site of the monument and the dialect of the
inscription, which is pure Northumbrian and another great
boon to the student of that rather rare dialect. The appearance
of some of the lines in identical form within the text of *The
Dream of the Rood* does not, however, demonstrate Caedmon's authorship of that obviously later poem. As a matter of
fact, *The Dream of the Rood*, in its almost mystical effects
and its lyrical tone, is much nearer to Cynewulf than to Caedmon. Probably it was written, if not by Cynewulf, at least by
a poet of Cynewulfian persuasion who knew of an older poem
(conceivably by Caedmon, or Caedmonian) and who in his
composition made use of certain shreds of the older poem. The
Ruthwell Cross inscription is probably a passage from that
same older poem. At any rate, if Cynewulf wrote *The Dream
of the Rood*, it was his masterpiece.

A work involving beliefs and traditions which are general
Indo-European rather than specifically Germanic is *The
Phoenix*,[52] a poem somewhat Cynewulfian in style but going
even farther than the signed poems of Cynewulf in the direc-

tion of Christian symbolism. It is to be found in *The Exeter Book*. The first half of the poem—the description of the bird and of the Earthly Paradise in which it lives—is adapted from the fourth century poet Lactantius's *De Ave Phoenice*; the second half, the portion involving the symbolism, is the work of an Anglo-Saxon writer. The subject-matter is Oriental in origin, although a symbol of immortality in the form of a bird is virtually universal, and so is the conception of an Earthly Paradise. In consequence of this Oriental background, the most remarkable lines of the poem are those which give a more lush, more tropical landscape than can be found elsewhere in Old English literature.

> Neither hail nor frost falls there to the ground;
> Nor is there a wind-blown cloud; nor does the water descend,
> Driven by the tempest; but there the streams
> Wondrous and splendid gush welling forth;
> They water the land with fair springs,
> Winsome waters from the midst of woodlands,
> Which well forth ocean-cold from the soil,
> Sometimes purling joyously through a whole grove.
> It is the Lord's desire that the beautiful currents
> Should cross that lovely land twelve times.
> The groves are hung with blossoms, with fair fruits;
> There the trappings of the forest, holy under heaven,
> Never will fade; nor will the yellow fruits,
> The glory of the trees, fall ever to the ground;
> But the branches of the tree will ever be
> Splendidly laden, the fruit ever new.
> On the grassy plain the brightest of groves stands green,
> Joyously decked by the Holy One's power;
> The woodlands will keep their colors ever unfading.
> There the sacred fragrance fills the land with joy.
> That will never suffer change till He
> Who shaped it in the beginning shall bring
> The old, long-established work to an end.   [60-84]

Also unusual is the attention given to the musical song of the phoenix:

The harmony of that song is sweeter
And fairer than all music, and lovelier
Than any melody. Neither trumpets nor horns,
Nor the sound of the harp, nor the voice of any man on
    earth,
Nor the peal of the organ, nor the sweetness of singing,
Nor the swan's plumage, nor any delight
Which God has devised to gladden man in this dreary world
Can equal that outpouring.   [129-136]

The relation of such a poem as *The Phoenix* to the *Physiologus*,[53] or *Bestiary*, also in *The Exeter Book*, is obvious: both
are didactic; both use the habits, actions, and physical peculi-
arities of animals real or fabulous to illustrate and point moral
teachings. As such, they partake less of the epic than of other
forms of literature. The *Physiologus*, however, demonstrates
the natural interest of untutored people in animals; and there
is good reason to believe that England was actually the cradle
of the medieval fable.[54] But from before the Norman Conquest only this little group of didactic narrative and descriptive poems called the *Physiologus*, or *Bestiary*, has come down
to us. We have here an account of a panther and a whale, and
a small fragment which seems to describe a partridge. The
work is built on an Oriental foundation; at least it is of ancient
folk-origin. The religious didactic interpretation, however,
was evidently the contribution of the Church in Western Europe. When all is said and done, the Old English *Physiologus*
cannot compare in humor or in general human interest with
the famous Middle English or French bestiaries of the twelfth
and thirteenth centuries. *The Phoenix* and the *Physiologus* are
both old, let it be granted, in sources and in purpose; but while
the *Physiologus* is simple in its symbolism, *The Phoenix* is
ornate. The most effective didactic Christian writing in Old
English times, however, is found in the prose; the most effective didactic secular literature comes in the lyric poetry. It is
to the lyric that we must therefore turn.[55]

NOTES TO CHAPTER FOUR

1. In Bede's *Ecclesiastical History of the English People*, edited by Thomas Miller (London, 1890), Book II, chapter 1 (pp. 97ff.); but see notes 33 and 35 to Chapter VII below.

2. In Bede's *Ecclesiastical History*, Book II, chapters 9 and 10 (see note 1 above).

3. See III, 2 above.

4. See note 2 above.

5. The popular ballad, as we understand the term, does not exist in any surviving specimen of the vernacular before the thirteenth century. At the same time, the epic product of mute, inglorious Miltons and village-Homers probably was in existence long before. It is quite likely that there were numerous minstrels among the churls as well as more lordly *scops* among the earls; but if so, their work has been completely obliterated. Perhaps Beowulf's feats were celebrated among the lowly hallmen and kitchen-mechanics as well as among the *duguth* on the mead-benches; perhaps the nameless feats of forgotten churls had their little moments of glory. We know nothing of these, however, and can base our belief that they existed at all only on the uncertain and unsatisfactory foundation of mere likelihood.

6. The standard English works on the beginnings of the drama in England are still E. K. Chambers, *The Mediaeval Stage* (Oxford, 1903; 1925) and Karl Young, *The Drama of the Mediaeval Church* (Oxford, 1933). See also E. K. Chambers, *The English Folk-Play* (Oxford, 1933) and his *English Literature at the Close of the Middle Ages* (Oxford, 1945).

7. Emile Legouis and Louis Cazamian, *A History of English Literature* (New York, 1935), 6. Legouis, who wrote this portion of the book, gives in general an excellent account of English literature to 1660, but he consistently underestimates the literature composed in England before Chaucer and is obviously not in sympathy with the standards and ideals of English literature before the Conquest.

8. See the passage quoted in IV, 4 below. The runic alphabet in Anglo-Saxon shown in V, 7 below.

9. In Bede's *Ecclesiastical History of the English People*, Book I, chapter 12 (see note 1 above). For the story of Caedmon, see Book IV, chapter 25 of the same work.

10. *Caedmon's Hymn*, of course, appears in the West Saxon version in all editions of Bede's *Ecclesiastical History* (see Chapter VII and note 33 below). The Northumbrian version is printed in H. Sweet, *The Oldest English Texts*, volume 83 of *Publications of the Early English Text Society, Original Series* (London, 1885). A new, comprehensive edition, however, is in A. H. Smith, *Three Northumbrian*

Poems (London, 1933). See also M. G. Frampton in *Modern Philology*, XXII, 1-15. Still more recent is E. V. K. Dobbie, *The Manuscripts of Caedmon's Hymn and Bede's Death-Song* (New York, 1937). Two good notes are L. W. Chappell, "The Caedmon Story" in *Englische Studien*, LXIX, 152-154, and Louise Pound, "Caedmon's Dream-Song" in the *Klaeber Miscellany* (Minneapolis, 1929), 232-239. A good study is C. L. Wrenn, *The Poetry of Caedmon* (London, [1947]). See also Chapter V and note 15 below.

11. The Junius Manuscript has been referred to before (see Chapter III, note 9 above). The Columbia edition, edited by G. P. Krapp (New York, 1930), is the most satisfactory.

12. There were evidently two poems on the subject of Daniel in Old English literature. One is the Caedmonian poem just mentioned as found in the Junius Manuscript. The other does not survive in its entirety. But in *The Exeter Book* is a poem known as *Azarias*, some portions of which (1-75) are virtually the same as another portion of *Daniel* (280-365). It is now generally assumed that *Azarias* represents at least a part of a second poem on Daniel. The question arises as to the relationship of the two poems, more particularly as to the relationship of the two similar passages. According to one theory, the scribe of *Daniel* noted that the prayer of Azarias was missing from the Caedmonian poem and so copied it from the second poem on Daniel, which we call *Azarias*. But this theory, advocated particularly by Grein and Craigie, has been discredited, because in point of fact there are many dissimilarities in phraseology, word-order, and even dialect between the two poems. Perhaps the scribe of *Daniel* had the lines from *Azarias* in mind without actually copying them into *Daniel*. There the matter rests at present. Since *Azarias* is not otherwise in any way distinguished, no further comment on it in the present work seems necessary. See, however, O. Hofer, "Über die Entstehung des angelsächsischen Gedichtes *Daniel*" in *Anglia*, XII, 158-204, and especially 184-191.

13. There are some separate editions of individual pieces in the Caedmonian cycle; the oldest is Theodore W. Hunt, *Exodus and Daniel* (Boston, 1889). The same two poems were edited also by Francis A. Blackburn (Boston, 1907). Wilhelm Schmidt has an edition of *Daniel*, "Die altenglischen Dichtungen Daniel und Azarias" in *Bonner Beiträge*, XXIII, 1-84. Merrel D. Clubb edited *Christ and Satan* (New Haven, 1925). The editions of *Genesis A* and *Genesis B* are mentioned below in note 19. As to translations, the best is that by Charles W. Kennedy, *The Caedmon Poems* (London, 1916); that by R. K. Gordon in his *Anglo-Saxon Poetry* (No. 794 of the Everyman Library; London, 1927), is not complete. Partial translations have been frequent. Krapp's edition of the Junius Manuscript, already

mentioned (Chapter III, note 9 above), contains an exhaustive bibliography of the entire Caedmonian cycle.

14. Eduard Sievers, *Der Heliand und die angelsächsische Genesis* (Halle, 1875).

15. Not, as it happens, the Old Saxon Christian epic *Heliand* itself, but another poem probably by the same author, of the early part of the ninth century. Sievers's views as to the structure of *Genesis* are developed more fully in his "Caedmon und Genesis" in *Britannica* (the Max Förster *Festschrift*) (Leipzig, 1929), 57-84. See also F. Klaeber in *Anglia*, LIII, 225-234. The German poetic fragments found in the Vatican Library were published by Karl Zangemeister and Wilhelm Braune, *Bruchstücke der altsächsischen Bibeldichtung* (Heidelberg, 1894). Sievers reviewed the matter in *Zeitschrift für deutsche Philologie*, XXVII, 534-538 and changed his opinion slightly: instead of regarding the poem as by the author of the *Heliand*, he thought it might be the work of a pupil or an imitator.

16. See S. J. Crawford, *Anglo-Saxon Influence on Western Christendom, 600-800* (Oxford, 1933) and W. Levison, *England and the Continent in the Eighth Century* (Oxford, 1946).

17. The definition of a kenning is implicit in the illustrations given a few lines below. Interesting monographs on the subject of this pronounced stylistic characteristic of Old Germanic and Celtic poetry are the following: Francis B. Gummere, *The Anglo-Saxon Metaphor* (Halle, 1881); A. Hoffmann, "Der bildliche Ausdruck im Beowulf und in der Edda" in *Englische Studien*, VI, 163-216; Wilhelm Bode, *Die Kenningar in der angelsächsischen Dichtung* (Darmstadt-Leipzig, 1886); James W. Rankin, "A Study of the Kennings in Anglo-Saxon Poetry" in *Journal of English and Germanic Philology*, VIII, 357-422 and IX, 49-84; H. Van de M. Scholtz, *The Kenning in Anglo-Saxon and Old Norse Poetry* (Oxford, 1929), and H. Marquardt, *Die altenglischen Kenningar* (Halle, 1938).

18. See Walther Paetzel, "Die Variationen in der altgermanischen Alliterationspoesie" in *Palaestra*, XLVIII (Berlin, 1913).

19. Before considering this matter, the reader should first know the editions of *Genesis* in Krapp's Junius Manuscript edition (Chapter III, note 9 above) and Gollancz's edition of the Caedmonian poems (see the same note). In addition to the all-important work of Sievers already mentioned (see notes 14 and 15 above), there are Wilhelm Bruckner, *Die altsächsischen Genesis und der Heliand, das Werk eines Dichters* (Berlin-Leipzig, 1929); P. E. Destoor, "Legends of Lucifer in Early English and in Milton" in *Anglia*, LIV, 213-268; F. Klaeber, *The Later Genesis and Other Old English and Old Saxon Texts Relating to the Fall of Man* (Heidelberg, 1931) and "Zur altsächsischen und altenglischen (jüngeren) Genesis" in *Anglia*, LV, 393-396; Wil-

helm Bruckner, "Zu den Versen 564-567, 599-620, 666-677, 772ff. der angelsächsischen *Genesis B* und zur Frage nach der Heimat des Dichters" in *Halle Beiträge*, LVI, 436-441; and Laurence Michel, *"Genesis A* and the *Praefatio"* in *Modern Language Notes*, LXII, 545-550. See also Otto Behaghel, *Heliand und Genesis* (Halle, 1903; 1934), which is the standard edition of the Old Saxon (Low German) poems. Lawrence Mason has translated *Genesis A* separately (New York, 1915).

As for the influence of the Junius Manuscript on Milton, it is still not outside the bounds of speculation, but there is absolutely no good evidence of it. R. P. Wülker, in "Caedmon und Milton" in *Anglia*, IV, 401-406, broached the subject. The parallels have been noted especially in J. H. Hanford, *A Milton Handbook* (New York, 1936), 226-227, and they are interesting enough. But there are other works of similar subject-matter which it is certain that Milton knew. Junius was in England until 1651, when he received the Caedmon manuscript from Bishop Ussher preparatory to his edition of this manuscript (1655). Milton's biographer Masson thinks (*Life of Milton*; London, 1881; VI, 557 and note) that Milton must "almost certainly have been acquainted with Junius." There is little to show, however, that Milton would have been capable of reading Anglo-Saxon in 1651; and by the time of Junius's edition of 1655 Milton had already been blind for three years. I think that the resemblances between *Genesis B* and *Paradise Lost* are fortuitous—parallels and little else. Two poets, working in different ages upon the same theme, achieve a certain similarity in concept of character and action. Such instances have occurred time and again. See Stephanie von Gajsek, *Milton und Caedmon* (Vienna, 1911).

20. Especially Legouis in E. Legouis and L. Cazamian, *A History of English Literature* (New York, 1935), 38-39. See note 7 above. "If, for a moment, these Anglo-Saxon poems are not read indulgently, if we cease to make allowances for them, almost as we do for the sketches of children and savage peoples, but, like some critics, overpraise them, the heavy pompousness of the paraphrases at once becomes evident, in contrast to the sober and sublime vigor of the Bible. . . . Indisputably, the Anglo-Saxon diverges from his model; he is himself. But the sum of his originality is his promiscuous piling-up of words, which hides, rather than reveals, the great outline of the primitive chaos. Above all, it drags out the act of creation, which showed the might of God by its very swiftness. The God of the Anglo-Saxons fumbles awkwardly before he lights up the world. . . . Mr. Stopford Brooke praises what he calls the 'vivid realistic way' of the Anglo-Saxon poet in the paraphrase, but it is a very childish realism which consists in making Moses describe the phenomenon to his people

as he accomplishes it. . . ." This criticism, while it is unnecessarily harsh, has some truth in it and is a partial indictment of much Old English poetry.

21. But see Kenneth Sisam, *Cynewulf and his Poetry* (Oxford, 1933). Another important account is that by A. S. Cook, *The Old English Elene, Phoenix, and Physiologus* (New Haven, 1919), xiii ff. Aside from this edition by Cook, the majority of the poems in the Cynewulfian cycle have been issued only in editions of separate pieces, of which *Elene* seems to be the favorite.

22. E. Sievers in *Paul und Braune's Beiträge*, IV, 235 and note; also in the same publication, X, 209ff. and 464-475; also in *Anglia*, XIII, 10ff.

23. Grimm in his edition of *Andreas und Elene* (Cassel, 1840), l-li.

24. See notes 29ff. below.

25. These were treated fully in A. S. Cook, *The Christ of Cynewulf* (Boston, 1900), lxxii-lxxvi.

26. The identification of the poet as Bishop Cynewulf of Lindisfarne hinges upon the fact that he is supposed to be Northumbrian rather than a Yorkshireman. Cook places the author at York, but Carleton F. Brown in *Publications of the Modern Language Association*, XVIII, 308-334 and again in *Englische Studien*, XXXVIII, 225-233, favors the Bishop of Lindisfarne. Brown was following the cue of Trautmann in *Anglia Beiblatt*, XI, 325.

27. This is the specific view of A. S. Cook, as presented in his edition of *Christ* (note 25 above). He tends to withdraw his original points in the face of Brown's articles (see note 26 above and the introduction to Cook's *Elene, Phoenix, and Physiologus*; New Haven, 1919, xiii, n.3). It must be admitted that Lindisfarne would be as good as Dunwich for a good appreciation of the sea.

28. In addition to the articles and prefaces by Cook mentioned in notes 25, 26, and 27 above, there is the article by F. S. Tupper in *Publications of the Modern Language Association*, XXVI, 240-244. One objection to accepting Bishop Cynewulf of Lindisfarne as the poet is the very presence of the *Cynwulf* signature, for Bishop Cynewulf died in 783. But the matter of ten or fifteen years' leeway in the use of a particular phonetic form, which is often a mere matter of orthography, is scarcely a fatal objection.

Separate editions of the four signed poems of Cynewulf have appeared from time to time. *The Fates of the Apostles* was edited along with *Andreas* by G. P. Krapp (Boston, 1906). *Elene* was edited by Cook (see notes 21 and 27 above); the best is probably that by F. Holthausen, *Cynewulfs Elene* (Heidelberg, 1905; 1937). These two supersede the older editions by J. Zupitza (Berlin, 1877; 1899) and Charles W. Kent (Boston, 1889). *Christ* was edited by A. S. Cook (note 25 above), and *Juliana* by William Strunk (Boston, 1904). The best complete translations are those in prose by Charles W. Kennedy, *The Poems of Cynewulf Translated into English Prose* (London-New York, 1910). This is a rendering of no less than nine Cynewulfian poems. Much space is given these poems in R. K. Gordon, *Anglo-Saxon Poetry* (No. 794 in the Everyman Library; London, 1927). Helpful articles and monographs are the following: O. Glöde, "Cynewulfs Juliana und ihre Quelle" in *Anglia*, XI, 146-158; P. J. Cosijn, "Cynewulfs Runenversen" in *Verslagen en Mededeelingen der koninklijke Akademie van Wetenschappen*, Reeks III, Deel. 7., pp. 54-64; Eduard Sievers, "Zu Cynewulf" in *Anglia*, XIII, 1-25; Frank J. Mather, "The Cynewulf Question from a Metrical Point of View" in *Modern Language Notes*, VII, 193-213; Moritz Trautmann, "Der sogenannte Crist" in *Anglia*, XVIII, 382-388—which disputes the unity of the poem, as does more or less Philip, Brother Augustine, "The Exeter Scribe and the Unity of Christ" in *Publications of the Modern Language Association*, LV, 903-909—Trautmann is answered by F. A. Blackburn, "Is the *Christ* of Cynewulf a Single Poem?" in *Anglia*, XIX, 89-98. See also Johannes Bourauel, "Zur Quellen- und Verfasserfrage von Andreas, Crist, und Fata" in *Bonner Beiträge*, XI, 65-132; Moritz Trautmann, "Berichtigungen, Erklärungen, und Vermutungen zu Cynewulfs Werken" in *Bonner Beiträge*, XXIII, 85-146; Gordon H. Gerould, "Studies in the *Christ*" in *Englische Studien*, XLI, 1-19; Samuel Moore, "The Old English *Christ*; Is it a Unit?" in *Journal of English and Germanic Philology*, XIV, 550-567; B. S. Monroe, "The Anglo-Saxon *Juliana*" in *Modern Language Notes*, XXXI, 55-56; Edward Burgert, *The Dependence of Part I of Cynewulf's Christ upon the Antiphonary* (Washington, 1921); Eduard Sievers, "Zu Cynewulf" in *Neusprachliche Studien (Die Neueren Sprachen)*, VI, 60-81 (1925); Edwin J. Howard, "Elene" in *Modern Language Notes*, XLV, 22 and "Cynewulf's Christ, 1665-1693" in *Publications of the Modern Language Association*, XLV, 354-367; and F. Holthausen, "Zur Quelle von Cynewulfs Elene" in *Anglia Beiblatt*, XLV, 93-94.

29. The runic alphabet in Old English is given in a later chapter (V, 7 below). In this alphabet the letter C(K) is named *cen*, which is presumably cognate to the Old High German *kien, ken*, "resinous pine-wood" or "torch." In most Old English manuscripts a *K* is interchangeable with a *C* before front vowels.

30. The runic letter Y is called *Yr*, and its meaning is very obscure; nor does the passage in *Elene* help us. It has been tentatively identified with the Old Norse *yr*, "bow." Here, as elsewhere, the discussion of the various runic letters by Bruce Dickins in his *Runic and Heroic Poems* (Cambridge, 1915) is very helpful.

31. The runic letter N is called *nyd*, and has been equated to the Old English word for "need" or "trouble."

32. The runic letter E is called *eh* or *eoh*, cognate to the Latin *equus*, "horse."

33. It is a little doubtful whether the runic letter W is *wen*, "hope," "expectation" or a dialectal form of *wyn*, "bliss," "joy." Both meanings would fit this particular passage and others in the Cynewulfian poems.

34. The runic letter U is called *ur*, the old name of the aurochs, or buffalo, the wild ox described by Caesar. Its horns were greatly prized among North European peoples. The form of the word, however, approaches so closely to that of the possessive pronoun, first person plural, that it is so used here.

35. The runic letter L is called *lagu*, one of the great number of Old English words for "ocean" or "sea."

36. The runic letter F, the first letter in the runic alphabet, is called *feoh*, "wealth."

37. E. K. Chambers, *The Mediaeval Stage* (London, 1903; 1925), II, 7ff.

38. See Chapter VI, note 5 below.

39. A. S. Cook, *The Christ of Cynewulf* (Boston, 1900), xxv ff.

40. Edited by Merrel D. Clubb (New Haven, 1925).

41. See Chapter III, note 9 above.

42. There is a separate edition in the old Belles-Lettres Series by A. S. Cook, *Judith* (Boston-London, 1907). See his introduction in general and pp. x ff. in particular. The ascription to Cynewulf is given further attention in Moritz Trautmann, *Kynewulf, der Bischof und Dichter* (Bonn, 1898).

43. Since this poem is in *The Vercelli Book*, it has received ample editorial treatment in G. P. Krapp, *The Vercelli Book* (New York, 1932). There is, however, an old separate edition by Krapp, *Andreas and the Fates of the Apostles* (Boston, 1906). Bearing especially upon the Cynewulfian problem implicit in *Andreas* are Friedrich Ramshorst, *Das altenglische Gedicht vom heiligen Andreas und der Dichter Cynewulf* (Berlin, 1885); Julius Zupitza, "Zur Frage nach der Quelle von Cynewulfs Andreas" in *Zeitschrift für deutsches Altertum*, xxx, 175-185; Moritz Trautmann, "Der Andreas doch von Cynewulf" in *Anglia Beiblatt*, VI, 22-23; Gregor Sarrazin, "Noch einmal Kynewulfs Andreas" in *Anglia Beiblatt*, VI, 205-209; A. S. Cook, "The Authorship of the Old English Andreas" in *Modern Language Notes*, XXXIV, 418-419, and "The Old English Andreas and Bishop Acca of Hexham" in *Transactions of the Connecticut Academy*, XXVI, 245-332 (New Haven, 1924).

44. Πράξεις Ἀνδρεού καὶ Ματθείς εἰς τὴν πόλιν τῶν ἀνθρωποφάγων edited

by Bonnet in *Acta Apostolorum Apocrypha* (Paris, 1892; 1930), Vol. I, part 2, 65-116.

45. Unfortunately Bertha Thompson, *The Old English Poems of St. Guthlac* remains an unpublished doctoral dissertation in the University Library at Leeds, as of 1931. There is no edition that could be called up-to-date except that in the editions of *The Exeter Book* as a whole (see Chapter III, note 9 above). Critical treatments of the poem have also been scarce enough, but the following are useful: P. Lefèvre, "Das altenglische Gedicht vom heiligen Guthlac" in *Anglia*, VI, 181-240—discussing the unity and authorship of the poems; N. Forstmann, "Untersuchungen zur Guthlac-Legende" in *Bonner Beiträge zur Anglistik*, XII, 1-40; Hubert G. Shearin, "The *Phoenix* and the *Guthlac*" in *Modern Language Notes*, XXII, 263— calling attention to some parallels between the two poems named; Gregor Sarrazin, *Von Kädmon bis Kynewulf* (Berlin, 1913); Gordon H. Gerould, "The Old English Poems on St. Guthlac and their Latin Source" in *Modern Language Notes*, XXXII, 77-89; and Charles W. Jones, *Saints' Lives and Chronicles in Early England* (Ithaca, 1947).

Of the poem found in *The Exeter Book*, the first 818 lines constitute *Guthlac A*; the remainder (through line 1379) comprises *Guthlac B*.

46. Bede's *Ecclesiastical History* (note 1 above), Book IV, chapter 26.

47. There is always a tendency in medieval literature to keep the body and the soul separate until it comes to the matter of physical torment or death; then the soul and the body both suffer *physical* pain and are virtually indistinguishable in their sufferings. See the material in the Dialogues of the Body and the Soul (V, 4 below).

48. In "The Old English Poems on St. Guthlac and their Latin Source" in *Modern Language Notes*, XXXII, 77-89.

49. See J. E. Wells, *A Manual of Writings in Middle English, 1050-1400* (New Haven, 1916; 1934) for bibliographical information (especially pp. 815-816), and W. H. Schofield, *English Literature from the Norman Conquest to Chaucer* (New York, 1906), 397ff. The device of the vision is so common throughout medieval literature, however, that no single reference can be entirely satisfactory.

The Dream of the Rood, as a poetic member of the collection in *The Vercelli Book*, has been edited in G. P. Krapp, *The Vercelli Book* (New York, 1932). Separate editions have been numerous—the most recent is that of Bruce Dickins and A. S. C. Ross, *The Dream of the Rood* (London, 1934). The older standard edition is that by A. S. Cook, *The Dream of the Rood* (Oxford, 1905). For general critical discussions of the piece, see A. Brandl, "Zum angelsächsischen Gedichte

Traumgesicht vom Kreuze Christi" in *Sitzungsberichte der königlich-preussischen Akademie der Wissenschaften* (1905), 716-723; and W. Bütow, "Das altenglische 'Traumgesicht vom Kreuze'" in *Anglistische Forschungen*, LXXVIII (Heidelberg, 1935).

50. This inscription is printed in H. Sweet, *The Oldest English Texts*, volume 83 of *Publications of the Early English Text Society*, *Original Series* (London, 1885). Charles D. Chretien has an unpublished doctoral dissertation in the Harvard University Library, summarized in *Summaries of Theses* (Cambridge, Mass., 1927), "The Relation of *The Dream of the Rood* to the Ruthwell Cross and to the Veneration of the Cross." Extremely valuable is the article by A. S. C. Ross, "The Linguistic Evidence for the Date of the Ruthwell Cross" in *Modern Language Review*, XXVIII, 145-155.

In the treasure-chamber of St. Gudule's at Brussels there is a reliquary of the Cross, about which runs a thin plate of silver; on this plate is the inscription in Roman letters of about the tenth century: "Rood is my name; of yore I bore the Mighty King, trembling I was drenched with blood. This rood Aethelmaer had wrought, and Aethelwold his brother, in honor of Christ, for the soul of Aelfric their brother." The matter is discussed by Logeman, *L'inscription anglosaxonne du réliquaire de la vraie croix au trésor de l'église de SS. Michel et Gudule, à Bruxelles* (London, 1891). The reliquary has since been known as the Brussels Cross. Its relation to *The Dream of the Rood* appears to be the same as that of the Ruthwell Cross. See S. T. D'Ardenne, "The Old English Inscription on the Brussels Cross" in *English Studies*, XXI, 145-164 and 271-272. For a similar kind of runic inscription, see H. Harder, "Das Braunschweiger Runenkästchen" in *Archiv*, CLXII, 227-229.

51. At these points the runes become illegible.

52. Published in the editions of *The Exeter Book* (see Chapter III, note 9 above) and separately, first by N. F. S. Grundtvig (Copenhagen, 1840), again by Otto Schlotterose, "Die altenglische Dichtung Phoenix herausgegeben und erläutert" in *Bonner Beiträge zur Anglistik*, XXV (Bonn, 1908), still later by A. S. Cook, *The Old English Elene, Phoenix, and Physiologus* (New Haven, 1919). Critical discussions of the authorship and the sources are contained also in the following, although Cook's introduction to his edition leaves little to be desired: Herman Gaebler, "Ueber die Autorschaft des angelsächsischen Gedichtes vom Phoenix" in *Anglia*, III, 488-526—a strong plea for Cynewulf's authorship; Friedrich Kluge, "Zu altenglischen Dichtungen" in *Englische Studien*, VIII, 472-479; Edward Fulton, "On the Authorship of the Anglo-Saxon Poem *Phoenix*" in *Modern Language Notes*, XI, 146-149; Oliver F. Emerson, "Originality in Old English Poetry" in *Review of English Studies*, II, 18-31—an ex-

tremely significant article which confines itself chiefly to an analysis of the work of the Phoenix Poet; and Henning Larsen, "Notes on the *Phoenix*" in *Journal of English and Germanic Philology*, XLI, 79-84 —which relates the Old English poem to an analogous Scandinavian work.

53. Published in all editions of *The Exeter Book* (see Chapter III, note 9 above); separate editions are by A. S. Cook, *The Old English Elene, Phoenix, and Physiologus* (New Haven, 1919)—with a definitive introduction; and again by A. S. Cook, *The Old English Physiologus*, with verse translation by James H. Pitman (New Haven, 1921). The critical discussion has centered about the problem as to whether or not the poems and a fragment, which also was recovered, represent the whole or the part of the design of the Anglo-Saxon poet. The older critics believed that this design was very ambitious, though incomplete; since the time of Miss Peebles's article, mentioned a few lines below, the tendency has been to regard the Old English poem as virtually complete except for the fact that the poem on the Partridge is unfinished. The controversy began with A. Ebert, "Der angelsächsische Physiologus" in *Anglia*, VI, 241-247; then followed A. S. Cook, "The Old English Whale" in *Modern Language Notes*, IX, 129-135; E. Sokoll, "Zum angelsächsischen Physiologus" in *XXVII. Jahresbericht der Staats-Oberrealschule in Marburg*—no longer readily accessible, but the gist of Sokoll's monograph is available through summaries by G. Sarrazin in *Englische Studien*, XXVII, 135ff. and by Mann in *Anglia Beiblatt*, XI, 332ff. and by A. Brandl in Paul's *Grundriss der germanischen Philologie*, II, 1, 1047. A good account of the whole *Physiologus* or *Bestiary* tradition in European literature is Lauchart's *Geschichte des Physiologus* (Strassburg, 1899). An excellent bibliographical article, now unfortunately somewhat dated, is Max F. Mann, "Zur Bibliographie des Physiologus" in *Anglia Beiblatt*, X, 274-287, with addenda in *Anglia Beiblatt*, XII, 13-23 and XIII, 236-239.

Miss Peebles's article, already referred to, is "The Anglo-Saxon Physiologus" in *Modern Philology*, VIII, 571-579. See also Frederick Tupper, "Notes on Old English Poems" in *Journal of English and Germanic Philology*, XI, 82-103.

54. See Moll in *Zeitschrift für romanische Philologie*, IX, 161, and particularly Joseph Jacobs, *The Fables of Aesop* (London, 1889), I, 158 and 180.

55. For all the poems considered in this chapter, see especially Charles W. Kennedy, *The Earliest English Poetry* (New York, 1943).

V · Miscellaneous Old English Poetry

1. THE ELEGIAC POEMS

ALTHOUGH the Anglo-Saxon may seem too restrained in emotion for the taste of many and too fond of the somber grays and browns of nature to the exclusion of the brighter hues, it still does not follow that he was deficient in real feeling and inarticulate in the utterance of that feeling. The warrior class —if one is to judge by what has been left us—reacted to life in such a way as to produce a rather grim outlook on the world, an awareness of the difficulties and cruelties of the northern winter, a melancholy but not hopeless realization of the fleeting nature of all living, and an acceptance of the brutal immensity of the ocean, which may well have suggested to its originally pagan mind the nothingness of the hereafter. The Christian teacher was to turn these raw materials to his own uses; he was to keep the grimness, the melancholy, and the sense of vastness; but he would make them the foils to his brighter promise of a blissful life to come. Of the two elements in the Old English lyric—the pagan and the Christian—the pagan is much superior both as regards depth and as regards vividness, for it is not a period of great hymn-writing in England, and the religious note is sounded with monotonous consistency at too low a poetic level.

It is therefore proper to insist that the Anglo-Saxon possessed a true lyric gift, although one pitched in a minor key. He also exercised an unusual amount of restraint, as if he were ashamed to exhibit his emotions too clearly. Some have seen in his difficult climatic environment a cause for this restraint, a kind of slow poetic circulation of the blood. The fact is, however, that he was physically extremely active; the present-day psychologist would have called him a most emphatic extrovert. Such people are more inclined to deeds than to any excessive cerebration. There is an old saying to the effect that the English temperament is as fire beneath snow; allowing for the exaggeration in any such neat phrase, there is aptness in the description. But this fire is most likely to show itself in action at a time of stringent crisis. It is not surprising, therefore, that there should be a very intimate blend of the lyric and the epic in Old English lyrical poems. Sections of *Beowulf* and the Christian epics can stand alone as detached lyrics. The flights of song in Old English poetry, however, are usually short and of only moderate height; sooner or later they will sink back into narrative advance or into dramatic contrast or into stagnant didactic moralizing.

From the appearances of lyrics like the lay of the bereaved father in *Beowulf* (2444ff.) or, better still, the lay of the last survivor in the same work (2247-2266), it is clear that the *scop* had occasional recourse to the lyric; and this fact becomes even more obvious when we consider the detached lyric pieces. The Anglo-Saxon lyric seems certainly to have been produced by the warrior's class, along with the heroic epic. In fact, one is led straight to the belief that the lyric, like the epic, had an aristocratic bardic tradition to support it even into the sobering days of the spread of Christianity.

Fortunately there remains at least one separate piece which exists in a strictly lyric form before any Christian allusion comes in to mar the picture. *Deor's Lament,* or *The Song of Deor,*[1] is a poem in *The Exeter Book*. It is a work fairly bristling with difficult references and occasionally incomprehensible readings; it is of great antiquity, although probably not so old as portions of *Widsith* (III, 2). It purports to be the utterance of a cast-off bard who is consoling himself by comparing his misfortunes with the greater woes of legendary and historical heroes, heroines, and nations. The bard, Deor, belongs in legend only. It is now generally held that the author was a poet of perhaps the early eighth century who assumes imaginatively the position of a fictitious *scop* named Deor. On the other hand, both the poem and the poet may be older.

Whether or not it is autobiographical, however, we shall call
it a lyric; and the situation in which Deor finds himself,
deprived of lord and patron, is one which the Anglo-Saxon
aristocratic tradition would call tragic.

Incidentally, the poem illustrates well the status of the
Germanic bard in society, his high rank and the royal favors
he enjoyed. Deor, who depends upon an individual king, is
more characteristic of his class than the itinerant bard who
moved from place to place, although the latter type of *scop*
was not unknown. At any rate, having lost the patronage he
needs, Deor sits

> . . . Weary of heart; his joy has departed,
> His soul grows dark. It seems to him
> That his share of sorrow will be endless.   [28-30]

But then he thinks of the woes of the smith Wayland, held
captive by his foes, of Beadohild bewailing her pregnancy, of
the fierce king Eormanric, whose "wolfish thoughts" weighed
heavily upon his people[2]—and he realizes that, as the troubles
and perils which beset those people passed away, so will it be
with his own anguish. "That passed away; so can this" is an
approximate translation of the difficult refrain. And, at least
by implication, the bard of *Deor*, supplanted by another, one
Heorrenda, sounds the same note that will be sounded more
than a thousand years later by another Englishman:

> The flesh will grieve on other bones than ours
> Soon, and the soul will mourn in other breasts.

In this thought the Old English poet takes comfort; he would
not, as did Shakespeare's Richard II, deride such a viewpoint as

> Thoughts tending to content flatter themselves
> That they are not the first of Fortune's slaves,
> Nor shall not be the last; like silly beggars,
> Who, sitting in the stocks refuge their shame,
> That many have and others must sit there;
> And in this thought they find a kind of ease,

Bearing their own misfortunes on the back
Of such as have before endured the like.
[RICHARD II, V, v, 23-30]

Unusual, since they are found in but one other Old English poem, are the refrain and the strophic structure of *Deor's Lament*. The refrain, already quoted, is matched by that of *Wulf and Eadwacer*, to be discussed in a moment; it is the earliest example of such a poetic device in Germanic literature, for although some of the Scandinavian heroic poems may make use of a refrain, those poems are not nearly so old as *Deor's Lament*. The strophic form, too, is found in Norse literature, but the same limitations of relative age apply here. The stanzas in *Deor's Lament* are irregular—sometimes they are of only three or four lines; sometimes more than a dozen. All are concluded with the refrain.

Such external matters as the refrain and the stanzaic form afford one important significance to *Deor's Lament*. But the poem is at least as interesting to the student of the epic as to the student of the lyric, because in its various allusions and half-told incidents of Germanic legendry, it is more than half epic in nature. The subjective lyric element is held in abeyance until the last dozen lines.

The idea at the core of *Deor's Lament* is virtually universal in the Old English lyric: time passes, and mankind with it. This leaning toward a celebration of the most permanent of all eternal verities—change—should not surprise anyone familiar with the environment of the Anglo-Saxon. Coldness, grayness, and violence will inevitably stimulate a mood which would turn to such a theme. *Sic transit gloria et ubi sunt?* So passes all glory, and where are those who were glorious?

The nightingale that in the branches sang,
Ah whence and whither flown again, who knows?

These two motifs are the prime motifs of Old English lyric poetry; they are also the prime motifs of Middle English secular lyric poetry later on. We may attribute the liking for these themes to the genius of the Anglo-Saxon's temperament or to his climate, his way of living, his physical and spiritual discomforts. We can just as easily attribute it, however, to the work of the churchman. Granted that life was to these people hard and cruel, still the joys of the heavenly kingdom may never seem so convincing as the fact of this life, for all its transitoriness. Yet it was to the interest of medieval Christianity that men's minds should be turned away from the joys of this world—such as they are—and anything to make this world less attractive would serve. No doubt the hardy persistence of these themes into the Middle English period, when life was probably a little more comfortable, even worthwhile, can be explained by the fact that they served to promote the doctrine of unworldliness which the medieval Church tried hard to inculcate.

It would probably be unwise, however, to suggest that the Anglo-Saxon was unable to develop his own lyrical moods or to compose his own threnodies of the spirit without the help of the priest. On the contrary, the true Old English lyric is, as has been stated, an outgrowth of the epic, in so far as one has any right to dogmatize about its origins. For after all, the lonely heart has never been without a habitation and a name.

Thus the solitary exile in *The Wanderer* thinks of his lord and people, from whom he has been separated by fell circumstance and by death, and he voices his sorrow from the depths of his soul:

> Whither went the steed? Whither went the kinsman?
> Whither went the seats of feasting?
> Where are the revels in the hall?
> Alas, the bright cup! Alas, the byrnied warrior!
> Alas, the glory of the prince! How time has departed,
> Darkened under the helmet of night, as if it had never been!
> [THE WANDERER, 92-96]

For this wanderer, possessions, friends, men and women are all transitory; "All the foundations of the earth will be empty and useless!"

This somber, powerful poem[3] is at first glance the lyrical

utterance of a warrior or bard who has been bereft of all that
he had held dear. Specifically, he has lost his lord and patron;
he is wandering about, virtually a man without a country,
looking fruitlessly for a new home. The piece is highly subjective and dramatic; and its author, a poet of high order,
belongs to the eighth century.

The Wanderer is clearly elegiac in tone; its message and the
message of the lay of the last survivor in Beowulf⁴ are much
the same. The Germanic mind has always tended to be intro-
spective, and when not turned to physical activity easily assumes a brooding cast. The Wanderer exhibits this tendency
even better than most poems of its time, because it is relatively
free from traditional Christian formulas and exhortations. It
is, in spite of its melancholy, stoical in tone; and only the last
few lines of the poem, which are weak and intrusive, seek the
conventional road of Christian teaching, with a stress on
acceptance in terms of the belief in salvation and a better existence hereafter. This is one case where pagan negation is
artistically triumphant over Christian assurance.

The structure of The Wanderer raises difficulties. The poet
gives the words of the friendless man, and the friendless man
in turn records the speech of one who broods upon ruin. At the
beginning the Wanderer speaks of himself in the first person
and then generalizes himself into the third person. At the end
come some moralizing lines which have nothing in particular
to do with the Wanderer. About half-way through, the scene
shifts from the sea, where

> He sees before him the yellow waves,
> The sea-birds bathing and preening their wings,
> The falling of frost and snow mingled with hail,
>
> [46-48]

which is the principal mise-en-scène, to a mead-hall, thence to
a ruined edifice. In other words, the continuity of the poem is
not based upon logic, but upon the inconsecutiveness of a
dream, either waking or sleeping. The final lines of the poem,
most likely a sop to Christianity from the hands of some pious

scribe, succeed in being an anticlimax, for the heart of the poem is beating with triumphant pessimism.

The Wanderer has for its companion *The Seafarer*; the two poems form a striking pair of vignettes. *The Seafarer*, also in *The Exeter Book*,[5] was likewise composed in the early eighth century by someone who knew the sea and the life of a seaman. The older theory[6] that the poem is a dialogue between an ancient mariner, tired of constant voyaging, and a youth, enthusiastic but uninformed about life on the ocean, would account for the change in viewpoint shown in the middle of the poem. This theory, however, is now out of fashion. It is possible to maintain that the speaker is the same individual throughout the work—a man who loves the sea and hates it, who has had cause to remember the sufferings it has brought but who cannot resist the spell that it has wrought on him and so must return to its bosom. The first sixty-four lines of *The Seafarer* offer vivid glimpses of the ocean and the frail little cockle-shells of boats which labor on its surface, as well as the hardships of the sailor. We soon come to the typical elegiac melancholy:

> The groves take on their blossoms; the towns grow fair,
> The meadows beautiful; the world revives;
> All things urge on the hearts of the eager-minded
> To the journey, the hearts of men who bethink them
> To depart far over the flood-ways.
> Yet the cuckoo sings a warning with its mournful notes,
> The guardian of the summer bodes forth sorrow
> Bitter in its breast-hoard. No man can know,
> Who dwells in comfort, what they endure
> Who lay their paths of exile far and wide!
>   So now my thoughts go roaming;
> My spirit is with the sea-flood
> Beyond the home of the whale; it hovers afar
> Over the expanses of the world; it returns to me
> Greedy and yearning. The solitary flier cries out;
> It drives me irresistibly on the whale-road,
> Over the wastes of the sea. . . .   [48-64]

The remainder of the poem is static and pious and has no intimate relation to the earlier portion, although it does not necessarily form any illogical disunity. An old man feels the call of the sea, but he is infirm and must experience his adventures only vicariously; he therefore yields to the inevitable and speaks in a resigned fashion of the heavenly kingdom. To be sure, these later lines may have been added by some later poet. But *The Seafarer*, with its celebration of the sea, is an indestructible tribute to the mariners of England; as it appeared in the eighth century, so Masefield's *Sea-Fever* appears in the twentieth century to keep alive the tradition. Still, it is reasonably clear that *The Seafarer*, for all its pagan vitality, did not escape the almost inevitable Christian adulteration. It ends on the note:

... Therefore more ardent for me
Are the joys of the Lord than this dead life
Transitory on earth. . . . [64-66]

... Blessed is he who lives humbly;
Mercy will come to him from the heavens;
And the Lord will establish him in courage,
For he has trusted well in His strength. [107-108]

Only a fragment though it may be, *The Ruin* sounds magnificently the pessimistic climax of all these Old English elegiac verses. Like its predecessors just described, it appears in *The Exeter Book*.[7] Itself a ruin, and a small one at that, there are in its lines, however, an intensity and a passionate regret that make it one of the most notable of Old English poems. The contemplation of a ruined city inspires the poet to describe the

Wondrous wall-stones broken down by Wyrd,
The crumbling work of giants, undermined by eld. . . .
[1-2]

The place has sunk into ruin, levelled to the hills,
Where in times past many a man,
Light of heart and bright with gold,
Adorned with splendor, proud and flushed with wine,

Shone in war-trappings, gazed on treasure,
On silver, on gems, on riches, on possessions,
On costly jewels, on this bright fortress
Of the spacious kingdom. . . .   [31-37]

The text of the poem is badly mutilated. The meanings of
some of the words and phrases are often more than uncertain.
Yet the glory of its lyrical melancholy will never be tarnished.

2. PERSONAL LYRICS

It is true that the Old English lyric does not seem to have
much concern for everyday subjects. The "natural sorrow,
loss, or pain" which may present themselves are abstract
enough. The emotional force of the poems, indeed, is ex-
pended largely upon the relation of warrior to chieftain, of
earl to king. Probably the aristocratic tradition of the epic has
much to do with this. In *The Exeter Book*, however, there
will be discovered a trio of short, dramatic little pieces of
poetry. They are especially interesting because of the presence
in them of a sexual element distinctly foreign to the general
conventions of Old English poetry. These three poems are
The Wife's Lament,[8] *The Husband's Message*,[9] and *Wulf
and Eadwacer*.[10] The last-named of these, because it comes in
The Exeter Book immediately before the *Riddles* (V, 4), was
for a long time known as the *First Riddle*. Such a title, however, is utterly misleading, for no matter how enigmatic the
text may be, it cannot be considered at all similar in form, content, or purpose to the *Riddles* themselves.

The first two pieces, *The Wife's Lament* and *The Husband's Message*, may be connected in some way. It was Grein
who first observed that the two poems "appear to belong to a
greater whole."[11] Such a view, of course, is hardly substan-
tiated by the respective contents of the two pieces; it is much
more justifiable to regard them as two similar though distinct
poems, affording examples of a wife's love for her husband
and of a husband's love for his wife. In *The Wife's Lament*, a
woman separated by captivity from her husband calls down

reproaches and curses on her foes and prays that they may some day feel her own bitterness of exile and loneliness.

> There are loving friends alive on the earth;
> They have their bed; while alone at dawn
> I pass through this earth-cave to beneath the oak tree,
> Where I sit a long summer's day. [33-36]

The tone of the latter part of this lyric is that of a kind of softened Babylonian sorrow, elegiac in atmosphere, and endued with a fierce enmity which has been weakened by the conventions of the Old English heroic tradition. Germanic poetic vagueness and indirection supplant the Hebrew concreteness and directness of the 137th Psalm. *The Husband's Message*, on the other hand, is a lyric expressed through the instrumentality of the letter which a husband in a far land writes to his wife at home, explaining that he will rejoin her when the cuckoo is heard once more in the spring. In this little touch of nature and in the reference to the sea, "the home of the gull," the poem shows a certain kinship to *The Seafarer*. At the end of the piece appear some runic letters, in the manner of a Cynewulfian signature; but they do not seem to form any word or spell any man's name and are usually explained as some kind of code-message from the husband which the wife, and the wife alone, could be expected to understand.

Wulf and Eadwacer, like *Deor's Lament*, has a strophic structure with refrain and presents at least the possibility of being one of the truly unusual works of the period. I say "possibility," for the poem is very obscure and consequently is capable of several interpretations.[12] As long ago as 1888, Henry Bradley[13] made the statement that the poem was to be regarded as a dramatic monologue comparable to *Deor's Lament* and *The Wife's Lament*.[14] The speaker is a woman, and probably a captive in a foreign land; she yearns for Wulf, her lover, and bristles at the thought of Eadwacer, her unloved and possibly brutal husband. And so there comes a passage unparalleled in Old English literature—

I waited for my Wulf with far-raging desire,
When it was raining and I sat weeping.
When the warlike man wound his arms around me,
It was pleasure to me; but it was also pain.
O Wulf, my Wulf, my yearning for thee
Has made me sick, thy visits but seldom,
A woeful heart and not lack of food. . . .   [9-15]

—unparalleled because the presence of a domestic triangle
and more than the mere suggestion of a passionate sex-intrigue
is altogether out of the ordinary in Anglo-Saxon writings, the
makers of which seem to possess a temperament which leads
them to regard sex as a fundamental matter to be taken for
granted and therefore not to be discussed. Such few examples
of the treatment of sex as come into the pages of Old English
literature are handled ingenuously and usually in rather awkward fashion, and always with a notable reticence. We are reminded for the moment of the brief allusion to the assignation
of King Cynewulf in *The Anglo-Saxon Chronicle* for the year
755, of the occasionally obscure *Riddles*, or of the charmingly
inept account of the sorceress Circe in the Alfredian translation
of Boethius's *Consolation of Philosophy* (VIII, 2). In *Wulf
and Eadwacer*, however, true passion comes to the surface in
an unexpected manner. Even so, neither here nor in any other
passage in Old English literature is there that preoccupation
with sex which marks the writings of the twentieth century.

3. RELIGIOUS LYRICS

OF THE true religious lyric there is very little at this time. To
be sure, there was much religious verse, but it belongs for the
greater part either to the epic or the didactic class of writing.
As we have seen, there has been ample evidence to indicate
that the early Anglo-Saxon was incapable of either long or
lofty lyrical flights. His inspiration seemed to express itself
best in terms of physical action, as might be expected, or it
might smoulder in protracted solitary brooding; but for him
ecstatic vision translatable into impulses of lyrical rapture is

particularly rare. Many centuries are to go by before we find
an English writer, Richard Rolle of Hampole, diffusing the
dulcor, calor, and *canor*—the sweetness, warmth, and lyricism
—which are associated with all great religious poetry. Indeed,
so far as the Old English period is concerned, the most successful pieces of religious lyricism appear in reflective verse. Occasionally the rhetoric of a Wulfstan or an Aelfric will, in a
prose homily, soar to the height of poetic enthusiasm; frequently Bede's simple faith will touch even higher poetic
levels. The jeremiads of Wulfstan in the days of the Danish
invasion are pieces of striking intensity of emotion. So, too, is
the Vision of Drihthelm in Bede's *Ecclesiastical History.* But
there are only *Caedmon's Hymn* and the chain of religious
lyrics in *Doomsday* which have survived still singing their
original devotional song, unless we ignore completely the
epic elements of *The Dream of the Rood* and include that fine
poem in this catalogue.

Caedmon's Hymn, already mentioned (IV, 3), is the name
given to a short poem of nine lines which occurs in several
Old English versions in the blank spaces of various Latin
manuscripts of Bede's *Ecclesiastical History.* The most valuable of these versions is that of the Moor Manuscript; it is in
the Northumbrian dialect, and hence probably was written
before the collapse of Northumbrian culture in the 730's. This
Northumbrian text is generally believed to be nearest to the
original of the poem.[15] Whether Caedmon actually wrote it
can be neither disproved nor established; there is no inherent
impossibility, however, in his having written it. If so, it is the
only work of his about which scholars could be at all sure, and
even here there is an unwillingness to accept his authorship.
The poem is a hymn to God the Creator, who first made the
heavens and the earth and the sun to illumine mankind. This,
according to Bede, was Caedmon's first song, and was inspired
by the angel who came to him in the shippen and encouraged
him to sing. In *Beowulf* (90-98) we are told that the *scop* in
Heorot sang a song of similar import to the warriors gathered
in the mead-hall. Here again is the sort of literary parallel

comparable to the case of *The Dream of the Rood* and the few lines of the Ruthwell Cross and Brussels Cross inscriptions; and here once more it is impossible to diagnose the situation clearly. One may assume, however, that the lines in *Beowulf* are no more than an echo of the little lyric known as *Caedmon's Hymn*. Or perhaps *Caedmon's Hymn* and lines 90-98 of *Beowulf* were inspired by some work which preceded them. The Book of *Genesis* would be the ultimate fountain-head.

Doomsday, in a manuscript of Corpus Christi College at Cambridge, is a work inspired directly by a Latin poem, *De Die Judicii*, which has been attributed to Bede and again to Alcuin (VII, 2).[16] The Old English version, however, shows considerable freedom from its source. The speaker is a man sitting apart from his fellow-men and obsessed with the fear of punishment on the dreadful day of the Lord. The English poem, which is considerably longer than the Latin poem, contains three lyric bursts, all fairly well sustained. But the inherent liking of the Anglo-Saxon for narrative intervenes and cuts short the lyric flight. The opening lines of each of these lyric sections will make clear the achievement of the poem as a whole.

> O unhappy mind, I ask thee,
> Why dost thou linger so long that thou canst not
> Show thyself to thy Physician?
> Or thou, sinful tongue, why art thou still? . . .
>
> [65-68]
>
> O flesh, why dost thou not purge away
> Thy grievous sins in the shedding of tears?
>
> [78-79]

Whereupon the lyric outburst drops down into didactic meditation and thence to the dramatic spectacle of the hills falling and perishing. Terror will pervade all, "heart-searchings and bitter lamentations," and all the wicked will be turned to stone while awaiting their miserable doom.

> O flesh, what dost thou? With what
> Art thou now busy? How canst thou at that time
> Lament thy woes? Alas! thou servest now thyself,

And art living here gladly in wickedness,
And dost urge thyself on with the mighty goads of pride.

[175-178]

For the flames and the ice of Hell will descend upon the wicked;[17] and yet the tortures will not be all physical tortures, but a vague and undefined spiritual torment as well. Still, there is hope. At the end of the poem comes a glimpse of the joyous lot of the redeemed:

Ah! happy will he be and more than happy,
Yea, the happiest of all beings for ever and ever,
Who knows well how to escape in bliss
These tremblings and disasters, and can at once,
While blessed in this world, serve his Lord.
Then can he possess the kingdom of Heaven. . . .

[246-252]

And like the despairing Job in the great third chapter of the Book of *Job*, he reflects that

Sorrow comes not there, nor pain, nor worn-out eld,
Nor is there any toil, nor hunger, nor thirst,
Nor unhappy sleep; nor is there fever nor sickness,
Nor sudden plague, nor crackling fire, nor hateful cold. . . .

[255-259]

But peace reigns there, and happiness
And goodness with the everlasting God,
Glory and honor, and worship and life. . . .   [267-270]

4. DIDACTIC POEMS OF LYRICAL NATURE

MORE often, however, the religious lyric in Old English literature merges with the general moralizing poetry of the period, which needs comment at this point. One cannot look to any single preëminent work in the surviving poetic library of Old English literature which will be sufficiently representative in itself of this strong didactic element. The fondness for aphorism, for rules of conduct, for what one ought or ought not to do, can be observed in almost any piece of writing for which an Englishman is responsible, and scarcely any more at one period of his literary history than at another. This predilection seems an integral part of the Germanic psychological make-up. As has been noted again and again, the English-speaking peoples demand of "good" or "great" literature that it give a message, that it "make sense," or, to use Matthew Arnold's happy phrase, that it demonstrate a "moral idea"—whatever the morality. It merely goes to confirm this trait that we should find the same tendency among our oldest pieces of literature as well as among the most left-wing of twentieth-century poetic fledglings. Therefore, if we concentrate for the moment entirely upon Old English writings, we shall discover that even our most venerable poems show didactic elements mixed with the epic or the lyric, as the case may be. Thus whole sections of *Beowulf*, such as Hrothgar's long harangue (1700-1784), to say nothing of short reflections in the same poem (20-25; 183-188; 1384-1385; 2029-2031—to pick but a few at random), illustrate the didactic tendency in the epic, a tendency which is baldly imitated in *The Battle of Maldon*, for instance. *The Wanderer* and *The Seafarer* obtrude their moralizing most unscrupulously upon the lyric mood; and what is true of these poems is true in greater or less degree of the other important pieces of Old English elegiac verse. One of the oldest pieces in Northumbrian Old English, the curious little *Bede's Death-Song*,[18] is pure didacticism:

> Before the necessary journey, no one
> Is wiser than he should be,
> Who considers before his going hence
> What may be judged of his soul for good and evil
> After the day of his death.

This poem is preserved in a manuscript of St. Gall, Switzerland, in a Continental hand of the ninth century and is virtually pure Northumbrian. That it is what it purports to be, a composition by Bede, is not impossible. We shall see, however, that there was a rather widely circulated Bede legend, and so the ascription of this little verse to the abbot of Jarrow remains merely an academic possibility. The piece may perhaps be by Caedmon, or it may be the work of Cuthbert.[19]

These didactic or (as they are usually called in speaking of Old English literature) "gnomic" features of Anglo-Saxon poetry and prose are mainly religious and ethical moralizing. Some of them are traceable directly to the churchman. Some, on the other hand, are merely expressions of human experience altogether apart from either religious doctrine or dogma.

A striking example of the Christian didactic poem is the fragment *The Address of the Soul to the Body*, found in one version in *The Vercelli Book* and in another in *The Exeter Book*. A prose homily on the same subject is also extant.[20] The soul, angered by the sins which the body has committed during life, is reproving the body for having consigned them both to Hell. The grim quality of this poem, most awesome in the *Vercelli Book* version, has been encountered before in Old English literature. The immediate subject, of course, is general throughout medieval European writings. An excellent example is the famous Middle English *Debate of the Body and Soul* of the mid-thirteenth century. A discussion of this Middle English poem would be out of place in the present book;[21] but it is a fine instance of the medieval debate, a literary form fostered by the religious scholasticism of the Middle Ages. In the Middle English version, the body is allowed to reply to the soul, and the debate waxes hot until hell-hounds rush in and carry off the victims to a nameless Hell. Now in the Old English *Address of the Soul to the Body* there is a short piece telling of the gratitude of a saved soul to the body, which by its self-denial made possible the soul's salvation; such a note in the usual chorus of denunciation of matters corporeal is extremely rare in this age. The Old English poem, however disjointed it may be, prefers exposition to argument; its lyrical note is pitched to the shriek of horror and the terror of dissolution, reaching a climax in

> The head is cloven, the hands unloosed;
> The jaws gape wide, the mouth torn open;
> Sinews are melted; the neck gnawed in two;
> Fingers rot away; feet are broken;
> Eager worms strip the ribs, thirsting for blood;

In swarms they drink from the corpse;
The tongue is rent into ten portions
For the satisfying of the hungry;
Therefore it cannot exchange words of wisdom
With the unhappy spirit. . . .

[*Vercelli Book* Version, 108-115]
[*Exeter Book* Version, 103-110]

The shorter fragment in the *Vercelli Book* version offers a most pleasing contrast to the charnel atmosphere of the preceding:

Dearest friend, though the eager worms
Yet busy themselves about thee,
Now I thy soul have come, fairly adorned,
To my father's kingdom, surrounded by mercies.
Alas! my lord, could I but bring thee with me
That we two might behold all the angels,
Likewise the glory of the heavens. . . .　　[135-141]
I would tell thee not to be troubled,
For we twain shall be gathered together
At the great judgment of God.　　　　　[156-158]

Clearly such a piece is the very stuff of medieval Christian doctrine. On the other side of the coin, there are the more impersonal and less pietistic observations upon life and living. Some three hundred lines of such gnomic poetry have come down to us, most of them in *The Exeter Book*, although some are in Manuscript Cotton Tiberius B I,[22] and are known simply as *Gnomic Verses*, or *Maxims*. These brief and often platitudinous notes in verse are the kind of human commentary of which the celebrated Biblical Book of *Proverbs* is representative; they offer indeed an interesting parallel to the scriptural book of wisdom. Perhaps some of the *Gnomic Verses* are influenced directly by *Proverbs*. On the other hand, they are more likely parallels and nothing more. After all, "the way of a serpent on the rock, the way of the eagle in the air, the way of a ship on the sea, and the way of a man with a maid" are things of universal appeal and can be discussed as spontaneously on the shores of the North Sea as in Palestine or the Garden of Ophir. The *Gnomic Verses* yield nothing of the magic of the Oriental poetry; they are bare, arid, often very obscure and detached thoughts on natural phenomena, human conduct, religion, and counsel. Still, at times they afford glimpses of the life of the people—of the hunter, of the warrior, of the gamester at the chess-board and the dice, of the felon to be hanged, of the clouds in the sky and of the wild hawk swooping down from them. These glimpses are of the briefest, and kaleidoscopic in nature; the net impression left is that of sudden vistas almost at once obscured. The general coloring of even these often quite pagan apothegms is, however, mainly Christian, as would be expected of any considerable amount of Old English verse from about the ninth century.

Closely allied to the *Gnomic Verses* is the little pair of poems in *The Exeter Book* known as *The Arts* (or *Gifts*) *of Men* and *The Fates* (or *Fortunes*) *of Men*[23]—allied, because these two poems are nothing more than gnomic verses on a particular subject. In *The Arts of Men* we hear of the various possible states and occupations for a gifted man—the poet, the warrior, the rich man, the poor man, the sage, the architect, the harper, the runner, the shooter, the seaman, the swimmer, the horseman, the chessman, the fowler, the hawker. God has scattered His gifts far and wide. In *The Fates of Men* one is confronted with a list of methods by which a man can leave this dreary world—by hunger, by the tempest, by the spear, by the gallows; one shall fall from a tree; one shall be consumed by flames; one shall die violently in drink. Here, as elsewhere, we are struck by the rarity of a natural death in Anglo-Saxon literature when the writing is not of definitely clerical origin. The social commentator may speak his mind, although sweeping generalities are as usual dangerous.

Undoubtedly the most famous Old English poems of wisdom, however, are the many *Riddles*. There are over ninety of these *Riddles* in *The Exeter Book*; these were probably put into form during the eighth or the early ninth century. The Anglo-Saxon, layman as well as learned cleric, had an obvious liking for intellectual exercise of this type, a fact which gave much popularity to the writing of enigmas. The same is true of other Germanic peoples. Latin collections of riddles, starting originally with the enigmas of a certain Symphosius, who flourished during the twilight of the Roman Empire,[24] were compiled in the Old English period by Aldhelm (VII, 2), Bishop of Sherborne; Tatwine, Archbishop of Canterbury; and Eusebius, Abbot of Wearmouth. Aldhelm's collection came to an even hundred riddles; his source, Symphosius, he followed closely, especially in regard to the personification of the subject of the riddle and the use of the first person. Tatwine and Eusebius confined themselves more to Christian subjects; Tatwine's collection is relatively short.

The *Riddles* of *The Exeter Book*[25] are related to the Latin tradition, but they are in the vernacular, handled in the customary alliterative verse with great freshness of treatment. It is apparent now that the collection cannot be by a single writer; but Cynewulf, the Christian epic poet, was at one time nominated as their author, and the First Riddle, now known as *Wulf and Eadwacer* (V, 2), was in particular attributed to him.[26] The opinion now held, however, is that the collection is the work of several writers, some laymen and some educated, some earls, some clerics, some even churls. The result of this multiple authorship is a heterogeneous mass of topics, a varied style, and a miscellaneous approach. Some riddles are merely picturesque, some witty, some ingeniously obscene, and some lyrics of beauty and impressive power in the portrayal of nature. But in the manuscript none of the riddles is given a title; those equipped with a rubric in a modern text are tokens of the fact that the editor, with patience and industry, has solved the riddle and made the answer the title of the poem.

It is customary for the riddle to describe its subject neatly but most equivocally. At least three noteworthy riddles describe a storm; and here one finds the accepted Anglo-Saxon poetic technique at work in the portrayal of the tempest—the foggy headlands, the driving sea, the rack of heaven in confusion, the roll of thunder over the towns, the fatal flash of lightning. Unfortunately these powerful pieces of nature-description must be quoted in full to be properly appreciated, and space forbids. The riddles having for their subjects common objects, implements of war, or the birds of the air and beasts of earth, are shorter. The "shield" is a lonely dweller, wounded by weapons, wearied in battle, but not looking for comfort, and never finding a physician to heal his wounds, which grow ever wider with deadly blows day and night. The "swan" treads the earth in silent plumage, or flies aloft a wandering spirit. The "cuckoo" was given up for dead by his father and mother but was rescued by a kinswoman, who cared for him. Because of the bird's traditional ingratitude, however, he turned upon the young of his foster-mother. The "horn" is an armed warrior—sometimes men kiss him; sometimes he summons men to battle with song; sometimes he lies stripped on the table while men drink. The "anchor" must fight against wind and wave, must go to seek the earth overwhelmed by billows. Some of the *Riddles,* such as "Month," are more esoteric, almost allegorical. Some, like "Book," describe in detail the operation of some trade. Some are satirical —the "bookworm" has devoured the song of man and yet is no whit wiser for having swallowed the words. Some, such as "One-eyed Seller of Leeks," are merely grotesque. All, however, have a certain relation to the kenning, which imparts to the imagery of Old English verse its typical qualities; the riddles, indeed, are frequently nothing more than elaborate, successive kennings. And what is perhaps more significant, the sort of mind which made current the kenning and the enigma came to a more ambitious expression later in the medieval allegory, with some of its attendants—complex theology and the occult inquiry into astrology and alchemy.

5. POEMS ON INDIVIDUAL MATTERS

No DISCUSSION of a body of poetry, no matter what its scope, can ever avoid the category of the miscellaneous. So it is in

Old English poetry: there are a half-dozen and more titles which refuse to be fitted conveniently into any of the foregoing subdivisions. None of them is especially important; one or two are decidedly obscure. But we are fortunate in having them before us, even if a few can be hurried over. We have, for example, the fragment of verse found among the letters of Winfrid or Bonifacius, the German churchman (d.755). The individual letter in which the verses occur is from a nameless monk of nameless nationality, though presumably English. The fragment has been virtually ignored by the nineteenth-century editors of Old English poetry, and only the pedant would be interested in its discussion here.[27]

More important is a piece from *The Exeter Book*, recounting the story of Christ in Hell during the three days of His sepulture on earth (the "Harrowing of Hell" Legend),[28] which has been taken by some to be a portion of Cynewulf's *Christ* and is assuredly Cynewulfian in style:

> And John saw the doors of Hell shining with light
> Which erst had long been locked
> And covered with darkness. . . .   [50-55]

Logically, however, it seems to be a separate poem. In spite of the moving image of the gates of Hell flooded with light at the approach of the Saviour, *The Harrowing of Hell* is overshadowed by the fact that there is a long and eloquent prose account of the same scene in the Old English version of the *Gospel of Nicodemus* (X, 5), and on the whole the poetic presentation is distinctly inferior.

The Exeter Book, in fact, contains many minor poems.[29] Similar in their definitely homiletic nature to *The Harrowing of Hell* poem just mentioned are two works in verse on the not uncommon general subject of pride and overweening spirit, *The Presumption of Man (Vainglory)* and another counterblast at man's wickedness, *The Failings of Man*,[29] from *The Vercelli Book*. The basis of the second poem, which is a fragment but much the more interesting of the two, is the text from *Psalms*, xxviii, 3-4: "Draw me not away with the wicked, and with the workers of iniquity, which speak peace to their neighbors, but mischief is in their hearts. Give them according to their deeds, and according to the wickedness of their endeavors; give them after the work of their hands; render to them their desert." *Resignation*, or *The Exile's Prayer*,[30] the cry of a depressed man (though not necessarily an exile), is notable more for its curious passivity and self-abasement—

> Yet that is best, when a man
> Cannot of himself avert his fate
> But can endure it   [117-118]

—than for any distinctive poetic virtue.

A curious isolated piece in *The Exeter Book* is *The Riming Poem*.[31] This title was given the work by Thorpe in his 1842 edition, but he regarded the poem as "extraordinary and unintelligible." His belief was that it represented a "very free paraphrase" of Chapters xxix and xxx of the Book of *Job*. The subject-matter of the poem, however, does not follow the Biblical passage at all closely. A rich man is in Purgatory or Hell itself and is bemoaning the pomp and circumstance of his earlier life, contrasting in rather sibyllic fashion his former well-being with his present misery. This honored medieval theme is later made famous by Dante's lines in the fifth canto of his *Inferno*, but the reader will no doubt remember some similar expressions in *The Wanderer*. What is most significant about the poem is the presence of end-rime in addition to alliteration. Many of the words, however, are badly mutilated in order to bring about the rime. In substance the work resembles the autobiographical portions of Cynewulf's *Elene* (IV, 4). The theory that this entitles Cynewulf to consideration as the author of *The Riming Poem* is nevertheless unwarranted. The general opinion now is that this poem is in the nature of a metrical experiment, perhaps influenced by the riming Latin hymns of this general period. The Norse skaldic poems, which also exhibit this combination of alliteration and

rime, are of too late a date to have offered any influence—
perhaps, indeed, they are imitative of the Old English.[32]

Still another poem in *The Exeter Book*, apparently complete, is *The Father's Counsel*. The domestic flavor of the
title suggests the pair of personal lyrics already discussed,
The Wife's Lament and *The Husband's Message*. But there
is nothing of the dramatic or the emotional in this piece; it is
instead another didactic product, in which a father bestows,
Polonius-like, a series of ten precepts upon his son—precepts
which represent in the main the Decalogue. It is barely possible that the poem was in use in the church schools of the
time. Ten Brink[33] suggests a parallel with the Book of *Proverbs*—Chapter VII, for instance—which is obvious enough
and could be suggested also for the instruction of a son by his
father in any Christian nation. For that matter, *The Father's
Counsel* is analogous to *The Proverbs of Alfred* (VIII, 2).

The Last Judgment,[34] from *The Exeter Book*, is once more
a didactic poem which implies a relationship in topic, though
obviously not in style or treatment, with Cynewulf's *Christ*
as well as with *The Phoenix* and *Doomsday*, all of which have
appeared previously. *The Last Judgment*, however, even in
this matter of substance and theme, is more general and conventional and less distinguished than any of the other poems,
and therefore suffers badly in comparison with *Doomsday*. It
treats of the final judgment in most undetailed fashion, whereas *Christ* speaks particularly of and for sinners, *The Phoenix*
considers the redemption of the righteous through Christ, and
Doomsday makes clear in vivid manner the physical tortures
of Hell.

The Wonder of Creation, or *The Order of the World*,[35]
from *The Exeter Book*, may or may not be a fragment, because the ending is abrupt, and the main body of the piece
certainly disconnected and incoherent. As for substance, it is
a quasi-lyrical treatment of Creation, wordy and rambling;
and its more than one hundred lines say less than the tiny
Caedmon's Hymn (IV, 3) says in nine.

Another small poem of nine lines on the virtues of almsgiving, *Alms*, which may well be a portion of a longer piece; and a poem of eight lines, known as *Pharaoh*, asking what happened to Pharaoh's army and replying that he and his thousands went to the bottom of the Red Sea—these complete the list of miscellaneous minor poems in *The Exeter Book*. Concerning the date of these minor poems it is almost impossible to be categorical, but the consensus of scholars is that they all belong to the latter half of the eighth and the first half of the ninth century.

6. MINOR HISTORICAL POEMS

NOT all the lesser monuments of Old English poetry, however, belong to the realm of the didactic or the religious or the doctrinal. There are several pieces of epic and heroic stuff which have been fashioned here and there into a verse-form— just another example, in other words, of the vitality of the heroic tradition in our early poetry. Mention has been made (III, 4) of *The Battle of Maldon* and of *The Battle of Bru-nanburh*, the latter of which appeared in *The Anglo-Saxon Chronicle* as the entry for the year 937. There are five other similar poetic entries in the *Chronicle*, or in certain manuscripts thereof.[36] First comes *The Liberation of the Five Towns*, a title which has no reference to the famous Cinque Ports of Middle English history. In 942, King Edmund of Wessex was obliged to make an expedition against the Mercians, who were harrying the five towns of Derby, Lincoln, Nottingham, Stamford, and Leicester. The expedition, which from the West Saxon point of view was entirely successful, was celebrated by this verse-narrative in the *Chronicle*.[37] Second, we have a pair of poems based upon the life of King Edgar of England (d. 975).[38] One reports his coronation by Dunstan and is dated, in the six various manuscripts of this portion of the *Chronicle*, between 972 and 974. The same piece, in four of the six manuscripts, describes Edgar's death; in the other two, the parts dealing with his passing are separate entries for the year 975. Another manuscript gives also a prose account. Third in the list of these heroic pieces from the *Chronicle* is *The Capture and Death of Alfred*. The Alfred here is not Alfred the Great of Wessex, most remarkable of all Anglo-Saxon kings, but the "blameless Alfred, son of Ethelred the king," as he is called in the opening prose section of the C Manuscript,[39] for the year 1036. He was captured by Harold Hardrada, son of the former King Canute. Some of Alfred's followers were killed, some hamstrung and otherwise maimed,

> The most bloody deed that was done in the land
> Since the Danes came hither and made peace.

Alfred was blinded and given over to the monks, where he lived until his death. The poem is not much more than doggerel. The fourth remnant is an account in two of the manuscripts of the Chronicle[40] of the death of King Edward the Confessor in 1065, at the outermost portals of the Old English period. It recounts the comparatively peaceful years of Edward's reign until the angels came to bear away the soul of the faithful one into the light of Heaven. A few lines naming Harold as the successor of Edward conclude the piece, which, while not of the same martial vigor and eloquence as *The Battle of Brunanburh*, is nevertheless the most noteworthy of these several scraps of verse from the *Chronicle*. As for *The Durham Poem*, which might be considered along with these *Chronicle* poems, it existed in a manuscript which was burned in the Cotton Library fire (1731); but another manuscript, edited originally by Sommer,[41] gives the poem at the conclusion of the *Historia Ecclesiae Dunelmensis*, written at Cambridge by Simon of Durham. From the standpoint of mere chronology, this poem belongs outside the present discussion. But it should be remembered that the writing of chronicles is an important activity among churchmen during the Anglo-Norman period, which was to follow the Norman Conquest, and the chronicles preserved in the vernacular during those years are of remarkable conservatism of language and style. They are allied much more closely to Old English prose than anything else written in the early Middle English period. Still, to judge from an historical fact alluded to in *The Durham Poem*, the opening of Saint Cuthbert's tomb (1104), it is obvious that this interesting *Encomium Urbis*, whatever its affinities to the poems of *The Anglo-Saxon Chronicle*, is on chronological grounds a representative of Middle English literature.[42]

7. PAGAN RELICS IN ANGLO-SAXON VERSE

Not the least attractive of surviving minor Old English verse is that all too scanty collection of material which forms an integral part of the pagan past. Hitherto we have noted a reasonably fair balance between warrior and priest in Old English poetry; indeed, all Anglo-Saxon literature may be said to have put on Christian clothing to cover its pagan nakedness. Mention has already been made of the hardiness of some of this heathen folklore and its present-day survivals.[43] One should no doubt relegate such manifestations of the older order to the anthropologist, but the spirit which prompts these manifestations is also the spirit which produces Old English literature.

In a manuscript in the British Museum (Caligula A VII) is a charm, very obscure as to interpretation, against bewitched land. Similarly, there is a charm against a sudden stitch in the side; the stitch is evidently attributed to witches ("mighty women") who ride about tormenting their victims. Against these predatory females, feverfew and the red nettle must be boiled in butter and the charm must then be invoked:

> Loud were they, O loud, as they rode over the hill;
> They were resolute, as they rode over the land.
> Take care now of thyself, that thou mayest survive their
>   hatred! . . .
> Out, little spear, if herein thou be!
> Out, spear! be not in, spear!

The charm runs on for nearly twenty lines, with the occasional recurrence of the "out, little spear" refrain. Another charm against a swarm of bees is short enough to quote in full. It is found in a Cambridge manuscript (Corpus Christi College Cambridge 41).[44] The opening prose directions should be noted.

> Against a swarm of bees. Take earth, cast it with thy right hand under thy right foot, and say:
>
>> 'I take it under foot; I found it.
>> Lo! earth will prevail against all creatures
>> And against hate, and against forgetfulness,
>> And against the mighty tongue of man!'
>
> Throw dirt over them, when they swarm, and say:
>
>> 'Settle, victorious women, sink to earth!
>> May you never fly wild to the wood!
>> May you be as mindful of my good
>> As every man is of food and shelter!'

A series of verses in Manuscript Harleian 585[45] celebrates the names of plants and herbs with healing properties. These have been tentatively identified as nine in number (mugwort, waybroad, water-cress, setaria viridis, blind nettle, maythe, crabapple, chervil, fennel) and the verses have been labelled by Wülker *The Sign of the Nine Herbs*. There is a great deal of doubt, however, both as to the identity of the herbs actually named and as to the completeness of the herbarium. But all of the plants in the list are spoken of as antidotes to poison, or fever, or witchcraft. Then come several short charms, none of which needs any expatiation here. There is one against a dwarf, which presumably means against the illnesses which in popular fancy could be blamed upon the influence of a dwarf—lameness, faintness, epilepsy, and convulsions. Another is a charm for pregnant women; another for a journey; another against what is called "water-elf's disease," presumably dropsy.

Two equally fascinating antiquities in the literature of the period are *The Anglo-Saxon Runic Poem* and the inscription on the Franks Casket. The *Runic Poem*, transcribed by George Hickes before the manuscript containing it was consumed in the Cotton Library fire,[46] consists of twenty-nine short stanzas.

Each stanza describes a runic letter, that is, a letter of the runic alphabet, the alphabet used by the ancient Germanic peoples.[47] The method is precisely that in use in many present-day children's books, where our alphabet is illustrated in short verses applying each letter to a word in common use for which that letter is the initial. Each letter in the old runic alphabet had a name; the þ, in general use throughout the Old English period for the spirant consonant which we spell *th*, is known, for example, as a *thorn*; and all other letters were named in similar fashion. The order of the letters in the runic alphabet used by the Anglo-Saxons is maintained in consistent manner, as follows (the names are given under each letter):

ᚠ	ᚢ	ᚦ	ᚩ	ᚱ	ᚳ	ᚷ	ᚹ	ᚻ	ᚾ	ᛁ	ᛄ
f	u	þ	o	r	c	ȝ	w	h	n	i	j

feoh (feh) ur thorn os rad cen gyfu wen haegl nyd is ger

ᛇ	ᛈ	ᛉ	ᛋ	ᛏ	ᛒ	ᛖ	ᛗ	ᛚ	ᛝ	ᛟ
i(h)	p	z	s	t	b	e	m	l	ng	oe

eoh peorth eolh sigel tir beac eh man lagu ing ethel

ᛞ	ᚪ	ᚫ	ᚣ	ᛡ	ᛠ	ᛢ	ᛣ	ᛥ	ᚸ
d	a	ae	y	io	ea	cw	c?	st	g

daeg ac aesc yr iar ear — — — —

To illustrate, the first three stanzas of *The Runic Poem* are quoted. The key-word or name of the runic letter is always translatable as a common noun in the language. Thus,

> *Feoh* ["wealth"] is a comfort to every man;
> Yet every man must bestow it freely
> If he wishes to gain glory in the sight of the Lord.

> *Ur* ["the aurochs, an ancient wild ox"] is proud and has
>   great horns;
> A very savage beast; he fights with his horns,
> The noted moor-ranger;[48] he is a brave creature.

Thorn ["thorn"] is exceeding sharp; for any thane
An evil thing to touch, immoderately rough
For any man who rests among them.

Similar runic poems are found among the Norse peoples, particularly the Norwegian and the Icelandic, with some slight variations in the alphabet.[49] The Old English *Runic Poem*, however, seems to be older than the others, for it cannot possibly be later than the early part of the ninth century. A date of 775 would probably be approximately right. Some scholars, however, would place the poem earlier than that.

The Franks Casket is a casket of walrus-bone carved with a runic inscription in the Northumbrian dialect.[50] The story, as given by the antiquarian Franks,[51] from whom the box derived its name, is both involved and fascinating. According to Franks, this piece of antiquity was once in the possession of an Anglo-Saxon, whether cleric or layman could not be determined, who gave it to a church in France, where it remained for more than a thousand years. In the nineteenth century it came into the hands of an antiquarian in Paris, from whom Franks purchased it in the 1850's. Previously one Matthieu, at Clermont-Ferrand, France, appears to have held it for a while; it was his statement that the casket had been in the home of a citizen of Auzon, in Département Haute-Loire, where the woman of the house had used it for a work-basket. The silver clasp had been broken; when Franks acquired it, it was already in fragments, and some pieces are still missing.

The runic inscription on The Franks Casket is actually a matter of interest entirely secondary to the figuration made on the casket; this figuration represents the birth of Christ and the adoration of the Magi. Beside this undoubted Christian picture is a scene from the Wayland Saga, part of which is alluded to in the second stanza of *Deor's Lament* (V, 1). Beadohild, the princess, is bringing the necklace to Wayland for him to forge; on the ground lie the corpses of her two brothers slain by Wayland. Also on the cover are portrayed Romulus and Remus being suckled by the she-wolf, and a

fight between the Jews and the Emperor Titus. The text itself, fragmentary as it is, serves to confirm the picturization
on the casket:

> Far away Romulus and Remus, brothers twain,
> The she-wolf fed them in Rome town,
> Here fight Titus and the Jewish people.
> This whale-bone the fish-flood
> Cast up on Ferry Hill;
> Angry was the ocean,
> Where it came swimming to land. . . .

It is tempting, in view of the presence of runic letters in the
inscription, to assign the casket a date of great age; and yet
the Northumbrian dialect exhibited here should make the
early eighth century a generally satisfactory date, although
an apologetic question-mark can be added to salve the con-
science of the painstaking scholar.

8. MINOR DIDACTIC POETRY

SUCH relics as the *Charms*, *The Runic Poem*, and The Franks
Casket, with their evident antiquarian value, however much
their occasional tintings of Christianity may impress the
reader with their incongruity, belong nevertheless to that dim
past which is considered pagan; and their didactic import,
where any exists, is likewise in limbo. On the other hand,
there are various little pieces of literature, predominantly
Christian and moralizing as well, which now call for brief
attention.

In two manuscripts, both from Corpus Christi College,
Cambridge (Mss. 41 and 422), comes a poem known as *Salomon and Saturn*. In its surviving form, it is pretty much of a
hodgepodge of verse and prose, and the work as a whole is
rather incoherent.[52] It is better not to refer it to the prose
Dialogues of Solomon and Saturn (see Chapter XI), with
which it seems to have little in common save the title, although one small section of the poem, in the form of enigmatic questions, resembles in method the prose *Solomon and*

Saturn. Instead, the poem treats in general of the fall of the angels, the world to come, and the good and evil spirits that follow every man through life. It might be defined as an abstract discourse, chiefly in verse, upon the divinity of Christ. Morley[53] has commented upon the non-Anglo-Saxon qualities of the piece. Its rather mature mysticism and scholasticism bespeak rather the Continental churchman, and we know of French and German-Latin parallels. Hammerich[54] has even called it "somewhat baroque." Like the Norse *Wafþrudnismal* of later date, it is at times a gnomic type of dialogue. There was a Jewish apocryphal didactic legend, a true Book of Wisdom, which placed the wise King Solomon in opposition to Marcolis, the Mercury or Hermes of classical mythology. This name appears in the Germanic "Marcolf" and is actually used in some versions of the prose *Dialogues of Solomon and Saturn*. It is Ten Brink's contention[55] that Marcolis was confused with Malcol, which in turn was a form of Moloch, the ancient Oriental divinity identifiable in the main with the Roman Saturn.

Whatever its origins, the verse *Salomon and Saturn* breaks rather obviously into two parts. The second may well be older than the first. Taking them in the order in which they appear in the text, however, we see that the first part discusses the power of Almighty God and furnishes a discourse upon the nineteen initial letters of the *Pater Noster*. Then comes some sort of lacuna; the second part, of rather controversial quality, follows apace. Saturn has traveled much and has many questions to ask. These questions, nevertheless, are not always answered; instead a new question may be posed in reply to Salomon. Sometimes, in fact, Salomon's answers are given in terms of his own life-experience, with the result that we get direct exposition. In the midst of his account of good and bad angels, the poem ends abruptly; but it is to be inferred from the trend of the discourse that Salomon is to be the ultimate victor in the controversy. Dating such a work is extremely difficult, because the two parts differ somewhat in style, but a period from 800 to 850 seems safe.

Akin to the *Salomon and Saturn* poem are the translations of the Meters in Boethius's *Consolation of Philosophy*. But inasmuch as a discussion of these Meters necessarily involves one in a discussion of the whole of Boethius's magnum opus, and inasmuch as this magnum opus is always associated in the Old English period with the Alfredian translation, comment on these poems must be reserved until a later page (VIII, 2).

In a late eleventh-century manuscript which contains also the Alfredian *Orosius* (VIII, 2), there is a small portion of *The Anglo-Saxon Chronicle* known as the *Abingdon Chronicle*, and with it lies another curiosity in the form of a bipartite poem. The entire work was first published by Hickes in 1705 and again in 1830 by the Reverend Samuel Fox, who gave it the name *Menologium*,[56] a name by which this particular poem is now generally called. The first part certainly deserves the name, for it is a kind of poetic calendar, giving in the margins the Old English name of the month and in the text itself a brief description of that month in terms of Christian church-holidays.

> [*February*].... And so four weeks
> And Sol-Month ("February") comes to town,
> Lacking two nights; so in times past
> Wise folk called it stormy February,
> Old folk, very wise. And about a night thereafter
> We hold the feast of Mary,
> Mother of the King, for on that day Christ,
> The Son of God, she brought to the temple.

In April comes Easter; in June Peter and Paul preached in Rome; in September comes Michaelmas; in November Martinmas; in Jul-Month (December) the feast of Our Saviour.

Another piece in a late eleventh-century manuscript[57] is *Admonition to a Christian Life*, which, however, seems to have been composed at least a century earlier. The pungent line, "The world is at an end," suggests a date very close to the year 1000, when the millennium would be complete and Judgment Day would descend upon all mankind. This point must be raised again in discussing the *Blickling Homilies* (X, 2), for the expected doom of the world on a certain date must have had a definitely deterring effect upon all of men's activities. As it is, this extremely dull poem tells an "old battle-warrior" how he may win salvation on that dire day— let him pray to God, render to God a pure life, and to his fellow-men a generous, almsgiving spirit; let him fast and shun gluttony and debauchery. The poem, it should be added, stands in the same manuscript as *Doomsday* (V, 3), and this fact suggests a common consideration of the two poems, although they are actually not connected in any way save by subject-matter. Quite negligible, since it is nothing more than an obscure fragment, is the piece which Thorpe called *Maxims*, at the end of *The Exeter Book*;[58] it must be added to this list of didactic poems for the sake of completeness but for no other reason.

We should linger for a moment, however, on the minor verse of purely Christian doctrine or ritual. None of these pieces has the power or the eloquence of *Doomsday*. There is, first of all, a metrical paraphrase of the *Gloria in excelsis*, probably from the second half of the tenth century; then a little triptych, as it were, on the Lord's Prayer. These three pieces are from different manuscripts: one, "Thou art Our Father, Ruler of all," in the same Cambridge manuscript as *Doomsday*; the second, "Father of mankind, I pray Thee for consolation," in Manuscript Bodleian Junius 121;[59] the third, "Holy Father, who dwellest in Heaven," in *The Exeter Book*. There is also, in this same Junius manuscript, a metrical paraphrase of the *Credo*.

Next to be considered is a small group of hymns and prayers. They should be regarded as true religious lyrics of a personal nature quite unusual for the period. One, "Help me, O holy Lord!" from *The Exeter Book*, has been attributed to Bishop Cynewulf (IV, 4),[60] whom some have identified with the Christian epic poet Cynewulf. Modern scholarship, however, views askance any such ascription. Still, it is true that this poem is from the mouth of an old man:

To adorn me for my journey forth and to try myself
For the adventure on which I must set out.   [71ff.]

or again:

...God have I
Mightily angered, the Jewel of mankind,
Because of that I was sorely chastised in this world;
So my deserts were great in the sight of man,
For that I suffer now deepest martyrdom,
Nor am I a wise judge, prudent as this world goes;
And so I speak these words burning in my bosom.

[78-84]

The poem is the same as *Resignation* (V, 5). Now it is conceivable enough that these words are spoken by a man in
worldly or churchly authority. Other lines indicate that he
has been punished, whether or not justly, for a particular of-
fense; he acknowledges, at any rate, that he has been guilty of
overweening worldly pride. He is even friendless, as was the
Wanderer. The poem has a certain amount of somber force;
the somberness, however, often approaches obscurity. Yet the
general performance here is much superior to that in the run
of these minor poems.

Among the Cottoniana (Julius A II) in the British Museum is a trio of hymns—"O dear Lord!", "O bright master!", "O light of light!"—which serve as feeble forerunners
of the Richard Rolle poems of the fourteenth century, although they can be referred more immediately to the Cynewulfian cycle, particularly because of their mystical tone. Another Cottonian manuscript (Vespasian D VI) gives the
hymn, "Let us glorify the Lord of mankind"; and, finally,
in Manuscript Cambridge Corpus Christi 201 appears the
poem, "Then take pity," half in Old English and half in
Latin, with an invocation to Mary—a device which foreshadows the hymns to the Virgin of the thirteenth and fourteenth
centuries.[61]

Coming to matters of psaltery, we must note briefly the
presence of a metrical version of Psalm 50, in Manuscript

Cotton Vespasian D VI, from the early part of the ninth century, and of a free translation of the Psalms in an eleventh
century manuscript found in Paris.[62] The Psalms from 1 to
50 are in prose; those from 51 to 150 in alliterative verse,
with both the beginning and the end of the verse portion somewhat incomplete. These versions, especially the poetic portions, have been assigned by some to the eighth century and
by others to King Alfred. Many point out what they consider
to be Kentish characteristics in the dialect. But if it is Kentish,
it is not unadulterated Kentish. Another theory attributes
these poems to Aldhelm (VII, 2). Yet the general feeling is
that they are too late for Aldhelm, though not too early for
Alfred, that they show a rather crude metrical technique
which can hardly be granted to any known poetic school in
Anglo-Saxon literature, and that they may possibly represent
what is left of a complete metrical translation of the Psalms,
now unfortunately lost in part. The dialect is probably West
Saxon with Kentish admixture, rather than pure Kentish, as
is the case in the version of Psalm 50 in Manuscript Cotton
Vespasian D VI.

We will conclude this brief discussion of Old English didactic verse with the latest, most stoical, and most eloquent of
all such shorter poems. *The Grave*,[63] in Manuscript Bodleian
343, is in a handwriting of the twelfth century, and a few final
lines are in a hand of the thirteenth. It may therefore be regarded technically as a piece of Middle English poetry, although it was probably written not long before 1100. Late as
it is, it is all the more valuable to serve as a reminder that the
Englishman has, for all his remarkable and steadfast activity,
an inner core of pagan negation and an unflinching ability to
face the inevitable end. Most of the time, no doubt, he will
follow the mighty lines of that great Book of Wisdom:
"Whatsoever thy hand findeth to do, do it with thy might;
for there is no work, nor device, nor knowledge, nor wisdom,
in the grave, whither thou goest." But the author of *The
Grave* was thinking only, in grim intensity of vision, of the

final resting-place, where all men's labors will follow after them:

> For you a house was built before ever you were born,
> Earth marked out ere you came from your mother.
> Yet it was not prepared, nor its very depth measured,
> Nor yet was it certain how long it should be.
> Now men bring you where you must and shall lie;
> Now men measure you, and the ground thereafter.
> This house you have is not raised up high,
> But low and even when you lie there within it.
> And low are the sills, and low the walls;
> Close to your breast the roof is reared.
> All cold shall you lie in that dwelling of earth,
> All darkness and dimness; the den will decay,
> Dwelling without door and all dark within.
> Long will you be locked there; only Death has the key.
> Hateful that earth-house and loathly to live in;
> There you shall lie and be eaten by worms.
> Thus are you laid away, leaving your dear ones,
> Never a friend will journey to see you,
> Or seek to find how you like that abode,
> Or open the door and come down to join you,
> Thus soon you will rot and be hateful to see ...
> Soon shall your head be deprived of its hair,
> And all the fairness of your locks be minished;
> Soft fingers shall fondle them never again.

Grim, macabre, but vivid and unforgettable; the quintessence of the elegiac; the essence of the terror of death, but with no Judgment Day to break the spell; sans wine, sans singer, and sans end.[64]

NOTES TO CHAPTER FIVE

1. In all editions of *The Exeter Book* (see Chapter III, note 9 above). The best separate edition is that by Kemp Malone, *Deor* (London, 1933); another good one is that by Bruce Dickins, *Runic and Heroic Poems* (Cambridge, 1915). It has been customary to

print at least the text of *Deor* in the standard editions of *Beowulf* (as do Klaeber, Sedgefield, and Holthausen; see Chapter III, note 11 above). Critical discussions of the poem have had to do chiefly with details of the text and allusions therein; but see W. W. Lawrence, "The Song of Deor" in *Modern Philology*, IX, 23-45; L. Forster, "Die Assoziation in Deors Klage" in *Anglia*, LXI, 117-121; F. Norman, " 'Deor': a criticism and an interpretation" in *Modern Language Review*, XXXII, 374-381, as well as his "Deor and Modern Scandinavian Ballads" in *London Mediaeval Studies*, vol. I, part II (1938), 165-178; and L. Whitbread, "The Third Section of *Deor*" in *Modern Philology*, XXXVIII, 371-384. A good parallelism with the Old Norse is suggested by F. P. Magoun, "Deors Klage und *Guúrnarkviþa* I" in *Englische Studien*, LXXV, 1-5.

2. For the allusion to Wayland made here, as found in the first strophe of *Deor*, see K. M. Buck and Alfred H. Mayhew, *The Wayland-Dietrich Saga* (London, 1930), but Malone's and Dickins's editions (see note 1 above) will give further bibliographical aid. As for Eormanric, he appears in *Beowulf*, where he is something of a symbol of a tyrannical, unjust king, although such a conception is not absolutely in line with known historical facts. Nevertheless, there is a full-grown saga about Eormanric in Germany and Scandinavia; see Caroline Brady, *The Legends of Ermanric* (Berkeley, 1943); also see O. L. Jiriczek, *Deutsche Heldensagen* (Leipzig, 1894) and the discussions of the matter in both R. W. Chambers, *Widsith* (Cambridge, 1912) and Kemp Malone, *Widsith* (London, 1935).

3. In *The Exeter Book* and all editions thereof (see Chapter III, note 9 above). *The Wanderer* has been something of a favorite for all compilers and editors of anthologies and readers of Old English literature and is therefore easily accessible, both in and out of translation (see Chapter II, note 11 above), for which the following are indispensable: I. Gollancz, *The Exeter Book: an anthology of Anglo-Saxon Poetry* (Part I, London, 1895; and Part II, London, 1934 —continued by W. S. Mackie); R. K. Gordon, *Anglo-Saxon Poetry*, No. 794 of the Everyman Library; N. Kershaw, *Anglo-Saxon and Norse Poems* (Cambridge, 1922); Kemp Malone, *Ten Old English Poems* (Baltimore, 1941); W. A. Craigie, *Specimens of Anglo-Saxon Poetry* (Edinburgh, 1931); and J. D. Spaeth, *Old English Poetry* (Princeton, 1922). These works will be referred to from time to time.

There is, however, no separate edition of *The Wanderer*. Illuminating discussions of the poem are the following: C. C. Ferrell, "Old Germanic Life in the Anglo-Saxon *Wanderer* and *Seafarer*" in *Modern Language Notes*, IX, 402-407; R. C. Boer, "Wanderer und Seefahrer" in *Zeitschrift für deutsche Philologie*, XXXV, 1-28—which suggests that the two poems we have as *The Wanderer* and *The Seafarer* can be broken down into three separate poems; W. W. Lawrence, "*The Wanderer* and *The Seafarer*" in *Journal of English and Germanic Philology*, IV, 460-480; Rudolf Imelmann, *Wanderer und Seefahrer im Rahmen der altenglischen Odoaker-Dichtung*—a not very convincing attempt to connect the two poems, together with *Wulf and Eadwacer*, *The Husband's Message*, and *The Wife's Complaint*, as part of an Old English Odoacer Saga (see note 10 below). It is probably better to accept the general viewpoint expressed by Bernard F. Huppé, "*The Wanderer*: theme and structure" in *Journal of English and Germanic Philology*, XLII, 516-538, which presents the poem as a work "unified" by a single theme—we may paraphrase the theme as "the vanity of human wishes." Huppé, however, does not in my opinion stress sufficiently the non-Christian qualities of the poem.

4. *Beowulf*, 2247-2266.

5. Many of the discussions of *The Seafarer* are concerned also with *The Wanderer*, since the two poems have frequently been considered together; see therefore the items mentioned in note 3 above. As in the case of *The Wanderer*, there is no separate edition for *The Seafarer*, although the poem has been printed as often as any Old English poem, not only in all editions of *The Exeter Book* (see Chapter III, note 9 above) but also in most of the Old English readers and anthologies. The poem, along with *The Wanderer*, has been translated into alliterative verse especially well by Charles W. Kennedy in *Old English Elegies* (Princeton, 1936), but see other translations mentioned in note 3 above. There is a special translation by Gavin Bone in *Medium Aevum*, III, 1-6, and there are the usual prose renderings. An exceptionally good critical study is O. S. Andersson Arngart, *The Seafarer: an interpretation* (Lund, 1937), and see also the following: N. Kershaw, *Anglo-Saxon and Norse Poems* (Cambridge, 1922)—especially the introduction—and other articles or monographs such as Friedrich Kluge, "Zu altenglischen Dichtungen—Der Seefahrer" in *Englische Studien*, VI, 322-327; Marjorie Daunt, "Some Difficulties of *The Seafarer* Reconsidered" in *Modern Language Review*, XIII, 474-479; and L. L. Schücking, "Heroische Ironie im angelsächsischen Seefahrer" in the *Deutschbein Festschrift* (Leipzig, 1936).

6. Particularly set forth by M. Rieger, "*Seefahrer* als Dialog hergestellt" in *Zeitschrift für deutsche Philologie*, I, 334-339 and by E. Hönncher, "Zur Dialogeinteilung im Seefahrer(A) und zur zweiten homiletischen Partei(B) dieses Gedichtes" in *Anglia*, IX, 435-446.

7. In all printed editions thereof (see Chapter III, note 9 above). Separate editions are those by Heinrich Leo, *Carmen anglosaxonicum in codice Exoniensi servatum quod vulgo inscribitur Ruinae* (Halle, 1865)—with translation into German; and by J. Earle, "The

Ruined City" in *Academy*, XXVI, 29—with translation into English. It is included in Ernst Sieper, *Die altenglische Elegie* (Strassburg, 1915) and L. L. Schücking, *Kleines angelsächsisches Dichterbuch* (Cöthen, 1919), as well as in N. Kershaw, *Anglo-Saxon and Norse Poems* (Cambridge, 1922) and W. A. Craigie, *Specimens of Anglo-Saxon Poetry* (Edinburgh, 1931), Vol. III. The poem has not received the attention, however, that it deserves. There is a pleasing translation by Cosette Faust and Stith Thompson in *Old English Poems* (Chicago, 1918) and another in Charles W. Kennedy, *Old English Elegies* (Princeton, 1936). There have been a few short articles on individual lines in the poem, and see especially Alois Brandl, "Venantius Fortunatus und die angelsächsischen Elegien *Wanderer* und *Ruine*" in *Archiv*, CXXXIX, 84; Stephen J. Herben, "*The Ruin*" in *Modern Language Notes*, LIV, 37-39 (see also LIX, 72ff.); and Cecilia A. Hotchner, *Wessex and Old English Poetry, with Special Consideration of 'The Ruin'* (New York, 1939). Herben and Miss Hotchner differ as to the identification of the locale of the poem. Herben maintains that it is the old Roman wall which is the subject of the lament.

8. Published in all editions of *The Exeter Book* (see Chapter III, note 9 above) and in several of the anthologies of Old English poetry already mentioned, notably in Craigie, Sedgefield (*An Anglo-Saxon Verse-Book*; Manchester, 1922), Kershaw, Schücking, Kluge (*Angelsächsisches Lesebuch*; Halle, 1888; 1915), Wülker (*Kleinere angelsächsische Dichtungen*; Halle, 1882), Ettmüller (*Engla and Seaxna Scopas and Boceras*; Quedlinburg-Leipzig, 1850), all the way back to J. J. Conybeare, *Illustrations of Anglo-Saxon Poetry* (London, 1826), which is about the earliest of such collections. See also the translations cited in note 3 above. There is no separate edition. Critical discussions of the poem, such as they are, have usually found it necessary to quote the whole piece. These would include F. Kicketier, "*Klage der Frau, Botschaft des Gemahls*, und *Ruine*" in *Anglia*, XI, 363-368—which suggests that all three poems may be riddles; L. L. Schücking, "Das angelsächsische Gedicht von der Klage der Frau" in *Zeitschrift für deutsches Altertum*, XLVIII, 436-449—an excellent study; Rudolf Imelmann, *Die altenglische Odoaker-Dichtung* (Berlin, 1907)—see note 10 below; W. W. Lawrence, "The Banished Wife's Lament" in *Modern Philology*, V, 387-405; Svet Stefanovic, "Das angelsächsische Gedicht *Die Klage der Frau*" in *Anglia*, XXXII, 399-433; Rudolf Imelmann, *Forschungen zur altenglischen Poesie* (Berlin, 1920)—a kind of summary of Imelmann's theory stated in 1907; and F. Klaeber, "Zu altenglischen Dichtungen" in *Archiv*, CLXVII, 36-41. In any case, *The Wife's Lament* must be considered critically with *The Husband's Message* (see note 9 below) and *Wulf and Eadwacer* (see note 10 below).

9. Published in all editions of *The Exeter Book* (see Chapter III, note 9 above) and in L. F. Klipstein, *Analecta Anglo-Saxonica* (New York, 1849), vol. II—the first American Anglo-Saxon reader—and in the anthologies of Ettmüller, Wülker, Kluge, Sieper, Schücking, Wyatt, Sedgefield, Gollancz, Kershaw, and Spaeth already mentioned (see note 3 above); also in Craigie, Vol. III. There is no separate translation or edition. In addition to the poetic translations mentioned above, there is the English prose translation in A. S. Cook and C. B. Tinker, *Select Translations from Old English Poetry* (Boston, 1902); other good ones are those in Faust and Thompson's *Old English Poems* (Chicago, 1918) and J. D. Spaeth's *Old English Poetry* (Princeton, 1922). The critical discussion of this poem is bound up with that of *The Wife's Lament* and *Wulf and Eadwacer*, for which see note 8 above and note 10 below, especially the items by Imelmann and Moritz Trautmann, "Zur Botschaft des Gemahls" in *Anglia*, XVI, 207-225, which is virtually a separate edition.

10. Published in all editions of *The Exeter Book* (see Chapter III, note 9 above); also in the following readers or anthologies already mentioned (see notes 3, 7, 8, and 9 above): Kluge, Sieper, Schücking, Sedgefield, Craigie (vol. III), Gollancz, Gordon, Malone. Translations are also to be referred to the list of anthologies cited. The poem has received a considerable critical manhandling. Is it a riddle, a personal lyric, a bit of dramatic dialogue, or the fragment of an epic poem? The last suggestion—that it is a piece of an epic—was chiefly the product of Rudolf Imelmann's fertile mind. He believed that *Wulf and Eadwacer*, *The Wife's Lament*, *The Husband's Message* and (later) *The Wanderer* and *The Seafarer* were all parts of an Old English epic version of the Odoacer legend or saga. The three publications of Imelmann constructing this theory are (1) *Die altenglische Odoaker-Dichtung* (Berlin, 1907); (2) *Wanderer und Seefahrer im Rahmen der altenglischen Odoaker-Dichtung* (Berlin, 1908); and (3) *Forschungen zur altenglischen Poesie* (Berlin, 1920). Imelmann's theory has not made much headway in recent years. For one thing, the five poems which he collects are much less epic than other pieces, and it would be a remarkable epic fragment which yielded only five lyrics among its remains!

Odoacer, usurping ruler of the Western Empire in the late fifth century, was finally defeated and killed by Theodoric the Great, the Dietrich of Germanic saga. In legend Odoacer became more or less identified with Ermanric or Eormanric (see note 2 above), and lived the life of an exile hanging upon the fringes of the Dietrich-Saga. The similarity, if not the actual identity, of Odoacer's name with that of Eadwacer, and the fact that all five of the poems selected by Imelmann have exile as a chief theme, both lend some credence, however, to Imelmann's theory.

Wulf and Eadwacer was known for a long time as *The First Riddle* and as such was regarded, along with other *Riddles* in *The Exeter Book*, as the work of Cynewulf. Leo and Dietrich were the earliest and most convincing champions of this theory. See note 25 below. The theory of Cynewulf's authorship is hardly tenable now; see F. Tupper, *The Riddles of The Exeter Book* (Boston, 1910) and his introduction for an excellent outline of riddle-literature in general and of the Cynewulf problem in particular. But the following items in the course of a discussion of the *Wulf and Eadwacer* question will repay reading: Heinrich Leo, *Quae de se ipse Cynevulfus . . . poeta Anglosaxonicus tradiderit* (Halle, 1857)—the first propounding of the Cynewulf-for-author theory: F. Dietrich, "Die Rätsel des Exeterbuchs: Verfasser, Weitere Lösungen" in *Haupt's Zeitschrift*, XII, 232-252; Henry Bradley, in a review of Dietrich published in *Academy*, XXXIII, 197-198—the first identification of *Wulf and Eadwacer* with the theory that it is a dramatic fragment; Georg Herzfeld, *Die Räthsel des Exeterbuches und ihre Verfasser* (Berlin, 1890)—backing up Bradley; I. Gollancz in *Academy*, XLIV, 572—romanticizing Bradley's theory into the decidedly extreme statement that *Wulf and Eadwacer* is a "life-drama in five acts"; W. W. Lawrence, "The First Riddle of Cynewulf" in *Publications of the Modern Language Association*, XVII, 247-261; Edmund Erlemann, "Zu den altenglischen Rätseln" in *Archiv*, CXI, 49-63; Moritz Trautmann, "Das sogenannte erste Rätsel" in *Anglia*, XXXVI, 133-138; Ferdinand Holthausen, "Zu den altenglischen Rätseln" in *Anglia Beiblatt*, XXX, 50-55; H. Patzig, "Zum ersten Rätsel des Exeterbuches" in *Archiv*, CXLV, 204-207— the last important statement that *Wulf and Eadwacer* is a riddle. Further references to material on the *Riddles* are given in note 25 below.

11. C. W. M. Grein, *Bibliothek der angelsächsischen Poesie* (Göttingen, 1857-1858), I, 10.

12. See note 10 above.

13. See note 10 above.

14. See note 10 above.

15. See Chapter IV, note 10 above. This little poem is published, in its Northumbrian version, in Henry Sweet, *The Oldest English Texts*, volume 83 of *Publications of the Early English Text Society, Original Series* (London, 1885), and more recently in a good separate treatment in A. H. Smith, *Three Northumbrian Poems* (London, 1933). See also E. V. K. Dobbie, *Anglo-Saxon Minor Poems* (New York, 1943). Excellent discussions are to be found in W. G. Frampton, in *Modern Philology*, XXII, 1-15, and in Louise Pound, "Caedmon's

Dream-Song" in the *Klaeber Miscellany* (Minneapolis, 1929), 232-239. See also R. S. Watson, *Caedmon* (London, 1875).

16. Edited by J. Rawson Lumby, *Be Domes Daeʒe—De Die Judicii*, volume 55 of *Publications of the Early English Text Society, Original Series* (London, 1876). This poem must be distinguished from *The Last Judgment* in *The Exeter Book* (see note 34 below). *Doomsday* has been badly neglected by scholars; see A. Brandl, *"Be Domes Daege"* in *Anglia*, IV, 97-104 and G. Grau, *Quellen und Verwandschaften der . . . germanischen Darstellungen* (Halle, 1908).

17. Observe how this tallies with the many accounts of the torments of the damned, culminating in Dante's treatment of the material in the later cantos of the *Inferno*.

18. In E. V. K. Dobbie, *Anglo-Saxon Minor Poems* (New York, 1943), and with general introduction in A. H. Smith, *Three Northumbrian Poems* (London, 1933). The older edition is that in Henry Sweet, *The Oldest English Texts*, volume 83 of *Publications of the Early English Text Society, Original Series* (London, 1885). The piece is actually a fragment of a Latin prose passage in English paraphrase (see note 19 below). It is believed that Bede, in his later days, was working on a translation of the Gospel of John. See also R. Brotanek, *Texte und Untersuchungen zur altenglischen Literatur- und Kirchengeschichte* (Halle, 1913), 151-157.

19. The Latin passage of which *Bede's Death-Song* is a portion in an Old English version turns up in an epistle of a certain Cuthbert to a certain Cuthwin. It is known that Cuthbert, who is not to be confused with the important Bishop Cuthbert (St. Cuthbert) of Lindisfarne (d.687), was a pupil of Bede, and it is presumed that Cuthwin was another pupil. Cuthbert attributes the Latin passage in question, however, to his master Bede.

20. See X, 2 and Chapter X, note 15 below. Aside from the editions given in all printings of *The Exeter Book* (see Chapter III, note 9 above) and *The Vercelli Book* since that published by Grein and Wülker in their *Bibliothek der angelsächsischen Poesie* (Cassel-Leipzig, 1883-1889), II-a, 92-107, the best text is in Rudolph Willard, "The Address of the Soul to the Body" in *Publications of the Modern Language Association*, L, 957-983. For the idea behind these poems, including the Middle English versions as well, see B. P. Kurtz, "Giver the Worm: an essay toward the history of an idea" in *University of California Publications in English*, vol. II, no. 1, 235-261 (Berkeley, 1929) and T. Batiouchkof, "Le débat de l'âme et du corps" in *Romania*, XX, 1-55; also J. Zupitza, "Zu Seele und Leib" in *Archiv*, XCI, 369-381, and particularly J. D. Bruce, "A Contribution to the Study of 'The Body and the Soul': Poems in English" in *Modern Language Notes*, V, 385-401 and R. Buchholz, "Die Fragmente der

Rede der Seele an den Leichnam" in *Erlanger Beiträge zur englischen Philologie*, vi. The Middle English poem survives in no less than six manuscripts; good editions are those of Linow in *Erlanger Beiträge zur englischen Philologie*, i, and of Thomas Wright in *Latin Poems Commonly Attributed to Walter Mapes* (London, 1841) and in several readers and anthologies of Middle English literature. For an interesting analogue, see also Eleanor K. Henningham, *An Early Latin Debate of the Body and Soul* (New York, 1939).

21. See note 20 above. But attention should be called here to *The Grave*, discussed below (see V, 7 and note 63 below).

22. The standard edition and reference-work is Blanche C. Williams, *Gnomic Poetry in Anglo-Saxon* (New York, 1914; 1937). Good discussions in addition to Miss Williams's monograph are the following: J. Strobl, "Zur Spruchdichtung bei den Angelsachsen" in *Zeitschrift für deutsches Altertum*, xxxi, 54-64; H. Müller, *Über die angelsächsischen Versus Gnomici* (Jena, 1893); C. Krüger, *Beiträge zur gnomischen Dichtung der Angelsachsen* (Halle, 1924); C. C. Batchelor, "The Moralistic Poetry of the British Isles and Iceland before 1066" in *Summaries of Theses, Harvard University* (Cambridge, Mass., 1932), 241-244; and Kemp Malone, "Notes on Gnomic Poem B of *The Exeter Book*" in *Medium Aevum*, xii, 65-67.

23. *The Arts* (or *Gifts*) *of Men* is sometimes known by the Old English title *Bi Monna Craeftum; The Fates* (or *Fortunes*) *of Men*, by the Old English title *Bi Monna Wyrdum*. Both are printed in all complete editions of *The Exeter Book* (see Chapter III, note 9 above). There are no separate editions, nor have the two pieces been included in the readers or anthologies of Old English literature except in O. T. Williams, *Short Extracts from Old English Poetry* (Bangor, 1909) and W. A. Craigie (see note 3 above), vol. iii. The critical discussion of these poems has not been significant, except where they touch the immediate problem of the *Gnomic Verses* (see note 22 above).

24. Just when, however, is a matter of much dispute. Symphosius has been placed anywhere from the second to the sixth century. A brief but useful outline of the matter is given in F. Tupper, *The Riddles of The Exeter Book* (Boston, 1910), xxix ff.

25. The *Riddles* have been published in all editions of *The Exeter Book* (see Chapter III, note 9 above) and have been treated generously in anthologies and readers. The edition of Moritz Trautmann, *Die altenglischen Rätsel* (Heidelberg, 1915), has the mixed value of being the work of one of the most feverish yet erratic authorities on the subject. The most extensive translation of these pieces is doubtless in I. Gollancz and W. S. Mackie, *The Exeter Book: an anthology of Anglo-Saxon Poetry* (London, 1895; 1934), but many are rendered in prose in R. K. Gordon, *Anglo-Saxon Poetry* (No. 794 of the

Everyman Library; London, 1927). The most useful, for the general reader's consumption, of the editions of the *Riddles* are those by F. Tupper, *The Riddles of The Exeter Book* (Boston, 1910) and by A. J. Wyatt, *Old English Riddles* (London, 1912)—particularly Tupper's, because of its invaluable introduction, discussion of the solution of the riddles, and text. Moreover, no student of the subject could afford to miss the discussion in Charles W. Kennedy, *The Earliest English Poetry* (New York, 1943), 131-146.

The critical literature on this topic is moderately bulky; see especially F. Dietrich, "Die Räthsel des Exeterbuches" in *Zeitschrift für deutsches Altertum*, XII, 232-252; Moritz Trautmann, "Cynewulf und die Rätsel" in *Anglia*, VI, 158-169; August Prehn, "Komposition und Quellen der Rätsel des Exeterbuches" in Körting's *Neuphilologische Studien*, III, 143-285; Georg Herzfeld, *Die Räthsel des Exeterbuchs und ihre Verfasser* (Berlin, 1890); Albert S. Cook, "Recent Opinion Concerning the Riddles of *The Exeter Book*" in *Modern Language Notes*, VII, 20-21; Moritz Trautmann, "Die Auflösung der altenglischen Rätsel" in *Anglia Beiblatt*, V, 46-51; August Madert, *Die Sprache der altenglischen Rätsel des Exeterbuches und die Cynewulffrage* (Marburg, 1900); F. Tupper, "Originals and Analogues of the Exeter Book Riddles" in *Modern Language Notes*, XVIII, 97-106; Moritz Trautmann, "Alte und neue Antworten auf altenglische Rätsel" in *Bonner Beiträge zur Anglistik*, XIX, 167-215; F. Tupper, "Solutions of the Exeter Book Riddles" in *Modern Language Notes*, XXI, 97-105; Moritz Trautmann, "Zum Streit um die angelsächsischen Rätsel" in *Anglia*, XXXVI, 127-133; Fritz Lowenthal, *Studien zum germanischen Rätsel* (Heidelberg, 1914), particularly pp. 14-51; Moritz Trautmann, "Die Quellen der altenglischen Rätsel" in *Anglia*, XXXVIII, 349-354 and "Zeit, Heimat, und Verfasser der altenglischen Rätsel" in *Anglia*, XXXVIII, 365-373 and "Die Zahl der altenglischen Rätsel" in *Anglia Beiblatt*, XXV, 272-273 and "Weiteres zu den altenglischen Rätseln und metrisches" in *Anglia*, XLIII, 245-260; Erika von Erhardt-Siebold, "Old English Riddle No. 4" in *Publications of the Modern Language Association*, LXI, 620-623, "Old English Riddle No. 39" in *Publications of the Modern Language Association*, LXI, 910-915, "The Anglo-Saxon Riddle 74 and Empedokles' Fragment 117" in *Medium Aevum*, XV, 48-54, "Old English Riddle No. 57" in *Publications of the Modern Language Association*, LXII, 1-8, and "Old English Riddle No. 95" in *Modern Language Notes*, LXII, 558-559; also Laurence K. Shook, "Old English Riddle I" in *Mediaeval Studies*, VIII, 316-318.

26. See note 10 above.

27. The piece survives in a Vienna and a Mainz manuscript. The

Vienna manuscript has been transcribed by H. Massmann in *Kleine Sprachdenkmale des achten Jahrhunderts* (Vienna, 1937) and again by J. Kemble in *Archaeologia*, XXVIII, 257. M. Rieger included it in one of the oldest anthologies of Old English literature, *Alt- und angelsächsisches Lesebuch* (Giessen, 1861).

28. In all complete editions of *The Exeter Book* (see Chapter III, note 9 above). There is a separate critical text, with no apparatus, by Julius Cramer, "Quelle, Verfasser, und Text des altenglischen Gedichtes Christi Höllenfahrt" in *Anglia*, XIX, 137-174. A fine recent critical discussion is Genevieve Crotty, "The Exeter *Harrowing of Hell*: a reinterpretation" in *Publications of the Modern Language Association*, LIV, 349-358. See also Richard Wülker, *Grundriss zur Geschichte der angelsächsischen Litteratur* (Leipzig, 1885), 186 for a discussion of the older view concerning the relation of this poem to Cynewulf's *Christ*. Finally, see the text in E. V. K. Dobbie, *Anglo-Saxon Minor Poems* (New York, 1943).

29. See Chapter III, note 9 above re both *The Exeter Book* and *The Vercelli Book*.

30. In all complete editions of *The Exeter Book* (see Chapter III, note 9 above), although the title may vary slightly. It was known by Wülker as the fourth of the poems he called *Prayers*; most editors, however, have preferred to associate the piece with an exile or wanderer, either as a supplication or a complaint. It appears but seldom in anthologies, but see Ernst Sieper, *Die altenglische Elegie* (Strassburg, 1915); L. L. Schücking, *Kleines angelsächsisches Dichterbuch* (Cöthen, 1919). It has received scant critical attention, but see F. Klaeber, "Zu altenglischen Dichtungen" in *Archiv*, CLXVII, 36-41.

31. In all complete editions of *The Exeter Book* (see Chapter III, note 9 above), Thorpe's being the earliest. Separate printings appear in only a few anthologies, such as F. Kluge, *Angelsächsisches Lesebuch* (Halle, 1888; 1915), Ernst Sieper (see note 30 above), Schücking (see note 30 above), and W. A. Craigie, *Specimens of Anglo-Saxon Poetry* (Edinburgh, 1931), vol. III. But the best such treatments are those in Ferdinand Holthausen, "Das altenglische Reimlied" in *Festschrift für Lorenz Morsbach* (Halle, 1913), 190-200 and in *Englische Studien*, LXV, 181-189; and an English one, with translation, by W. S. Mackie, "The Old English Rhymed Poem" in *Journal of English and Germanic Philology*, XXI, 507-519. For textual and critical notes, see especially Eduard Sievers, "Zum angelsächsischen Reimlied" in *Paul und Braune's Beiträge*, XI, 345-354 and F. Holthausen, "Zum altenglischen Reimliede" in *Anglia Beiblatt*, XLI, 39-40 and XLVI, 83.

32. See G. Neckel, *Beiträge zur Eddaforschung* (Dortmund,

1908), 367ff. and particularly Lee M. Hollander, *Old Norse Poems* (New York, 1936).

33. In his *Geschichte der englischen Litteratur* (Berlin, 1899), 77. Beyond the fact that this piece is printed in all complete editions of *The Exeter Book* (see Chapter III, note 9 above), it has attracted comparatively little scholarly attention. It has been published separately, however, by L. F. Klipstein in *Analecta Anglo-Saxonica* (New York, 1849), II; by R. P. Wülker in *Kleinere angelsächsische Dichtungen* (Halle, 1882); by W. J. Sedgefield in *An Anglo-Saxon Verse-Book* (Manchester, 1922); and by W. A. Craigie in *Specimens of Anglo-Saxon Poetry* (Edinburgh, 1931), vol. III. There are some textual notes by James W. Bright in *Modern Language Notes*, x, 136-137. Krapp and Dobbie, in their edition of *The Exeter Book* (New York, 1936), refer to the poem as "Precepts."

34. Which might more accurately be called the *Exeter Last Judgment*, to distinguish it from the *Corpus Christi Last Judgment*, which is found in Manuscript Corpus Christi College Cambridge 201. For these two poems and other scattered references to Old English eschatological material, see W. Deering, *The Anglo-Saxon Poems on the Judgment Day* (Halle, 1890). The *Exeter Last Judgment* is printed in all complete editions of *The Exeter Book* (see Chapter III, note 9 above) and also in O. T. Williams, *Short Extracts from Old English Poetry* (Bangor, 1909). For an analogy between this piece and Cynewulf's *Christ*, see Albert S. Cook, "Cynewulf's Principal Source for the Third Part of *Christ*" in *Modern Language Notes*, IV, 341-352.

35. Printed in all complete editions of *The Exeter Book* (see Chapter III, note 9 above). Wülker, in his *Grundriss zur Geschichte der angelsächsischen Litteratur* (Leipzig, 1885), 235, and Alois Brandl, in Paul's *Grundriss der germanischen Philologie* (Berlin, 1898), vol. II, 1, 1047, are dubious about the genuineness of the closing sections of this poem. As a whole it is obviously a loose mixture of markedly Cynewulfian derivation.

36. For *The Anglo-Saxon Chronicle*, see Chapter VIII, note 7 below. These pieces have been described in R. Wülker, *Grundriss zur Geschichte der angelsächsischen Litteratur* (Leipzig, 1885), 338-347. Particular attention has been paid by Klaeber to a poem on King Oswald's death, in *Philological Quarterly*, XVI, 214; by Margaret Schlauch to *The Durham Poem* in "An *Encomium Urbis*" in *Journal of English and Germanic Philology*, XL, 14ff.; and by F. Liebermann to *The Death of Edmund I* in *Archiv*, CXLVIII, 96. See also note 42 below.

37. The piece has been published in editions of *The Anglo-Saxon Chronicle* (see Chapter VIII, note 7 below) and separately as long

ago as L. Ettmüller, *Engla and Seaxna Scopas and Boceras* (Quedlinburg-Leipzig, 1850).

38. Usually published in editions of the *Chronicle* (see Chapter VIII, note 7 below), and first published separately by Ettmüller (see note 37 above); cf. M. Förster, "König Eadgars Tod" in *Englische Studien*, LXXII, 10-13.

39. That is, in Manuscript Cotton Tiberius B I, the Abingdon Chronicle. This was first discussed at length in J. Earle, *Two of the Saxon Chronicles Parallel* (Oxford, 1865); see Chapter VIII, note 7 below.

40. Again, in the Abingdon Chronicle (see note 39 above) and in the Worcester Chronicle (Manuscript Cotton Tiberius B IV); see Chapter VIII, note 7 below.

41. From Roger Twysden, *Scriptores X* (London, 1652); see also Miss Schlauch's article cited in note 36 above.

42. Before dropping the matter of the poems from *The Anglo-Saxon Chronicle*, one should give attention to the convenient survey of the subject in the introduction to W. J. Sedgefield, *The Battle of Maldon and Short Poems from the Saxon Chronicle* (Boston-London, 1904).

43, A handy little manual is A. R. Wright, *English Folk Lore* (New York, 1928), but the most specific record on the folklore of the Anglo-Saxons is E. A. Philippson, *Germanisches Heidentum bei den Angelsachsen* (Leipzig, 1929). Of considerable value is the special treatment in G. Storms, *Anglo-Saxon Magic* (The Hague, 1948). See also F. P. Magoun, "On Some Survivals of Pagan Belief in Anglo-Saxon England" in *Harvard Theological Review*, XL, 33-46 and Chapter XIII, note 24 below.

44. The fullest treatment of the *Charms* is found in F. Grendon, *The Anglo-Saxon Charms* (New York, 1930); but see G. Storms, *Anglo-Saxon Magic* (note 43 above). See also *Journal of American Folklore*, XXII, 105-337. Most of the surviving *Charms* were printed by O. Cockayne, in *Leechdoms, Wortcunning, and Starcraft of Early England* (London, 1864-1869). More generalized is F. Hälsig, *Zauberspruch bei den Germanen* (Leipzig, 1910). Brief discussions of various aspects of individual charms include the following: A. R. Skemp, "The Old English Charms" in *Modern Language Review*, VI, 289-301; J. H. G. Grattan, "Three Anglo-Saxon Charms from the *Lacnunga*" in *Modern Language Review*, XXII, 1-6; F. Holthausen, "Der altenglische Reisesegen" in *Anglia Beiblatt*, XL, 87-90 and XLI, 255; F. Holthausen, "Die altenglischen Neunkräutersegen" in *Englische Studien*, LXIX, 180-183 (see Chapter XIII below); Bruce Dickins, "Runic Rings and Old English Charms" in *Archiv*, CLXVII, 252; F. P. Magoun, "Zu den altenglischen Zauberspielen"

in *Archiv*, CLXXI, 17-35, and "Strophische Überreste in den angelsächsischen Zaubersprüchen in *Englische Studien*, LXXII, 1-6; L. K. Shook, "Notes on the Old English Charms" in *Modern Language Notes*, LV, 139-140; and Howard Meroney, "Irish in the Old English Charms" in *Speculum*, XX, 172-182.

45. In the British Museum.

46. In 1731; see the reference to this in relation to the Beowulf Manuscript (III, 3 above).

47. There has been a considerable recent outburst of scholarship on the Germanic runes. Perhaps the most celebrated of the older works is L. F. A. Wimmer, *Die Runenschrift* (Berlin, 1887), with translation into German by F. Holthausen; another famous treatment, at least from a pictorial standpoint, is G. Stephens, *The Old Northern Runic Monuments of Scandinavia and England* (London-Copenhagen, 1866; 1901). There are four excellent additional monographs with slightly varied opinions as to the origins of the runes, in the following items: O. Von Friesen, "Runenschrift" in J. Hoops's *Reallexikon der germanischen Altertumskunde* (Strassburg, 1911-1919), which points out the probability that the runic alphabets were derived not only from Latin capitals (which is Wimmer's point of view) but also from Greek letters adapted; C. D. Buck, "An ABC Inscribed in Old English Runes" in *Modern Philology*, XVII, 219-224—which rejects Wimmer and substitutes an Italic but non-Latin origin for the Runes; S. Agrell, *Runornas talmystik och dese antike förebild* (Lund, 1927)—which returns more or less to Wimmer; and S. Feist, "Zum Ursprung der germanischen Runenschrift" in *Acta Philologica Scandinavica*, IV, 1-25—which leans towards Buck. In my opinion, von Friesen's theory seems best to fit the facts. More specific treatment of the problem, at least in reference to the Anglo-Saxon runes, are the following: Helmut Arntz, *Handbuch der Runenkunde* (Halle, 1935)—probably the best of the recent studies; H. Harder, "Die Inschriften angelsächsischer Runenringe" in *Archiv*, CLXIX, 224-228; Wolfgang Jungandreas, *Die germanischen Runenreihe und ihre Bedeutung* (Stuttgart, 1936); W. Keller, "Zur Chronologie der altenglischen Runen" in *Anglia*, LXII, 24-32; and W. Krause, *Runenschriften im älteren Futhark* (Halle, 1937).

As for *The Runic Poem* itself, it has been published in Grein and Wülker's *Bibliothek der angelsächsischen Poesie* (Cassel-Göttingen, 1883-1898); in G. Körting, *Grundriss der Geschichte der englischen Literatur von ihren Anfängen bis zur Gegenwart* (Münster, 1919); and in Bruce Dickins, *Runic and Heroic Poems of the Old Teutonic Peoples* (Cambridge, 1915), which last-named book is especially useful for its comparisons of the Runic Poems found elsewhere in Germanic literatures. Apart from the introductions to the texts just cited, the best discussions of the Old English *Runic Poem* are T. Grien-berger, "Das altenglische Runengedicht" in *Anglia*, XLV, 201-220 and W. Keller, "Zum altenglischen Rungedicht" in *Anglia*, LX, 141-149.

48. A notable kenning.

49. The different runic alphabets are conveniently accessible in Bruce Dickins, *Runic and Heroic Poems of the Old Teutonic Peoples* (Cambridge, 1915), x.

50. This is the most famous of many Anglo-Saxon relics, particularly of those which are inscribed. Others of this sort would include the Bewcastle Cross, the Falstone Ring, the Ruthwell Cross (see IV, 5 above), the Mortain Casket, the Brunswick Casket, the Urswick Inscription, the Sheffield Brooch, and the Brussels Cross (see Chapter IV, note 50 above). Two indispensable works covering all of these antiquities, and some others as well, are W. G. Collingwood, *Northumbrian Crosses of the Pre-Norman Age* (London, 1927) and G. Baldwin Brown, *The Arts in Early England* (London, 1937), volume VI. The text of the Franks Casket has been printed by Henry Sweet in *The Oldest English Texts*, volume 83 of *Publications of the Early English Text Society, Original Series* (London, 1885) and by A. S. Napier in "The Franks Casket" from *An English Miscellany* (Oxford, 1901). In addition there has been some intensive study of the Franks Casket in recent years—see particularly Eleanor G. Clark, "The Right Side of the Franks Casket" in *Publications of the Modern Language Association*, XLV, 339-353; and the excellent studies by Philip W. Souers: "The Franks Casket: Left Side" in *Harvard Studies and Notes in Philology and Literature*, XVIII, 109-209; "The Top of the Franks Casket" in *Harvard Studies and Notes in Philology and Literature*, XVI, 163-179; and "The Magi on the Franks Casket" in *Harvard Studies and Notes in Philology and Literature*, XIX, 249-254. These studies go far beyond the research of R. Imelmann in his *Forschungen zu altenglischen Poesie* (Berlin, 1920).

Other valuable works on these miscellaneous relics, in addition to those already mentioned, are Maurice Cahen and Magnus Olsen, *L'inscription unique du coffret de Mortain* (Paris, 1930)—reviewed somewhat challengingly in *Anglia Beiblatt*, XLII, 257-258; H. Harder, "Das Braunschweiger Runenkästchen" in *Archiv*, CLXII, 227-229, and "Die Runeninschrift der Silberspange von Sheffield" in *Archiv*, CLXIV, 250-252; W. G. Collingwood, "A Rune-Inscribed Anglian Cross-Shaft at Urswick Church" in *Transactions of the Cumberland and Westmoreland Antiquarian and Archaeological Society*, vol. XI, New Series, 462-468; and M. Olsen, "Notes on the Urswick Inscription" in *Norsk Tidsskrift for Sprogvidenskap*, IV, 282-286.

51. Sir Augustus Wollaston Franks (1826-1897), one of the most

distinguished of British nineteenth-century antiquarians, and for years president of the Antiquarian Society, as well as vice-chairman of the Division of Antiquities in the British Museum. He tells the story of the Franks Casket in *Archaeological Journal*, XVI, 391ff. (1859), under the title, "Memoir on the Casket."

52. In addition to the old text published in Grein and Wülker, *Bibliothek der angelsächsischen Poesie* (Cassel-Leipzig, 1883-1898), vol. III b, 58-82, there is an older edition in J. M. Kemble, *The Dialogue of Salomon and Saturnus* (London, 1848)—which contains also the *Hadrian and Ritheus* (see Chapter XI below)—and two later texts: that by J. Schipper, "Salomo und Saturn" in *Germania*, XXII, 50-70 and A. R. Von Vincenti, *Die altenglische Dialoge von Salomon und Saturn* (Leipzig, 1904), which constitutes also no. 31 of the *Münchener Beiträge*. But by far the best edition is that by Robert J. Menner, *The Poetical Dialogues of Salomon and Saturn* (New York, 1941). Kemble's text has been discussed by Henning Larsen, "Kemble's *Salomon and Saturnus*" in *Modern Philology*, XXVI, 445-450; and there are two articles on details of the poem by Robert J. Menner: "The *Vasa Mortis* Passage in the Old English *Salomon and Saturn*" in the *Klaeber Miscellany* (Minneapolis, 1929), 240-253, and "Nimrod and the Wolf in the Old English *Salomon and Saturn*" in *Journal of English and Germanic Philology*, XXXVII, 332-354.

53. Henry Morley, *English Writers* (London, 1895), vol. I.

54. F. Hammerich, *Älteste christliche Epik der Angelsachsen, Deutschen, und Nordländer* (Berlin, 1874).

55. B. Ten Brink, *Geschichte der englischen Literatur* (Berlin, 1877-1899), I, 112-114.

56. The definitive study of this piece is, however, R. Imelmann, *Das altenglische Menologium* (Berlin, 1902). One of the works to which Imelmann was clearly indebted, nevertheless, is F. Piper, *Die Kalendarien und Martyrologien der Angelsachsen* (Berlin, 1862). The piece has, of course, been printed in Grein and Wülker, *Bibliothek der angelsächsischen Poesie* (see note 52 above).

57. Manuscript Corpus Christi College Cambridge 201. The poem is known also by its Old English title of *Lar* ("Lore") and as "Exhortation to Christian Living." It is printed in Grein and Wülker, *Bibliothek der angelsächsischen Poesie* (see note 52 above), but the best edition and discussion of the work is J. R. Lumby's in his edition of *Be Domes Daege* (see note 16 above).

58. In all printed editions of *The Exeter Book* (see Chapter III, note 9 above); Krapp and Dobbie's edition (New York, 1936) dubs it *Homiletic Fragments II*.

59. Published, with translation and commentary, by E. Thomson in *Godcunde Lar and Theowdom* (London, 1875).

60. See the reference to *Resignation* in note 30 above. The ascription to Cynewulf was made by F. Dietrich in *Disputatio de Cruce Ruthwellensi* (Marburg, 1865), but this view was opposed shortly afterwards by Max Rieger in "Über Cynewulf" in Zacher's *Zeitschrift für deutsche Philologie*, I, 323ff., and virtually every one following Rieger has sided with him against Dietrich.

61. These hymns and others like them have been printed, with discussion, by J. Stevenson in *The Latin Hymns of the Anglo-Saxon Church, with an Interlinear Anglo-Saxon Gloss*, volume 23 of *Surtees Society Publications* (Durham-London, 1851); by E. Thomson in *Godcunde Lar and Theowdom* (London, 1875), 213-225; by J. R. Lumby in his edition of *Be Domes Dæge* (see note 16 above); by Henry Sweet in *An Anglo-Saxon Reader* (Oxford, 1922), 177-188; and as usual in Grein and Wülker, *Bibliothek der angelsächsischen Poesie* (see note 52 above).

62. The prose version is printed and discussed in J. Wright and R. L. Ramsay, *Liber Psalmorum* (Boston, 1907); the poetic version, in B. Thorpe, *Liber Psalmorum* (Oxford, 1835), 129ff.; in Grein and Wülker, *Bibliothek der angelsächsischen Poesie* (see note 52 above); and in G. P. Krapp, *The Paris Psalter and the Metres of Boethius* (New York, 1932). Other good discussions are the following: J. D. Bruce, *The Anglo-Saxon Version of the Book of Psalms* (Baltimore, 1894); H. Bartlett, *The Metrical Division of the Paris Psalter* (Baltimore, 1896); A. S. Cook, *Biblical Quotations in Old English Prose Writers* (New York-London, 1898); and E. Brüning, *Die altenglischen metrischen Psalmen in ihren Verhältnis zur lateinischen Vorlage* (Königsberg, 1921).

63. The comparative neglect of this magnificent little poem can be accounted for only on the ground that its date makes it seem too late for students of Old English literature and perhaps too early for a student of Middle English. It was edited first in J. Conybeare, *Archaeologia*, XVII, 173-175 and by B. Thorpe, *Analecta Anglosaxonica* (London, 1868), 153ff. It was translated by none other than Henry Wadsworth Longfellow. The best modern edition is, however, that by Schröer in *Anglia*, V, 289-290. For a time it was considered a part of the "Soul and Body" material (see note 20 above), for which see F. Kleinert, *Über den Streit zwischen Leib und Seele* (Halle, 1880) and R. Buchholz, "Die Fragmente der Reden der Seele an den Leichnam" in *Erlanger Beiträge*, VI. But the absence of a specific Christian bias in the poem has invalidated this theory. The best study of the poem is, in my opinion, Louise Dudley's article in *Modern Philology*, XI, 429-442.

64. Once the Old English poems discussed in the three preceding chapters (III, IV, and V) have been considered, the following studies will be found extremely helpful: Emile Pons, *La thème et le sentiment de la nature dans la poésie anglo-saxonne* (Oxford, 1925); Bertha S. Philpotts, "Wyrd and Providence in Anglo-Saxon Thought" in *Essays and Studies*, XIII; R. A. Kissack, *The Sea in Anglo-Saxon and Middle English Literature* (St. Louis, 1926); Anne Treneer, *The Sea in English Literature* (Liverpool-London, 1927); H. C. Wyld, "Diction and Imagery in Anglo-Saxon Poetry" in *Essays and Studies*, XI, 49-91; and Aldo Ricci, "The Chronology of Anglo-Saxon Poetry" in *Review of English Studies*, V, 257-266. Indeed, these works might well be read in reference to all Old English literature, poetry as well as prose.

The same is true in even greater degree of C. W. Kennedy, *The Earliest English Poetry* (New York, 1943).

VI · A Note on Old English Literature and the Drama

THE Anglo-Saxon had a strong epic sense and a moderate feeling for the lyric. Inevitably the question will arise as to the expression of his dramatic instincts. Is there any Old English drama? So far as a set dramatic form is concerned, the answer must be in the negative. Nor is there any surviving evidence that the Anglo-Saxon enjoyed any public dramatic presentations. And yet it is possible for the special student of dramatic literature to engage in interesting conjectures. The mimetic instinct is never wholly lacking in the constitution of a whole people, particularly when they are in an unsophisticated, not to say backward or primitive, state of culture. Most folklorists would agree that this mimetic instinct is among the strongest, most basic artistic impulses of mankind. It is also agreed, however, that the strength of the dramatic urge may vary greatly among different peoples; and so, if the Anglo-Saxon was slow to fancy and repressed in emotional utterance, then the absence of an Old English drama would not be remarkable.

In reviewing the field of Old English poetry, where fancy and emotional expression can have freest play, we are struck by the semi-dramatic structure of a few poems. Most remarkable of these is Cynewulf's *Christ* (IV, 4), three sections of which are virtually in dialogue form. And dialogue in narrative verse is a fair enough approximation of poetic drama. Thus, in Section VI of *Christ* (164-213) we have a passage in dialogue between Mary and Joseph, which is direct enough and personal enough to suggest a portion of some play in verse. There are also other lines in the same poem which, while not so lengthy or so obviously dramatic, nevertheless imply drama. For example, in Section III (71-103) comes an invocation to Mary, and Mary replies, after the slight "stage-direction" effect of one line to indicate the speaker. Similarly, in Section XIII (558-585) there is a speech which has some of the characteristics of a dramatic monologue. It seems most unwise, however, to interpret the monologue itself as drama. Whole pieces of Old English poetry could then be represented as dramatic presentation or exhibition. The point is, of course, that we can have the dramatic without the drama, for the drama, in the usual sense of the word, demands the interplay of two or more characters. Such interplay requires at least a dialogue. Of such dialogues, Section VI of *Christ* remains the classic example in Old English poetry. Perhaps one might so consider *The Seafarer*, although, as already noted (V, 1), the viewpoint held at present is that *The Seafarer* has an essential subjective unity. In any event, poems like *The Seafarer* and *The Wanderer* or the lines concerning Satan in *Genesis B* illustrate a dramatic atmosphere which is extremely common in Old English poetry. But to return momentarily to the works which introduce two personages in verbal exchange. The poetic *Salomon and Saturn* is in part a dialogue (V, 8), although expository rather than dramatic in purpose; *Wulf and Eadwacer* (V, 2) also has the potentialities of dialogue, but is primarily, in my opinion, a lyrical utterance.

It is a fundamental fact, of course, that the English drama, like all western European drama, had its origins in religious observance and ritual.[1] Once more we are brought back to the fact that the one poem in Old English literature which comes nearest in form to a play is Cynewulf's *Christ*, a basically religious poem in which, as we shall see in a moment, ritual exercises a most important influence. The first portion of *Christ* is, indeed, a string of religious lyric intermezzi, broken by a scene between Mary and Joseph. The invocation to Mary at the beginning of Section III suggested to Wülker[2] the expression of the inhabitants of Jerusalem in chorus, to whom Mary responds. This by no means fanciful suggestion, however, and other theories as to the dramatic possibilities of

Christ will collapse for lack of support in the literature following Cynewulf.[3]

There, in short, lies the most cogent argument against the idea that the Anglo-Saxons possessed a real drama. If there had been any appreciable amount of true dramatic dialogue-composition in the days of Cynewulf—that is, late in the eighth century or early in the ninth—there should be, granting the influence of Cynewulf upon subsequent Old English literature, some sort of surviving dramatic material from the ninth, tenth, and eleventh centuries. Such pieces either did not exist or else have not survived, more likely the former. In other words, Cynewulf's *Christ* exhibits flashes of dramatic composition more advanced than the liturgical drama or tropes of the beginnings of medieval drama; and yet these specimens stand virtually alone in the whole Anglo-Saxon period. Such a fundamentally negative fact is simply not in harmony with the existence of any true Old English drama.

To put it in another way, one may say that the earliest surviving miracle-plays from the thirteenth century are bound to treat the same religious subject-matter which appears also in the literature of the Old English period. Such a play as *The Harrowing of Hell*, however, which takes its place in the Middle English drama-cycles, has no apparent connection with Old English versions of the same story. In other words, a true dramatic tradition is not discernible. And as in the case of *The Harrowing of Hell*, so with the dozens of other Biblical stories which both the Old English and the Middle English literatures treated frequently. Moreover, the Old English Glosses (see Chapter XIII), which are crude and often highly inaccurate translations of difficult Latin words, show a general ignorance of the meaning of Latin theatrical terms. A favorite word to cover the Latin *ludus, amphitheatri, gymnasio,* and *palestrarum*[4] is the Old English *plega* (Modern English "play"); but this word is applied as well to the wagging of Cerberus's tail and to the dancing of Salome. On one occasion, in Alfred's *Orosius* (VIII, 2), the Latin *theatrum* is carried over bodily into the Old English as *þeatr*, a nonce-word.

Now it is altogether probable that the Anglo-Saxon, like every other untutored, unsophisticated individual, resorted to mimetics; he may have been either skilled or unskilled in pantomime or mummery. Of that there is no record. To judge from the literature which he has left behind him, however, it is difficult to see him as the possessor of any strong dramatic sense or the mimetic artist of vivacity and imagination. There is nothing to show that he professed any knowledge of or curiosity about the Roman theater; even his clergy did not produce such a person as the German nun Hrostvitha of the ninth century,[5] who wrote plays on the model of the comedies of Terence, although without his dangerous worldliness. And yet it is altogether probable that the Church had begun as early as the ninth century to make use of dramatic dialogue in its Easter and Christmas rituals. There is a trope surviving from Winchester Cathedral at the end of the tenth century— the famous *Quem Quaeritis?* Authorities are agreed, however, that the more fully developed mystery-play, as it has survived, was not composed until two or three centuries later. It is possible that the Norman Conquest hastened the appearance of dramatic representation in England; we have evidence of a play in the reign of William II (William Rufus), who died in 1100—a miracle-play in honor of St. Katharine.[6] This seems, however, to have been clearly the exception rather than the rule, for such representations had become fairly common only by 1200. All this, therefore, merely goes to show that one cannot justifiably hold the view that the Anglo-Saxon had a drama, a theater in any conceivable form, or public actors.

Where, then, did Cynewulf or the unnamed author of *Christ* derive this dramatic structure for his poem? Almost entirely from the Roman office for the celebration of Advent, from the greater antiphons sung on the occasion of that holy day. This is to say that he owes much to the dramatic nature of the Church ritual,[7] which obligation underlies our later

English drama. Cynewulf is only making individual use of certain literary devices which in themselves go to make up the medieval theater many centuries after his time. As for *Wulf and Eadwacer*, I reject it as dramatic dialogue; and as for the combination of subjective and dramatic obvious in many of the individual poems in Old English literature— any collection of human utterances written down with the least pretense of conscious art will show that much.[8]

NOTES TO CHAPTER SIX

1. It is obviously out of place to attempt here any full bibliography of the early drama in England. A few titles, however, would be of general interest to the reader of Old English literature as well as Middle English literature. The two best introductions to the whole subject are E. K. Chambers, *The Mediaeval Stage* (Oxford, 1903; 1935) and Karl Young, *The Drama of the Medieval Church* (Oxford, 1933). In Chambers's work the first volume deals particularly with the breakdown of the classical theater and the developments of folk-elements of a dramatic nature; the second volume treats specifically of the medieval drama, and the opening chapters are especially germane to the material of the present work. On the other hand, Young's study devotes much of the first volume to the relationship of the Church ritual to the early drama; his second volume parallels in general the corresponding volume of Chambers. In addition to these two excellent works, there are dozens of writings on the genesis of the English drama, on its historical and topical growth, and on its relation to religion and folklore. Of these the following are likely to be helpful to any student of Old English literature: Allerdyce Nicoll, *British Drama* (London, 1925) and *The Development of the Theatre* (London, 1927)—the first for a survey of the literary type, the second for a study of its practical aspects; Hennig Brinkmann, *Zum Ursprung des liturgischen Spieles* (Bonn, 1929); Oscar Cargill, *Drama and Liturgy* (New York, 1930); Joseph R. Taylor, *The Story of the Drama* (Boston, 1930), particularly Volume I; E. K. Chambers, *The English Folk-Play* (Oxford, 1933), for an amplification of much of the material in the first volume of his *The Mediaeval Stage* mentioned above; Allerdyce Nicoll, *The English Theatre* (London, 1936)—a short and rather technical treatment of dramaturgy; Virgil R. Stallbaumer, "The Easter Trope: the major source of the English

drama" in *Catholic World*, cxxxiv, 652-659; and W. J. Perry, "The Dramatic Element in Ritual" in *Folk Lore*, xxxix, 39-67. For further details and for further references to individual phases of medieval drama, the bibliographies in Chambers and Young are highly recommended.

2. Richard Wülker, *Grundriss zur Geschichte der angelsächsischen Literatur* (Leipzig, 1885), 385.

3. The relation of *Christ* to a potential Old English drama has been exhaustively discussed on several occasions by Albert S. Cook; see his edition of *Christ* (*The Christ of Cynewulf*; Boston, 1900), xxxv-xliii, and "A Remote Analogue to the Miracle Play" in *Journal of English and Germanic Philology*, iv, 421-451, for a more direct presentation. Poems like *The Seafarer* (V, 1 above) or *The Harrowing of Hell* (V, 5 above), as we have seen, certainly contain the germs of drama. But—to anticipate—when we see what happens to the legend of The Harrowing of Hell in a miracle-play of the thirteenth century, let us say, it is not possible to maintain the existence of an Old English drama in any way equivalent to the thirteenth-century version. At least there is no way to demonstrate the presence of a stage, however rough and ready, or of an actual actor, however elementary his art, until after the Norman Conquest.

4. Glosses, as such, will be mentioned briefly later (Chapter XIII). A lengthy list of Latin words bearing upon the drama and their curious Anglo-Saxon equivalents is given in R. Wülker, *Grundriss zur Geschichte der angelsächsischen Literatur* (Leipzig, 1885), 386.

5. The best edition of Hrostvitha's plays is that of Helene Homeyer, *Hrostvit: Werke* (Paderborn, 1936). There is an English translation of Hrostvitha by Christopher St. John, *The Plays of Roswitha* (London, 1923). Two critical and biographical essays are to be found in Evangeline W. Blashfield, *Portraits and Backgrounds* (New York, 1917) and Alice Kemp-Welch, *Of Six Mediaeval Women* (London, 1913). For the particular relationship of Hrostvitha to classical literary tradition, see J. Abbick, "Roswitha and Terence" in *Classical Bulletin*, xxiii, 31-32.

6. See Chambers (note 1 above), ii, 64.

7. See Young (note 1 above), i, 79-111. In reference to this, mention should be made once more of Edward Burgert, *The Dependence of Part I of Cynewulf's Christ upon the Antiphonary* (Washington, 1921).

8. For the *Wulf and Eadwacer* matter and its implications as drama, see Chapter V, note 10 above.

VII · Anglo-Latin Literature in the Old English Period

1. GILDAS AND NENNIUS

Any account of Old English poetry in its fullest aspects must in the long run end upon the theme of the churchman dominant. In all fairness to the cleric, however, it must be emphasized that he was interested in the older poetry of the *scop*—had he not been so, much less Anglo-Saxon poetry would have survived than did survive, perhaps none in the older tradition. No doubt the Saxon in the Church at that time carried some of the bardic literature into his private life, and he must have enjoyed some of it for its own sake. We have seen that he composed poetry in the manner of the *scop*—poetry which he ably turned to his own Christian uses. It is therefore just as well to concede that none of the important collections of Old English poetry[1] would be in existence today had it not been for the churchman.

The priest, however, was by profession a preacher and a teacher, and to preach and teach he would turn most frequently to the medium of the intellect, prose. If he has exerted influence on all surviving Old English poetry, the same thing is true to an even greater extent of Old English prose. In fact, all the important prose of the Old English period before the days of King Alfred the Great (849-901) is prose written in Latin by princes and servants of the Church. All these writers conceived of the vernacular as barbaric and ephemeral, and not until a true king of the people made his entrance upon the scene was there to be any attention to the writing of prose in English. As a consequence of this attitude of the early churchman and also of the historical fact of Alfred's existence, it is most convenient to consider Old English prose first under the general head of Anglo-Latin literature in the Old English period, for Anglo-Latin poetry at this time is entirely ancillary to the prose writings. There may have been copious composition by the two great Irish missionaries of northern Britain before the coming of Augustine in 597, namely St. Columba (521-597)[2] and Bishop Aidan (IV, 1).[3] But if so, this writing has not survived. All that is known about these pioneers in religious education in Britain has been derived from the words of later writers like Bede and Aelfric. The first considerable writer, in point of time, to transmit his work to posterity was Gildas (ca. 500-570). Little is known of his life beyond a few chance facts dropped into the pages of his writings. Two lives of Gildas from the eleventh and twelfth centuries are rather confused and basically unreliable.[4] The very place of his birth is unknown, although one may well believe that he was a Welshman. There is little doubt that he was a cleric; he tells us that he was inspired to write in zeal for the sake of God's house and holy law, and he scatters Biblical quotations and allusions throughout his writing. It seems that he went to France in his thirties and there wrote the chronicle which bears his name. His death, probably in Brittany, is given in the *Cambrian Annals*[5] as having taken place in 570.

Gildas's work, usually known simply as *The Book of Gildas*, bears a variety of titles in subsequent references,[6] but it is commonly called *Gildae Sapientis de Excidio Britanniae Liber Querulus.*[6, 7] Another work, of which he is probably no more than the putative author, the *Lorica*, will be mentioned among the miscellaneous "scientific" works in a later chapter.[8] *The Book of Gildas* is in three parts. A preface explains the mental struggles which Gildas underwent in the preparation of his work and tells of his Christian submissiveness. It foreshadows the misgivings which he feels about the state of Britain and its hopeless future. Then follows a history, recounting the events in Britain from the invasion of the Romans until Gildas's own time; necessarily, as a devout churchman, he must consider certain other events of importance in the general history of the Christian world. Thus he discusses in particular the introduction of Christianity to Britain in the days of the Roman emperors (which must have concerned the Irish for the greater part), the spread of this Christianity and also the Arian heresy,[9] the invasions of the Picts and Scots, the decline of Roman power in Britain and the abandonment of the island by the Romans, and finally the Anglo-Saxon invasions. Most interesting is his brief sketch of the career of Ambrosius Aurelianus, a great leader of the Romano-Britains against the Saxons and a possible prototype of King Arthur.[10] He brings to a close this historical portion of his work with a masterpiece of sustained anticlimax, for the issue of the conflict between Britons and Saxons was still unsettled in his own day, although from the standpoint of a Celtic Briton he might indeed fear the worst. As a matter of fact, the historical portion of his work is relatively brief and irritatingly vague. Gildas is almost never specific in his statements and shows a tendency to wander, on the least excuse, into abstract reflection.

The final part of his work, much the longest of the three, is an epistle full of gloomy thoughts on the parlous state of Britain, a land for which Gildas sees no faint ray of hope, for he has been left alone "as a withering tree in the midst of a field." A series of jeremiads addressed to the British kings of his day is followed by discourses upon kings of the Old Testament—a few good ones, such as Samuel, but mostly bad ones, such as Jeroboam and Baasha. The figures of the major prophets, such as Isaiah and Jeremiah, and of a great potentate, such as Solomon the Wise, appear in procession and inveigh against the depravity of the clergy in Britain and the simony of the ecclesiastical officials. From the Gospels and the Pauline Epistles he draws further warnings, examples, and strict homiletics.

Viewed as a piece of historiography, *The Book of Gildas* has some degree of value, since it is the only piece of its kind written in England during the sixth century—so far as we know; but it is singularly unsatisfactory history-writing— somber, vague, and grossly biased in the direction of national and spiritual pessimism and despondency. Yet Gildas was for his day a learned man. He knew three important chroniclers before him—Eusebius, Jerome, and Orosius—and he seems to show at times a knowledge of Virgil. As for his influence on others, Bede unquestionably knew him, and after Bede writers like Nennius and even perhaps Alfred.[11]

Another work the value of which is historical rather than intrinsic is the *Historia Britonum*.[12] The opening sentence of its prologue states that Nennius, a disciple of St. Elbotus (Elbodugus or Elvod, a bishop of Bangor, who died in 809), put together the ensuing "ears of grain," having gleaned them from various sources. The date is given as 858, the twenty-fourth year of King Mervin of the Britons. That, however, would be the year 896 of the Christian Era. The fact is that this prologue, and a short apologia which follows, must strike the expert as composed in a Latin far superior to the very poor brand of Latin which serves for the History itself. It is probable that Nennius speaks the truth; he did not in all likelihood write the History but rather the prologue and the apologia only.

The ultimate author of the *Historia Britonum*, then, remains unknown, but he was obviously a Briton, probably of the latter half of the seventh century, since his chronicle does not go past that time. The material of the History is extremely heterogeneous in nature and was most likely gathered from several sources and possibly by several scholars. Nennius mentions in the apologia Jerome, Eusebius, Isidorus, Prosper, and the annals of the Scots and the Saxons as having contributed to the History. In addition, we should undoubtedly take into account a powerful influence of the Bible, more particularly of the chronicles of the Old Testament, and a moderate obligation to Virgil and to Julius Caesar. After all these considerations have been weighed, the thoughtful reader will be inclined to agree that Nennius is merely the redactor who, as he says, is making a compilation and rescension of several fragments of historical matter. The date of Elbodugus's death (809) makes a date of 858, to say nothing of 896, wholly improbable for Nennius; he belongs not far from 800.

When one reads the bald, sibyllic pages of the *Historia Britonum*, one recognizes that only a flagrant example of what Matthew Arnold called the "historical estimate" could ever credit Nennius with ability either as an historian or as an editor of historical materials. The work sketches rapidly the generations and years from Adam through the Roman emperors, the list of whom is very much telescoped; next comes a catalogue of the important settlements in Britain; after that some description of the geography and topography of the island; finally we are launched into an account of the descendant of Aeneas, one Brutus, who ruled over Britain "at the time Eli the high-priest judged Israel."[13] Long rows of genealogy obtrude themselves, and then the reader comes suddenly upon the story of the Roman invasions of Britain, and after that the coming of the Saxons. The tale of the ill-fated Vortigern and his foolish relations with Hengest and Horsa (I, 3) is told with some detail, and is probably the best part of the whole work. The finding of the boy Ambrose, the "lad without a father," is interesting in the light of the later legends about King Arthur. And here Arthur himself makes briefly his first entrance into the pages of written literature:

> The magnanimous Arthur . . . [*dux bellorum*] fought against the Saxons. And though there were many more noble than himself, yet he was twelve times chosen to be their commander, and was as often conqueror.[14]

The account of the twelve battles follows; the last is the celebrated battle of Mount Badon. The figure of Arthur then disappears; in his place we meet Saint Patrick. After that genealogies of the royal houses of Bernicia, Kent, East Anglia, Mercia, and Deira allow the work to trickle out in the sandy desert of forgotten kings.

Undoubtedly the greatest single stimulus to the Anglo-Latin writings in the Old English period was the coming of Theodore of Tarsus, who was made Archbishop of Canterbury in 668, and of his able assistant, Abbot Hadrian.[15] These two men were in their day the most influential churchmen in

England. They were well equipped for teaching because their intellectual background was rich: not only were they possessed of the churchman's usual fluency in Latin, but they knew Greek also. Although there is nothing surviving from the pens of these two, their presences were felt in the increase of writing which will be noted almost immediately after their arrival in Canterbury. The arts of bookmaking and of illumination were fostered together[16]—from this late seventh century come the *Gregorian Gospels* (in Manuscript Corpus Christi College Cambridge 286); the *Graeco-Latin Acts of the Apostles* (in Manuscript Laud 35), a remarkable curiosity; the beautiful *Lindisfarne Gospels*[17] of Northumbria, with their Anglo-Saxon interlinear glosses to the Latin text so precious to the student of the tenth century Northumbrian dialect; and the *Codex Amiatinus* of the Latin Bible, originally done at Wearmouth and Jarrow about 700, but now preserved in Florence, Italy. Of this little group, the *Lindisfarne Gospels*, for the reason just mentioned, is the most important member; it remains, along with the *Rushworth Gospels* of the next century,[18] invaluable to the linguistic expert. More than that, it is a superb specimen of the scribe's art.

2. ALDHELM AND HIS GROUP

WITH this potentially wealthy intellectual foundation, it is scarcely remarkable that the Church in England during the later seventh and early eighth century should have produced at least two noteworthy writers. The first of these chronologically was Aldhelm; the second, the Venerable Bede. Of these two, Bede is beyond cavil the greater. He is, in fact, one of the four significant prose writers in England before the Norman Conquest and far above the other Anglo-Latin writers of the period.

Aldhelm (ca. 640-709),[19] however, cannot be ignored. We know about him only a few meager details. He was somehow related to King Ina of Wessex, who reigned until 726. He was educated by Irish clerics and traveled in France and Italy. It appears also that he studied under Abbot Hadrian at Canterbury; if this is true, he received what must have been the best training of the time in scientific knowledge. Having settled in England, he rose in the Church and became famous for his learning. A Scottish prince sent some of his works to Aldhelm, begging that the wise man "give them the last polish by rubbing off their Scottish rust." Ultimately he became Bishop of Sherborne and died in 709.

Aldhelm's position is that of the first English writer to compose in Latin both prose and verse which have survived, and of all the writers considered in this chapter his talent in verse was the most pronounced. He seems to have been an almost popular song-writer. Some two hundred years after his death King Alfred had for his favorite song a piece by Aldhelm. This aspect of his work, unfortunately, has not lived to undergo our scrutiny. But he was a tireless worker in the Church; and the presence of his *Riddles*, at least, suggests that his were very broad interests. It is perhaps unnecessary to dwell for long on his individual works—some of them need not even be mentioned by name. Several, however, call for special attention.

It is not possible, in this case, to follow a strict chronological order. There is, for example, a series of letters by Aldhelm to colleagues and students, at least three of which[20] are well worth the effort of reading his resonant though often turgid and unlicensed Latin. The first of these is to Geraint, a Welsh king, in which Aldhelm complains of the lack of harmony between Welsh and English churchmen, of their lack of uniformity in such matters as tonsure or the fixing of the date of Easter, the latter a burning question in Aldhelm's day and for at least a century later. The most elaborate letter is an epistle to Eahfrid, presumably a student who has just returned from Ireland. Aldhelm speaks of his training and how much better it could have been accomplished in England; and, as if to benumb and bedazzle the unfortunate Eahfrid and thereby to make him regret his choice of academic pastures, Aldhelm turns to pyrotechnics of style and vocabulary, committing excessive alliteration and dragging in Greek, Latin, and Hebrew words out of sheer scholastic gasconade. No other work of his will show better his brilliant, rhapsodic, and fundamentally Celtic tendencies of mind; nor does any other work exhibit so well the essential scholarship of the man and the degree to which he took to heart the lessons of Hadrian or possibly of Theodore of Tarsus himself. A third epistle of great value is that addressed to Hedda, Bishop of Winchester, for the letter is autobiographical, giving many details of Aldhelm's schooling and priestly training and more than one glimpse of the academic life of the time, as no other piece of contemporaneous writing can do it.

Enough of the letters, however—when all is said and done, Aldhelm, who founded the abbey at Malmesbury, Wiltshire, was first and last a worker in the vineyard of the Lord. As a good example of his homiletics, consider his prose treatise on virginity.[21] This thoroughly medieval document is addressed to a school of nuns. It begins with an account of various men and women of the scriptures or of hagiology who were notable exemplars of chastity—Elijah, Jeremiah, Daniel, John the Baptist, and Paul among the men of the Bible (there are many other names, of course); Clement, Ambrose, Martin, and Felix among the Church Fathers; the Virgin Mary, Cecilia, Lucia, Agnes, and Eulalia, to name but a few canonized virgins. The discourse ensuing is remarkable not so much for subject-matter, which is indeed highly conventional, as for style. It is florid and rotund, so that Aldhelm often becomes a kind of Swinburne among Old English writers of prose; in the interests of his oratorical and rhetorical effects, he wages a stern war on sense as well as sound.

Next, to illustrate the literary versatility of Aldhelm, one should look at a metrical version of the treatise on virginity.[22] The arrangement of this poem is not unlike that of the prose treatise, but the style is even more elaborate. Some of the examples of the prose version are omitted and new ones are added; a section is subjoined at the end, describing the eight principal vices and concluding with an exhortation to prayer and a deprecation of slander or unfavorable criticism. The form, especially of the beginning, is nevertheless arresting, because the poem opens with a double acrostic. The initial letters of the lines form a complete hexameter verse; the final letters of the same lines give that verse in reverse, so that the hexameter can be read twice—once downward in the initial letters and once upward in the final letters.

The work by Aldhelm, however, which will probably challenge the interest of the average reader most consistently is a miscellany in prose.[23] This opens with a discussion of the number seven, in a manner which is reminiscent of the famous discussion of the quincunx by Sir Thomas Browne about a thousand years later. Then follows an explanation of verse-meters in general and of the hexameter in particular, with plentiful illustrations drawn from an astonishing array of writers in Latin. Here Aldhelm's reading is evident in a most impressive form. Among the classical writers represented are Virgil, Ovid, Lucan, and the prose writers Cicero, Pliny, and Sallust. Horace, Juvenal, and Persius, however, are apparently unknown to Aldhelm. He none the less compensates partly for these deficiencies by furnishing an endless list of Christian Latin poets none of whom, with the possible exception of Cyprianus, is remembered today. Another group of authorities is Spanish. The list closes with Lactantius (IV, 5) and the ubiquitous Orosius.

The treatise itself is for the greater part an intellectual curiosity and little else, although one must pay tribute to the industry and, for his time, the catholicity of the author's reading. In the midst of this treatise, however, come the *Riddles*, much the most attractive of Aldhelm's surviving writings. The position of these *Riddles*, in relation to the noted collection of *The Exeter Book*, has already been touched upon (V, 4). Suffice to say here that the collection is probably the best of those which were written in Latin during this period. Unlike his obvious model, Symphosius, Aldhelm is most capricious as regards length of stanza; and, as Tupper has observed,[24] his achievement is more romantic and often less effective, for the epigrammatic quality of the riddle, as a riddle, is lost if the stanza is too long. Essentially, however, Aldhelm's *Riddles* are not so much exercises of wit as they are somewhat mystical observations of nature—mystical, in that they clothe all nature with the glory of God's kingdom. But even to those unsympathetic toward mysticism, Aldhelm's *Riddles* are very fair examples of his Latin verse and of his highly-seasoned metrical devices: alliteration (a tendency which is markedly Germanic rather than Latin), internal rime, and a straining after synonyms. As we have seen, these devices are also highly characteristic of the Old English *scop's* tradition. Certain parallels, in fact, have been pointed out[25] between the Aldhelm style and the style of *Beowulf*, parallels which raise interesting though probably insoluble problems concerning the relation of this ecclesiastical and scholastic Latin prosody to the Old English bard's system of composition.

Aldheim's *Riddles* are prefaced by a prologue of thirty-six lines, which contain the same metrical devices as the prologue to the verse treatise on virginity—the acrostic. Here the initial and the final letters of each verse are identical, and the acrostic spells out in parallel columns—as one reads downward—the Latin verse "Aldhelmus cecinit millenis versibus odas." There are scarcely a thousand lines in the collection, but the approximately eight hundred perhaps come near enough. There is no reason to suppose that any are missing.

We have no opportunity here to individualize each of these hundred *Riddles*. As their author heads them, they are composed "about various created things" (*ex diversis rerum creaturis composita*). An enumeration of their topics would repeat most of what has already been said about the *Riddles* of *The Exeter Book*. Picking at random through the list, one finds descriptions of such widely different things as clouds, the Pleiades, organs, ant-lions, balances, minotaurs, lions, writing-tablets, night-ravens, leeches, swallows, milfoils, double-boilers, eagles, unicorns, doves, mills, yews, springs of water, hornets, wine-casks, morning stars, steers, shields, palms, dwarf elders, elephants, camels, and a concluding poem of great

nobility on Nature. There is no apparent system in this bewildering catalogue, but in that lack of system lies much of the
attractive quality of the whole collection. Three or four sam-
ples are in order.[26]

ALPHABET

We seventeen sisters, voiceless all, declare
Six others bastards are, and not of us.
Of iron we are born, and find our death
Again by iron; or at times we come
From pinion of a lofty-flying bird.
Three brothers got us of an unknown mother
To him who thirsts for instant counsel, we
In silence quickly bring out hoarded words.

This riddle is useful for the academic information it yields—
six letters, according to Aldhelm's immediate source for this
piece, Isidore of Seville's *Origines*,[27] are not native: *h*, *k*, *q*,
x, *y*, *z*. It should be remembered that *w* is not Latin: *u* is *v*, and
j is *i*. The "three brothers" are the thumb, forefinger, and
middle finger, which hold the pen from the "pinion of a lofty-
flying bird." Again,

UNICORN

Though on the lofty hills the hunter urge
His vainly barking dogs with empty din,
And speed his iron shafts, I fear no risk
Of savage Mars, but trusting in my might,
I boldly set upon tall elephants
And fell them, wounded sore. Yet cruel Fate,
Alas, has tricked me slyly; I who slay
The mighty, by an unarmed girl am caught;
For a fair maiden, laying bare her breast,
May take me, doing as she will with me,
And to her high-built city lead me back.
My horn has given me my name in Greek;
Thus, too, the Latins call me in their tongue.

This would be familiar to those who know the old legend
about the unicorn, as told by Pliny in his *Natural History* and

transmitted through the medieval French version of the
Physiologus, or *Bestiary*.[28] For a third illustration, consider

WOMAN IN LABOR WITH TWINS

Six eyes are mine; as many ears have I;
Fingers and toes twice thirty do I bear.
Of these, when forty from my flesh are torn,
Lo, then but twenty will remain to me.

But few have the bareness and simplicity of this last-quoted
riddle. The final Praise of Nature is too long to give here in
its entirety, but the concluding lines (80-96) are characteristic:

..... Thus does my wisdom far surpass the lore
Of wise philosophers; yet was I taught
By no rich-lettered books, nor ever learned
The rhyme and reason of a syllable.
Drier than summer blazing from the sun,
Yet am I dripping dew, more wet than brooks
That rise from welling springs; and far more salt
Than the broad bosom of the heaving sea,
But fresher than cool inland streams I flow,
Adorned with all the lovely varied hues
That beautify the structure of this world,
Yet am I robbed of all fair coloring.
  Hear and believe my words, scarce to be cleared
By any schoolman skilled in speech; and yet
That reader who denies them, at the end
Will think them far from trifling! Now I ask
Puffed-up philosophers what name I bear.

It would be much easier to get a fair perspective on Aldhelm if the many songs which, according to William of
Malmesbury,[29] he wrote in the vernacular had only survived.
Alfred regarded him as the greatest English poet. His interest
in music is obviously authentic, to judge by his letter to Bishop
Hedda;[30] and the picture of him standing by a bridge-head,
making songs to the harp, in the manner of a gleeman, is not
inconceivable in reality. No vestige of his work in the vernac-

ular remains, however, and his great reputation is now based entirely upon hearsay.

But even if it is impossible to appraise Aldhelm as a poet except upon the rather uncertain basis of his Latin verse, the fact must be granted that he left behind him an influence which was instrumental in the shaping of later poetry. There is a sort of Aldhelmian school of Latin verse, just as there is a Cynewulfian school of verse in the vernacular. A group of five little poems[31] in Latin will serve to illustrate. The first, possibly addressed to Aldhelm, was written by some cleric at Malmesbury and describes a storm in June which blew the roof off a dormitory. The second, by one Aethelwald, otherwise unknown, describes a visit to Rome, one of the few compositions left us on what must have been a common experience among Old English churchmen. The third is a short prayer. The fourth is a poem in praise of Aldhelm. The fifth is considered to be Aldhelm's reply, but it need not have been written by him.

Three individuals, of much more exalted station than the obscure Aethelwald, subscribe to the Aldhelm tradition. Tatwine, Archbishop of Canterbury, who died in 734, has already been mentioned (V, 4) as a writer of riddles; he continues in particular Aldhelm's writing of acrostics into the body of the riddles—the initial letters and final letters of each line are eventually resolved into a hexameter line. Abbot Eusebius, who officiated at Wearmouth after the year 716, also wrote a collection of riddles which is merely subsidiary to Tatwine's. Saint Boniface (680-735), the effective missionary, whose Christian activities in Germany were crucial in the conversion of that region, was born an Anglo-Saxon and followed the learning of the England of his time. Besides indulging in an extensive correspondence, he left an acrostic in verse, a series of riddles or enigmas on the Virtues and the Vices, which he wrote in Aldhelmian hexameters.

With the exception of Eusebius, about whom there is at best some uncertainty,[32] the writers of the Aldhelmian school belong to the south and the west—in general to Wessex. It remains to consider the fruit of learning in the north of England. One fact is important in such a consideration: the see of Canterbury, largely because of the training and background of its first great occupant, Theodore of Tarsus, was given perhaps more than the see of York to the Christianity of Alexandria and the Levant rather than to the Christianity of Rome. Naturally there were no fundamental schisms in Britain; but the Oriental color of some writer like Aldhelm is in sharp contrast to the simple occidentalism of Bede, and what is true of the respective protagonists of the south and north is true in general of the two schools which they represent.

3. BEDE

THE life of Bede[33] evidently fell into smooth and placid ways. He was born near Durham in 673; his parents died soon thereafter, and he was brought up by Benedict, a Northumbrian earl turned churchman, one of the most enlightened men of an intellectually vital region. Benedict was a builder, both of churches and of learning; he imported skilled architects and artisans and workers in glass. He knew Latin and probably Greek and satisfied his bibliophiliac tendencies by gathering for himself a comparatively large library.

It is not surprising, then, that Bede should have developed as he did. His first training came at Benedict's monastery at Wearmouth; then, in 682, the monastery at Jarrow being completed, Bede moved there and, like Goethe at Weimar, stayed there the rest of his life. Jarrow, his congenial home, became also his world.

Bede seems to have worked assiduously and unobtrusively at all the business demanded of him by the Benedictine Rule. Since this life imposed upon him no necessity for haste, he studied quietly all the learning of his day. He became so thoroughly recognized as a scholar that Dante, writing six centuries later, placed him in the Region of the Sun.[34] Moreover, his scholarship was of a liberal cast, for it included not only the usual fields of theological and linguistic training expected of any clerical scholar but also the natural sciences, mathematics, medicine, history, and poetry. Bede appears to have assimilated this diverse knowledge with a true love of learning for its own sake, but he was also sufficiently human to be sympathetic even with those whose ideas clashed with his own. Perhaps it is enough to say that he was tolerant in an age not noted for tolerance. His great predecessor Aidan entertained what Bede considered heretical notions about the dating of Easter, yet Bede respected him; even a true enemy, such as Bishop Wilfrith, emerges in the *Ecclesiastical History* as an agent of good. Nothing could shake his implicit faith in the teachings of his Church; his mind was a strange blend of the scholiast's, the knowledge-seeker's, and the human being's.

Most of Bede's writings have to do with the interpretation of the Scriptures. Some of them are allegorical. There are also many works, however, on a wide variety of subjects, as will appear shortly, and a series of saints' lives, miscellaneous biographies of worthies and church dignitaries, culminating in his chief work, *The Ecclesiastical History of the English Nation*,[35] which became a model for subsequent chroniclers and early historians. For Bede exerted influence not only as a writer but also as a teacher of able disciples. Thus one of his students, Ecgbert, was instrumental in making York a center of learning. From York went forth such men as Alcuin (VII, 4) to revive learning under Charlemagne in France, whence the plant which became a Renaissance tree.

In considering the various works of Bede, one will find Plummer's chronology most convenient.[36] There is no possibility, however, of fixing a Bede Canon with any great assurance, although we happen to be unusually privileged to hear so much about an important author of those times from his own words. His writings began shortly after his eighteenth birthday and continued steadily until his death. To the 690's we may refer his tracts *On Metrics, On Orthography, On the Tropes of the Scriptures*.[37] The first of these, *On Metrics*, opens with a discussion of the alphabet, in which Bede's acquaintanceship with Greek is at once made probable; next comes a definition of the syllable; then a discussion of the importance in verse of the syllable. Following this are descriptions and definitions of the important metrical feet in general and of the dactyl in particular; then a summary of common classical metrical forms—the sapphic, the anacreontic, and others—in which summary the stanzaic forms are confused with the forms of the individual line. Finally there is a brief enumeration of the common types of poetry. On the whole, nothing in this work is noteworthy. *On Orthography* is another account of the alphabet, with a plethora of illustrations, most of which possess a strong churchly flavor. *On the Tropes of the Scriptures* has for its main thesis the idea that all authority for the Scriptures is divine, "both for useful purposes, since they lead to eternal life, and for veneration." It contains a brief definition of the various tropes, which appear in rather an astonishing number, and then a series of examples. It is no accident that the section on allegory should bulk the largest in the treatise.

De Temporibus,[38] written about Bede's thirtieth year, is sufficiently comprehended from the first sentence of the opening section: "Time is divided into moments, hours, days, months, years, centuries, and ages." The current astronomical information, which was evidently Bede's in amplitude, is then poured forth, carefully organized in approved scholarly fashion. The perennial question of the dating of Easter raises up its head. Was not this controversy, apart from its obvious implications of dogma, fascinating also in this period largely because it gave men an opportunity to apply their mathematical and scientific instincts to their religious beliefs? The sections on the ages of the world in *De Temporibus* resolve themselves into catalogues of chronology, derived from Isidore of Seville's *Origines*, and are worthless as literature. Some twenty years later (about 725) Bede expanded this tract into the more ambitious and scholarly *De Tempora Ratione*.[39] This work opens with a review of the methods of counting. What follows is, as just remarked, an elaboration of Bede's earlier treatise: days and nights, days of the week and their origins, months—

both Roman and Greek (*sic*), as well as the English, which reminds one of the *Menologium* (V, 8)—the signs of the zodiac, the phases of the moon and its motions, "the harmony of moon and sea," the equinoxes and solstices, a sketch of contemporary geography, and the most definite arguments hitherto observed in English literature for the fixing of Easter, followed by a very extensive account of the ages of the world, with a great deal of historical fact included. All this goes to form the soundest work on astronomy and geography which Britain was to produce for centuries.

Since *De Tempora Ratione* has been described, it is appropriate to point out at this time that it has a companion-piece which serves to round out the conception of Bede as a kind of pioneer Encyclopedist. His *De Natura Rerum*[40] belongs also to a date near 725. It is a shorter and more objective composition than *De Tempora Ratione* and is indebted as much to Pliny as to Isidore of Seville. "The divine Operation, which created and governs the universe" is the theme of the discussion—that, and the way in which the Operation manifests itself to mankind. The formation of the world; what the world is; the elements; the heavens; the stars and planets and their courses; comets, eclipses, and clouds; thunder, lightning, and the rainbow; the oceans of the world—these are the topics which Bede treats in short sections. Only one earthly phenomenon, pestilence, does he try to explain in terms of his science; it arises, he says, in the air from dryness or from heat or from excess of rains[41] and descends upon man, who acquires it by breathing or eating. It is obvious from these works that Bede's scientific interests and information are chiefly astronomical and meteorological. There is also extant, however, a treatise on phlebotomy[42] ascribed to Bede, which shows him to be at least conversant with the medical knowledge of his day. By and large, of course, Bede's scientific knowledge is not at all original. But, as Plummer observes,[43] he has performed at least one great service through his interest in "time": he consistently dates from the birth of Christ and so aids greatly in establishing a reliable plan of historical chronology.

Shortly after the earlier *De Temporibus* (ca. 703), Bede wrote a metrical *Life of Saint Cuthbert*,[44] the subject being the seventh century saint, successor to Aidan, hermit of Holy Island and later Bishop of Lindisfarne (IV, 1). As a saint's life this piece is perhaps overshadowed by the similar prose work of Aelfric (IX, 2), for Bede is not at his best in verse; his mind does not seem to have the ability to cast itself in the required florid expression. All the main incidents in the biography are there, however—the exhortation of the Blessed Infant who turned Cuthbert to a life of holiness; Cuthbert's prayers on the beach; his vision of Aidan's death; the sign of the two seals on the beach; the adventure of the eagle; the miracle of the burning house; the prophecy concerning King Edfrith; various healing incidents and recallings of the dead to life; Cuthbert's friendship with Herbert and Elfled; his elevation to the episcopal see; and his return to a hermitage, followed shortly by his death. At the end of the work comes the accepted prayer for Cuthbert. In short, the piece is a typical medieval saint's life, the didactic purpose of which speaks for itself.

To the fourth decade of Bede's life belong his many epistles and Biblical commentaries. The epistles are addressed for the most part to Bishop Acca[45] and are frequently further expositions of the Gospels, or of the Temple of Solomon, or of the first chapter of *Genesis*. Specifically, the Biblical commentaries are brief essays expounding the books of *Revelation*, *Acts*, the Pauline Epistles, *Luke*, and the two books of *Samuel*. These pieces are a part of the church history of the period and are valuable otherwise only for the light they shed upon the intense earnestness and devotional steadfastness of their author.

The Lives of the Holy Abbots,[46] a brief chronicle of the lives of the five abbots of the monasteries of Wearmouth and Jarrow, appears to have occupied Bede during the years from 716 to 720. This has, on a small scale, all the virtues of his more famous *Ecclesiastical History*. It is from this account that we have virtually all our information about Benedict, Bede's spiritual and intellectual mentor. Easterwine, the second of the abbots, stands out as a model ascetic churchman; the account of his death parallels closely the fuller account of the passing of Caedmon in the *Ecclesiastical History*. The departure of the abbot Ceolfrid, old and weak, on his pilgrimage to Rome, is a colorful and moving incident. Having completed *The Lives of the Abbots*, Bede composed his prose *Life of St. Cuthbert*,[47] longer and more detailed than his poetic version, and a *Life of St. Felix*, as well as a calendar of the saints, with biographical notes on their natal days. At about the same time he finished his commentaries on the books of *Ezra* and *Nehemiah*.

It remained for Bede, however, to reserve his most important work for his last years. His *Ecclesiastical History of the English Nation* (*Historia Ecclesiastica Gentis Anglorum*) was completed, according to the author's own statement, in 731. It begins with a brief description of the British Isles and proceeds forthwith to the first visit to Britain of Julius Caesar and the subsequent Romanization of the island under Claudius and his successors. The story has already been outlined and is thoroughly familiar. As for the *Ecclesiastical History* as a whole, it has been most carefully compiled and is written with Bede's characteristic transparent simplicity; it is, therefore, unquestionably the most important historical writing composed in England before the Norman Conquest, and it is doubtful whether the many histories and chronicles written in England during the Middle English period can in any way surpass it. Probably it is the best history written by an Englishman before the seventeenth century. Moreover, it happens that the *Ecclesiastical History*, although generally the only piece of contemporary historiography that is anywhere near trustworthy in its chief statements, has an inherent value intangible but appreciable. Many of its passages are notably eloquent; many, indeed, achieve a true poetic eminence. From the first dim beginnings of Christianity in Britain under the Romans, and the martyrdom of St. Alban, to the installation of Theodore of Tarsus as Archbishop of Canterbury in 668, the narrative of the *Ecclesiastical History* runs a smooth-flow-ing course, almost entirely, it is true, in religious channels. For Bede is careful to define the limits of his work in its title. We can do no more here than point the finger at certain portions of this imposing book. Probably the most notable pages in it are those which treat of the introduction of Christianity by the Roman missions of Augustine and Paulinus. Of almost equal power, from the viewpoint of the present-day reader, is the account of the Anglo-Saxon conquest, which Bede does not recognize until the advent of Christianity has become a fact. Imbedded in the work are several occasional biographical sketches of prominent churchmen—Aidan, Gregory the Great, the Abbess Hild. Notable also is the story of the heavenly vision of the householder of Cunningham, Drihthelm, for it is the only example in Old English literature outside the quasi-scriptural account of the *Harrowing of Hell* (V, 5), of the classical journey to the other world.

> Radiant in face and look and in bright apparel was he who guided me. . . . We arrived at a valley of great breadth and depth, and of infinite length. . . . One part was very dreadful, being full of boiling flames; the other not less intolerable through the chill of hail and snow. Both were full of men's souls, which seemed to be cast to either side in turn, as though by the overpowering violence of a great storm. When they could not endure the force of the excessive heat, they sprang away in their misery into the midst of excessive cold; and when they could find no rest there, they sprang back into the midst of the burning fire and the unquenchable flame.[48]

This, and more, the assiduous reader will recognize as an essential part of that great body of medieval vision-literature which a supreme poet, nearly six centuries after Bede, was to turn into one of the ultimate expressions of medieval literary art. The relationship between Dante and Bede has already been hinted at. Further consideration of Bede's *Ecclesiastical History* may well be postponed until the discussion of the Alfredian translation of that work into the English language (VIII, 2). It is only fitting to observe at this point, however, that the placid ghost of Bede stands beside all the Latin

chroniclers of the Anglo-Norman period, such as William of
Malmesbury, Henry of Huntingdon, and even Geoffrey of
Monmouth, *romancier* that the last-named happens to be. For
that matter, there is much of the religious fictionist in Bede,
for all his sober historiography.

Between the time of the completion of the *Ecclesiastical
History* and Bede's death in 735, there are only a few rather
minor works which can safely be attributed to the churchman
of Jarrow. It is possible that the martyrological calendar already referred to should be placed within these last four
years.[49] Certainly a poetic martyrology of much greater brevity[50] belongs here. So do the *Hymns*,[51] a series of fourteen
metrical compositions. The topics of these poems may be listed
as follows: (1) the order of the seasons; (2) the celebration
of the four seasons; (3) the various rules for computing the
seasons; (4) the works of the God of the Universe; (5) the
feasts of the Innocents; (6) the ascension of the Saviour; (7)
the birthday of Saint Agnes; (8) the birth of Saint John the
Baptist; (9) the apostles Peter and Paul; (10) the passion of
Saint John the Baptist; (11) the birthday of the holy Mother
of Christ; (12) the birthday of Saint Andrew; (13) a hymn
spoken to the cross of Saint Andrew on his feast-day; (14)
Judgment Day. The first three of these hymns are in hexameters; those from 4 to 13 are in trimeters; the last one is
hexametrical.

Probably to the last period of Bede's life belongs also the
little *Retraction to the Acts of the Apostles*.[52] It is clear that
virtually all writers of medieval Christendom were wont to
close their works with prayer or to demand forgiveness for the
shortcomings both of their works and of themselves. No doubt
the convention—and it becomes a well-established convention,
as the poems of Chaucer, Dante, and even Spenser bear witness
—originated in a sincere humility; and it is presumptuous to
suppose that Bede the naïve would undertake a specious "retraction" merely as a concession to convention. Yet he cites in
this little work the example of Saint Augustine, whom he "is
pleased to imitate," and he therefore makes certain specific

statements of belief which his commentary on *Acts* left either unsaid or merely vague. Whatever the sincerity of the sentiments, however, they add a graceful final touch to Bede's works. Whether or not they are the true epilogue to his writings is not susceptible of proof, but they may well stand as an unofficial epitaph. "His rest and his sepulchre will be glorious."

Bede was a good man, a good writer, and a good scholar and teacher as well. Naturally, therefore, there were many works attributed to him beyond what the present-day investigator is willing to allow him.[53] *Bede's Death-Song* (V, 4), for one, is probably not his, although the chief reason for refusing it to him is that it is in the vernacular. It may possibly have been suggested, however, by an item or passage in Bede's many Latin works, for its sentiment is almost universal in medieval literature, and it is stated over and over again in Bede's known writings. More difficult either to admit or to deny to Bede's authorship are some miscellaneous pieces—a little dialogue between Spring and Winter, with Palaemon the umpire;[54] various scriptural expositions; a discourse on holy places.[55] There can be little doubt about the fifty-nine *Homilies*,[56] partly exhortatory, partly exegetical, on the Gospels; but these do not illustrate Bede at his best, either as regards freshness and originality or literary craftsmanship. Only the confirmed devotee of the Middle Ages would have the courage to plow through their dreary wastes. But Bede's greatest achievements have already been enumerated. It remains only to pay tribute once more to both his accomplishment and his influence, which cannot easily be measured in books or lists of writings. That his fame became international is a truism, but he remained the Latinized Englishman writing in England, and he has every right to be considered a particular star in the English firmament of his day.

4. ALCUIN AND OTHERS

THE same cannot in all accuracy be said of Alcuin, the last of the major Anglo-Latin writers in the Old English period to be considered. He was born in the year in which Bede died (735) and lived until 804; it is not possible, then, for him ever to have been taught by Bede. Instead, he was educated in his native Yorkshire, in the center of learning at York which had come into prominence during Bede's lifetime. His teacher seems to have been that Archbishop Ecgbert to whom some of Bede's epistles are addressed. Little is known of Alcuin's career in England; a rumor has it that he was a bishop at Canterbury.[57] It is certain, however, that he was once sent to Rome, that on the journey homeward he met Charlemagne and made a great impression upon the King of the Franks, who invited him to live and teach at his court. The invitation was accepted; on only one subsequent occasion (790-792) did Alcuin return to England. His death, while Abbot of Tours, in 804 brought to a close a life so earnestly and ably dedicated to the cause of learning that he is now hailed as the brightest light in the renaissance which took place under the greatest prince of his age and the first Holy Roman Emperor. Yet all this has little to do with English literature. Moreover, Alcuin as a writer is far inferior to Bede both in literary skill and in versatility, although the actual range of his subject-matter may not be very far behind that of Bede. His compositions are of three general types: tracts upon the Bible; tracts upon doctrine, discipline, and morality; and historical pieces, in addition to which should be mentioned his many letters and a few poems.

In his theological works Alcuin's didactic purpose is expressed in somewhat eclectic fashion. He has no scruples about culling from the works of preceding commentators. At the same time, he is not devoid of variety in his method. For instance, his commentary on the book of *Genesis* departs from straight exegesis and assumes the form of a dialogue. Unlike the method, however, the thought here is altogether unoriginal. Nor do his treatises on doctrine, discipline, and morality differ in essentials from the great host of similar treatises by other writers on the same topics. *De Virtutibus et Vitiis*, perhaps his best known work in this category, is typical.[58] Open-

ing with the general thesis that true wisdom is to be found
only in obedient service to God, Alcuin proceeds with an exhaustive enumeration of the virtues and graces, and, by negative reference and implication, of the important sins. The
same kind of exposition is obvious in *De Animae Ratione*;[59]
but this work is also a description, based on St. Augustine, of
the human soul and its component parts. In the *Pueri Sancti
Martini*[60] Alcuin leaves aside the more wooden exposition to
adopt a homiletic tone, the homily in this case being a discourse on confession. The bulk of Alcuin's theological writing,
however, is directed in a controversial manner against the
rather obscure Adoptionists,[61] who demanded a belief in the
twofold aspect of the single personality of man. The fuller
details of this dogma have no place in the present paragraph
but belong rather to the specialist in the church history of the
period. Alcuin's three chief rebuttals of the Adoptionist point
of view, the *Liber Albini contra haeresim Felicis*, the *Libri vii
adversus Felicem*, and the *Libri iv adversus Elipandum*,[62] adhere, of course, to the strictly orthodox trinitarian views of
the Athanasian creed. They are in the main polemic and are
intended as immediate answers to his opponents' opinions as
they are presented. Since the tracts of Felix and Elipandus
are not closely knit pieces of argumentation, neither are Alcuin's answers. These important works of Alcuin are therefore
difficult to follow logically and strike one as entirely oblivious
to either form or order, nor are they in any way original or
stimulating. When, however, Alcuin writes independently of
controversy, in direct expository composition, as in his *De
Fide Sanctae Trinitatis*,[63] he achieves an earnestness and a rev-
erence which may often be stodgy in their conservatism but
which have the unquestionable qualities of sincerity and obedience to authority.

Alcuin's educational work is, after all, his chief contribution; it is a contribution, however, which belongs to the history of European thought rather than to the narrower limits
of Old English literature, with which it has to do only indirectly. And yet one can understand better the work of Alfred

the Great by understanding Alcuin's position and achievement. It is evident that European Continental scholarship had fallen upon mediocre days during the sixth and seventh centuries, as many chroniclers of the time complained.[64] Nor were matters much better in the eighth century until the accession of Charlemagne. This monarch was determined that his kingdom should be preëminent in every way and in no activity more than in the business of the intellect. Unlike Alfred, Charlemagne was not himself a learned man, but he teemed with ideas. His first and most desperate need, that for scholars, was satisfied by his inviting the most erudite men of Europe to his court. In that respect his transcending of national limits was remarkable for his time. Of these many scholars, Alcuin seems to have been best suited to Charlemagne's intellectual temper, for he was Germanic, learned, an excellent teacher and devoted student, very orthodox and steady, scrupulous as a man and as a Christian. Alcuin's activity under Charlemagne, which dates from 781, began as teacher of the king himself; it spread then to the reorganization of the entire educational system of the realm. There is a certain parallel between the work of Alcuin among the Franks and the work of Aldhelm at Malmesbury—both enjoyed the position of early laborers in the vineyard of learning under the benefits and auspices of an ambitious and acquisitive intellectual milieu.

And so Alcuin put new life into Charlemagne's educational endeavors by stamping his learning upon a group of young clergy. There is a likely probability that Alcuin himself was responsible for the famous *Capitulary*,[65] a circular letter addressed by Charlemagne to all the important churchmen of his kingdom, a document which is a sort of Charter of Education during the Middle Ages and clearly sets forth Charlemagne's design as no other surviving document has done it. In his later days at Tours, Alcuin served well the art of writing and gathered together materials to promote the study of ecclesiastical history. Scholars flocked to him from all parts of the western world. And yet his own educational works, as he has left them behind in writing, are not nearly so impressive as the works either of some of his predecessors, such as Bede, or of some of his successors, such as Alfred. His *Grammar*[66] is an arid performance, far below the standard of his sources, Priscian and Donatus. His dialogue *De Rhetorica et Virtutibus*[67] is an extremely unconvincing conglomeration of Cicero, Aristotelian theory, and the Bible. His *De Dialectica*[68] is a weak compilation of medieval philosophy, as far inferior to the obvious source of it, Boethius's *De Consolatione Philosophiae* (VIII, 2), as anything of its sort could well be. To judge Alcuin, in other words, by his creative work alone is entirely misleading. His greatest effectiveness came obviously from his personality, which must have been impressive. There must have been a personal vitality in his teaching which counterbalanced the shortcomings of his own scholarly equipment and expression; he lives more by what his students and followers accomplished than by what he himself achieved.

This personality glowed in Alcuin both as a churchman and as a human being. He made all kinds of collections of liturgical material—votive masses, breviaries, ritual-books, sacramentaries. He participated in a reform of church music in England to suit better the Roman pattern, a reform which he seems to have accomplished himself before he actually left England. He may have had a direct hand in the revisions of the texts of the Vulgate Bible carried out under the patronage of Charlemagne. This, however, cannot be shown directly, but occasional oblique references to the matter in some of his correspondence add weight to the supposition. It is in these letters that we have much the best opportunity to see Alcuin's character. He is not by nature a pioneer of the same heroic mold as Aidan, Columba, Saint Patrick, or Saint Cuthbert, but he is a shining example of the true servant of the Lord.

5. ASSER

WITH a consideration of Alcuin and his work, we come to the last important figure among the Anglo-Latin writers of the Old English period. The Welshman Asser (Asserius Menevensis) of Pembrokeshire, preceptor and companion of King Alfred after the year 880 and finally Bishop of Sherborne until his death in 910, is the author of a biography of King Alfred (*De Vita et Rebus Gestis Alfredi*),[69] which was presumably written in the year 893—in other words, during the king's lifetime. The work was for some time denied to Asser's authorship, and it remains true that our existing manuscript may date from a time subsequent to the death of Asser. This date, however, cannot be past the third quarter of the tenth century, and any idea that it is a Middle English forgery can be at once discarded.[70] This biography is characteristic of the historical writing of the time. It begins with a careful genealogy, tracing the ancestry of Alfred back to a god Geta, whom "the heathen long worshipped as a god." Next comes the genealogy of Alfred's mother. But naturally enough the important events of Alfred's lifetime are the incursions of the Danes. Their story Asser unfolds with clarity and a due regard for historical antecedents. Alfred's early years, until he attains literacy, are hurried over. With the account of the inspiration of the young prince to learning through a book of poems— either Aldhelm's or Alcuin's(?)—the biography turns its attention to the manner in which Alfred absorbed learning:

> After this he learned the daily course, that is, the celebration of the hours, and afterwards certain Psalms, and many prayers, contained in a book which he kept day and night in his bosom, as I myself have seen, and always carried about with him, for the sake of prayer, through all the bustle and business of this present life. But, sad to relate, he could not gratify his ardent wish to acquire liberal art, because, as he was wont to say, there were at that time no good teachers in all the kingdom of the West Saxons.

The "liberal art" referred to comprised the famous medieval *trivium* of the universities (grammar, logic, and rhetoric) and the more advanced *quadrivium* (arithmetic, geometry, music, and astronomy). Unfortunately, when the young man had the opportunity to learn, he had no masters; when he was older, he was so busied with military and state affairs that he could not study. For the Danes were upon him. Asser's biography furnishes extended accounts of the many battles in which Alfred was involved, culminating with the battle of Edington and the Treaty of Wedmore (I, 5). We hear, incidentally, that Alfred was a rather sickly man—something that one would scarcely suspect from his character and his achievements.

The latter portion of Asser's work is concerned chiefly with a general eulogy of Alfred's character—very much in the manner of a fulsome nineteenth-century laudatory biography —which is illustrated by many anecdotes exemplifying his sense of justice, his constructive Christianity, his quest of learning, which, it must be observed, he followed unremittingly in spite of all handicaps.

> But if any one, from old age or the sluggishness of an untrained mind, was unable to make progress in literary studies, he would order his son, if he had one, or one of his kinsmen— or, if he had no one else, his own freeman or servant, whom he had long before advanced to the office of reading—to read Saxon books before him night and day, whenever he had any leisure. And then they would lament with deep sighs from their inwardmost souls that in their youth they had never attained to such studies. They counted happy the youth of the present day, who could be delightfully instructed in the liberal arts, while they considered themselves wretched in that they had neither learned these things in their youth, nor, now that they were old, were able to do so. This skill of young and old in acquiring letters, I have set forth as a means of characterizing the aforesaid king.

At least Asser has not spared himself in giving us such details as he could of Alfred's career. He is not too accurate as historian, of course, because he does not discriminate correctly enough between fact and legend; but that is a general failing of historical writers throughout the period, not excepting Bede, and on the whole we have in Asser's work an intelligent and generally thoughtful delineation of a great man.

6. MINOR LATIN WORKS OF THE PERIOD

THERE are also many scattered works by authors almost unknown or else completely anonymous. We have, for example, an anonymous *Life of Gregory the Great*,[71] which must have served as a source of Aelfric's later biographical homily (IX, 2); there are two similar pieces, a *Life of Wilfrid of York*, by Eddius Stephanus,[72] and the *Life of Saint Guthlac*, by Felix of Croyland,[73] both from the eighth century. Here, too, should be included the *Chronicle* of Aethelweard,[74] who died in 998. It is a piece of slovenly Latin and is chiefly useful for its relation to *The Anglo-Saxon Chronicle* (VIII, 3), because three of its four sections (from the year 449 on), when they are not indebted to Isidore of Seville's *Origines* or Bede's *Ecclesiastical History*, lean heavily upon *The Anglo-Saxon Chronicle*—to such an extent, in fact, that one may suspect Aethelweard of making use of some lost manuscript of *The Anglo-Saxon Chronicle*. It is hardly proper to include here the works of the Irish-born John Scotus of the ninth century, although Alfred brought him to Malmesbury as a teacher not long before the Irishman, who had spent his life for the greater part teaching in Paris, died a violent death under rather mysterious circumstances.[75]

There is, further, a small group of Visions of the Otherworld. Two examples are to be found in Bede's *Ecclesiastical History*: one of these, the celebrated Vision of Drihthelm, has already been mentioned on a previous page. Two others are included among the letters of Bishop Boniface,[76] not otherwise noted as a literary man but rather as a teacher and missionary of importance. These all belong to the apocalyptic school of literature, of which the early Church Fathers were very fond. Some of these apocalypses, as a matter of fact, are to be referred to the not inconsiderable number of revelatory scriptures, such as the Gospel of Nicodemus, the Revelation of Paul, and the Revelation of Peter.

Into this miscellaneous heap must be thrown the poem by Aethelwulf, presumably a Lindisfarne monk of the early ninth century.[77] This poem is a history of some particular monastery as yet unidentified, as it is likely to remain, and it is important only because it contains also a vision of the Otherworld, this time in verse. Under these circumstances the poem is unique for the period.

As final items, there remain to be named the occasional Latin devotional writings—the prayer, the hymn, Church laws and penitentials,[78] and various examples of the ordinances of Church councils. Much of this material still exists in manuscript only and is therefore one of the few fields in Old English literature still comparatively untrampled by the scholar. Taking into account the general worth of this material, however, we may construe such a statement as a compliment to the thoroughness with which contemporary experts have sifted surviving Anglo-Saxon writings, however much may still be unknown to them.

The Anglo-Latin writers in Old English literature constitute something of a special domain. They have little to do with the full tradition of English literature, save where the great talents of a Bede transcend the limitations of his subject-matter and his environment. The Anglo-Latin writings in question contain little of largeness or the spacious view. Perhaps, however, we have no right to take such things for granted anywhere in Old English literature. Nevertheless, these Anglo-Latin writings cannot compare in their appeal to the modern reader with the Old English vernacular poetry, nor, for that matter, with most of the vernacular prose soon to be treated. Always, to be sure, there is the exception of the Venerable Bede—at least in occasional passages. He and Aldhelm still stand as the major figures in the whole body of this Anglo-Latin literature in the Old English period. One of these belongs to the north and the other to the south. By and large, however, the Anglo-Latin writers of the south, save for Aldhelm, seem mediocre, even feeble. But, considering the general dates of this Anglo-Latin literature, such weakness is not extraordinary, because the eighth century is not the time of West Saxon or Kentish intellectual leadership.[79]

NOTES TO CHAPTER SEVEN

1. See Chapter III, note 9 above.

2. The old Latin saint's life of Columba by Adamnan, who became Abbot of Iona in 670, has been edited and translated by J. T. Fowler (Oxford, 1894). Another biographical sketch is that by H. F. O. Abel in G. H. Pertz et al., *Die Geschichtschreiber der deutschen Vorzeit* (Heidelberg, 1898); still another is Justus Jones, *Life of St. Columba* (Philadelphia, 1899). But the best as well as the most recent biography is Lucy Menzies, *St. Columba of Iona* (London-New York, 1920), which might be supplemented by the article of Halliday Sutherland, "Columba on Iona" in *Month* (March, 1939), 240-249. For general considerations, there is W. Douglas Simpson, *The Celtic Church in Scotland* (Aberdeen, 1935).

3. Not much has been done with Aidan, for obvious reasons. See the article on Aidan in *Dictionary of National Biography*. There is always, however, some passing reference to him and his work in all the English histories covering the Old English period; see especially, therefore, R. H. Hodgkin, *A History of the Anglo-Saxons* (Oxford, 1935), I, 335-336 and elsewhere. Fuller accounts are the older ones in William Bright, *Chapters in Early English Church History* (Oxford, 1888) and in John R. Green, *The Making of England* (New York, 1882).

4. These two medieval lives were written by individuals who were evidently not sure of their subjects and who probably confused the identities of more than one man named Gildas. They are, in short, valueless. The first published edition of Gildas is that of Polydore Vergil in 1525; it is most unsatisfactory. Josselyn's edition of some forty years later is better, but Thomas Gale's (Oxford, 1691) is much the best of the early editions. The standard modern edition of Gildas—as well as of Nennius (see note 12 below)—is Theodor Mommsen's, in *Monumenta Germaniae Historica: Auctorum Antiquissimorum* (Berlin, 1898), XIII. This text has been reprinted, virtually intact, by Hugh Williams in his edition, *Cymmrodorion Record Series*, No. 3 (London, 1899-1901). Still helpful, however, is the edition by J. Stevenson for the English Historical Society (1838); and still the most accessible translation is that of J. A. Giles, either in *Works of Gildas and Nennius* (London, 1841) or in the valuable collection, *Six Old English Chronicles*, in Bohn's Antiquarian Library (London, 1848).

For critical comment, see R. H. Fletcher, "The Arthurian Material of the Chronicles, especially those of Great Britain and France" in *Harvard Studies and Notes in Philology and Literature*, X; also C. E. Stevens, "Gildas and the Civitates of Britain" in *English Historical Review*, LII, 193-203; Charles J. Singer, "The Lorica of Gildas the Briton" in *From Magic to Science* (London, 1928)—see note 8 below; and A. Anscombe, "The Author and Date of Gildas' *De Excidio Britanniae*" in *Academy*, XLVIII, 206 and 411, reviewed by W. H. Stevenson in *Academy*, XLVIII, 522.

5. Edited by J. W. Ab Ithel (London, 1860) and by E. Phillimore in *Y Cymmrodor* (1888), IX, 141ff.

6. Usually as *De Excidio Britanniae*, sometimes as *De Excidio et Conquestu*. Habington, a seventeenth-century translator of the second part of Gildas's work, refers to it as the *Epistle of Gildas*, but this "epistle" is a homily rather than a historical treatise and should be thought of as separate from the history itself.

7. Gildas had the nickname of "Sapiens" ("the wise").

8. See Chapter XIII below.

9. Arius, a Cyrenaican churchman of the early fourth century, was the begetter of the "first great heresy" in the history of the Church. This heresy is virtually the forerunner of Unitarianism; that is, Arius insisted on the unity and "unoriginateness" of God and on the "originateness" of Christ. "We believe in one God alone without birth, alone everlasting, alone unoriginate. . . . We believe that this God gave birth to the only begotten Son before eternal periods, through whom He made those periods and all things else; that He gave birth to Him, not in semblance, but in truth, giving Him a real existence, at His own will so as to be unchangeable, God's perfect creature, but not as other creatures, not . . . a development; nor again . . . a consubstantial part, nor . . . as Son and Father at once. . . . While there are three persons, yet God is alone the Cause of all things and unoriginate." The resulting schism in the Church was serious; and it was not resolved by the Council of Nicaea (325), for although Arianism was there officially defeated, it maintained a strong hold upon millions of Christians, particularly among the young Germanic nations of the time of the great migrations.

10. That is, "possible" from the standpoint of historical possibility, at least within the fifth century. There is a strong tendency among Arthurian scholars, however, to look for the historical prototype of Arthur in a period before the fifth century; for example, see W. A. Nitze, "Bédier's Epic Theory and the Arthuriana of Nennius" in *Modern Philology*, XXXIX, 1-14, which sums up a view—in my opinion a rather extreme one—regarding the historical sources of Arthur which would go back to Roman Britain of the second century to find the original Arthur. Many of Nitze's approaches have tended toward a Roman background, in any case, for the historical figure underlying the legendary King Arthur. This seems highly probable, at that. Geoffrey of Monmouth, the twelfth-century chronicler unquestionably more responsible than any other individual for the Arthurian legend, identifies Ambrosius with Merlin, Arthur's great magician.

The matter is of vast complexity and is probably irrelevant here; see, however, J. D. Bruce, *The Evolution of Arthurian Romance* (Baltimore, 1923), I, 134 and note.

11. For the matter of the *Lorica Hymn*, generally attributed to Gildas, see Chapter XIII below.

12. The standard edition is that of Mommsen (see note 4 above). The first important work to give the *Historia Britonum* its proper due was Heinrich Zimmer, *Nennius Vindicatus* (Berlin, 1893). Rudolf Thurneysen, in his reviews of Zimmer (*Zeitschrift für deutsche Philologie*, XXVIII, 80ff.) and of Mommsen (*Zeitschrift für celtische Philologie*, I, 157ff.) had the benefit of an additional manuscript of the *Historia Britonum*. But Thurneysen suggests that Nennius became engaged on the compilation of his material as early as 826. Both Zimmer and Thurneysen take a date after 670 for the composition of the original History (the "pre-Nennius"). The ninth-century date set by Thurneysen (826) seems too exact to be trusted, but anywhere between 800 and 830 is probable.

The translation by J. A. Giles in *Six Old English Chronicles* (see note 4 above) is still very useful. So is Fletcher's monograph (see note 4 above) indispensable for Nennius as well as for Gildas. The following are also recommended: Alfred Nutt's review of Zimmer's *Nennius Vindicatus* in *Academy*, XLIV, 132 and 151; César Boser, "À propos de Nennius" in *Romania*, XXIII, 432ff.; A. O. Anderson, "Nennius's Chronological Chapter" in *Antiquity*, VI, 82-84; Kenneth Jackson, "Nennius and the Twenty-Eight Cities of Britain" in *Antiquity*, XII, 44-55; and especially two French studies: Edmond Faral, *La légende arthurienne* (Paris, 1929) and J. Loth, "Remarques à l'Historia Britonum dite de Nennius" in *Revue Celtique*, XLIX, 150-165 and LI, 1-31.

13. *Historia Britonum*, section 11. The translation used is that by J. A. Giles in *Six Old English Chronicles* (London, 1848). The allusion is to the Brutus Legend, according to which Britain was founded by Brutus, a descendant of Aeneas. The long metrical chronicles of Wace and Laȝamon in the later twelfth century and shortly thereafter bear the name of the *Brut* to perpetuate the legend. The idea that the British were descended from the Trojans lends considerable popularity during the Middle Ages to the story of Troy and also handicaps the spread of the Greek side of the story. Homer told lies, according to medieval belief, largely because he was a Greek.

14. *Historia Britonum*, section 50.

15. There are good accounts of these men and their works in William Bright, *Chapters in Early English Church History* (Oxford, 1888); in A. W. Haddan and W. Stubbs, *Councils and Ecclesiastical Documents Relating to Great Britain and Ireland* (Oxford, 1869-

1878); in John H. Green, *The Making of England* (New York, 1882); and particularly in Walter F. Hook, *Lives of the Archbishops of Canterbury* (London, 1860-1869).

16. Two excellent treatments of this subject are J. A. Herbert, *Illuminated Manuscripts* (London, 1911), particularly Chapter VII, entitled "English Illumination to A.D. 1200" and (better still) the exhaustive work by E. G. Millar, *English Illuminated Manuscripts from the Tenth to the Thirteenth Century* (Paris-Brussels, 1926)—which contains a lavish number of plates for illustration. The most authoritative general work on medieval writing is W. Wattenbach, *Das Schriftwesen im Mittelalter* (Leipzig, 1896), and a standard general treatment of medieval English handwriting is E. M. Thompson, "The History of English Handwriting, A.D. 700-1400" in *Transactions of the Bibliographical Society*, V, 109-142. Somewhat later comes another good treatment of English palaeography: W. Keller, *Angelsächsische Palaeographie*, volume 43 of *Palaestra* (Berlin, 1906). The volumes of the Palaeographical Society are from time to time of great historical as well as artistic value.

17. See Chapter X and note 32 below.

18. See Chapter X and note 32 below.

19. In considering Aldhelm, as well as Bede and Alcuin, a few general works should be remembered, for they will contribute immeasurably to a thorough knowledge of the intellectual conditions under which these three men labored. There is first of all the article by J. M. Campbell, "Patristic Studies and the Literature of Medieval England" in *Speculum*, VIII, 465-478. Next comes George R. Stephens, *The Knowledge of Greek in England in the Middle Ages* (Philadelphia, 1933). Third is the doctoral dissertation of J. D. A. Ogilvy at Harvard, which was expanded into *Books Known to Anglo-Saxon Writers from Aldhelm to Alcuin* (Cambridge, Mass., 1936); see also his *Anglo-Latin Scholarship*, 597-780, in *University of Colorado Studies*, XXII, 327-340. Finally there is the contribution by Ramona Bressie, "Libraries of the British Isles in the Anglo-Saxon Period" in James W. Thompson, *The Mediaeval Library* (Chicago, 1939), 102-125.

For Aldhelm himself, there are Clyde Furst, "An Anglo-Saxon Saint" in *A Group of Old Authors* (Philadelphia, 1899), and Montague R. James, *Two Ancient English Scholars* (Glasgow, 1931). The best study of biographical material is A. S. Cook, "Sources of the Biography of Aldhelm" in *Transactions of the Connecticut Academy of Arts and Sciences*, XXVIII, 275-293. There are one or two full biographies, of which, in my opinion, George F. Browne's *St. Aldhelm: his life and times* (London, 1903) is better, although O. Bönhoff, *Aldhelm von Malmesbury* (Dresden, 1894), is very satisfactory.

Other biographical contributions can be pieced out from the many scattered articles which have appeared from time to time, such as A. S. Cook, "Aldhelm's Legal Studies" in *Journal of English and Germanic Philology*, XXIII, 105-113; and "Aldhelm's Rude Infancy" in *Philological Quarterly*, VII, 115-119; or Erika von Ehrhardt-Siebold, "Aldhelm in Possession of the Secrets of Sericulture" in *Anglia*, LX, 384-389 and "The Hellebore in Anglo-Saxon Pharmacy" in *Englische Studien*, LXXI, 161-170. See also Alois Brandl, "Zu den angeblichen Schreiben des altmercischen Königs Aethelweard und Aldhelm" in *Archiv*, CLXXI, 70, and Putnam F. Jones, "Aldhelm and the Comitatus Ideal" in *Modern Language Notes*, XLVII, 378. The question of Sherborne is treated in F. P. Magoun, "Aldhelm's Diocese of Sherborne *bewestan wuda*" in *Harvard Theological Review*, XXXII, 103-114.

The standard edition of Aldhelm's works is *Aldhelmi Opera*, volume XV of *Monumenta Germaniae Historica: Auctorum Antiquissimorum*, edited by Rudolf Ehwald. An excellent edition of the *Riddles*, with English metrical translation, is James H. Pitman, *The Riddles of Aldhelm* (New Haven, 1925). At the same time was published a more comprehensive study by Erika von Ehrhardt-Siebold, *Die Lateinischen Rätsel der Angelsachsen* (Heidelberg, 1925).

20. See Ehwald's edition (note 19 above). The letter to Geraint turns up also in the correspondence of the great St. Boniface, English-born missionary in Germany (d. 755).

21. *De Laude Virginitatis*, published by Ehwald (see note 19 above) and also among Bede's *Opuscula* (see note 32 below).

22. It is generally assumed that the metrical version was written after the prose version.

23. The *Epistola ad Acircium*; Acircius was King Aldfrith of Northumbria, who ruled from 685 to 705. See Ehwald (note 19 above). The work is known also as the *Liber de Septenario*; see J. A. Giles, *Sancti Aldhelmi . . . Opera* (Oxford, 1844), which is an adequate edition.

24. Frederick Tupper, *The Riddles of The Exeter Book* (Boston, 1910), xxxii.

25. A. S. Cook, at least, was willing to commit himself; see "The Possible Begetter of the Old English *Beowulf* and *Widsith*" in *Transactions of the Connecticut Academy of Arts and Sciences*, XXV, 335-339.

26. The translations used in these quotations are those of James H. Pitman, in *The Riddles of Aldhelm* (New Haven, 1925).

27. Isadorus or Isidorus Hispaniensis was one of the most influential writers of the early Middle Ages, who succeeded his brother as Bishop of Seville in the early years of the seventh century. His contempora-

neous reputation for learning was great, and he seems to have been a relatively prolific writer. His most ambitious work was the *Etymologiarum Libri XX*, or the *Origines*, the Encyclopaedia Britannica of the time. Also influential were his book on synonyms (the *Differentiarum*) and his short treatise, *De Natura Rerum*. He died in 636.

28. Also in Isidore's *Origines* (Book 12, part 2, Chapter 12). For the *Physiologus* tradition, see Chapter IV, note 53 above, and especially Lauchart, *Geschichte der Physiologus* (Strassburg, 1889).

29. Probably the most distinguished of the many twelfth-century chronicle-writers in England and the one most directly in the tradition of the Venerable Bede. He was born about 1095 and for most of his life was associated immediately with the abbey at Malmesbury, on the borders of Wiltshire and Gloucestershire. His death is believed to have taken place in 1142. His major work was a *Chronicle of the Kings of England* (ca. 1128); he wrote also a *Chronicle of the Popes* (ca. 1125) and a number of saints' lives and miracle-stories. One of these lives is a life of Aldhelm. See Montague R. James, *Two Ancient English Scholars* (Glasgow, 1931).

30. This letter is preserved in William of Malmesbury's *Chronicle of the Popes* (*Gesta Pontificium*)—see note 29 above. It has been published also by N. E. S. A. Hamilton in the *Rolls Series* (London, 1870), LII, 341.

31. These appear in the correspondence of Boniface (see also note 20 above). The letters, invaluable for the light they throw upon the life of the times, are to be found in E. Emerton, *The Letters of Saint Boniface* (New York, 1940); also in J. A. Giles, *Bonifacii Opera Omnia* (London, 1844); Philipp Jaffé, "Monumenta Moguntina" in *Bibliothek Rerum Germanicarum* (Berlin, 1866); or—the best of the older editions—in Ernst Dümmler, *Monumenta Germaniae Historica: Auctorum Antiquissimorum*, VII (Berlin, 1892). There is an English translation, based on Dümmler's text, by E. Kyrlie (London, 1911).

32. Bede tells us about Tatwine in his *Ecclesiastical History* (see Chapter I, note 4 above), Book V, Chapters 23 and 24; see also Adolf Ebert, "Die Rätselpoesie der Angelsachsen" in *Berichte über die Verhandlungen der königlich-sächsischen Gesellschaft der Wissenschaften zu Leipzig, Phil.-Hist. Classe*, XXIX, 20-56, especially p. 25; also Heinrich Hahn, "Die Rätseldichter Tatwin und Eusebius" in *Forschungen zur deutschen Gedichte*, XXVI, 601ff. The riddles of Tatwine are presented by Thomas Wright in *Anglo-Latin Satirical Poets* in the *Rolls Series*, II, 525-534. There are some further comments in Frederick Tupper, *The Riddles of The Exeter Book* (Boston, 1910), xxxiv, upon the relationship of Tatwine and Aldhelm.

As for Eusebius, he is treated in the monographs mentioned in the preceding paragraph. Ebert, for instance, can say no more about him than that he was a contemporary of Tatwine; Hahn identifies him as a friend of Bede, probably Hwaetbert, Abbot of Wearmouth (680-ca. 750). Ebert, in his *Allgemeine Geschichte der Litteratur des Mittelalters im Abendlande* (Leipzig, 1889), I, 603, and M. Manitius, in his *Geschichte der christlich-lateinischen Poesie bis zur Mitte des achten Jahrhunderts* (Stuttgart, 1891), both accept Hahn's suggestion. See also Ebert in *Haupt's Zeitschrift*, XXIII, 200 and Frederick Tupper in *Modern Language Notes*, XXI, 97ff.

33. There has been a great deal of fruitful research on Bede during the past few years, particularly on the occasion of the twelve-hundredth anniversary of his death. The most distinguished treatments of Bede's full career are H. M. Gillett, *Saint Bede the Venerable* (London, 1935) and R. W. Chambers, "Bede," in *Proceedings of the British Academy*, XXII (London, 1937). Smaller works in this category and of the same approximate date are Ruby Davis, "Bede's Early Reading" in *Speculum*, VIII, 179-195; M. L. W. Laistner, "Bede as a Classical and a Patristic Scholar" in *Royal History Society Transactions*, XVI, 69-94; Bede Jarrett, "The Venerable Bede" in *Dublin Review*, CXCVII, 73-82; E. E. Kellett, "The Venerable Bede" in *Spectator*, CLIV, 869; J. Scott Lidgett, "The Venerable Bede" in *London Quarterly Review*, CLX, 289-293; A. L. Maycock, "Bede and Alcuin" in *Hibbert Journal*, XXXIII, 402-412; and H. Schreiber, "Beda als Dichter" in *Zeitschrift für deutsche Geistesgeschichte*, I, 326-327.

The most ambitious of the recent books is A. H. Thompson, *Bede, his Life, Times, and Writing* (Oxford, 1935). See also G. F. Browne, *The Venerable Bede* (New York, 1879) and Karl Werner, *Baeda der Ehrwürdige und seine Zeit* (Vienna, 1875); there are good treatments also in both William Bright, *Chapters in Early English Church History* (Oxford, 1888-1897) and in W. P. Ker, *The Dark Ages* (New York, 1904), especially pp. 141ff. The most recent study is in Eleanor S. Duckett, *Anglo-Saxon Saints and Scholars* (New York, 1947).

A detailed description of the Bede manuscripts is Charles R. Beeson, "The Manuscripts of Bede" in *Classical Philology*, XLII, 73-87. The most easily accessible edition of Bede's complete works would be J. A. Giles, *The Venerable Bede's Miscellaneous Works in Latin, with Translation of the Historical Works* (London, 1843; 1848). The historical works have been printed recently in the Loeb Classical Library, with English translation by J. E. King, *Baedae Opera Historica* (London, 1930). Editions of the *Historia Ecclesiastica Gentis Anglorum* have been numerous; the most noteworthy are those by John Smith (Cambridge, 1722), George H. Moberley (Oxford, 1881), Alfred Holder (Freiburg-Tübingen, 1882), and particularly that by Charles Plummer (Oxford, 1896). Reference has already been made (see Chapter I, note 4 above) to Miller's edition of the West Saxon Alfredian version. Plummer's edition, however, has an unusually good introduction. All have nevertheless contributed much to a knowledge and appreciation of Bede both as man and as writer. Other shorter treatments of certain aspects of Bede's writings are covered in the following: Putnam F. Jones, *A Concordance to the Historia Ecclesiastica of Bede* (Cambridge, 1929); Mary E. Harris, "A Translation of the Letters of the Venerable Bede"—unfortunately an unpublished doctoral dissertation, summarized, however, in *Abstracts of Theses* (Pittsburgh, 1932); W. Jaeger, "Bedas metrische Vita Sancti Cuthberti" in *Palaestra*, CXCVIII (Leipzig, 1935); W. Mohr, "Die geographische Beschreibung Englands in Bedas Kirchengeschichte" in *Zeitschrift für deutsche Geistesgeschichte*, I, 322-324; F. Strunz, "Beda in der Geschichte der Naturbetrachtung und Naturforschung" in *Zeitschrift für deutsche Geistesgeschichte*, I, 311-321; and Wendell Clausen, "Bede and the British Pearl" in *Classical Journal*, XLII, 277-280. Treatments of some of Bede's individual works are referred to below at the appropriate place. See also Chapter VIII below, and the notes under King Alfred's translation (note 19 in particular). For the *Ecclesiastical History* as a piece of historiography, see Charles W. Jones, "Bede as Early Medieval Historian" in *Medievalia et Humanistica*, IV, 26-36 and C. Grant Loomis, "The Miracle Traditions of the Venerable Bede" in *Speculum*, XXI, 404-418—also notable for the idea of nationalism inherent in Bede's *Ecclesiastical History*, for which see in addition R. M. Lumiansky, "The Beginnings of English Nationalism" in *Journal of the History of Ideas*, II, 248-249.

34. *Paradiso*, Canto X, 131. The Sphere of the Sun was reserved for great theologians and Christian thinkers.

35. See note 33 above and Chapter VIII, note 19 below.

36. As printed in the introduction to his edition of the *Ecclesiastical History* (see note 35 above).

37. According to Plummer's chronology; see also J. A. Giles, *Miscellaneous Works* (note 33 above), for a convenient text.

38. Again, if we follow Plummer's chronology, the work would fall in the year 703. There is a separate edition by Charles W. Jones, *Baeda Opera de Temporibus* (Cambridge, Mass., 1943); see the review of this work by H. Henel, "The New Edition of Bede's Computistical Treatise" in *Journal of English and Germanic Philology*, XLIII, 411-416.

39. In reference to this work and the shorter *De Temporibus* mentioned in note 38 above, see especially Charles W. Jones, "The Lost Sirmond Manuscript of Bede's *Computus*" in *English Historical Re-*

view, LII, 204-219; and H. Henel, "Studien zum altenglischen Computus" in *Beiträge zur englischen Philologie*, XXVI (Leipzig, 1934).

40. Charles W. Jones, "The Manuscripts of Bede's *De Natura Rerum*" in *Isis*, XXVII, 430-440.

41. There was an old theory, which must have been based ultimately upon the observation that extremes of climatic conditions led to a predisposition toward certain diseases, if not their outright incidence. Many of the leechdoms and prescriptions to be discussed later (Chapter XIII below) were assembled with an eye to the weather. Galen, the great second-century Graeco-Roman authority on medicine, had developed the theory of the Hippocratic humors to the point where he taught that the normal condition or "temperament" of a human body depended upon the proper mixture or proportion of the four elements —hot, cold, wet, and dry. It was Galen more than anyone else who underlay Bede's pronouncements on medicine, for no important advance was made in that science from the death of Galen until nearly two centuries after the death of Bede, when the Arab physicians made their important contributions.

42. The art of opening the veins for the purpose of letting blood, in order further to improve the condition of the patient. In general, phlebotomy became bound up with astrology during the course of the Middle Ages. Bede's treatise, however, is not much more than a description of the anatomy involved in vein-cutting.

43. In the introduction to his edition of the *Ecclesiastical History* (see note 33 above).

44. See Jaeger's monograph referred to in note 33 above.

45. Acca was Bishop of Hexham from 709 to 732, succeeding his great friend and companion, the missionary Bishop Wilfrid, of whom Eddius Stephanus wrote a life (see note 72 below). Acca was an accomplished musician and a skilled administrator, and his saintly life endeared him to his flock. For reasons that are not known, however, he was driven from his episcopacy in 732 and died in retirement in 740. Bede appears to have been an intimate of Acca and addressed many letters to him; there has survived one letter of Acca in reply. For an interesting speculation concerning this churchman, see A. S. Cook, "The Old English *Andreas* and Bishop Acca of Hexham" in *Transactions of the Connecticut Academy*, XXVI, 245-332 (New Haven, 1924).

46. See not only J. A. Giles, *Miscellaneous Works* (note 33 above) but also particularly the Loeb Classical Library edition of the historical works, translated by King (mentioned also in note 33 above).

47. The prose version is treated briefly in Jaeger's monograph (see note 33 above) and in the Loeb edition.

48. Book v, Chapter 13.

49. Plummer, however, is dubious. There is also a *Martyrologium Poeticum* which has been rejected by all except Werner (see note 33 above), since it refers to an event which did not take place until some years after Bede's death. Of course the passage containing this reference might have been interpolated. The *Martyrologium* itself, however, if carefully studied, will be found to be rather unlike Bede in many ways, and certainly below his usual nobility of character and refinement of style.

50. See note 49 above. It is more than likely that this piece should be rejected from the Bede Canon.

51. Printed by J. A. Giles in the *Miscellaneous Works* (see note 33 above). Following Giles's numbering, we observe that four of the hymns (1, 2, 3, and 14) are in hexameters; the remainder are in tetrameters. Plummer rather sardonically notes: "They may well be genuine, though there is nothing of Bede in them." (See his introduction to the 1896 edition of the *Historia Ecclesiastica*, mentioned in note 33 above, p. cliii.) There has never been any real disposition on the part of scholars to reject these hymns as spurious.

52. M. L. W. Laistner, *Baedae Venerabilis Expositio Actuum Apostolorum et Retractatio* (Cambridge, Mass., 1939).

53. Charles W. Jones, *Baedae Pseudepigraphia: scientific writings falsely attributed to Bede* (Ithaca, 1939).

54. *Cuculus, sive Veris et Hiemis Conflictus.* Dümmler and Plummer are inclined to assign it to Alcuin, because "Cuculus" was one of the pet names given by Alcuin to his disciples: see A. W. Haddan and W. Stubbs, *Councils and Ecclesiastical Documents Relating to Great Britain and Ireland* (Oxford, 1869-1878), III, 508-509.

55. *De Locis Sanctis.* For other dubious pieces in the Bede Canon, see C. W. Jones, *Baedae Pseudepigraphia* (note 53 above).

56. Of these fifty-nine, only seven have ever been questioned.

57. Not, however, Archbishop. Actually, it is not at all clear just how far Alcuin advanced in Church rank.

For biographical material on Alcuin, see particularly the articles on *Alcuin* in the *Dictionary of National Biography* and the *John Rylands Library Bulletin*, XIX, 273-275, as well as Ethel H. Thomson's study in *London Quarterly Review* for July, 1933, pp. 351-360. Further details can be eked out in H. L. Maycock, "Bede and Alcuin" in *Hibbert Journal*, XXXIII, 402-412, and in R. B. Hepple, "Alcuin's Visit to Wearmouth" in *Notes and Queries*, CLXXI, 82-83. There is a rather feeble biography by George F. Browne, *Alcuin of York* (London-New York, 1908); a better account in James Raine, "De Pontificibus et Sanctis Ecclesiae Eboracensis Carmen" in *Historians of the Church of York* (London, 1879-1894); and a still better study in Andrew F. West, *Alcuin and the Rise of the Christian Schools* (New

York, 1892). There is an extremely good short treatment in H. O. Taylor, *The Medieval Mind* (London, 1911; 1930), 214-221. Studies of Alcuin primarily as teacher and scholar are F. Watson, "Alcuin as an Educator" in *Academy*, XLIII, 344; B. W. Wells, "Alcuin the Teacher" in *Constructive Quarterly*, VII, 531-552; and E. M. Sanford, "Alcuin and the Classics" in *Classical Journal*, XX, 526-533.

No careful study of Alcuin, however, would be complete without a consideration of the following: C. J. B. Gaskoin, *Alcuin: His Life and Work* (London, 1904); F. Lorenz, *Alcuins Leben* (Halle, 1829) translated into English by J. M. Slee; J. B. Mullingar, *The Schools of Charles the Great* (London, 1877); J. E. Sandys, *A History of Classical Scholarship* (Cambridge, 1908); and the aforementioned life by Dean West. The best of the Continental biographies is still Karl Werner, *Alkuin und seine Jahrhundert* (Paderborn, 1876).

Duchesne's edition (Paris, 1617) is the first complete one of Alcuin's works; Froben's edition (Ratisbon, 1777) is better. But the most accessible texts today are in Migne's *Patrologiae Cursus Completus: Series Latina*, C and Ci; and Philipp Jaffé's "Monumenta Alcuiniana" in *Bibliothek Rerum Germanicarum* (Berlin, 1873), VI. Among the most useful critical works on Alcuin's writings, in addition to such references to them as have been given in the citing of other books, are M. Rule, "The Liturgical Libellus of Alcuin" in *Athenaeum*, I, 20-21 (1905); J. D. A. Ogilvy, "Alcuin's Use of Alliteration" in *Modern Language Notes*, XLVI, 444-445; Edward K. Rand, "A Preliminary Study of Alcuin's Bible" in *Harvard Theological Review*, XXIV, 323-396; George T. Flom, "Codex A M 619 Quarto" in *University of Illinois Studies in Language and Literature*, XIV (Urbana, 1929)—containing Alcuin's *De Virtutibus et Vitiis*; Margaret L. Hargrove, "Alcuin's 'Poem on York' "—an unpublished dissertation summarized in *Abstracts of Theses* (Ithaca, 1938). See also Ralph B. Page, *The Letters of Alcuin* (New York, 1909).

58. See the edition by Flom mentioned in note 57 above.

59. A good example of Alcuin's liturgical works.

60. Probably the best of Alcuin's saints' lives.

61. This name is applied to those who subscribed to a heresy which sprang up in the late eighth century, from the teachings of two Spanish bishops, Felix of Urgel and Elipandus of Toledo, that Christ was not the Son of God in the sense of being so by generation, except as to His Godhead, while as to His Manhood He was not begotten but adopted. Alcuin, in 800, held a public dispute with Bishop Felix, in which the latter acknowledged himself beaten. The effect of this controversy was

to call attention to the duality of man in his divine and in his human aspects.

62. These three doctrinal compositions, defending the Catholic faith against the Adoptionist heresy, are often regarded as Alcuin's best and most effective writings. It is presumed that they appeared before the Council of Frankfurt (794), which officially disposed of the heresy, although, as pointed out in note 51 above, Alcuin was combatting it as late as 800. Jaffé, in *Monumenta Alcuiniana* (see note 57 above) was inclined to believe that Alcuin was the author of the so-called *Caroline Books*, which appeared in the last decade of the eighth century as the work of Charlemagne.

63. This was written in Tours between 800, when Charles the Great became Emperor, and 804, when Alcuin died. The tract is indebted chiefly to St. Augustine's *De Sancta Trinitate*. Appended to Alcuin's works in Migne's text (see note 57 above) is his *Twenty-Eight Questions of the Trinity*.

64. Gregory of Tours (ca. 549-594) is the author of the *Historia Francorum*, an indispensable document for our knowledge of the obscure sixth century. As such, he is the first to call attention to this decline in learning. In addition to this work, he was responsible for a tract, *De Miraculis*. His history of the Franks, however, while it is prejudiced and unsystematic, is still an honest and important contribution to the chronicle-writing of the time; see O. M. Dalton, *Gregory of Tours and the History of the Franks* (Oxford, 1927).

65. Issued in 787; a second Capitulary in 789 gave more detailed instructions to the schoolmasters and teachers of Charlemagne's kingdom; see H. Brauer, "Capitula Caroli, angelsächsisch und althochdeutsch" in *Zeitschrift für deutsche Philologie*, LIII, 183-184. For a further study of the relations of Alcuin and Charlemagne, see note 67 below.

66. This work falls into two parts: (1) a dialogue between Alcuin and his pupils on philosophy and liberal studies in general; and (2) a dialogue between a young Frank and a young Saxon on grammar, which is conducted in the presence of Alcuin. "The vowels are, as it were, the souls, and the consonants, the bodies of words." One cannot avoid being appalled by the Alcuinian list of the parts of grammar. They comprise "words, letters, syllables, clauses, sayings, speeches, definitions, feet, accents, punctuation-marks, critical-marks, orthographies, analogies, etymologies, glosses, distinctions, barbarisms, solecisms, faults, metaplasms, figurations, tropes, prose, metres, fables, and histories." The performance of Aelfric (see Chapter IX and note 20 below) is infinitely better.

67. Alcuin's sophistical reasoning in this book reflects little credit on the logic of the age. If the following passage, quoted by West in his

Alcuin and the Rise of the Christian Schools (New York, 1902), 104-105, is not to be taken as a joke—and Alcuin is not one of the world's great humorists—then it is flat; but it is in any case worth repeating:

> ALCUIN: What art thou?
> CHARLES: I am a man (*homo*).
> ALCUIN: See how thou hast shut me in.
> CHARLES: How so?
> ALCUIN: If thou sayest I am not the same as thou, and that I am a man, it follows that thou are not a man.
> CHARLES: It does.
> ALCUIN: But how many syllables has *homo*?
> CHARLES: Two.
> ALCUIN: Then thou art those two syllables?
> CHARLES: Surely not; but why dost thou reason thus?
> ALCUIN: That thou mayest understand sophistical craft and see how thou canst be forced to a conclusion.
> CHARLES: I see and understand from what was granted at the start, both that I am *homo* and that *homo* has two syllables, and that I can be shut up to the conclusion that I am these two syllables. But I wonder at the subtlety with which thou hast led me on, first to conclude that thou wert not a man, and afterward of myself, that I was two syllables.

At any rate, most of *De Rhetorica et Virtutibus* is not so jocose. A recent valuable translation is that by W. S. Howell (*Princeton Studies in English, No. 23*; Princeton, 1941).

68. Indebted also to St. Augustine's apocryphal work on Aristotle's *Categories*. It is probable that this work, along with the *Grammar* (see note 66 above) and the *De Rhetorica et Virtutibus* (see note 67 above), comprised the *trivium* of Alcuin's Palace School curriculum.

69. The standard edition is that of W. H. Stevenson (Oxford, 1904); based on Stevenson is A. S. Cook's edition (Boston-New York, 1906). The *Life* is also included in J. A. Giles, *Six Old English Chronicles*, in Bohn's Antiquarian Library (London, 1848).

70. The manuscript is unique and not in good condition, and the first edition (that of Archbishop Parker in 1574) is adulterated with additions and miscellaneous interpretations from the *Lives of St. Neots*. Stevenson, however, in the introduction to his edition (see note 69 above), disposes of most of the objections to the authenticity of the original. The Welsh and Latin proper names and the forms of scriptural quotation point clearly to the tenth century and to the indubitable fact that the author was a Celt. Much of Asser's work borrows from *The Anglo-Saxon Chronicle* (VIII, 3 below), and he shows also that

he is familiar with Continental chroniclers. See also the appropriate material in R. H. Hodgkin, *The History of the Anglo-Saxons* (Oxford, 1935) and G. M. Stenton, *Anglo-Saxon England* (London, 1943).

71. This is printed by Paul Ewald in *Historische Aufsätze dem Andenken an Georg Waitz gewidmet* (Berlin, 1886) and is discussed at length by Charles Plummer in his edition of Bede's *Historia Ecclesiastica* (Oxford, 1896), II, 389-391. The *Life of Pope Gregory the Great* is apparently of English origin, presumably from Whitby in Yorkshire, and was written most likely before Bede's *Historia Ecclesiastica*, because Plummer has pointed out parallels between Bede and the *Life*, and yet the author of the *Life* complains bitterly of the lack of helpful material available—something which would be absurd if Bede's fine *History* had been already written and known to him. There is a translation in Charles W. Jones, *Saints' Lives and Chronicles in Early England* (Ithaca, 1947).

72. There has been a good new edition by Bertram Colgrave, *Life of Bishop Wilfrid* (Cambridge, 1927) and a study in Eleanor S. Duckett, *Anglo-Saxon Saints and Scholars* (New York, 1947).

73. See Chapter IV and note 45 above in reference to *Guthlac B*. Nothing of importance is known of Felix; see, however, *Acta Sanctorum* (Paris, 1865-1931) for April 11. There is a new translation in Charles W. Jones, *Saints' Lives and Chronicles in Early England* (Ithaca, 1947).

74. The *Chronicle of Aethelweard* was first printed by Savile in his *Scriptores post Baedam* (London, 1596), having been fortunately transcribed from the unique Cotton manuscript which was later consumed in the fire of 1731. It has been reprinted by T. D. Hardy in *Monumenta Historica Britanniae* (London, 1848); and translations are given by J. A. Giles in *Six Old English Chronicles* (London, 1848) and by J. Stevenson in *Church Historians of England* (London, 1863), xxvii.

75. See the article on John Scotus in the *Dictionary of National Biography*. His major work, *De Divisione Naturae*, does not come strictly into the province of Old English literature. Some attention has been paid recently to the glosses on Marcian attributed to him; see Cora E. Lutz, *Iohannis Scottis Annotationes in Marcianum* (*Medieval Academy of America*, No. 34; Cambridge, Mass., 1939) and Cornelia C. Coulter, "The Date of John the Scot's *Annotationes in Marcianum*" in *Speculum*, XVI, 487-488, and E. K. Rand, "How Much of the *Annotationes in Marcianum* is the Work of John the Scot?" in *Transactions and Proceedings of the American Philological Association*, LXXI, 501-523.

76. The letters of Boniface are included in J. A. Giles, *Opera*

Omnia (London, 1844); in Ernst Dümmler, *Poetae Latini Aevi Carolini* (Berlin, 1884); and in Philipp Jaffé, *Monumenta Moguntina* (see note 31 above). The best recent collection is that of E. Emerton, *The Letters of Saint Boniface* (New York, 1940). A few of these letters have been translated by G. W. Robinson in *Papers of the American Society of Church History*, series 2, VII, 157-186 (New York, 1923); see also Edward Kyrlie, *The English Correspondence of Saint Boniface* (London, 1924) and G. W. Robinson, *Willibald's Life of St. Bonifacius* (Cambridge, Mass., 1916). There is a new study of Boniface in Eleanor S. Duckett, *Anglo-Saxon Saints and Scholars* (New York, 1947).

77. See J. Mabillon, *Annales Ordinis Sancti Benedicti Occidentalium Monachorum Patriarchae* (Paris, 1703-1739).

78. Some individual items, useful especially because of their bibliographical interest, are the following: W. Berbner, *Untersuchungen zu dem altenglischen Scriftboc* (Bonn, 1907)—especially pp. 7-16 and the bibliography; C. Gross, *Sources and Literature of English History from the Earliest Times to about 1485* (London-New York, 1915)—again for bibliography; Benjamin Thorpe, *Ancient Laws and Institutes of England* (London, 1840)—for Old English and Latin texts; M. Bateson, "The Supposed Latin Penitential of Ecgbert and the Missing Work of Halitgar of Cambrai" in *English Historical Review*, IX, 320-325; J. Raith, "Die altenglische Version des Halitgar'schen Bussbuches" in *Bibliothek der angelsächsischen Prosa*, XIII (Hamburg, 1933); R. Spindler, *Das altenglische Bussbuch* (Leipzig, 1934); and John T. McNeill and Helena M. Gamer, *Medieval Handbooks of Penance; a translation of the principal penitentials* (New York, 1938).

79. General considerations bearing upon the subject of this chapter are presented in F. J. E. Raby, *A History of Christian Latin Poetry from the Beginnings to the Close of the Middle Ages* (Oxford, 1927); W. Levison, *England and the Continent in the Eighth Century* (Oxford, 1946); and—in a distinctly limited way—Sister M. Charlotte, "The Latin Riddle Poets of the Middle Ages" in *Classical Journal*, XLII, 357-360.

VIII · The Work of King Alfred

1. GENERAL OBSERVATIONS

THE attainment by Wessex of the leadership of the English people came late in the ninth century under the presiding genius of Alfred the Great. The most remarkable figure in the Old English period, Alfred was also the fountain-head of Anglo-Saxon prose. When he came to the throne of Wessex in 871, he found his kingdom in parlous state, thanks to the Danes, and so the early part of his reign was devoted to the career of a military man. But once he had brought about the Treaty of Wedmore (878), he found time to cope with the intellectual poverty of his nation. The very fact that he was willing to cope with it marks Alfred as heroic, for he had been brought up with zeal by good teachers and knew full well the formidable obstacles that would have to be overcome to reduce the appalling ignorance of his countrymen. His general plan, however, was as simple as all great plans should be: "that we render into the language that we all know some of those books that are most necessary for all men to know . . . and that all the youth in England born of English freemen, who have the means to do so, be set to study . . . until such times as they shall have learned well how to read English books."[1]

Alfred's career still needs some sharpening of details in order to be as clear as one would like to have it. This is true of any man who bears the epithet "great." It is particularly true of Alfred because he happens to have earned the sobriquet. That he was the savior of his nation in an almost hopeless situation, that he formulated wise laws and administered them even more wisely, that he desired above everything else the betterment of his people, especially in an intellectual way —these are now self-evident facts. His only rival in stature would be a churchman such as the Venerable Bede. But Alfred was greater than Bede because in him the influence of the priest was blended with that of the warrior and the man of action. He was the resultant of the two forces emanating respectively from the Church and from the tradition of the Germanic fighter.

Alfred was born in 849, amid conditions which are obvious enough to the student of history, for the Danes had penetrated Mercia and were pressing hard on Wessex, having acquired that peculiar momentum which is familiar to all military experts. The struggle between Dane and West Saxon was no series of sudden, impromptu raids. The two nations had been locked in critical conflict during the reign of Alfred's older brother Ethelred I. Almost as soon as he came to the throne in 871, Alfred suffered a defeat at Wilton and was obliged to make a temporary truce. He put this respite to good use, however, built a little navy, and harried the invaders from the southern coasts of England. The details may be passed over here;[2] it is enough to say that within seven years the Danes had been restrained by the Treaty of Wedmore to the Danelagh. At the risk of repetition it must be emphasized, in justice to Alfred, that seven years constituted a remarkably short time for such a successful conclusion, considering the sporadic and unsystematic nature of much of the warfare. The Danish occupation of the Danelagh is a matter still under the close scrutiny of scholars; the amateur may find romantic interest in the part played by the old Roman roads in effecting practical boundaries.[3] More specifically, the Danes, having been restricted to this territory, were obliged by treaty to become subjects of the kings of Wessex, and their leaders were to be baptized as Christians. The terms of this treaty, it may be added, were adhered to with reasonable fidelity. The general area assigned the Danes coincided approximately with the region of old Anglia, although most of the settlement was at first in Mercia and East Anglia. It has already been remarked that the occupation of the Danelagh was a potent factor in the great Scandinavian influence upon the English language, an influence which is much greater than is generally realized.[4] In passing it might be said that the Christianization of the Danes seems to have softened somewhat the fierceness of their warlike dispositions and reduced their aggressiveness.

But all this was not done in a day, a week, or even a year. The difficulties, reverses, and narrow escapes which Alfred and his troops underwent during those seven years can scarcely be exaggerated. The Danes, moreover, succeeded in drawing to themselves the disaffected Celtic population of Wales and sections of Somersetshire, Devonshire, and Cornwall. Several times, indeed, it seemed that nothing could save Alfred from disaster, so that his ultimate triumph at Ethandun (Edington) and the subsequent treaty are all the more remarkable.

The military ability of Alfred has been dwelt upon here in order to furnish the proper contrast to his peacetime activities. There was never a better example than Alfred's career to give point to Milton's observation that Peace has her victories no less renowned than War. Alfred was able to spend the remaining years of his life—he died in 901—amid comparative quiet, except for some isolated difficulties with more Danish invaders. There were some minor rebellions within the Danelagh and two that were rather serious. These were due in large measure, however, to the appearance of new Danish marauders who were able to incite their brothers of the Danelagh to rise. One of these periods of anxiety came when a group of Danes made a foray on Rochester in 885. This was quickly broken up by the English. More dangerous was a protracted succession of small and very troublesome raids in the years between 893 and 897, especially the one in 895, when the Danes set up fortifications within twenty miles of London. But, to counterpoise these bothersome interludes, there were many years of unbroken peace; it was during those years that Alfred was able to turn to the more tranquil arts, among which the pursuit of education was to him the most important. We know regrettably little about this more domestic side of Alfred's career. Many an interesting story has grown up about him, but such stories are more properly to be called legends, and however much they may show him to advantage, they must be rejected as history.

One fact is clear, however, and that is that at the beginning of Alfred's reign the condition of his people was one of great ignorance. The chief original impetus to the learning of the Anglo-Saxons had gone by. Bede and Aldhelm had been dead for more than a century; the influence of Alcuin remained, to be sure, but that influence was appreciable mainly on the Continent. As Alfred tells us in his Preface to the Alfredian version of Gregory the Great's *Pastoral Care* (VIII, 2), learning had so declined in England that

.... there were very few this side of the Humber who could understand the service in English or could translate one word from Latin into English; and I think that there were not many beyond the Humber. So few there were that I could not think of a single man south of the Thames, when I came to rule this kingdom.

Perhaps Alfred paints the picture in too dark colors, for the Church, after all, was alive and apparently in sound health throughout the ninth century. There is little doubt, however, that the Church in England had entered into a state of quiescence in its teaching and needed a good rousing. We have no real evidence as to what the state of learning in the island may have been when Alfred died, but we know what he tried to do during his lifetime.

There are definite literary achievements which belong to his reign and are rightfully associated with his name; the only questionable point that arises in the minds of later readers has been the extent to which Alfred himself was the writer of these works. Did he actually undertake or did he merely superintend or influence the translations of standard works of learning?[5] In this same Preface to Gregory's *Pastoral Care*, he sounds as if he himself were the translator:

When I brought to mind how the knowledge of the Latin tongue had declined before this [Alfred's accession] throughout England, and nevertheless many knew how to read English writing, then I began among other varied and manifold businesses of the kingdom to turn that book into English which is called in Latin *Pastoralis*, and in English *Shepherd-Book*, sometimes word by word, sometimes sense by sense, just as I learned it from my archbishop Plegmund and from my bishop Asser, and from Grimbold my mass-priest and from John my mass-priest.

The first person pronoun in the singular may have no special significance, but the whole sentence reads like a very personal, direct statement in most characteristic Alfredian simplicity.

And so Alfred undertook—or possibly supervised, depending perhaps upon the individual case—the translation into English of the five most authoritative works of the period, as he conceived them: Boethius's *Consolation of Philosophy* (*De Consolatione Philosophiae*), a philosophical work of the sixth century based largely upon a Platonic foundation; Bede's *Ecclesiastical History of the English Nation* (VII, 3); Orosius's *Compendious History of the World*; the *Soliloquies* of Saint Augustine; and Gregory the Great's *Pastoral Care*, on the duties and responsibilities of the episcopal office. The books which he chose for translation illustrate the essentially wide interests of the man and scholar Alfred. There are in these works a wealth of commentary and happy attempts here and there to bring the works up to date; these additions it is difficult to assign to any other than the earnest, kindly, simple Alfred himself. In short, Alfred made accessible to the Englishmen of his kingdom a body of human knowledge remarkably well rounded for the time, touching as it did the best history of the nation, the most exhaustive geography and world-history of the age, a well-defined code of religious conduct, the steadying influence of an idealistic philosophy which had the further advantage of being closely akin to the teachings of Christ, and the essence of the patristic and ascetic spirit.

To Alfred's credit also must be entered the codification of the laws of Anglo-Saxon England, a collection which shows a strong Biblical influence.[6] Here again it is well to let him explain in person. He begins with a version in the vernacular of the Ten Commandments and adds some other important

stones in the edifice of Mosaic law. "These are the judgments which the Almighty God Himself spoke to Moses and
charged him to observe. . . ."

One of the most valuable activities of Alfred's reign, for
which we must doubtless thank the king himself, was the
stimulation of the writing of chronicle and history, as illustrated by *The Anglo-Saxon Chronicle*.[7] This represents a kind
of national journal, an account given in annual entries of the
notable events taking place in the kingdom during that year,
and with some few references to events outside the realm,
generally those having to do with the Church. It is, moreover,
in many passages a most spirited narrative in its own right.
The *Chronicle* possesses the further virtue of being informal,
sometimes to the point of being ungrammatical; it is not the
polished work of a Bede or the stylized story of an Aelfric,
but it is genuine. It is of varied authorship, editorship, and
scribal accomplishment and comes from different parts of
England. Its tradition is so hardy that it can be found even
after the middle of the twelfth century. Within the years following Alfred's accession we encounter more detail and more
verisimilitude, for it may be presumed that the entries for the
years before his accession were written by Alfred's strict contemporaries with an obvious purpose of bringing the chronicle
up to date, or else they were rewritings of old, bare entries
not known by the Alfredian scribes at first hand. Once the detail and verisimilitude have been clearly mastered, the qualities are retained, and again one feels that it is Alfred's influence which is responsible. The final entry for the *Chronicle*
is for the year 1154.[8]

The ascription to Alfred of sayings and epigrams, in the
special shape of *The Proverbs of Alfred*[9]—sayings which he
himself probably never originated—is but another tribute to
the remarkable influence of this king among kings. The *Proverbs* represent the sort of legendary, apocryphal utterances of
a mythical, all-wise, all-seeing hero of an Alfred; they are
paralleled, to take only two examples, by the mass of supposed proverbs attributed to Charlemagne[10] and to Solomon.[11]

But it remains now for us to look at the Alfredian works in somewhat greater detail, because they are by far the most varied and withal human documents surviving in all Old English vernacular prose.

2. THE ALFREDIAN WRITINGS

WE ARE indebted for most of the known details about Alfred and his works to Bishop Asser, whose *Life of Alfred* has been already described (VII, 5), along with a brief outline of Asser's own career. According to this Welsh churchman, he first met Alfred at Chichester in 884, and after a three-day conference he returned to his native Wales with the promise that he would thenceforth spend six months in the year with Alfred. He was delayed by illness for a year or more but began his sojourns in 885. He further observes that Alfred's *Handbook*, or *Encheiridion*,[12] a work which has been lost to us, was completed in 887, whereupon Alfred began his translations.

This *Handbook* appears to have been known somehow to the chroniclers of the twelfth century such as William of Malmesbury and Florence of Worcester. It would seem to have been Alfred's only absolutely original work; but its substance, on the other hand, was probably drawn mostly from the Bible or from the Church Fathers. It is altogether likely, however, that it contained some kind of history of the Anglo-Saxons; perhaps it included some of Aldhelm's songs (VII, 2); perhaps, again, it was in part a collection of wise saws and modern instances, whence the ascription to Alfred of *The Proverbs of Alfred*. As a matter of fact, several scholars have attempted to develop some sort of further connection between this book and Aldhelm's work.[13] Unfortunately there is nothing left to this question but speculations about the possible answer, since Asser's account of the *Handbook* is too vague. Regretfully, then, one must virtually ignore the *Handbook* as such and concentrate upon its value as an instrument for dating the general beginnings of Alfred's creative literary life.

As for the translations themselves, there is little on which to base a chronological order. The authorities have differed in the most astonishing way.[14] A composite of all their arguments would probably lead to the sequence: Boethius, Orosius, Gregory, Bede, and Augustine;[15] and there seems in fact to be a general agreement that the Boethius and the Orosius belong to a period somewhat earlier than that of the Bede and the Gregory. It is known that Asser used Boethius in his teaching of Alfred. Yet little beyond personal opinion can decide the matter; one might argue that the Boethius was a beginning, that Alfred's mind turned next to a consideration of the history of his own people, whence the translation of the Bede, that it moved next to the contemplation of the world, whence the translation of the Orosius, and then turned finally to the education of his people, as the preface to Gregory shows. There is no insistent logic in such a view, however, certainly no more than in one which would present the works in an exactly reversed order. Nevertheless, it is scarcely likely that Alfred would have undertaken the education of his people without having acquired some education of his own, unless, like Charlemagne, he was content to serve as sponsor—and student—of the educational endeavors of Asser and others. It would be fully as reasonable to insist that the *Pastoral Care* represents his first translation, as the opening gun in a serious campaign, for its educational purpose and program are practical enough. The nature of the *Pastoral Care* would then suggest to Alfred a history of the Church in England, of which Bede's fine work was a better than adequate representative. In order to achieve a kind of supplement to the Bede, he would next translate the Orosius. Ultimately, as he approached middle age, the significance of the Boethius would have special appeal to him.

Before undertaking a survey of these five major pieces of Alfredian prose, it might be convenient to dispose of the *Law Codes*. Since these are founded upon scriptural precedents, it is probable that they belong to the year 888, at which time, so Asser says, Alfred was finished with his Biblical study. The

Law Codes are in different sections: a *corpus* of Alfred's laws; a corpus of the laws of a predecessor, Ina, King of Wessex from 688 to 726; and a final section containing the Treaty of Wedmore between Alfred and King Guthrun of the Danes. The nature of these law-codes is best explained by comparing them with their Biblical antecedents (*Exodus*, xx-xxiii) and particularly the Golden Rule. In the corpus of Alfred's laws, however, comes this long but arresting sentence:

> I, then, Alfred the King, gathered these together, and had written down many of the laws which our predecessors observed insofar as they pleased me; and many of those which did not please me I rejected with the consent of my *witan* and bade them to be observed in other fashion; for I did not dare presume to set down many of my own in writing, because it was unknown to me which of my laws would be pleasing to those who were to come after us; but those which I found either in the days of Ina my kinsman or of Offa, King of the Mercians,[16] or of Ethelbert who first received baptism in England—those which seemed to me more just I gathered herein, and the others I abandoned.

This sentence explains the presence of Ina's code. Unfortunately the codes of both Offa and Ethelbert have been lost, except for a fragment here and there. It may be assumed that Alfred was thinking in terms of making his code eclectic but judicious; in this selective process he shows his true discretion and his remarkable liberalism. The details of his *Law-Codes* are for the social historian; we may content ourselves with the well known comment of Lees:[17]

> In spite of inconsistency and obscurity, Alfred's vernacular dooms, with their core of ancient custom, form a unique and invaluable record of early English law. Curt, elliptical, disjointed, their very heterogeneity is characteristic. They show a State in the making, inchoate still and weak, but reaching out towards centralization, and finding it, to a certain extent, in the person of the king. They show, moreover, the king gathering up the broken fragments of the older tribal society, and fitting them into some sort of coherent whole.

Strong as was the force of custom, Alfred at least was able to rearrange the custom-law, to decide in what way one or another part of it should be observed, and to frame new rules to meet new cases. If he did not dare to set down much of his own in writing, it was no small matter that he dared to innovate at all, for it meant that the king was powerful enough to be a constructive statesman.

Let us now return to the matter of the Alfredian translations. The *Pastoral Care* is preserved in seven manuscripts,[18] three from Alfred's time or shortly thereafter, and the others from as late as the eleventh century. The piece is not interesting literature, but it is extremely valuable, first, as indicating Alfred's whole plan, and again for the manner in which it exemplifies the technique of the Alfredian translations. Unlike the other works, the translation of the *Pastoral Care* contains almost no original matter, with the exception of the Preface, and it is in fact a fairly faithful paraphrase rather than an exact translation. In other words, Alfred here is prone to adopt a "sense by sense" rather than a "word by word" rendering. Since the most significant part of the work, the Preface, has already been touched upon, we may proceed to the next piece.

The Alfredian version of Bede's *Ecclesiastical History of the English Nation* survives in four complete manuscripts and in portions of a fifth.[19] Alfred himself is not named in any of these, but Aelfric and William of Malmesbury both credit him with being the translator. In a sense, of course, Alfred is merely Bede's mouthpiece; but, after all, Alfred is speaking in the vernacular, and his medium is simpler, more naïve, more uncultivated than Bede's dignified Latin, and so the flavor of the Alfredian version is often altogether different. There are a half-dozen passages in this work which should receive honorable consideration in any history of English prose. One occurs in the account of the landing of Augustine and of his preachings before Ethelbert of Kent.[20] Finer still is the story of the conversion of Edwin of Northumbria by Paulinus;[21] indeed, these particular lines are regarded by many as the high point of Anglo-Saxon literature, whether prose or poetry:

When the king heard these words, he answered and said that it was both his desire and duty to receive the faith which the bishop taught. Yet, he said, he would speak and take counsel with his friends and wise men, and if they agreed with him, all together would be consecrated to Christ in the fount of life. Then the king did as he said, and the bishop assented. So he conferred and took counsel with his wise men, and asked all of them separately their opinion about this new doctrine and worship of God, which was taught therein. Then the chief priest, called Coefi, answered: "Consider for your part, O king, what this doctrine is that is now preached to us. I truly confess to you, what I have learned for certain, that the religion we have held and maintained hitherto is without all use or excellence. For none of your followers devoted himself more closely or cheerfully to the worship of our gods than I did, but nevertheless many have received more gifts and promotion from you than I, and in all things have prospered more. Well, I am sure if our gods have any power they would help me more, for I more zealously served and obeyed them. Therefore, if you consider this religion to be fairer and stronger, which is newly preached to us, it seems wise to me that we should receive it." Another of the king's counselors, one of his chief men, assented to his words, and taking up the speech spoke thus: "O king, the present life of man on earth, in comparison with the time unknown to us, seems to me as if you sat at table with your chief men and retainers in winter-time, and a fire was kindled and your hall warmed, while it rained and snowed and stormed without; and there came a sparrow and swiftly flew through the house, entering at one door and passing out through the other. Now as long as he is within, he is not beaten by the storms of winter; but that is only the twinkling of an eye and a moment of time, and at once he passes back from winter into winter. So then this life of man appears for but a little while; what goes before, or what comes after, we know not. And so if this new doctrine reports anything more certain or apt, it deserves to be followed."[22]

The thoughtful reader can well ponder the spread of Christianity through the pagan world of Anglo-Saxon Britain in terms of the last sentence in this quotation. Again, consider the accounts in Bede of Aidan[23] and of the herdsman Caedmon.[24] The first of these explains as almost no other passage in English literature the thoroughgoing zeal of the early churchman. The second of these gives us our only information about Caedmon, explaining that this humble cowherd was unable to partake of the gift of song, as did his more fortunate fellows in the establishment of the Abbess Hild; yet he was visited by an angel and thenceforth became a master of holy story in poetry (IV, 3). When it came his time to die, he, like all the holy people in Bede's history, departed in blessedness. But there is a strange, peaceful impressiveness about the story of Caedmon's passing that is distinguished:

> For when it grew near the time of his death and departure, fourteen days before that he was oppressed and afflicted with bodily infirmity, yet moderately so that he could all the time speak and walk about. There was close at hand a house for the sick, into which it was their custom to bring those who were infirm and those who were at the point of death, and tend them together. Then he bade his attendant, on the evening of the night on which he was to depart from the world, to prepare a place for him in that house, that he might rest. Then the attendant wondered, why he should ask this, for it seemed to him that his death was not so near; nevertheless he did as he had said and directed. And when he went to bed there, and cheerfully spoke and jested with those who were in the house, then after midnight he asked them, whether they had the Eucharist in the house. Then they answered and said: "What need have you of the Eucharist? It is not so near to your death, seeing that you speak thus cheerfully and brightly to us." He repeated: "Bring me the Eucharist." When he had it in his hand, he asked whether they all felt peaceably and cheerfully disposed towards him, without any rancor. They all answered, and said that they had no malice towards him, but all were most friendly disposed to him; and they in turn prayed him to feel kindly towards them. Then he answered and said:

"Dear brethren, I feel very friendly towards you and all God's servants." And so he fortified himself with the heavenly viaticum, and prepared his entry into another life. Then once more he asked, how near it was to the hour that the brothers should arise and raise the song of praise to God and sing lauds. Then they answered: "It is not far off." He said: "Good! Let us indeed await the hour." And he prayed and signed himself with the token of God's cross, and laid down his head on the pillow and fell asleep for a time; and so in quiet ended his life. And so it came to pass, that as with pure and simple heart and with tranquil devotion he served his Lord, so he also by a peaceful death left the earth and appeared before God's presence. And the tongue which composed so many words of salvation in praise of the Creator, concluded its last words to His glory, as he crossed himself and commended his spirit into His hands.

This passage and the foregoing one, while long, are necessary to illustrate just what Bede was doing in addition to chronicling the events which he considered important in the unfolding of English history. A final passage, the unusual Vision of Drihthelm, has already been mentioned (VII, 3).[25] One cannot resist the temptation, however, to call attention to the truly Dantesque tone in:

As I was being led there, suddenly my guide disappeared, I knew not where, leaving me in the midst of darkness and my fearful vision. And while these masses of fire incessant shot up on high or sank down again into the bottomless pit, I looked and saw that all the points of the ascending flames were full of men's souls, which, like ashes ascending with smoke, were now cast up on high; now again, as the fiery vapor subsided, slipped back once more to the bottomless abyss. And an intolerable foulness steamed up with the fiery vapor, and filled all the place of darkness. When I had stood there for a long time in terror, and knew not what to do, where to go, or what was coming to me, I suddenly heard behind me a loud sound of violent, piteous weeping, as well as loud cackling laughter, as if a rude mob were mocking its captive foes. And when the sound came nearer to me, I saw a crowd of accursed spirits dragging and leading into the midst of darkness five men's souls lamenting and sorrowing, and they exulted, laughing exceedingly. . . . Meantime there rose up some of the dark spirits out of the abyss and place of torment, and surrounded me. They had fiery eyes and blew foul fire out of mouth and nostrils; and they held in their hands fiery tongs, and they beset me, and threatened to seize me with them and hurl me to destruction. But though they thus terrified me, still they dared not touch me.

Perhaps it is the account of the miraculous which is most striking in the *Ecclesiastical History*, precisely the kind of thing which weakens Bede's work in the eyes of scientific twentieth-century historians. For Bede has a somewhat romantic mind. The factual elements in his history, however, are sound enough most of the time, and his method is acceptable even to a modern. We are privileged as readers of his literature to receive both the miraculous and the factual and to appraise the fact and fiction as we choose.

A goodly amount of attention has been bestowed upon the Alfredian *Orosius*,[26] partly because of its subject-matter, but chiefly because in this work Alfred contributed much of his own; scarcely a chapter goes by without some alterations of the original. In the early fifth century, Paulus Orosius, a Spanish monk who was an avowed disciple of the great Church Father St. Augustine, undertook on his own initiative a kind of outline history of the world as he knew it, and dedicated it to his spiritual progenitor. The *Compendious History of the World*, as it is now generally known, is poor stuff both as regards history and as regards prose composition, but it was the best that the age possessed for its purpose. That Alfred should have selected it as a work of educational value cannot therefore be held against him.

As it happens, however, Alfred makes a great many additions, subtractions, and general corrections in the *Orosius*, but these changes are in the general direction of a condensation. The most important of his insertions occurs near the beginning, where he fills out the geographical information—which, since it was written originally by a southern European, is concerned mainly with the Mediterranean world—with some further direct information about the world to the north and east of England. He relies for this on the tales of two travelers: a Norwegian named Ohthere, who gives an account of his experience in the most northerly parts of the Scandinavian peninsula, and a Dane named Wulfstan, who traveled in the Baltic.

The work begins, however, in a manner characteristic of the Middle Ages, with an enumeration of the "divisions of the world." Europe, Asia, and Africa are broken down into their proper districts, although some of the details, such as the Blessed Isles beyond the Mount of Atlas, place the sure stamp of antiquity upon the information. The description of Europe closes with a brief allusion to the Scandinavian countries, whereupon Alfred inserts first an enumeration of the various tribes and regions of northern and central Europe, and then the stories of the voyages of Ohthere and Wulfstan.

The sections devoted to these voyages have all the usual interest which any travel-story will possess; taken together, they constitute the first travelogue in English literature and are intimately associated with the great English sea-tradition. Ohthere went north along the coast of Norway, around the North Cape into the White Sea; he gives a sketchy indication of the wildness and desolation of the region and how the few inhabitants eke out a poor existence from the soil and depend largely upon their fishing for sustenance, particularly upon their walrus-hunting, for these creatures have "very noble bones in their teeth." Unlike the Germanic tribes, the Permians living along the shores of the White Sea plough with horses instead of oxen. Wulfstan's voyage carried him from "aet Haethum" (Haddeby) in Sleswick eastward through the Baltic to what is now the Frische Haff, the large freshwater inlet to the south of the Gulf of Danzig. At the outset, Wulfstan's account is as factual a catalogue of place-names as Ohthere's; but when he comes to the point where he encounters the Esthonians, he tells much of the funeral customs of these people, of their method of distributing inheritance, and of their mysterious devices for thermal control, because they had some principle of refrigeration and the preservation of food. Lord Bacon, in the seventeenth century, would have been fascinated by this achievement of the Esthonians, but in Alfred's narrative it is merely a statement of fact and nothing more. Thus does the medieval differ from the modern.

Little of interest remains in the *Compendious History*. As remarked before, the geographical information is presented in dried-up fashion and is besides none too accurate. The episodes from Greek and Roman history are often promising from a dramatic point of view, but their dramatic potentialities are sadly wasted. So it is with the stories of Leonidas, of the siege of Rome by the Gauls, and of the fine epic material concerning Alexander the Great—material which it remained for the Middle English period to develop more fully for English literature. The account of Hannibal is something of an exception to the depressing rule. It is lively and not untouched by the tragic aspects of the protagonist. Particularly inadequate, however, is the tale of Antony and Cleopatra. It should not be charged to Alfred that these stories are ineptly told; his source is obviously to blame. Yet it is a pity that he did not inject his own personality into this work to the same degree that he did into the others.

The Alfredian *Boethius* (*De Consolatione Philosophiae*[27]) survives in two versions, represented (1) by Manuscript Cotton Otho A VI,[28] approximately contemporary with Alfred, and (2) by Manuscript Bodleian NE.C.3.11,[29] about two centuries younger. The essential difference between these two versions lies in the fact that the older one has translated the Meters of Boethius into Old English alliterative verse; the younger, into Old English prose. There has been much dispute over the question whether or not Alfred did the metrical translations;[30] if so, they represent his only work in the field of Old English verse. This question is virtually impossible to answer. If, as most scholars believe, the translation was completed in Alfred's later years, when he had achieved maturity in the art of translation, the versifying would be quite credible. Indeed, both versions attribute the entire translation, verse as well as prose, to Alfred himself without qualifications. There is unfortunately no indication that these prefatory ascriptions were written in Alfred's time. The consensus, however, which assigns the *Boethius* a date late in Alfred's career, is based upon the general success and skill of his translating and paraphrasing. Such a basis would make plausible Alfred's unprecedented writing of verse. He is known to have had a fancy for songs and poetry in his boyhood, and there is little reason to assume that he was incapable of poetic speech in the approved tradition of the *scop*.

A side-glance at Boethius's *De Consolatione Philosophiae*, which is probably the most important single philosophical influence upon the literature of the Middle Ages, would not be amiss at this moment. Of the author it is known that he was born in the later years of the fifth century of a prominent Roman family; his father was consul in the year 487; his father-in-law also occupied that office. Boethius was admitted to the Senate while still in his twenties, served as consul in 510, and saw his two sons serve as consuls in 522. This was during the reign of Theodoric. His fortunes were suddenly reversed, however, soon after his golden year of 522: he was charged with attempting to put the power of the Senate above that of the Emperor, was imprisoned, and was put to death in 524. According to his own testimony, he had contemplated a modernization and translation of all the writings of Plato and Aristotle. He was never able to carry out this plan, although he did complete Aristotle's *Categories* and *De Interpretatione*. It is not known for certain whether or not he was officially a Christian, but he joined in the controversy among Catholic churchmen in which he maintained an orthodox position against Nestorianism,[31] as Alcuin was to do three hundred years later.[32]

But *De Consolatione Philosophiae*, written, as he tells posterity, while he was in prison awaiting what proved to be the end, is at once Boethius's contribution to the future and the chief monument to his name, although he is still remembered among musicologists for his work on early Occidental music. Broadly speaking, *De Consolatione Philosophiae* is permeated with Platonic ideas. Its form is rather peculiar—apparently an imitation of a somewhat similar work by Martianus Capella (ca. 400), *De Nuptiis Philologiae et Mercurii.*[33] It consists of five books, and is alternately in prose and in verse; the prose being more expository or dialectic, the verse more lyrical. The verse itself is facile and often pretty and is derived in large measure from Seneca. In the first book, after some autobiographical passages, Boethius explains how Sorrow has aged him. In his grief, an impressive-looking woman makes her appearance; he has some difficulty recognizing her, but she finally reveals herself to be his beloved guardian, Philosophy (Wisdom). She is determined to bring him consolation and so begins to cross-examine him to that end. She elicits from him the belief that God rules the world; but he deplores the fact that he has no self-knowledge. This lack, she assures him, is the very cause of his woe. So ends the first book. In the second, Philosophy introduces Fortune to Boethius. Fortune advertises herself as a bringer of blessings, but Philosophy shows that these blessings are all untrustworthy and unsatisfactory. In the third book, Philosophy holds out to Boethius the possibility of attaining true happiness, which lies only in God Himself—God is the highest good, and the highest good is true happiness, therefore God is true happiness. God furthermore, being omnipotent and not wishing evil, negates all evil. In the fourth book, Boethius, who is not at all convinced of the non-existence of evil, asks how it is that evil can appear to exist, if God is truly good. Why do the virtuous suffer, and why do the wicked prosper? Philosophy replies, with demonstrations, that this evil is apparent, not real; no wickedness is unpunished and no virtue is unrewarded. She turns to the difficult problems of Providence, Freewill, and Destiny, and shows that every fortune is good. In the fifth and final book, man's freewill and God's foreknowledge are balanced against each other; and an attempt is made to show that neither is inconsistent with the other, or with God. The conclusion is reached, in happy summation, that the omnipresent eternity of God's vision agrees with the future quality of our actions, dispensing rewards to the good and punishment to the wicked.

Whatever the circumstances underlying the two versions of the Alfredian *Boethius*—whether they are translated, in accordance with the Boethian scheme, in alternate prose and metrical passages, or rendered entirely in prose—one fact is clear. The arrangement of the original has been altered. Boethius's work was in five books; Alfred has divided the whole into forty-two chapters, with occasional references to the plan of the original. These many chapters are subdivided into often as many as half a dozen sections; the divisions are logical enough, but, since they do not conform in any way to the design of Boethius's book, it is awkward to refer from the translation to the original. Moreover, it is well to remember that Alfred has several opportunities to contract and to expand in his typical fashion—opportunities which he seizes with great effectiveness. It is no doubt unnecessary to enumerate here all the additions, subtractions, insertions, and corrections in the Alfredian versions for their own sakes; a brief indication of the purple passages with which the original is decked and which Alfred has doggedly tried to reproduce in substance if not in essence, will certainly be in order.

There is, for example, the noted Boethian Meter descriptive of the Golden Age,[34] a classical motif which needs no discussion here. It is an instructive though a rather lengthy business to compare the prose version in the later Bodleian manuscript with the metrical version in the earlier Cottonian manuscript, for the comparison illustrates very well the kind of difficulty which the relationship of the two versions will present. First, the prose:

> O, how happy was the first age of this wide world, when to every man there seemed enough in the fruits of the earth! There were then no splendid homes, nor various sweetmeats

nor drinks; nor were they desirous of costly garments, for they were not yet, nor did they see or hear anything of them. They cared not for any luxury, but very moderately followed Nature. They always ate once in the day, and that was in the evening. They ate the fruits of the trees and the herbs. They drank no pure wine, nor knew they how to mix any liquor with honey, nor cared they for silken apparel of many colors. They always slept in the shade of trees. They drank the water of the clear springs. No merchant visited island or coast, nor did any man as yet hear of any ship-army, nor was there even talk of war. The earth was not yet stained with the blood of slain men, nor was any one even wounded. They did not look upon evil-minded men; such had no honor and no man loved them. Alas! that our times cannot now become such! But now the covetousness of man is as burning as the fire in that Hell, which is in the mountain called Aetna, in the island that is called Sicily. The mountain burns ever with brimstone, and burns up all the near places about. Alas! who was the first greedy man, who first began to dig the earth after gold, and after gems, and found the dangerous treasure, which before was hidden and covered by the earth. . . .

Truly a comprehensive statement of the cult of the primitive in literature and philosophy, such as would make a Rousseauist water at the mouth! Now, as to the metrical version:

Lo! that first age was for every dweller
Over the expanse of earth a thing availing,
Then, when the fruits of the earth seemed to each
Sufficient. It is no longer thus!
There were not throughout the world splendid homes,
Nor various food and drink;
Nor did they care aught for garments,
Which lordly men now regard so highly;
For there were none such as yet.
Nor did they behold seafarers,
Nor did they hear of any about.
Lo! they were not wicked in their sinful lusts,
But only lived as they could with measure,
Following Nature, as Christ fashioned her;

But once a day did they eat
In the evening the fruits of the earth,
Of herbs and woodland; no wine did they drink
Bright from the beaker. There was no rascal
Who knew how to mix meat and drink,
Or liquor and honey; nor did they sew
Silken garments; nor in their artifice
Did they weave costly weaving or rear great palaces;
But ever they rested themselves
In sleep beneath a shade-tree; water from the brook
They drank, cold from the spring. No merchant saw they
Bearing noble wares over the mingling of waves;
Nor knew the peoples of ship-armies;
Nor even did a man talk of war.
The earth was not yet stained
With the blood of a warrior, when the sword reddened him,
Nor indeed did earth-dwellers behold
A wounded man under the sun. None since was of worth
In this world, if they perceived his mind
Did harbor evil among men—he was hated by all.
Alas! that it might be so, or that God would have it,
That on earth now in these days of ours
Throughout the wide world there might be such
Anywhere under the sun! But it is slacker now,
For greed has marred the heart
Of every man, so that he has a care no longer;
But it burns and wells up in his mind,
Even such greed, as has no bottom
Sleeps blackly in each, like indeed
To the mountain which the sons of men
Call Aetna, that on the island
Sicily burns in brimstone—
Men call it Hell-fire far and wide,
Because it is ever and ever burning
And about it all neighboring places
It burns blue with its bitter flames.
Alas! who was the first
Avaricious man in this world,
Who grubbed in these fields
For gold and precious gems?

> Lo! he has found a miserable treasure
> Concealed in the world beneath water and earth!

The juxtaposition of these two versions affords a fair estimate of the relative merits of the two, as prose and as poetry, and it is equally fair as an illustration of the Boethian Meters in their Old English shape and form. He who has read sufficiently in Old English poetry whether epic or elegiac will recognize at once, even from a Modern English translation, the inferiority of technique in these Boethian poems. The Alfredian verses are, moreover, heavily didactic in a more wordy manner than the prose version alone; they intrude Christian reflection—where there is no convincing evidence that Boethius was himself a Christian—and they exhibit a homiletic turn in characteristic though inartistic fashion.

In considering further noteworthy passages in the Alfredian prose version, however, we come upon this typical distrust of fame:[35]

> Whoever desires to have vain fame and unprofitable glory, let him behold on the four sides of him, how spacious the expanse of the heaven is and how narrow the space of the earth, though it seem large to us.

What has become of great men like Brutus or Cato? To the names of these Roman figures Alfred adds the name of Wayland, the mythical Germanic smith. The passage is paralleled at greater length in the metrical version. Another section somewhat farther along[36] celebrates the Creator and His wonders, the seasons and their control, the powers of nature and their signs. These ideas Boethius relates clearly to a monotheistic principle; Alfred, in keeping with the tradition of other Christian translators of pagan or near-pagan works of literature, chooses to equate this monotheistic principle to the Christian God, "the same God" who "joins people together in friendship and unites families in cleanly love, who brings together friends and companions, that they faithfully may hold their compacts and their friendships." The metrical version of this passage follows the prose version perhaps more closely than is usually the case. Still another Boethian Meter of eloquence is that which treats of the nature of all creatures and their dispositions and the way in which God influences them.[37]

> There is no creature formed which desires not to come thither whence it came before, that is, to rest and tranquility. The rest is with God, and it is God. But every creature turns on itself like a wheel; and so it thus turns that it may again come where it was before, and be the same that it was before. . . .[38]

To judge from the whole product, it would appear that the Alfredian work translates the Boethian Meters effectively enough as to substance; they are essentially poetic in the original anyhow, and though derivative, often graceful. Some suggestion, at least, of their charm comes through in the Alfredian translations—particularly in the prose translations, indeed, for these achieve some of the simplicity and freshness of the original, whereas the metrical translations in the main are awkward and pedestrian. From the standpoint of the pure philosopher, the dialectics of Boethius are poor, and his prose sections suffer in consequence. But in these prose sections there are nevertheless many arresting lines. There is, for instance, the passage on the limitations of kings,[39] and the wretchedness of the tyrant with the Damoclean sword over his head must have appealed to Alfred, the responsible ruler of his people. In fact, the theory of natural equality in Chapter xxx is prophetic of the democratic Englishman:

> Why do you then exalt yourselves above other men on account of your birth, without cause, since you can find none who are not noble, if you are willing to remember the creation and the Creator, and the birth of every one of you?

The long Meter in praise of this Creator is one of the noblest sections of *The Consolation of Philosophy* and does much to explain the hold which Boethius had upon the medieval world:

> O my Lord, how Thou art almighty,
> Great and wonderful. . . .
> Lo! thou eternal God of all Creation,
> Who created wondrously well
> The invisible as indeed the visible. . . .[40]

Or to pick up the prose version: "Good is not to come to Thee from without, but it is Thine own." The passages on Providence and Freewill are involved and not convincing,[41] as Alfred gives them; the philosophical problem seems too weighty for him, as indeed it does for Boethius, although Boethius at least is glib.

It is in the lines from Boethius which contain allusions to figures of classical legend or history that Alfred finds his best opportunity to insert his own personality. As in the case of the voyages of Ohthere and Wulfstan from the *Orosius*, he speaks here as an Englishman of the ninth century. Thus in Boethius there is a chance reference (Book III, prose 12) to the wars of the Titans against Jupiter; this suggests to the English Christian the story of Nimrod and the Tower of Babel, and he tells it briefly. More extended are the narratives of Orpheus and Eurydice[42] and of Ulysses and Circe.[43] The treatment of a poetic ancient Greek legend by an earnest English medieval teacher, while incongruous, is none the less illuminating and even downright amusing. The symbolism and the exquisite poetic possibilities of these stories are beyond Alfred; but they convey to him a message, and so he tells the legend, or as he calls it, the "lying tale" to serve as an illustration, or *exemplum*, of the idea that

> Every man desires to flee the darkness of Hell, and to come to the light of the true God, that he look not about him to his old vices, so that he practise them again as fully as he did before.[44]

The Hellenist may well resent the suggestion that hapless Eurydice should personify vices, but to the medieval Christian this conception was in no way repellent. And in telling the story Alfred achieves an artless simplicity which is quaint and charming in its naïveté:

It happened once that there was a harper in the country called Thrace, which was in the kingdom of the Greeks. The harper was very immeasurably good. His name was Orpheus. He had a peerless wife. She was called Eurydice. Then they came to say concerning this harper, that he could harp so that the wood wagged, and the stones stirred themselves for the sound, and wild beasts would run up and stand as if they were tame; so still, that though men or hounds went against them, they would not shun them. Then, they said, the harper's wife had to die, and her soul must be led to Hell. Then the harper was said to be so sorry that he could not be among other men, but took to the woods and sat on the mountains, both by day and by night, weeping and harping, so that the woods trembled and the rivers stood still, and no hart shunned any lion nor hare any hound; nor did tame animals know any hatred or fear of others for the pleasure of that sound. Then it seemed to the harper that nothing in the world would please him, and that he would seek the gods of Hell and try to soothe them with his harping, and pray them, that they give him back again his wife. . . .

Orpheus goes to the entrance to Hell; there he meets aged Charon and particularly Cerberus, the hell-hound; "he was said to have three heads; and he began to rejoice with his tail and play with him for his harping." The Parcae appear, and Orpheus sees many of the famous prisoners of the lower world, such as Tantalus and Ixion and Tityus. "When he had harped for a long time, then spoke the king of the people of Hell, saying: 'Let us give the man his wife, for he has earned her by his harping.'" Eurydice is granted to Orpheus, on the familiar condition that he lead her away without looking back at her.

But love one can restrain with difficulty or not at all: well-away! Lo! Orpheus led his wife with him until he came to the boundary of light and darkness. . . . When he came forth into the light, then he looked behind his back toward the woman; and she was then immediately lost to him.[45]

This incident has been quoted at some length, for it is necessary that it should speak for itself. In its picturesqueness it surpasses the episode of Ulysses and Circe, which is found also in the metrical versions.[46] The chief interest in this account of Ulysses and Circe arises from the general inadequacy of Alfred's treatment of an exotic sex-situation, and specifically from the clumsy narrative of Circe's magic spell:

> As soon as she saw the king driven thither . . . whose name was Ulysses, then she began to love him, and each of them the other, beyond all moderation; so that he for love of her forgot all his kingdom and his family, and dwelt with her until the time that his thanes would no longer remain with him. . . . And it is said that she by her sorcery overthrew the men, and cast them into the bodies of wild animals, and afterwards threw them into chains and fetters. Some, it is said, she transformed into lions, and when they would speak, then they roared. Some became wild boars, and when they would lament their wretchedness, then they grunted. Some became wolves. They howled when they would speak. Some became that kind of wild beast that men call tiger.[47]

The metrical version adds nothing and is far less coherent as narrative.

Of course the metrical versions, since they draw upon the same material as the prose versions, are bound to be reasonably close to the prose translation. To some scholars[48] the closeness of the metrical versions to the prose is remarkable. The Old English Boethian Meters are further significant in that their metrical scheme is freer than is usually the case in Anglo-Saxon poetry—instead of the customary four-beat alliterative measure with marked caesura, there are many more half-lines with more than the two primary stresses which are normal. These hypermetrical lines, so it has been suggested,[49] are due to the closeness with which the Meters follow the prose translations of the original Latin verse; that is, in order to keep as nearly as possible the language of the prose translations, Alfred (or whoever the poet was) feels obliged to extend his lines beyond the customary four feet. Such a suggestion, of course, implies that the prose version was done first.

The Meters, however, so far as substance goes, contribute nothing that will not be found in the prose version, do not say what they have to say any better, and have the additional drawback of not representing completely the form of the original anyway. All this quite apart from the fact that they are generally poor poetry as poetry. There are thirty-nine Meters in the original *De Consolatione Philosophiae*; there are only thirty-one Alfredian Meters. The remaining eight have either been absorbed into the neighboring prose sections or else have been omitted entirely.

The first Alfredian Meter, for example, contains material which Boethius assigned to prose, and quite properly, since it is preliminary historical exposition. Because the subject-matter, however, is that of the Goths and their conquest of Rome, it has been put into verse and is about as vigorous narrative as anything in these Meters. The third Alfredian Meter is a somber and effective lyric, for its brevity commends it to the lyrical spirit:

> Alas! in what grim and bottomless abysm
> Labors the darkening spirit,
> When the strong storms of worldly cares
> Beat down upon it. . . .

Sometimes there is an incisive bit of nature-worship:

> When the sun shines brightest
> And clearest down from Heaven,
> Straightway are they darkened,
> All other stars over the earth;
> For their brightness is as naught
> When set beside the light of the sun.[50]

When, however, we find introduced such figures as Nero or Ulysses, with an attempt to draw the obvious morals which these figures suggest, then the result in these Meters is prosaic and inconclusive, and the blame can be divided here between the poetic ineffectiveness of the original and the not unexpected failure of the translation to enhance the Boethian material. And again,

> . . . . Thus it will be
> That to every man the weather will be fairer
> If storms have come upon him a little before,
> And a stark wind from the north and east.
> To none would the day be a gracious thing,
> If dim night had not sooner brought terror to men.[51]

Or the interest in nature may take the form of some manifestation of moral didacticism:

> Lo! the wild bee, though she be wise,
> Will altogether perish
> If in her rage she stingeth aught;
> So shall every soul straightway be lost,
> If the body be spotted with whoredom,
> If repentance come not to the heart,
> Before one passes hence.[52]

The twentieth Meter, the hymn in praise of the greatness of God, treats in substance what has already been mentioned. This theme is unquestionably the most exalted in the entire collection—and the poem is the longest, if not the wordiest, of all the Meters. Far more effective in its joyous fervor is the one following:

> I have pinions swifter than the bird's;
> With them I can fly far from earth
> Over the lofty roof of the heavens.
> But now I must bepinion thy spirits
> And thy soul itself with my feathers,
> Until thou canst behold this mid-earth,
> Each earthly thing in all its fullness,
> Sport with thy pinions in the mighty heavens,
> Whirling about far up in the clouds
> Gazing down from above over all. . . .[53]
> . . . . If thou canst truly soar
> Till thou leavest behind thy highest sphere,
> Then canst thou have thy share of the true light . . .

Then wilt thou say and publish forthwith:
"This is all my true homeland,
My dwelling and nation; hence I came of yore
And was born through the midst of the All-knowing One;
Never will I depart from here,
But forever will stand here in comfort
Yet safe through the will of my Father."[54]

It is of course truly difficult to deny Boethius a direct affinity to Christian belief; and this affinity the West Saxon translator, be he Alfred or Alfred's man, has cultivated to the utmost. Again, we may be shown once more our ever-present companion, the sea:

Why must you ever trouble your mind
With unrighteous hate, as the waves of the sea-flood
Stir up the ice-cold ocean,
And heave it aloft before the wind?[55]

And now there is a new note to blend with the old elegiac paganism:

Why upbraid your fate, forasmuch as she has no power?
Why can you not await the bitter taste
Of death, which the Lord has shaped for you,
Towards which he hastens you each new day?[56]

Here, in fact, Wyrd has given away and become the handmaiden of Christian resignation.

In a manuscript of a twelfth-century hand, a manuscript now bound with that which contains *Beowulf*,[57] has survived a translation of the *Soliloquies* of St. Augustine. The translation was at first accepted as Alfred's, then rejected, then once more accepted.[58] Alfred's name is not attached to the work, but then it is not actually attached to any of the translations except in the case of the preface to Gregory's *Pastoral Care* and the highly debatable foreword to the *Boethius*.[59] The absence of the name, in other words, is of no special significance. The *Soliloquies* are not named in lists of Alfred's work like those of William of Malmesbury in the early twelfth century, but after all no complete catalogue of Alfred's work is in existence. And the fact remains that in Alfred's time no layman except the king himself seems of sufficient intellectual stature to have done the work, particularly in view of the personal style which seems to be evident in certain lines.[60] In the absence of positive testimony to the contrary, Alfred can be indicated as the translator.

This work comprises not only the two portions of St. Augustine's *Soliloquies* but also a third section in the form of a re-working of the same Church Father's *De Videndo Dei*.[61] The first part is a fairly close translation of the first book of Augustine; the second is a kind of anthology, a culling of "blossoms," of the important ideas and sentiments of the second book of the *Soliloquies*. The third section applies the dialogue form of the *Soliloquies* to the tract *De Videndo Dei*. After due consideration, it can be generally conceded that Alfred's translation belongs to the latter years of Alfred's life —whether or not after the *Boethius* is uncertain—for it shows a considerable maturity and skill in the handling of the difficult and bare original. It is apparent that in preparing the version of the *Soliloquies* Alfred had occasional recourse not only to the work of Augustine himself, but to Pope Gregory the Great's *Dialogues* and *Morals* and to St. Jerome's *Vulgate* and his *Commentary on Luke*.

The translation of the *Soliloquies* attempts the ambitious double task of explaining the nature of God and the nature of the human spirit. The first book is a search for the presence of God; the second has for its focal point the question of the immortality of the soul. The first book demonstrates the need of Faith, Hope, and Charity as guides to the finding of God; Truth is a fourth necessity. The second book is to the thoughtful philosopher an unsatisfactory piece of exposition, but so is Augustine's original. When Alfred begins his translation, he adheres to the Latin with much fidelity; but the farther he proceeds, the more he departs from his original. Thus in Book 1, Alfred makes four important insertions—in so far as the subject-matter will allow, they may be called original compositions—on the vicissitudes of nature, a rather elaborate

metaphor on the ship and the anchor, on seeing God and
working with Him, and the parable of the king and his subject.[62] We have seen this kind of insertion before, but nowhere
previously have they shown themselves to be so clearly artistic
improvements on the original. Indeed, the preface itself is an
excellent example of an authentic Alfredian contribution, and
its sentiments fit Alfred better than any other man of his day
in England:

> I gathered for myself cudgels, and stud-shafts, and cross-
> shafts, and handles for each of the tools I could work with,
> and arch-timbers and bolt-timbers for every work that I could
> carry out, the comeliest trees, as many as I could carry. Nor
> did I come home with a burden, for it pleased me not to bring
> all the wood back, even if I could have carried it. In each tree
> I saw something that I needed at home; and so I counsel each
> one who can, and has many carts, that he turn his steps to the
> same wood where I hewed the stud-shafts. Let him fetch more
> for himself, and load his carts with fair beams, that he may
> build many a neat wall, and rear many a fine house, and raise
> up a fair town, and therein may live merrily and quietly both
> winter and summer, in such manner as I have not yet done.
> But He who taught me, and to whom the wood was pleasing,
> has power to make me dwell more comfortably both in this
> transitory cottage by the wayside while I am on this world-
> pilgrimage, and also in the eternal home which He has prom-
> ised us through Saint Augustine and Saint Gregory and Saint
> Jerome.[63]

This tendency to add as he went along is characteristic of
Alfred's technique as a translator; it must be insisted that he
himself had a simple, direct mind, which either wearied of the
finespun subtleties of the Augustinian original or could not
find at its command an adequate English vocabulary. Since
Augustine frequently becomes tangled in his own arguments,
it is not surprising that Alfred should disregard minutiae, lest
he fall into the same snare.

The first book, as has been said, is an inquiry into the nature
of God, cast in the form of a dialogue between Augustine and

his reason. We cannot dwell here upon the theology involved; it is more important to understand the sort of interpretation which Alfred was trying to convey. As an example one may take the passage[64] on God the Creator. Augustine paints God as the Creator of all creatures, of the heavens and the stars, of the sun and the moon; the governor of the seasons and the celestial motions, "and so all stars change and vary in the same manner." Alfred, however, feels apparently that this is an insufficient statement; he continues, "likewise the sea and the rivers; in the same manner all creatures suffer change." The flower of the field, the fruit on the tree, all beasts and fowls are transformed in time;

> Yea! even men's bodies grow old, just as other creatures do, but just as they once lived more worthily than trees or other creatures, so shall they arise more worthily on Judgment Day, so that never afterward shall their bodies become naught nor grow old. . . . And all the creatures about whom we say that they seem to us unharmonious and fickle, have yet something of steadiness, because they are bridled with the bridle of God's commands.[65]

Therefore he returns to Augustine and observes that God gave freedom to men's souls. Such interpolations do not fit neatly into the gap in which they have been inserted, but to the reader they almost never fail to give a sense of concreteness and definiteness which Augustine's original all too often lacks. A characteristic addition is the metaphor of the ship and anchor previously mentioned.[66] It is not necessary to quote it now, except to remark that it yields, in its topic sentence, still another welcome glimpse of the Anglo-Saxon seafarer. Similar is the following passage, in which the Alfredian increment has been italicized:

> He who wishes to see the sun of wisdom with his mind's eyes must begin very gradually, and then little by little mount nearer and nearer by steps, *just as if he were climbing on a ladder and wished to ascend some sea-cliff. If he then ever comes up on the cliff, he may look both over the shore and*

over the sea, which then lies beneath him, and also over the
land that formerly was above him.[67]

In the second book the dialogue continues, but with more
and more Alfredian increments. Indeed, the actual translation
gives little more than the opening interchange between Augustine and his reason, which states the subject of the book—
the question of the immortality of the soul. The discussion
which follows is all Alfredian. His reason assures Augustine
that the soul is undying: "thou art eternal and shalt ever
exist." So will the intellect. But Augustine would know more
about the intellect, whether it will grow great or small after
death. The reason explains that this question cannot be answered in a few words and refers Augustine to "the book
which we call *De Videndo Dei*; in English the book is called
Of Seeing God."

The third book, then, is a free disquisition, still in the form
of a dialogue, on the theory that we shall never lose the wisdom which we now have, once the soul has parted from the
body. Indeed, the wisdom will be the greater, inasmuch as we
shall have greater freedom, and after Doomsday nothing will
be hidden.

> Therefore methinks that man is very foolish and very mis-
> erable who will not increase his intellect while he is in this
> world, and also wish and desire that he may come to the
> eternal life, where nothing is hidden from us.[68]

With the brief remark that Alfred "collected these sayings
from the book which we call in—" the piece ends. Presumably
the missing word or phrase, as Wülker supplied it,[69] was
"Latin, *De Videndo Dei*." The detail is immaterial. It is
pleasing to think that Alfred rounded out his literary career
with either the *Boethius* or the *Soliloquies*, for nowhere does
he show more convincingly that he is the gentle, kindly, sincere, gifted, and effective teacher and observer. In his additions, as in some of the homiletic literature of a later century
(see Chapters IX and X), one can study much of the life of

the times. When we have finished reading Alfred, we know most of the accessible thought of the world in which he lived.

There are a few works surviving which have from time to time been attributed to Alfred himself. In a few instances, there is some positive evidence which throws doubt upon the ascriptions. And yet there is still no cogent reason for denying them a place in an Alfredian cycle, as it were. One piece is a prose translation of the first fifty psalms,[70] which, in its remarkable freedom from the literal following of the original and in the wealth of individual comments, reminds one of the characteristic performance of Alfred. It is ascribed to Alfred by William of Malmesbury, whose crediting of other works to Alfred has not been seriously shaken. As we have seen, on the other hand, the celebrated *Proverbs of Alfred* did not originate with the king. These sayings belong, we are sure, to the middle of the twelfth century or a trifle before. It is conceivable that they may have been influenced by some work of Alfred, perhaps the *Handbook*, perhaps the *Boethius*. It is most likely, however, that the *Proverbs* is a representative compilation of wise thoughts gathered by an individual or individuals unknown, almost certainly clerical in source. The collection has been attached to the name of Alfred in view of Alfred's reputation as a man of literary activity, possibly as a tribute to the heroic stature of the king built up in the minds of his countrymen. The tendency thus to assemble sayings of popular wisdom is assuredly not new. The fact that the opening lines of *The Proverbs of Alfred* declare that it was at "Siford" that the king dispensed his wisdom only raises the question whether or not this is a literary device and nothing more. Little has been suggested that could make this work much older than the reign of Henry I (1100-1135); it will be assumed, therefore, that it belongs to Middle English literature and not to the province of the present study. It illustrates, nevertheless, the impressive hold which Alfred kept upon the wise men of later times, a hold which can be appreciated even more fully by a reading of the twelfth-century chroniclers.

3. WORKS WRITTEN WITHIN ALFRED'S SPHERE

A DESCRIPTION of the Alfredian cycle requires at least passing mention of some works which, while clearly not from the hand of the king himself, were doubtless inspired by his efforts or as a result of his teaching. One of these, a piece which serves to introduce in brief appearance another name in Old English prose, is the translation of the *Dialogues of Gregory the Great*,[71] the original work of him who was Pope from 590 to 604. The English translator was Waerferth, Alfred's Bishop of Worcester. For this we have the unqualified assertions of both the contemporary Asser and the indispensable William of Malmesbury. The work is prefaced by some lines from Alfred's own pen:

> I, Alfred, by God's grace made worthy with the name of king, have perceived and often learned from the reading of holy books, that we, to whom God gave so much worldly favor, have special need to humble and subject our minds to divine laws in the midst of earthly cares. Therefore I prayed my faithful friends that they would write down out of holy books about the miracles of the saints the following stories, that I, strengthened in the mind by admonition and love, might think upon divine things in the midst of my earthly cares.

The *Dialogues of Gregory the Great* will be seen to possess a form which is self-evident from the title. Gregory, sitting in dejection, is found and comforted by his deacon Peter, who listens to stories which serve to relieve the weight on Gregory's heart. They are short miracle-tales, of which there were countless numbers then and later. In fact, the second part of the *Dialogues* is a rather extensive treatment of the life of St. Benedict. The narrative is rather simple and its movement quite lively, so that the general effect is much more graceful than is usually the case with a medieval saint's life. It is at once the first and last appearance of Waerferth as a contributor to English literature.

The natural consequence of Alfred's activity was to stimulate the copying of the standard spiritual and intellectual works of his day and earlier. The monks had for a long time kept local records of important events that happened to come into their sphere. There came to be something of a chronicle tradition, which, however, was not always maintained directly by the clergy. In keeping with the general educational policy of Alfred, the business of chronicling was evidently encouraged during his reign, and the impulse thus imparted carried through the next two centuries. During the twelfth century there were several important chroniclers, but they were in a measure formal historians following in the path of Bede. On the other hand, the miscellaneous type of anonymous chronicle-writing in the vernacular which was accomplished between Bede and such a writer as William of Malmesbury—the virtual year-by-year diary, if the paradox be permitted—received in the conglomerate the name of *The Anglo-Saxon Chronicle*.

There are seven surviving manuscripts of *The Anglo-Saxon Chronicle*.[12] They obviously bespeak several editors and scribes. Their chronological sweep is from 60 B.C. to 1154. Of these manuscripts, the Christ Church manuscript (Corpus Christi College Cambridge 173) is probably the most interesting, but it is idle to pick any one for special consideration. The general opinion is that the composition of most of the versions took place in the late ninth century under Alfredian auspices and was then continued through the Old English period; the authors are unknown, but it is likely that they should be regarded as compilers of a mass of antecedent material to start with. After the entry for the year 891 there comes a change of handwriting in the Christ Church manuscript (known as Manuscript A, the Winchester or Parker Chronicle), and after that date until the close of the entry for 1070, the final entry in this particular manuscript, many hands appear to have been at work. The same story in greater or less degree is to be told for the six other manuscripts. Such prominent names as those of Alfred's archbishop Plegmund, Aelfric, Dunstan, Stigand, and Wulfstan—to name only a few—have been associated with the *Chronicle*. The whole study of this work bristles with aca-

demic hazards. Some of the scribes were evidently inclined to
poetry, and at least one effective battle-epic in the old manner,
The Battle of Brunanburh,[73] is the fruit of such inclinations.
Other poetic insertions have already been noted (V, 6).

A brief enumeration of the locations of the various manu-
scripts will be enlightening. The first (Corpus Christi College
Cambridge 173) comes from the library of Christ Church in
Canterbury. Its handwriting points to Winchester, whence it
is often called the Winchester Chronicle. The second (Cotton
Tiberius A VI), known sometimes as the Annals of Aethelflaed,[74] is tenth-century and runs only to 977. The third
(Cotton Tiberius B I) is tenth-century also, closing in 1066,
and is the Abingdon Chronicle. The fourth (Cotton Tiberius
B IV) is the famous Worcester Chronicle, which concludes
with the entry for 1079, although there is a Middle English
end-piece which runs to 1080. The fifth is the equally famous
Peterborough Chronicle of Peterborough Cathedral; it throws
its emphasis upon the eleventh and twelfth centuries, where
its vivid accounts of the black days of King Stephen's reign
are told with terse and tragic detail;[75] but it belongs more to
Middle English than to Old English literature. The sixth
(Cotton Domitian A VIII), from Canterbury, is also late—it
lapses occasionally into Latin and even into Norman French
and stops at 1058. The seventh (Cotton Otho B XI), another
Canterbury Chronicle, reaches only to 1001 and is strongly
West Saxon in both its language and its interest.

The various manuscripts open in different ways: two or
three present genealogies of West Saxon or Mercian kings;
one has a saints' calendar and some proverbs. This much can
be said for all: the material before 870 is largely second-hand.
The period from the beginnings through 730 and a trifle later
is derived largely from Bede's epitome of his *Ecclesiastical
History of the English Nation.* At the latter date (730) we
begin to get something approaching the outlook of the contemporary historian. The exact sources of some of the early
ninth century material will probably never be known; the
details are often such as to suggest that the writer was an eye-

witness. One stretch in the Winchester Chronicle, from 822 to 855, is so military and unecclesiastical as to imply that it was written by laymen; and similar stretches can be found in the other chronicles. Obviously, however, *The Anglo-Saxon Chronicle* is at its best in the narratives beginning with the reign of Alfred.

The many authors of the *Chronicle* differ widely in their narrative abilities. Consequently many significant events are often neglected, and by the same sign many obscure happenings are unduly magnified. The unknown author of the entry for 755 achieved something of an epic in prose in his celebrated account of the feud between King Cynewulf of Wessex and his atheling Cyneheard. It is a tale of fierce private warfare, of ambush and slaughter. But the followers of the slain king have all the loyal instincts of the *comitatus* in the old heroic epic:

> . . . . they said that no kinsman was dearer to them than their lord, and they would never follow his slayer. . . . And then they fought about the gate until they had penetrated within and slain the atheling Cyneheard and the men who were with him.

The story of the resurgence of the Danes in 893 and of the warfare between Alfred and the Danes during the next few years, is admirable military narrative, restrained and succinct, yet eloquent of the hardships which the West Saxons had to undergo.[76] Equally effective is the account of the coming of the Danes under Swein (1004), for here the enemy is met not so often by the swords and spears of the Anglo-Saxons as by the bribe-money of the ineffective Ethelred the Unready. The disturbances among the thanes under Edward the Confessor (1052) make up another interesting entry, especially in the Abingdon Chronicle. The description of the character of William the Conqueror (1086) in the Peterborough Chronicle is virtually unmatched by contemporary writers. For obvious reasons the Battle of Hastings (1066) receives comparatively weak treatment in the *Chronicle*; we must wait half a century and more to get the stirring account in William of Malmesbury's *Chronicle of the Kings of England* (*Gesta Regum Anglorum*).[77] The harrowing details of the reign of King Stephen (1137), also in the Peterborough Chronicle, have already been alluded to, but these are, strictly speaking, outside the boundaries of the present summary. On the whole, it is apparent to even the casual reader that Anglo-Saxon literature would be far poorer without *The Anglo-Saxon Chronicle*, because it is not only a prime source-book for the historians of the period, but is also an often spirited narrative in its own right, with the additional virtue that it imparts to the story the indefinable but authentic flavor that only the writings of a bystander could impart.[78]

A final item in the Alfredian cycle would be the *Martyrology*.[79] It is undoubtedly West Saxon and, to judge from the list of saints included, would be from the time of Alfred's reign, if not somewhat before it. As a piece of significance, the work is of little value except for the expert on Anglo-Saxon hagiology. One can find much better examples of this sort of thing among the Anglo-Latin writers of the period and later. The same can be said for the *Leech-Book*[80] of about the same time, except that its inherent interest in substance makes it necessary for us to consider it in a later chapter.[81]

NOTES TO CHAPTER EIGHT

1. From the Preface to Alfred's translation of Pope Gregory's *Pastoral Care* (see note 18 below).

2. These details belong, of course, to any biography of Alfred and to any history of England in the ninth century. In addition to those mentioned in Chapter I, note 44 above (section 11), there are further items which are essential to any study of Alfred. Probably the best biography of Alfred is that of B. A. Lees, *Alfred the Great, the Truth-teller, Maker of England* (New York, 1919); but Charles Plummer, *The Life and Times of Alfred the Great* (Oxford, 1902) is also unusually good. Asser's *Life of King Alfred* (see Chapter VII, note 69

above) is, of course, the first-hand source. Not so effective is F. H. Hayward, *Alfred the Great* (London, 1936).

3. See the items mentioned in Chapter I, note 13 above. These remain the best works on the subject of the Roman roads in Britain.

4. For this Scandinavian influence, the reader is referred to T. D. Kendrick, *A History of the Vikings* (New York, 1930) and L. M. Larson, *Canute the Great . . . and the Rise of Danish Imperialism during the Viking Age* (New York, 1912) and—from the standpoint of the language in particular—E. Björkman, *Scandinavian Loan-Words in Middle English* (Halle, 1900-1902), his "Zur dialektischen Provenienz der nordischen Lehnwörter im englischen" in *Språkvetenskapliga sällskapets i Upsala forhandlingar* (1901), 1-28; and his *Nordische Personnamen in England in alt- und frühmittelenglischer Zeit* (Halle, 1910); also A. Wall, "A Contribution towards the Study of the Scandinavian Element in the English Dialects" in *Anglia*, xx, 45-135; G. T. Flom, *Scandinavian Influence on Southern Lowland Scotch* (New York, 1900); H. Lindkvist, *Middle English Place-Names of Scandinavian Origin* (Uppsala, 1912); and Allen Mawer, "The Scandinavian Settlements in England as Reflected in English Place-Names" in *Acta Philologica Scandinavica*, vii, 1-30.

5. Most scholars now accept the fact that Alfred did his own work, and certain common traits in the translations lead to a fairly clear notion of his personality and style—see, for example, F. Klaeber, "Zu König Alfreds Vorrede zu seiner Übersetzung der Cura Pastoralis" in *Anglia*, xlvii, 53-65, or L. Borniski, *Der Stil König Alfreds* (Leipzig, 1931). The case for Alfred's translating of the works seems well established, but there is an occasional dissenter, such as P. F. Van Draat, "The Authorship of the Old English Bede" in *Anglia*, xxxix, 319-347. The subject of Alfred's style furnishes material for part of R. W. Chambers's admirable discussion, *On the Continuity of English Prose from Alfred to More and his School* (Oxford, 1932).

6. The great work on Anglo-Saxon laws and law-codes is F. Liebermann, *Die Gesetze der Angelsachsen* (Halle, 1903-1916), and Alfred's codes are discussed especially in Volume iii of that work. An excellent special discussion of Alfred's part in the picture is that in H. M. Turk, *The Legal Code of Alfred the Great* (Halle, 1893), and this work contains also an excellent text. Another fine version is that in F. L. Attenborough, *The Laws of the Earliest English Kings* (Cambridge, 1922), which has also a Modern English translation. Its complementary volume is A. J. Robertson, *The Laws of the Kings of England from Edmund to Henry I* (Cambridge, 1925). This Attenborough-Robertson combination bids fair to supplant Liebermann as the definitive work on the subject. For manner and style, see Dorothy

Bethurum, "Stylistic Features of the Old English Laws" in *Modern Language Review*, XXVII, 263-279.

7. The general matter of chroniclers and chronicle-writing is handled in Reginald L. Poole, *Chronicles and Annals: a Brief Outline of Their Origin and Growth* (Oxford, 1926). The *Anglo-Saxon Chronicle* was first printed by Benjamin Thorpe for the *Rolls Series* (London, 1861). This is still the only edition to run synoptically six parallel texts from different manuscripts. Plummer's edition, based on an earlier rescension by John Earle, contains the best of the earlier bibliographies (*Two of The Saxon Chronicles Parallel with Supplementary Extracts from the Others*; Oxford, 1892-1899). In this work see particularly Vol. II, cxxvii-cxxxvi. Salient passages from the *Chronicle* are too long for significant quotation in the present work.

The seven distinct manuscripts described later in the text (VIII, 3) are: (1) A Ms., from Christ Church in Canterbury, known as the Winchester Chronicle (sometimes as the Parker Manuscript)—see the reference to the Smith edition a few lines below—which runs to the year 1070; (2) B Ms., the Annals of Aethelflaed, which runs to 977; (3) C Ms., the Abingdon Chronicle, in Manuscript Cotton Tiberius B I, which goes to the time of the Norman Conquest—see in particular H. A. Rositzke, "The C-Text of the Old English Chronicle" in *Beiträge zur englischen Philologie* (Pöpinghaus, 1940); (4) D Ms., the Worcester Chronicle, in Manuscript Cotton Tiberius B IV, which has been attributed in part to Bishop Waerferth of Worcester (VIII, 3); (5) E Ms., the Peterborough Chronicle, which is not concluded until 1154—its most striking portions, however, belong to the years after the Norman Conquest, especially the dismal reign of King Stephen (1135-1153); (6) F Ms., the Canterbury Chronicle, in Manuscript Cotton Domitian A VIII, which ends in 1058—it contains larger proportions of French and Latin texts than the others, concerning which see in particular two articles by Francis P. Magoun: "The Domitian Bilingual of the *Old English Annals*: the Latin Preface" in *Speculum*, XX, 65-72 and "The Domitian Bilingual of the *Old English Annals*: Notes on the F-Text" in *Modern Language Quarterly*, VI, 371-380; and (7) G Ms., in Manuscript Cotton Otho B XI, which belongs in date to the eleventh century, although it runs only to 1001—it appears to be largely a transcript of A Ms., or so Thorpe thought. The lettering of these seven manuscripts was devised by Earle and is purely arbitrary, although the Winchester (Parker) Chronicle (A Ms.) is the fullest and, all things considered, the most circumstantial in its narrative. It has received a recent masterly treatment in A. H. Smith, *The Parker Chronicle, 832-900* (London, 1935). Various discussions of individual chronicles are available: see W. Keller, "Die litterarischen Bestrebungen von Worcester in angelsächsischer Zeit" in *Quellen und Forschungen*, lxxxiv (Strassburg, 1900); K. Jost, "Wulfstan und die angelsächsische Chronik" in *Anglia*, XLVII, 105-123; F. Viglione, *Studio critico-filologico su l'Anglo-Saxon Chronicle* (Pavia, 1922); Francis P. Magoun, "Cynewulf, Cyneheard, and Osric" in *Anglia*, LVII, 361-376 —for one of the most dramatic episodes in the *Chronicle*, mentioned also in VIII, 3; A. Jean Thorogood, "*The Anglo-Saxon Chronicle in the Reign of Ecgberht*" in *English Historical Review*, XLVIII, 353-363; and J. S. P. Tatlock, "The Chronicle Misunderstood" in *American Historical Review*, XLI, 703. Translations are offered in J. A. Giles, *Bede's Ecclesiastical History and The Anglo-Saxon Chronicle* (London, 1847; 1912); J. Stevenson, *The Church Historians of England* (London, 1853), II, part 1; E. E. C. Gomme, *The Anglo-Saxon Chronicles* (London, 1909); and the Everyman Library edition (No. 624) by J. Ingram (London, 1912).

8. As noted before, in the Peterborough Chronicle (E Ms.); as a piece of literature it is more significant for Middle English than for Old English. However, its compiler, of the middle of the twelfth century, was a man of vivid ability as a prose-writer.

9. The surviving manuscripts do not seem to go back of the middle of the twelfth century and so are Middle English in point of time. See the edition in volume 49 of *Publications of the Early English Text Society, Original Series* (London, 1872), and the definitive treatment by W. W. Skeat, *The Proverbs of Alfred* (Oxford, 1907), as well as all bibliographical references in J. A. Wells, *A Manual of the Writings in Middle English* (New Haven, 1916—), Chapter VII. The fullest recent treatments with valuable bibliographies are Helen P. South, *The Dating and Localization of the Proverbs of Alfred* (Bryn Mawr, 1931) and O. S. Anderson-Arngart, *The Proverbs of Alfred* (Lund, 1942). Useful also for the light they throw upon currents and tendencies of old sayings and their modern equivalents are B. J. Whiting, *Chaucer's Use of Proverbs* (Cambridge, Mass., 1934) and Archer Taylor, *The Proverb* (Cambridge, Mass., 1931). A more characteristic collection than *The Proverbs of Alfred* could hardly be imagined. For, although Alfred probably did make a book of quotations, as Asser says, he is scarcely responsible for the collection bearing his name except in so far as any man with a reputation for wisdom is given credit for pithy utterance. For the wise sayings credited to Winfrid (Boniface), for example, see especially F. Holthausen in *Archiv*, CVI, 347-348.

10. No doubt the preëminence of Alfred and Charlemagne as lawgivers contributed chiefly to their reputation as wise men. There is, however, no single collection attributed to Charlemagne comparable to *The Proverbs of Alfred* or *The Proverbs of Solomon*.

11. i.e., the Biblical Book of *Proverbs*.

12. See the edition by J. A. Giles, *The Whole Works of King Alfred the Great* (London, 1858), with introduction by R. Pauli (Vol. III, 6-7). William of Malmesbury, in his *Gesta Pontificium*, V, indicates what he calls three fragments; see also Ernst Gropp, *On the Language of the Proverbs of Alfred* (Halle, 1879).

13. Particularly Gropp in the work cited in note 12 above.

14. A good idea of this variation will be derived from a study of the tabulation given by Richard Wülker in his *Grundriss zur Geschichte der angelsächsischen Litteratur* (Leipzig, 1885), 393.

15. Although it happens that this is not the exact order preferred by any one of the older authorities. Most of them believe that the *Bede* should precede the *Gregory* but are not at all agreed about the relative positions of the *Boethius* and the *Orosius*.

16. Ina was King of Wessex from 688 to 726 and was an effective ruler; for his laws see R. H. Hodgkin, *A History of the Anglo-Saxons* (Oxford, 1935), 319-321. Offa was King of Mercia from 757 to 796; his reign marks the culmination of Mercian supremacy.

17. B. A. Lees, *Alfred the Great* (see note 2 above), 215.

18. These are (1) the Oxford Manuscript (Bodleian Hatton 20), from the end of the ninth century; (2) a London Manuscript (Cotton Tiberius B XI), from the end of the ninth century; (3) another London Manuscript (Cotton Otho B II), from the beginning of the tenth century—this and the preceding manuscript (2) were badly damaged by the Cottonian Library fire of 1731, although Junius had already transcribed Manuscript Cotton Tiberius B XI; (4) a Cambridge Manuscript (Corpus Christi College Cambridge 1); (5) a Bibliotheca Publica Manuscript, from the latter half of the eleventh century; (6) a Trinity College Manuscript, from the close of the eleventh century; and (7) a Cassel Manuscript in a fragment, possibly from the ninth century. The first three of these manuscripts were used by Henry Sweet in his *King Alfred's West-Saxon Version of Gregory's Pastoral Care*, in volumes 45 and 50 of *Publications of the English Text Society, Original Series* (London, 1871-1872). The Cassel fragment is printed in F. Dietrich, *Anglosaxonica* (Marburg, 1854). The Preface in particular has been reprinted in virtually all of the readers and anthologies of Old English literature published; some of this extensive bibliography, at least in reference to the earliest printings, is to be found in R. Wülker, *Grundriss zur Geschichte der angelsächsischen Litteratur* (Leipzig, 1885), 401-402. The "contemporary" treatment of the work, however, begins with Sweet's edition, which contains the Latin text, an English translation, and the usual notes and introduction excellently done. Two monographs—A. De Witz, *Untersuchungen über Alfreds des Grossen*

westsächsische Übersetzung der Cura Pastoralis Gregors und ihr Verhältnis zum Original (Bunzlau, 1889) and G. Wack, *Über die Verhältnis von König Aelfreds Übersetzung der Cura Pastoralis zum Original* (Colberg, 1889)—virtually exhaust the subject. F. Klaeber's penetrating analysis of the Preface, "Zu König Alfreds Vorrede zu seiner Übersetzung der Cura Pastoralis" in *Anglia*, XLVII, 53-65, is recommended for the light it throws upon Alfred's personality and general interests. The Cassel Fragment is discussed further by H. M. Flasdieck in *Anglia*, LXII, 193-233—with text.

19. For the Latin texts of the *Ecclesiastical History*, see Chapter VII, note 33 above. The four manuscripts of the Alfredian translation are (1) the Oxford Manuscript (Bodleian Tanner 10); (2) the Cambridge Manuscript (Corpus Christi College Cambridge 41); (3) the London Manuscript (Cotton Otho B XI), almost completely destroyed in the fire of 1731; and (4) the Manuscript Corpus Christi College Oxford 279. A fifth manuscript (Cambridge University Library K K 3, 18) dates from the eleventh century. The first edition was that of Abraham Wheloc (Cambridge, 1643); another one by John Smith is dated Cambridge, 1722. Pieces of this history have been reprinted in all of the readers and anthologies of general Old English literature, and so it would be impractical to refer to them all here. The best modern editions are those by T. Miller, *The Old English Version of Bede's Ecclesiastical History*, volumes 95, 96, 110, and 111 of *Publications of the Early English Text Society, Original Series* (London, 1890-1891) and in C. W. M. Grein and R. Wülker, *Bibliothek der angelsächsischen Prosa*, IV (Cassel-Göttingen, 1872—) by J. Schipper. The monograph by P. F. Van Draat arguing against Alfred's authorship has already been mentioned (see note 5 above). There has been a recent translation by T. Stapleton, *Bede's History of the Church of England* (Oxford, 1929). For general literary relations of this work, see the bibliography in Chapter VII, note 33 above, also the following: A. S. Cook, "Bede and Gregory of Tours" in *Philological Quarterly*, VI, 315-316; Simon Potter, "On the Relation of the Old English *Bede* to Waerferth's *Gregory* and to Alfred's Translations" in *Mémoires de la Société Royale des Sciences de la Bohême, Classe des Lettres* (Prague, 1930), 1-76; and H. Schreiber, "Beda-Überlieferung in Sachsen" in *Zeitschrift für deutsche Geistesgeschichte*, I, 278-285.

20. Book I, Chapters 13-17 in Miller's edition (see note 19 above).

21. Book II, Chapter 10 in Miller's edition (see note 19 above).

22. See IV, 1 above.

23. Book III, Chapters 3 and 12-14 of Miller's edition (see note 19 above).

24. Book IV, Chapter 25 in Miller's edition (see note 19 above).

25. Book v, Chapter 13 in Miller's edition (see note 19 above).
26. There are three manuscripts: (1) the Lauderdale Manuscript, known to Hickes at the close of the seventeenth century and issued by William Elstob (Oxford, 1699); (2) Manuscript Cotton Tiberius B I; and (3) a Junius transcription of a Cottonian manuscript. (1) and (3) formed the first edition and translation by D. Barrington (London, 1773). R. Pauli's edition (with translation by Benjamin Thorpe) appeared in Bohn's Antiquarian Library at London in 1853 and was reprinted in 1902. There is an edition by Henry Sweet in volume 79 of *Publications of the Early English Text Society, Original Series* (London, 1883), with the Latin original. Much interest has been directed toward Alfred's attainments as a geographer, and nearly all the recent scholarly discussions of the *Orosius* have to do with the identification and confirmation of localities mentioned in Alfred's addenda to the work. So G. Hübener, "König Alfred und Osteuropa" in *Englische Studien*, LX, 37-57—to pass over the introductions and incidental chapters in such collections as J. A. Giles, *The Whole Works of King Alfred the Great* (see note 12 above) or the biographies of Alfred mentioned in note 2 above. See also the following: H. Schilling, *König Alfreds angelsächsische Bearbeitung der Weltgeschichte des Orosius* (Halle, 1886); H. Geidel, "Alfred der Grosse als Geograph" in *Münchener Geographische Studien*, XV (Munich, 1904); F. Nansen (translated by A. G. Chater), *Arctic Exploration in Early Times* (New York, 1911), particularly Vol. I, 169-181; William A. Craigie, "The Nationality of King Alfred's Wulfstan" in *Journal of English and Germanic Philology*, XXIV, 396-397; Kemp Malone, "King Alfred's Gotland" in *Modern Language Review*, XXIII, 336-339; also his "King Alfred's North: a study in medieval geography" in *Speculum*, V, 139-167—a particularly good piece of research; Samuel H. Cross, "Notes on King Alfred's North" in *Speculum*, VI, 296-299; Gustav Hübener, "König Alfreds Geographie" in *Speculum*, VI, 428-434; and two definitive articles by Kemp Malone, supplementing his above-mentioned study in *Speculum*, V, 139-167: "On Wulfstan's Scandinavia" in *Studies in Philology*, XXVIII, 574-579 and "On King Alfred's Geographical Treatise" in *Speculum*, VIII, 67-78; also Francis P. Magoun, "King Alfred's Halgoland and Old Norwegian Syncope" in *Scandinavian Studies*, XVIII, 163-164 and B. J. Whiting, "Ohthere (Ottar) and the *Egils-Saga*" in *Philological Quarterly*, XXIV, 218-226.
27. For the best edition of the original text, see Mark Science, *Boethius: de Consolatione Philosophiae*, volume 170 of *Publications of the Early English Text Society, Original Series* (London, 1928).
28. Henry Sweet, *An Anglo-Saxon Reader* (Oxford, 1922), 43. In any case, however, it seems most likely that the manuscript dates

from a time subsequent to Alfred's death; see G. P. Krapp, *The Paris Psalter and the Meters of Boethius* ("Anglo-Saxon Poetic Records, Vol. V") (New York, 1932), xxxv ff.

29. Junius made a transcript of this, which actually constitutes a third manuscript, often referred to as Manuscript Junius 12. I quote Krapp (see note 28 above), xli ff.: "The Junius transcript, in Ms. Junius 12, comprises a copy in Junius' hand of the Anglo-Saxon prose translation of the Latin Meters and the Latin prose from Ms. Bodley 180 (NE.C.3.11), with variants from the prose of the Cotton manuscript. Inserted throughout the volume in the appropriate places are copies of the several Meters from the Cotton Manuscript, written on odd-sized leaves of paper and pasted in. This transcript of the Anglo-Saxon Meters is indispensable in the establishment of the text, and for the parts of the Cotton manuscript which are now lost, it is our only authority. By a systematic comparison of the Meters in the Cotton Manuscript, so far as they have been preserved, with the corresponding parts of the Junius transcript, it is possible to determine the exact value of Junius' work, and the reliance which may safely be put on it. The results of such a comparison show that Junius was a careful transcriber, who achieved a high degree of accuracy in his work, and in his entire text of the Meters . . . there are not more than a dozen errors of transcription which would be seriously misleading in the establishment of the text."

30. Among the older editors, Thomas Wright, in his *Life of King Alfred* (London, 1852) and three German irreconcilables—M. Hartmann in "Ist König Aelfred der Verfasser der alliterierenden Übertragung der Metra des Boetius?" in *Anglia*, v, 411-450; O. Zimmermann, *Über den Verfasser der altenglischen Metren des Boetius* (Greifswald, 1882); and A. Leicht, "Ist König Aelfred der Verfasser der alliterierenden Metra des Boetius?" in *Anglia*, VI, 126-170 —raise doubts, particularly Leicht. The others are either indifferent to the question, or undecided, although the tendency among almost all the older editors, from the seventeenth-century Hickes to some as late as Henry Sweet or Ten Brink, is to accept Alfred's authorship. The later discussions of the matter, wisely noncommittal, are best summarized in E. Krämer, "Die altenglischen Metra des Boetius herausgegeben und mit Einleitung und vollständigem Wörterbuch versehen" in *Bonner Beiträge zur Anglistik*, VIII, 1-149 and in F. Fehlauer, *Die englischen Übersetzungen von Boethius' De Consolatione Philosophiae* (Berlin, 1909), which give not only the best texts but admirable introductions, notes, and bibliographical matter. As already noted, however (see note 28 above), the most recent edition is that in G. P. Krapp, *The Paris Psalter and the Meters of Boethius* (New York, 1932).

For the original Latin text of *The Consolation of Philosophy*, see note 27 above. The Alfredian version is published in J. A. Giles, *The Whole Works of King Alfred the Great* (see note 12 above), with English translation in verse by M. F. Tupper and in prose by S. Fox, who is responsible for the edition in the Bohn Antiquarian Library (London, 1864). But the best modern edition is that of W. J. Sedgefield, *King Alfred's Old English Version of Boethius' De Consolatione Philosophiae* (Oxford, 1899), with a translation into Modern English (Oxford, 1900).

On Boethius himself, see especially Howard R. Patch, *The Tradition of Boethius* (New York-Oxford, 1935), and H. F. Stewart, *Boethius: an Essay* (Edinburgh, 1891), particularly pp. 170-178, as well as the chapter, "Boethius, first of the Scholastics" in Edward K. Rand, *Founders of the Middle Ages* (Cambridge, Mass., 1928) and E. T. Silk, "The Study of Boethius' 'Consolatio Philosophiae' in the Middle Ages" in *Transactions and Proceedings of the American Philological Association*, LXII, xxxvii-xxxviii. An excellent, thorough treatment is Helen M. Barrett, *Boethius* (Cambridge, 1940). K. H. Schmidt, *König Alfreds Boethius-Bearbeitung* contributes little that is new but is a good summary. Valuable also are two articles: the first, F. Holthausen, "Zur altenglischen Metra-Übersetzung" in *Anglia Beiblatt*, XLIII, 156-160; and the second, E. T. Silk, "Boethius' Consolatio Philosophiae as a Sequel to Augustine's *Dialogues* and *Soliloquia*" in *Harvard Theological Review*, XXXII, 19-39.

31. Nestorianism is the "heresy" named after the doctrines of Nestorius, patriarch of Constantinople from 428 to 431. It has been shown, however, that the fundamental point of Nestorianism—the thesis that the God-man has two complete persons, and not one—is not stated in the surviving doctrines of Nestorius himself. In short, it is difficult to discover the heretical nature of Nestorianism, for Nestorius seems to have been strictly orthodox in his interpretation of the *Credo*, of the matter of the Incarnation, and of the divine Maternity. It would appear that the discrediting of Nestorius was a matter of factional jealousy within the Church and of unpleasant politics all around. But overtly the dispute was brought to a head by the rather unwise speeches of certain followers of Nestorius, notably one Anastasius, who preached: "Let no one call Mary the mother of God, for Mary was a human being; and that God should be born of a human being is impossible." In defending his own position Nestorius resorted to some force; the matter became a kind of ecclesiastical brawl; and more powerful members of the Church were able to bring about his defeat.

32. See Chapter VII, notes 61 and 62, for Alcuin versus the Adoptionists.

33. This rare work is printed in the edition by B. G. Teubner in

Bibliotheca Scriptorum Graecorum et Romanorum Teubneriana (Leipzig, 1866). The important commentary by John Scotus is edited by Cora E. Lutz, *Iohannis Scotti Annotationes in Marcianum* (Cambridge, Mass., 1939), but see Chapter VII, note 75 above.

34. Book II, Meter 5 (Meter VIII in Krämer's edition; see note 30 above).

35. Book II, Meter 7 (Meter X in Krämer's edition; see note 30 above).

36. Book III, Meter 9 (Meter XI in Krämer's edition; see note 30 above).

37. Book III, Meter 10, Prose 10 and Prose 11 (Meter XIII in Krämer's edition; see note 30 above).

38. There is an interesting parallel here to the famous passage in *Matthew*, XI, 28: "Come unto me, ye weary." There are many such echoes in Boethius of Christian statement; and there can be no question of the tremendous influence of Plato and Christ combined upon Boethius' ideas and personality, although there is still no absolute proof that he was a professed Christian.

39. Book IV, Meter 2; it is Alfred's Chapter XXXVII.

40. Meter XX in Krämer's edition (see note 30 above); these are the opening lines.

41. This is in general the subject of Book V of Boethius; Alfred's version is a very free paraphrase.

42. Book III, Meter 12; it is Chapter XXXV of Alfred's version.

43. The reference in Boethius is very slight (in Book IV, Meter 3); Alfred makes it the first part of his Chapter XXXVIII.

44. At the close of Alfred's Chapter XXXV.

45. In Alfred's Chapter XXXV.

46. In Meter XXVI of Krämer's edition (see note 30 above).

47. See Alfred's Chapter XXXVIII.

48. The matter is summed up in F. G. Thomas, "Alfred and the Old English Prose of his Reign" in *Cambridge History of English Literature*, Volume I, Chapter VI, pp. 112ff.

49. For a particular discussion of the versification of the Boethian Meters, see Krämer's edition (note 30 above), 4-10. The "hypermetric" lines Krämer finds to be largely of three stresses to the half-line instead of the customary two (see II, 3 above).

50. Meter VI in Krämer's edition (which edition is referred to in notes 51-56 below; see note 30 above), lines 3-7.

51. Meter XII, 11-17.

52. Meter XVIII, 5-11.

53. Meter XXIV, 1-11.

54. Meter XXIV, 28-30; 44-54.

55. Meter XXVII, 1-4.

56. Meter xxvii, 4-8.

57. Manuscript Cotton Vitellius A xv. The *Soliloquies* is sometimes known as "The Blooms of Alfred." There are several good editions of the text, notably in O. Cockayne, *The Shrine* (London, 1864-1869), 163-204; W. H. Hulme, "'Blooms' von König Alfred" in *Englische Studien*, xviii, 332-356 and xix, 470; H. L. Hargrove, "King Alfred's Old English Version of St. Augustine's *Soliloquies*" in *Yale Studies in English*, viii (New Haven, 1902)—in my opinion the most accessible; and W. Endter, "König Alfred der Grosse: Bearbeitung der Soliloquien des Augustinus" in Grein and Wülker's *Bibliothek der angelsächsischen Prosa*, xi (Hamburg, 1922). The questions of source and authorship are discussed in the above; see also R. P. Wülker, "Über die angelsächsische Bearbeitung der Soliloquien Augustins" in *Paul und Braune's Beiträge*, iv, 101-131 and in F. G. Hubbard, "The Relation of the Blooms of King Alfred to the Anglo-Saxon Translation of Boethius" in *Modern Language Notes*, ix, 321-342. Hargrove has also a Modern English translation in *Yale Studies in English*, xxii (New Haven, 1904).

58. The first dissenter was J. M. Lappenberg, in his *History of England under the Anglo-Saxon Kings*, translated by B. Thorpe (London, 1881), i, 337ff.; and the old editor of Alfred's works, Pauli (see note 12 above), was sure that Alfred was not the translator. Wülker, however, in his *Grundriss zur Geschichte der angelsächsischen Litteratur* (Leipzig, 1885), 417, shows that the objections of Pauli are not convincing, and that the evidence is more or less favorable to Alfred's authorship. No scholars since Wülker have upset his position on this matter.

59. See notes 18 and 30 above.

60. Moreover, the whole business of translation and the personality of the text remind one more of Alfred than of any other known writer in this time or later.

61. An epistle of Saint Augustine (A.D. 147).

62. Hargrove's comment on these (see his edition mentioned under note 57 above, p. xliii) is worth quoting, because it sums up well the fundamental nature of Alfredian additions to the original text: "These longer excursions are interesting from several points of view. They are original, and yet grow naturally out of the subject in hand. They are written to make clear certain fundamental truths. There may be seen in them a vigor of expression not found in the parts translated. . . . What he [Alfred] might have become as an original artist is not entirely a matter of speculation. Although natural endowments, education (or lack of it), and environment conspired to make of him a man of affairs and a king of intense practicality rather than a man of letters or a philosopher, yet in the genuinely original prefaces to his

various translations we can but recognize a master-hand. These are veritable preludes—thematic chords—touched by an artist, who, we feel, had he possessed opportunity, might have wrought out a composition that would take rank as a classic."

63. Page 1, lines 1-20 of Hargrove's edition (see note 57 above).

64. Pages 4-11 of Hargrove's edition (see note 57 above).

65. Pages 10, 11, and 14-16 of Hargrove's edition (see note 57 above).

66. Hargrove, p. 22, line 2 to p. 26, line 5.

67. Hargrove, p. 45, lines 14-18. The Latin text is, as usual, printed below, so that comparisons of this nature are easy.

68. Hargrove (see note 57 above), p. 69, line 34 to p. 70, line 3.

69. In his article in *Paul und Braune's Beiträge*, IV, 119; see note 57 above.

70. G. P. Krapp, *The Paris Psalter and the Meters of Boethius* (New York, 1932).

71. There is a Preface in alliterative verse; it has been printed by F. Holthausen, "Die alliterierende Vorrede zur altenglischen Übersetzung von Gregors Dialogen" in *Archiv*, CV, 367-369, and again—with translation—in A. S. Cook, "An Unsuspected Bit of Old English Verse" in *Modern Language Notes*, XVII, 13-20. As for the Prose text itself, it is given a thorough treatment by H. Hecht in Grein and Wülker's *Bibliothek der angelsächsischen Prosa*, V (Hamburg, 1900-1907); for general discussion, see B. J. Timmer, *Studies in Bishop Waerferth's Translation of the Dialogues of Gregory the Great* (Groningen, 1934); H. Krebs, "Die angelsächsische Übersetzung der Dialoge Gregors" in *Anglia*, II, 65-70 and III, 70-73; H. Johnson, *Gab es zwei von einander unabhängige altenglische Übersetzungen der Dialoge Gregors?* (Berlin, 1884)—his answer is in the affirmative; W. Keller, "Die literarischen Bestrebungen von Worcester in angelsächsischer Zeit," volume LXXXIV of *Quellen und Forschungen* (Strassburg, 1900); P. N. U. Hartung in *Neophilologus*, XXII, 281-302 and S. Potter, *On the Relation of the Old English Bede to Werferth's Gregory and to Alfred's Translations* (Prague, 1931). There are three surviving manuscripts—Cotton Otho C I, which is incomplete after the beginning of Book IV; Corpus Christi College Cambridge S 10, which is the most complete; and Oxford Hatton 76, which is the least satisfactory. All three date from the middle of the eleventh century. See also the summary in R. M. Lumiansky, "A Modern English Version of the Old English *Dialogues of Gregory*" in *University of North Carolina Record*, No. 383 (Chapel Hill, 1942), 76-77.

72. See note 7 above.

73. See Chapter III and note 35 above.

74. So called because it gives particular attention to the career of Aethelflaed, daughter of Alfred the Great.

75. See note 7 above.

76. Francis P. Magoun, "King Alfred's Naval and Beach Battle with the Danes in 896" in *Modern Language Review*, XXXVII, 409-414.

77. See Chapter VII, note 29 above.

78. At this point, backward reference should be made to the *Chronicle* by Aethelweard; see Chapter VII, note 74 above.

79. The text and an account of the manuscripts are published in O. Cockayne, *The Shrine* (see note 57 above), 46-156. The catalogue of days in this martyrology is almost complete, running from December 31 to December 21. See also G. Herzfeld, *An Old English Martyrology*, volume 116 of *Publications of the Early English Text Society, Original Series* (London, 1900).

80. See Chapter XIII, note 15 below.

81. Here, too, the matter of the *West Saxon Prose (Paris) Psalter* should be revived. It has already been described (see Chapter V and note 62 above). According to William of Malmesbury, Alfred was responsible for a translation or paraphrase of *Psalms*. It is generally accepted now as likely that the *Paris Psalter* is based on the Alfredian Psalms, now lost. At least that was Wülker's belief (see his *Grundriss zur Geschichte der angelsächsischen Litteratur*; Leipzig, 1885, pp. 435-436), and no one has seriously challenged his views. Added to the bibliographical items mentioned in Chapter V, note 62 above, there should be included the interesting article by J. Wichmann, "König Aelfreds angelsächsische Übersetzung der Psalmen, I-LI excl." in *Anglia*, XI, 39-96, which argues convincingly for Alfred's authorship of the pieces now surviving. But the definitive bibliography on the subject is that in G. P. Krapp, *The Paris Psalter and the Meters of Boethius* (New York, 1932), xxxiii-xxxv.

IX · Aelfric and His Works

1. THE IDENTITY OF AELFRIC

With the death of Alfred in 901, there comes a period in which the efforts of the great king appear at first to have gone for little. A general stagnation seems to have descended upon the monasteries, now that Alfred's unflagging spirit had passed away; and there is no intellectual leader comparable in stature to Alfred who might pick up the tradition and carry learning in England to its next higher range. The first half of the tenth century, to be sure, shines in English history as the era in which Alfred's political gains against the Danes were maintained and even improved. But it seems military rather than spiritual.

The account of the ecclesiastical literature of the period, however, can be resumed with the accession of Edgar (959), for in the reign of this ruler three unusual men appeared in the English Church—Dunstan, Archbishop of Canterbury; Oswald, Bishop of Worcester; and Aethelwold, Bishop of Winchester. Earlier in the century there had been a reform of the *Benedictine Rule*,[1] beginning in France, and concurrently a renaissance in matters spiritual spread throughout Western Europe. The emergence of these three prominent English ecclesiasts coincides with the effect of this renaissance upon England. Aethelwold, in fact, executed a new rendering of the reformed *Benedictine Rule* and translated it into English, somewhere between 959 and 963.

During the later decades of this century, there was growing up in a monastery the youth who was to become the most important figure in English literature between the death of Alfred and the Norman Conquest. Aelfric, born about 955, whose parentage and origins are obscure,[2] lived in the monastery at Winchester until 987; then he apparently went to Cernel to instruct the monks in the Benedictine Rule. This experience evidently decided for Aelfric that he would be a teacher, and so he began his busy career as a writer on religious matters. His rise in the Church was not high, probably because of his pedagogic tendencies, but he became Abbot of Eynsham in Oxfordshire in 1005. He died some time between 1020 and 1025.

There were two other important churchmen of the same name; one was Archbishop of Canterbury from 995 to 1006; the other was Archbishop of York from 1023 to 1051. There was also a devoted pupil, Aelfric Bata. The two archbishops could have done much writing, and no doubt did, but the chances are great that the works which have come down to us under the name of Aelfric are the products of the industrious and placid-living abbot rather than of the busy primates of the Church.[3] It is dangerous to generalize, of course; but Aelfric of York led a rather checkered politico-ecclesiastical career and therefore, even aside from his late dates, does not fit well into the picture of a diligent, tireless teacher. Aelfric of Canterbury remains a possibility, but his character was that of a soldier rather than a churchman, and his chief activity took place during the parlous days of national emergency.

We have, then, a fairly good reason for assuming that Aelfric the writer is the young cleric of Winchester and the mature abbot of Eynsham. His output is, for the time, copious—some forty homilies, in one series, and another series of forty, both series completed between 990 and 994.[4] As a teacher of Latin, he wrote a Latin grammar (995). He gathered together some scientific information in the manner of Bede. No doubt his major work, however, is his *Lives of the Saints* (996). But he did a good deal of miscellaneous religious writing, as will appear from the pages to follow, and among these religious compositions are some actual translations of certain sections of the Old Testament.[5] In his most typical works, he is first and foremost a Latinist and pretty much a rhetorician, with a style that is elaborate and often flowery. At the same time, Aelfric is a landmark in the history of English prose, if only because he is the first important writer of monastic literature in the vernacular, for Alfred was not primarily monastic but popular, and Bede wrote in Latin. It is true, of course, that both Alfred and Aelfric were essentially teachers; but where Alfred was the layman spreading learning, Aelfric was the trained churchman. Aelfric's audience, moreover, is clearly twofold—he wrote the homilies, the saints' lives, and the Biblical commentaries, translations, and paraphrases primarily for his people (although other churchmen were doubtless expected to profit by them); but the Latin grammar and the scientific compilations he intended in the main for the cleric in the cloister.

2. AELFRIC'S WRITINGS

THE large collection of homilies by Aelfric represents the peak of this kind of literature in the Old English period,[6] although some of the earlier *Blickling Homilies* (X, 2) are fully as effective, and those by Wulfstan (X, 1), conceived in a different way, are more powerful. There are three categories of the many Aelfrician manuscripts surviving. First, there are those manuscripts which give the two collections of homilies as separate. Second, there are those manuscripts in which the two collections of homilies are combined in such a manner as to coincide with the church-calendar and thus form a kind of religious homiletic year-book. Finally, and most numerous of all, there are those manuscripts which give the homilies without any particular order and mixed with pieces not ascribed to Aelfric. It is to be presumed, however, that Aelfric, the precise teacher and churchman, conceived of the homilies as forming a consecutive plan of instruction appropriate to the religious calendar; and the second type of manuscript described is therefore probably the original type.

The opening of the first series of these so-called *Catholic Homilies* indicates that Aelfric composed the first forty homilies, at least, while at Cernel. He mentions no other works of his as completed. It is assumed, therefore, that these homilies represent his earliest significant work, particularly as he speaks of himself, in this first preface, as impelled by a sense of Christian duty to compose them. A Latin version of this preface is addressed, incidentally, to Sigeric, who was Archbishop of Canterbury from 990 to 994.[7] This first collection of forty homilies is swelled by the addition of four more, in a copy addressed to "Ealdormon Aethelweard."[8] The four additional pieces apparently were written at Aethelweard's express request. The second collection of forty homilies also has both a Latin and an English preface, this time a dissertation in the form of an "admonition" against drunkenness. The collection is also addressed to Sigeric, still spoken of as an archbishop; it must therefore have been finished by 994, particularly since Aelfric speaks of the damage wrought by "pirates," which probably has reference to the serious Danish raids upon England during that year. This second preface indicates furthermore that Aelfric thought of the two series as a unit. Dietrich observes[9] that the second collection is on a somewhat higher educational plane; it is not so didactic and is more concerned with the origins of Christianity in general and with the appearance of Christianity in England in particular.

Aelfric himself acknowledges[10] that the homilies are in large measure translations from St. Augustine, St. Jerome, Bede, Gregory the Great, and others. It is obvious, however, that Gregory is at once his chief source and his main inspiration.[11] Although he speaks of some works in English, he mentions only one piece of poetry as having influenced him—a metrical version of the Passion of St. Thomas. But it is clear that he often followed the devices of Old English poetry; echoes of phraseology from *Beowulf* and other Anglo-Saxon poems appear from time to time in the *Homilies*, and two devices in particular seem to have swayed him in his composition. These are alliteration and the tendency, already seen in Bede and Alfred, toward the pairing of synonyms or near-synonyms, not necessarily of alliterative nature, although such is frequently the case. Since it is clear, however, that alliteration is a stylistic device which is inherent in the English rhetorical temperament, it is obviously inappropriate to call Aelfric its originator in prose writing. Yet it is certainly true that he made use of alliteration more consciously and more boldly than his predecessors in Old English prose—in so far as the literature of this period can be said to have rhythmical, poetic prose, Aelfric is the developer of that type.[12]

As regards sentence-structure, too, Aelfric makes a notable contribution to the literature of his time. Alfred's prose style, as we have seen, was in general an unpretentious style, given to the simple and loose sentence; at times it was almost colloquial, particularly in those passages in his works which are known to be original. Aelfric's style has a much greater range. He has been well schooled in the Latin style of the grand old Church Fathers, a Latin prose style which stems for the most part out of such writers as Cicero and Tertullian; but he is well versed also in the poetic traditions of the Germanic peoples and of their Anglo-Saxon representatives of the preceding two or three centuries. Therefore we are justified in looking for the use, in Aelfric's writings, of repetition through synonyms, of alliteration, and of the coupling of similar ideas —all in the same sentence.

Extended comment upon the whole of the *Catholic Homilies* would probably be unnecessary. The first series seems to be constituted of a greater number of pieces of scriptural content than the second; the second series has in it more of the legendary than of the purely exegetical. The favorite topics of the first series are God; the Creative Principle; the Trinity; Christ, His personality and His service; man, his sinfulness and his redemption. The second series, on the other hand, has more to do with the organization of the Church and the means of salvation through the Church. Specifically, the homilies on baptism and on the Last Supper are to be recommended, as well as the legendary stretches of various other homilies— the stories of the great Gregory himself, and the missionary efforts which he set to work; the account of Saint Cuthbert, of whom we have heard before (VII, 3). Three distinguished homilies are those treating of the Second Coming of Christ.

Not all the best of Aelfric's homilies are those intended primarily for Sundays and Church holidays, and so named aptly by Wheloc[13] the *Catholic Homilies*. There are others, probably written later than the general collection and inserted by Aelfric at some subsequent date. For example, the homily on the birth of the Virgin (found in Manuscript Corpus Christi College Cambridge 188)[14] develops the theme that Holy Church is the bride of Christ. A homily, *For the Birthday of a Confessor*,[15] was written at the request of Bishop Aethelwold of Winchester about 1010. Particularly characteristic of medieval homiletics is the sermon on Holy Chastity, addressed to Aelfric's friend Sigeferth. The following indicates sufficiently the tone of the whole:

> There are three states which are altogether pleasing to God: marriage, widowhood, and chastity. . . . They who live wisely in marriage will have thirty-fold reward from Christ. . . . They who remain widows for Christ's sake will have sixty-fold reward . . . ; they who in the service of Christ live in chastity and in cleanness of heart from childhood shall receive a hundred-fold reward with Him forever.[16]

The homily addressed to Wulfʒeat[17] is a summary, punctuated with much Augustinian teaching, of Christian doctrine. The homily, *On the Sevenfold Gifts of the Spirit*,[18] sometimes ascribed to Aelfric, may be by Wulfstan (X, 1).

Translation will not bring to light many of the characteristics of Aelfric's style, except perhaps his sentence-structure, because his alliteration will not always suit modern vocabulary and idiom. On the other hand, the prefaces of the two collections of the *Catholic Homilies* are worth quoting in part:

> I, Aelfric, monk and mass-priest, nevertheless inferior to what is fitting for such positions, was sent in the days of Aethelred the king by Alphege the bishop, successor to Aethelwold, to a certain abbey which is called Cernel. . . . Then it occurred to me, I trust through God's gift, that I should turn this book from the Latin language into English speech; not from the confidence of great learning, but because I have seen and heard great error in many English books, which unlearned men through their simplicity had accounted of great wisdom; and I was sorry that they knew not nor possessed not divine teach-

ings in their writings, except those men alone who knew Latin, and except for those books which King Alfred had wisely turned from Latin into English.[19]

The rhetorical quality of Aelfric's style and the rather lengthy sentence which he favored are both obvious in these lines. In passing, it is important to note that his purpose in writing was expressly similar to Alfred's but more restricted to ecclesiastical matters.

In contrast to the *Homilies* is the *Grammar*,[20] which apparently followed closely after the second series of the *Homilies*. It was evidently written to continue the tradition of learning,

> . . . . lest holy teaching grow cold and fail in our days, even as happened among Englishmen only a few years ago, so that before the time of Archbishop Dunstan and Bishop Aethelwold no English priest was able to compose or understand a Latin epistle.[21]

The work is a translation and paraphrase of the Latin grammar of Priscian,[22] the Roman grammarian who flourished about 500. It was undoubtedly an extremely widely circulated work, for no less than fifteen manuscripts remain.[23] Some of these manuscripts have also a *Glossary* of Latin nouns and adjectives with their English equivalents, classified not alphabetically but by topics. The original grammar of Priscian was a competent working-grammar of Latin and was divided into two parts: the first (Priscianus Major) treated of phonology, word-formation, and morphology; the second (Priscianus Minor), of syntax. Aelfric has chosen judiciously from both. The classic illustration of his procedure is that of the opening section, for it serves to show precisely the method which he followed in his adaptation:

> *Partes Orationis sunt octo*—eight parts are there in Latin speech: *Nomen, Pronomen, Verbum, Adverbium, Participium, Conjunctio, Praepositio, Interjectio. Nomen* is a name, with which we name all things both in particular and in general; in particular by proper names: Eadgarus, Aethelwoldus; commonly: *rex*—king, *episcopus*—bishop, etc.[24]

Much more important than either the *Grammar* or its dependent *Glossary*, however, is Aelfric's *Colloquium*, better known as the *Colloquy on the Occupations*.[25] It is a Latin dialogue with English interlinear glosses. Evidently it was intended to serve as a practice-book for a cloister-school; the opening lines, spoken by a pupil, indicate as much. This first speaker is apparently a monk addressing the master; the master, after a little preliminary talk, asks who the companions of the monk are, and is told: "Some are farmers, some shepherds, some cowherds; some indeed are hunters, some fishers, some fowlers, some merchants, some cobblers, salt-workers, bakers." The master then quizzes some of these others about their daily tasks and their troubles—the farmer tells of his hard labor and his hard master; the cowherd, of his ungrateful environment; the hunter, of his dangers; the fisher likewise, and so on. A "counselor" appears in the group and is asked by the master what trade, of those there represented, seems the most important. The counselor's rather injudicious choice of the farmer starts controversy in the group, a controversy which the counselor allays thus:

> O companions and good laboring men, let us leave immediately this dispute, and let there be peace and harmony among us, and let each do for the other according to his trade, and agree with the farmer, whence we have food for ourselves and fodder for our horses. And this thought I give to all workers, that each of you go about his business with pleasure, because he who abandons his profession will be abandoned by that profession. Whosoever thou may be—mass-priest, monk, churl, warrior, observe that this rule holds for thyself: be what thou art, for it is a great shame and abasement for a man not to be what he is and what he ought to be.

The master then addresses the first pupil, who is a candidate for the clergy; and the piece, a thoroughly charming one, ends on a note of Christian exhortation. The English interlinear gloss is not by Aelfric but is probably two or three generations younger.

Such a work, of course, is scarcely characteristic of Aelfric;

nevertheless it remains for the twentieth-century layman the most attractive of all Aelfric's writings. The student of sociology will welcome this rare chance to see the common Anglo-Saxon people at work; and the piece serves further to demonstrate that the problems confronting the sociologist today are basically much the same as those confronting the people in the year 1000, no matter how much environments may change. For the special student of literature, moreover, the *Colloquy* has some passing importance in that it foreshadows a favorite literary form of the Middle English period—the debate, or dispute.[26] For that matter, the *Colloquy* reminds one in style of a catechism; and its method comes to be taken for granted later on in any piece of medieval literature involving a teacher and a pupil.

The Lives of the Saints, in three surviving manuscripts—Cotton Julius E VII, Cotton Otho B X, and Cotton Vitellius D XVII—is actually a third series of homilies.[27] There are about forty of these lives, although there is a slight variation in the total among the three manuscripts. In the foreword, addressed to Ealdormon Aethelweard,[28] Aelfric observes:

> You have already received from my hands, for the strengthening of your faith, writings which you never before had in your language. Thou knowest, friend, that in the two former books we translated the passions and the lives of those saints which the English nation honors with festival-days. Now, however, it has seemed good to us to write this book about the passions and lives of those saints whom the monks celebrate among themselves.

However, in spite of the desire on Aelfric's part to distinguish *The Lives of the Saints* from the *Catholic Homilies*, the two works are much the same in nature and purpose. Indeed, many of the pieces in the second collection of the *Homilies*, such as the sermons on Gregory, Martin, and Cuthbert, are virtually saints' lives. And in *The Lives of the Saints* many discourses of a generally didactic nature are strewn about.

The Lives of the Saints begins with one such discourse, that on Christmas. It is useless to do much more here than comment upon the characteristic performance; an enumeration of the separate lives would be altogether unnecessary. It should be observed, first of all, that *The Lives of the Saints* is not devoted primarily to English saints. Such well-spaced geographical distribution as that represented by Eugenia, Juliana, Agnes, and Sebastian appears among the first eight lives. Old Testament heroes emerge in the eighteenth *Life*; the stories of three Anglo-Saxon saints, Aethelred, Alban, and Swithin, follow immediately. There is a section on the Maccabees, immediately pressing upon which is the rather well-known life of St. Oswald of Northumbria, which Aelfric derived obviously from Bede's *Ecclesiastical History*. It must be admitted that several of these lives are of considerable eloquence, notably the life of Oswald just mentioned, the life of St. Swithin, and the two general discourses on Ash Wednesday and on Mid-Lent, the latter sometimes referred to as *The Prayer of Moses*. The natural tendency of Aelfric's sonorous style to fall into the metrical is afforded an extreme example in *The Lives of the Saints*; Skeat has printed most of them as verse-compositions.[29]

We must remember, however, that *The Lives of the Saints* cannot be regarded as merely a group of narratives. As usual, they are instruments of Christian teaching. Aelfric does not hesitate, in fact, to incorporate into this work long passages of homily, such as the discourses on the false gods[30] or on the twelve abuses[31] or on auguries.[32] His entire attitude, it should be noted, here as elsewhere is that of the cautious teacher who is fearful of revealing too much to his ignorant flock:

> I do not promise that I shall write many lives of saints in this tongue, for it is not fitting that many should be translated into our language, lest indeed the pearls of Christ be held in contempt. And for that reason I hold my peace concerning the book called *Vitae Patrum*,[33] in which are contained many subtle points which ought not to be revealed to laymen, nor indeed are we ourselves able to comprehend them all.[34]

There is a mixture here of the ingenuous with the sincere

teacher, but the sentiments somehow would not fit either Bede or Alfred.

Included in the manuscripts of *The Lives of the Saints*,[35] and found separately in several other versions,[36] is the piece known as the *Interrogationes Sigewulfi*, or *Queries of Sigewulf*. Although Aelfric's name is not immediately connected with it, the work is clearly his, and probably followed soon after the composition of *The Lives of the Saints*. The chief bases for the ascription to Aelfric are the presence of the piece among Aelfric's accredited writings, the characteristic alliteration and other stylistic devices, and the same painstaking treatment of the equally characteristic subject-matter. It might, indeed, be considered as another of his homilies. Alcuin's *Handbook on Genesis* (VII, 4), the aim of which, to paraphrase its author, was to gather pearls of wisdom which the weary traveler might carry with him, is the original of the *Interrogationes Sigewulfi*. Aelfric is merely translating Alcuin's work and abridging it in the process. The piece is a catechistical affair treating of the difficulties in the Creator's moral government and in the rational creation; it treats further of the glorious process of physical creation; of the Trinity as manifest in creation; of the origin of man and his divine potentialities; of the genesis of evil; of the ages of the history of the world from Adam through Abraham. It concludes with a confession and a doxology. Aelfric has shortened the number of questions in the catechism from nearly three hundred to sixty-nine, and has prefaced the work with a life of Alcuin; furthermore, he has inserted in the discussion of the physical creation Bede's account of the planets.[37] Probably the most interesting part of the *Interrogationes Sigewulfi* is the beginning, in which Aelfric explains the origin of Alcuin's work:

> There was in England a celebrated teacher named Albinus, or Alcuin, and he had great fame. He taught many of the English in the knowledge contained in books, as he well knew how, and afterwards went across the sea to the wise king Charles, who had great wisdom in divine and secular matters, and lived wisely. Albinus, the noble teacher, came to him, and,

there a foreigner, dwelt under his rule, in the abbey of Saint
Martin, and taught to many the heavenly wisdom which the
Saviour had given him. Then at a certain time, a priest, Sigewulf, questioned him often from afar about some difficulties
which he himself did not understand in the holy book called
Genesis. Then Albinus said to him that he would gather together all his questions, and send him answers and reasons.
Sigewulf asked him first in these words: "What is to be understood by this: the Almighty ceased from his works on the seventh day, when he had created everything; but Christ said in
his gospel, 'My Father worketh until now and I work'?"
Albinus answered him: "God ceased from the new creation,
but he renews the same nature every day, and will guide his
work until the end of this world."

The preface to this work, addressed to Aelfric's friend and
patron, Aethelweard, shows Aelfric's practical didacticism, in
that he tries to explain the whys and wherefores of the existence of his work; but it shows also the essential artlessness of
Aelfric's teaching and his thoroughgoing solicitude for his
audience:

> Now it seems to me, beloved, that this work is very perilous
> for me or any man to undertake, because I fear lest some fool-
> ish man read this book, or hear it read, and will suppose that
> he can live now in our new law just as the patriarchs lived in
> that time before the old laws were established, or as men
> lived under Moses's law.

Specifically, Aelfric is afraid that his flock may be misled by
the apparent sanction of polygamy in the lives of Abraham
and Jacob.

As would be expected of a writer and teacher so prominent
and influential as Aelfric seems to have been, there are many
pieces which have attached themselves to his name. The
scholars, in the main, have been prone to accept many of these
apocryphal works as Aelfric's without the usual amount of
demurral. For example, there is, among these ascribed pieces,
the *Hexameron*, in four or five manuscripts,[38] first published
in Norman's edition of 1849. The reasons for assigning this

tract to Aelfric are inherent in the similarity of style, phraseology, and substance to those of the accepted Aelfrician pieces.
The homily is in part an adaptation of an original work on the
six days of Creation by Saint Basil of the fourth century; but
much of it is based upon Bede's scientific writings and his commentary on *Genesis* (VII, 3). Much of it, on the other hand,
would seem to be Aelfric's own. The author explains at the
outset:

> In another sermon [the Catholic Homily *De Initio Crea-
> turae*] we said some time before that the Almighty God
> created all things in six days and seven nights; but it is so
> great and complex a subject that we could not say as much as
> we wished in the former sermon.

Following these introductory remarks comes an account of
the works on each of the six days of creation, of the seventh
day of rest, of the tempting and the sin of man, of the expul-
sion from Eden and of the redemption through Christ. References to the earlier homily and to the matter of Bede's *De
Temporibus* suggest a date, we think, between 991 and 998
for the *Hexameron*.

Of less significance than the *Hexameron* is a little metrical
homily on the birth of Mary. The author explains that the
day is difficult to calculate; moreover,

> .... we will not give the false story which heretics have told
> of Mary's birth, for wise teachers have forbidden it; nor speak
> of her death, for holy writers do not permit it. Her holy father
> was named Joachim, and her mother Anna.[39]

The sermon itself is on holy virginity and is a strong defense
of celibacy. Again, the homily *For the Birthday of a Confessor*,[40] based on *Matthew*, xxv, 13, resolves itself ultimately
into a laudation of the forbearance of God. Less certainly
Aelfric's is the tract on Abgar, the legendary king of Edessa,
printed by Stephens in 1853[41] along with a Danish and an
English translation.

A work which has received much attention is Aelfric's translation of and commentary on selected portions of the Penta-

teuch, the Book of *Joshua,* and the Book of *Judges.* It was given the title *Heptateuch*[42] by its first editor, Thwaites (1698). It is not clear to what extent Aelfric is directly responsible for the whole of this piece, but it is probable that he did the first twenty-four chapters of *Genesis,* the Book of *Numbers,* and the Books of *Joshua* and *Judges.* Probably, too, the other portions had already been done by someone else. The selections under consideration are generous in length and are complete; the more abstruse portions, the isolated minutiae of Mosaic law, the tiresome and meaningless catalogues of names, are omitted, and only the story of Samson in the Book of *Judges* is told in any special detail. To the more famous judges of Israel, Aelfric adds the last three victorious kings of Wessex: Alfred, Athelstan, and Edgar. Since Aelfric explains in his long introductory address that he undertook the task at the behest of his friend Aethelweard, we must date the *Heptateuch* generally before 998, because the assumption is that Aethelweard died in that year. This, the major endeavor of Aelfric in the field of Old Testament literature, does not seem to have moved its author to any particular degree of enthusiasm; he had misgivings about the fitness of translating the Vulgate into bald Old English vernacular. The work, however, is a most characteristic example of Aelfric's popularizing of scriptural history and authority; it should be called a historical homily.

Similar to the *Heptateuch* are the treatments of the Books of *Job* and *Esther.*[43] The *Job* is mentioned in Aelfric's *On the Old Testament* (IX, 2) as the tale of one, "concerning whom I once translated a sermon." It appears to be the same as the homily on Job from the second series of the *Catholic Homilies,* and its source is wholly the Bible. As for the *Esther,* it needs little comment; it is found with the *Job* in a single manuscript edited by William L'Isle in the seventeenth century; and it offers a complete account, in "metrical" prose, with typical alliteration, of the story of Esther and Ahasuerus, who had "a kingdom east from India to Ethiopia-land,"—a diverting bit of geographical information! Ahasuerus was brought by the queen "to the belief in and worship of God who controls all things. . . . And he was righteous and wise in his works, and he had for another name Artaxerxes."

Two sets of *Canones*, or *Pastoral Letters*, by Aelfric have come down to the present.[44] The first set was requested by Wulfsiʒe, Bishop of Sherborne from 993 to 1001. A short personal letter in Latin to Wulfsiʒe explains the circumstances of the writing and makes clear that the composition of this work took place about 998. It is couched in language of considerable boldness of tone. "Free your mind, therefore, and tell them what ought to be regarded by the priests and ministers of Christ, lest you yourself perish likewise, if you are accounted a dumb dog." The body of the letter, however, is addressed to the Benedictines whom Wulfsiʒe had invited to Sherborne. It explains the findings of the Nicene Council; it enjoins celibacy and deprecates second marriages by laymen; it sets forth the hierarchy in the government of the Church, the duties of the orders and of the priests; it enumerates the necessary books with which the priest should be familiar; it forbids venality, covetousness, drunkenness, and worldliness. In the later portions of the epistle, comprising about a third of the whole, is a series of instructions concerning the Eucharist. The entire work is written in Aelfric's alliterative style. The second set of *Canones* was written for Wulfstan, Archbishop of York and Bishop of Worcester. This set consists of two epistles, written originally in Latin for Wulfstan's own use and then translated "not word for word, but sense for sense" in order that Wulfstan's secular clergy might make use of them. In substance they are virtually the same as those addressed to Wulfsiʒe; they contain, however, even more details concerning the founding of the Church. The Latin original of the second half of this set is incomplete, and there is some hesitation in assigning it to Aelfric. But there is little doubt about the first part; it was presumably done in 1014, because it has occasion to quote from a law passed by Ethelred II in that very year.

3. AELFRIC'S CIRCLE AND HIS MINOR WORKS

IT HAPPENED that Aelfric's old master Aethelwold, Bishop of Winchester, and important in the introduction of the Benedictines to England, had prepared a compilation of texts on the *Benedictine Rule* which went under the title of *De Consuetudine Monachorum*.[45] The ultimate source of this compilation was most likely multiple: Aethelwold partially translated an older Latin version into English and then added some material of his own in Latin. Since no manuscript bearing Aethelwold's name has come down from the period, one can but conjecture. To Aethelwold also was ascribed the *Concordia Regularis*,[46] another compilation based upon the teachings of the *Benedictine Rule*, the monastic habits of Continental monasteries, and native English clerical customs. There is now some doubt about this ascription, but there can be no question about Aethelwold's part in the spread of Benedictinism in England or about his authorship of much of *De Consuetudine Monachorum*. Aelfric wrote an epistle, known as the *Eynsham Letter* (in Manuscript Corpus Christi College Cambridge 265) which has been taken as the message of Aelfric to the Benedictine brothers at Cernel. And since Aelfric refers to himself here as "abbot" and addresses the epistle to the monks under the rule of Aethelmer, the date of this composition must be 1005 or shortly thereafter. The epistle is followed by a long tract on the rules of monastic life and can have interest only to the experienced student of ecclesiasticism.

By 1006 there is an instance of Aelfric's reputation among laymen. Wulfȝeat of Ylmandun, a thane high in the favor of Ethelred the Unready, although later disgraced, borrowed some of Aelfric's writings for his own use, talked with Aelfric about them, and was rewarded when Aelfric sent him one of his sermons. The *Homily to Wulfȝeat*[47] is first of all a summary of Christian doctrine and then a disquisition on the text of *Matthew*, v, 25 ("Agree with thine adversary quickly, while thou art with him in the way"). The sermon, developing a doctrine of St. Augustine, teaches that the "adversary" here referred to is the word of God. The word is as healing as a leech and serves as the instruction of a kindly teacher. The adversary is in truth man's friend. A man may love drunkenness and deceit, but God's word forbids all such sins. Our life on earth is the way in which we are to agree with our adversary. We must agree with the word now; later there will be no opportunity to do so, for the word will be our judge. The Lord bids all who labor to come to Him. We are to be meek and gentle in heart, must take care of the foolish and reckless, because we are responsible for them. The devious reasoning of so many medieval homilies protrudes here in striking fashion, yet the illogical quality is Augustine's as much as Aelfric's.

Some time shortly after 1006[48] Aelfric composed a practical introduction to the scriptures intended for the layman. It is known as *On the Old and New Testaments*[49] and is one of the most typical pieces among Aelfric's didactic writings. The recipient of all this didacticism was admittedly Sigeward of East Healle, Mercia. Yet, as the opening lines say: "This writing was done for one man, but indeed it may benefit many." As with many another of Aelfric's treatises on the Bible, *On the Old and New Testaments* is constructed in two parts. At the beginning of each part is an address to Sigeward, and at the close of each is Aelfric's usual warning to the scribe. The nature of the work is self-evident when it is explained that it is in most respects a popularization of the usual carefully organized medieval exposition of the Bible. It discusses the seventy-two books of the Bible and their authors; and as each appropriate book is mentioned, Aelfric points out his previous activity in expounding the book. It is these references that help us to date the performance. And so we are taken through a story of Creation and the Fall of the Angels, after which the various books of the Bible pass in review. Of the prophets, Isaiah seems to command most attention, no doubt because of the Messianic chapters. The second part, as the title of the whole work indicates, is a similar treatment of the New Testament; it begins with John the Baptist, discusses the four great Evangelists and the life of Christ, proceeds to the Epistles, and finally to the Acts of the Apostles and to the Apocalypse. Most interesting is the three-fold conclusion or appendix. The first describes and compares the two covenants with the Seraphim whom Isaiah saw, a warning to teachers to adhere to "this holy book," a comparison of the seventy-two books of the Bible with the seventy-two tribes of men left after the Deluge, an account of the ages of the world, and full exhortations to all people to do their duty to God. The second appendix recounts the punishment wrought upon the Jews by the destruction of Jerusalem by Titus; and the third is a personal address to Sigeward, admonishing him to give over drunkenness. While there is evidence to indicate that Aelfric was familiar with Augustine's *De Doctrina Christiana*, still one should give chief credit here to the author himself for the working out of the plan of the homily and certainly for writing it himself without recourse to any known translation.

As a final unit in Aelfric's tireless work, let us consider a little group of eight miscellaneous pieces. (1) There can be small doubt that he wrote, about 1006, a Latin *Life of Aethelwold*,[50] a biography of his teacher, the friend of Archbishop Dunstan and King Edgar, and the founder of many monasteries (IX, 1). This Latin life was then rewritten with some additions and corrections by Wulfstan of Winchester, who is known also for a life of Saint Swithin.[51] (2) It is possible that Aelfric wrote the metrical homily on Judith,[52] although he expressly does not assume credit for this work in his comments upon scriptural books in *On the Old and New Testaments*. Assmann[53] and Miss White[54] accept his authorship; and, indeed, since Aelfric favored the homily in metrical lines, their points are well taken. Aelfric himself, in *On the Old and New Testaments*, observes that the homily on Judith was written "in our wise." Whether this implies actual authorship by the writer or merely an imitation of his style, the reader must judge for himself. (3) There is what might be called an "edition" of Bede's *De Temporibus* (VII, 3)—selected material comprising astronomical facts—which fits, as far as style and intention are concerned, into the Aelfrician pattern.[55] It is, moreover, imbedded in the midst of manuscripts which are all Aelfrician material, and there is consequently no good reason for rejecting it from the Aelfric Canon. (4) A homily, *On Chastity*, dedicated to his friend Sigeferth,[56] may fitly be described as a call to celibacy. (5) A little collection of prayers and statements of faith is included in the better manuscripts of the *Catholic Homilies*; these include the Paternoster; the Apostles' Creed; the Nicaean, or Mass-Creed; seven short prayers on the growth of faith, love, hope, patience, blessing, etc. Apparently they are direct translations of the Latin text and are well done. (6) Similarly, the Cambridge Manuscript of the *Catholic Homilies*[57] contains a particular sermon, *On Penitence*, in two parts: the first treating of the necessity of Penitence and Confession; the second of the importance of fasting. Once more, there is no special reason for doubting the authenticity of the work. (7) Whether Aelfric or Wulfstan (X, 1) is responsible for the homily, *On the Sevenfold Gifts of the Holy Ghost*, is still doubtful,[58] but the credit, in my opinion, should go in all probability to Aelfric. This homily expounds the benefits of the sevenfold gifts and then describes the seven gifts of the Devil. The later passages dwell upon the evils of hypocrisy and the seductions of the Antichrist. Possibly this later portion is the work of a younger redactor of the Aelfric homily contained in the first part of the piece. (8) The rather fragmentary *Admonition to a Spiritual Son*[59] is unquestionably Aelfric's; it shows knowledge of Benedictinism, of the work of Saint Basil, and in both style and manner it is entirely consonant with Aelfric's other works. The original, to be sure, is by Saint Basil; and Aelfric's part here is chiefly that of a translator and commentator combined. The nature of the piece is sufficiently clear from the treatment in it of the following topics: spiritual warfare, the virtue of the soul, the love of God, the love of one's neighbor, the desire for peace, chastity, the avoiding of the love of the world, the eschewing of avarice.[60]

Enough has been said of Aelfric and his work to warrant the statement previously made that he is the most important figure in English literature between Alfred and the Norman Conquest. As is clear from the foregoing, Aelfric has for his time an unusually wide intellectual interest; and, although he is always primarily the teaching churchman, and obviously more narrowly so than someone like Bede, still he travels with equal ease in the fields of homiletics, astronomy, grammar, hagiology, and the tenth-century equivalent of sociology.

NOTES TO CHAPTER NINE

1. The famous monastic Rule of poverty and obedience founded by Benedict or Nursia about the year 528. While it is impractical here to attempt a summary of the seventy-three chapters of this Rule, it should be emphasized that the Benedictine Order was directed against that type of order in which the monks lived together in twos or threes without a fixed set of laws or recognized superiors to enforce them, and also against that type of vagrant monk who was for centuries a discredit to the monastic life. Benedictinism therefore added to the customary three vows of poverty, humility, and chastity a fourth vow of stability, which bound the monk to continuance in his profession and even to residence for life in the monastery in which he was professed, unless temporary absence or permanent transfer were permitted by the authorities of the Order. The Rule was in general noted for its relative absence of austerity; living was plain and perhaps a trifle bare, but compared to a peasant's life then—or now—it was more than adequate. Combined with this plain living was enjoined high thinking, which accounts for the lead that the Benedictines took in the establishing of schools. The feature of the Rule most valuable to its vitality was the insistence upon the essential dignity of work.

The tenth century is officially a dark age in the history of monasticism. This depression is accounted for partly by the depredations of the Northmen, partly by the remarkable growth of the feudal system, which secularized the Church to a striking degree, transforming abbots into lords and cardinals into princes, and partly by the tendency of laymen of wealth and power to seize and appropriate monastic revenues. The three great leaders in the revivifying of Benedictinism were the French Abbot of Cluny, Berno; Dunstan in England; and Anno, Archbishop of Cologne, in Germany. Of these Berno was the earliest and the most effective. The new Rule actually established an order within an order; it was in many ways stricter than the original Order, particularly as regards fasting and silence, and it emphasized ritual and liturgical pomp. As for Dunstan in England, he subscribed to the reformed Rule and undertook also some special reforms directed toward the substitution of monks for secular canons and the introduction of the Benedictine Rule into the English monasteries to supplant the Augustinian code.

The critical literature concerning the Benedictine Rule may be considered rather irrelevant in a work such as the present one; but not only was Aelfric concerned directly with the effects of Benedictine reform—so too were many other anonymous and forgotten writers of the time. Intellectually, the effects of this reform upon Christian thought were profound. Bibliographical references to those works of Aelfric immediately concerned with monastic problems will be made later at the appropriate place. The text of the Benedictine Rule, however, as it was known in the Old English period, will be found in H. Logeman, *The Rule of St. Benet*, volume 90 of *Publications of the Early English Text Society, Original Series* (London, 1888). The *De Consuetudine Monachorum* will be mentioned later; it was edited by W. S. Logeman in *Anglia*, XIII, 365-454 and XV, 20-40. A very important and useful survey of the subject is F. Tupper, "History and Texts of the Benedictine Reform of the Tenth Century" in *Modern Language Notes*, VIII, 344-367. There is a short discussion in M. Förster, "Beiträge zur mittelalterlichen Volkskunde" in *Archiv*, CXXV, 39-71. A. S. Napier edits the Reformed Rule in volume 150 of *Publications of the Early English Text Society, Original Series* (London, 1916). For Aethelwold, the article by H. W. Keim, "Aethelwold und die Mönchreform in England" in *Anglia*, XLI, 405-443 is very important. Further editions of parts and the whole of the Old English Benedictine Rule are the following: A. Schröer, "Die angelsächsischen Prosabearbeitungen der Benedictiner-regel" in Grein and Wülker, *Bibliothek der angelsächsischen Prosa*, II (Cassel-Göttingen, 1885-1888); A. Schröer, "De Consuetudine Monachorum" in *Englische Studien*, IX, 290-296 and *Die Winteney-Version der Regula S. Benedicti: lateinisch und englisch* (Halle, 1888)—see note 45 below; and J. Zupitza, "Ein weiteres Bruchstück der Regularis Concordia in altenglischer Sprache" in *Archiv*, LXXXIV, 1-24. There has been profuse discussion of these pieces, among which the following works are particularly recommended: A. Schröer, "Die angelsächsischen Prosabearbeitungen der Benedictinerregel" in *Englische Studien*, XIV, 241-253; M. Bateson, "Rules for Monks and Secular Canons after the Revival under King Edgar" in *English Historical Review*, IX, 690-708; and Chapters I and XII of White's

life of Aelfric (see note 2 below). The part played by Aethelwold is
further considered by F. Liebermann, "Aethelwolds Anhang zur
Benedictinerregel" in *Archiv*, CVIII, 375-377. The best book on
Dunstan is J. A. Robinson, *The Times of Saint Dunstan* (Oxford,
1923), which contains a study of Aethelwold and Oswald as well as
of Dunstan himself and describes the important tracts in the English
Benedictine Reform.

2. The best single work on Aelfric and his position in English literature is still Caroline L. White, *Aelfric: a new study of his life and
writings* (New Haven, 1898). There is also a good introduction by
W. W. Skeat in his preface to the edition of Aelfric's *Lives of the
Saints*, which comprises volumes 76, 82, 94, and 114 of *Publications
of the Early English Text Society, Original Series* (see note 27 below). S. S. Gem, *An Anglo-Saxon Abbot: Aelfric of Eynsham* (Edinburgh, 1912), is weak on bibliography. As reading to be done prefer-
ably before a consideration of Aelfric's individual works, there are the
following: Karl Jost, "Unechte Aelfrictexte" in *Anglia*, LI, 81-
103 and 177-219; Robert J. Menner, "Two Notes on Medieval
Euhemerism: Aelfred and Aelfric" in *Speculum*, III, 246-247; P.
Meissner, "Studien zum Wortschatz Aelfrics" in *Archiv*, CLXV, 11-
19, CLXVI, 30-39, and CLXVI, 205-215; C. E. Wright, "Two
Aelfric Fragments" in *Medium Aevum*, VII, 50-55; and E. K.
Chambers, *Eynsham under the Monks* (Oxford Record Society,
1937). The canon of Aelfric's works, however, has been but little
disturbed since the publication of Miss White's biographical, bibliographical, and critical monograph; and all subsequent notes in this
chapter referring to Aelfric and his works should be checked against
the references given by Miss White.

3. The fundamental problem among older scholars was the identity of Aelfric and whether he was one or more persons. These earlier
views are summed up in R. Wülker, *Grundriss zur Geschichte der
angelsächsischen Litteratur* (Leipzig, 1885), 453ff.

4. See note 6 below, with special reference to the studies by Sisam.

5. See notes 42 and 43 below; also B. Assmann, *Angelsächsische
Homilien und Heiligenleben*, which is volume III of Grein and Wülker's *Bibliothek der angelsächsischen Prosa* (Cassel-Göttingen, 1889).

6. See also notes 38, 42, 43, and 59 below, for the works given
reference there can be classed as homilies or at least homiletic material. General reference should also be made here to Chapter X below.
The earliest collection of Aelfric's various homilies was made by Benjamin Thorpe, *The Homilies of the Anglo-Saxon Church* (London,
rev. ed., 1884-1886), part I. Individual homilies had been printed
from time to time since the beginnings of the Renaissance knowledge
of Anglo-Saxon; a list of these will be found in Richard Wülker,

Grundriss zur Geschichte der angelsächsischen Litteratur (Leipzig, 1885), 457-458. After Thorpe, the next good collection in point of time is R. Morris, *Old English Homilies and Homiletic Treatises*, volumes 29 and 34 of *Publications of the Early English Text Society, Original Series* (London, 1867-1868). Selected homilies are to be found in A. S. Napier, *Wulfstan* (Berlin, 1883); Henry Sweet, *Selected Homilies of Aelfric* (Oxford, 1885; 1896); B. Assmann, *Angelsächsische Homilien und Heiligenleben*, volume III of Grein and Wülker's *Bibliothek der angelsächsischen Prosa* (Cassel-Göttingen, 1889); R. Brotanek, *Texte und Untersuchungen zur altenglischen Litteratur-und Kirchengeschichte* (Halle, 1913), 3-27; R. D. N. Warner, *Early English Homilies from . . . Vespasian D XIV*, volume 152 of *Publications of the Early English Text Society, Original Series* (London, 1917). A most valuable appraisal of the homilies doubtfully ascribed to Aelfric is Karl Jost's study (see note 2 above).

Discussions of most of these homilies both as a group and individually are F. Dietrich, "Abt Aelfric" in *Zeitschrift für die historische Theologie*, XXV, 487-594 and XXVI, 163-256; and—much the best detailed study of Aelfric's source-materials—M. Förster, "Über die Quellen von Aelfrics exegetischen Homiliae Catholicae" in *Anglia*, XVI, 1-61, with additional material in *Englische Studien*, XXVIII, 421-423. K. Sisam's excellent "MSS. Bodley 340 and 342: Aelfric's *Catholic Homilies*" in *Review of English Studies*, VII, 7-22 (completed in volumes VIII and IX of that periodical) is an indispensable recent contribution. See also Charles R. Davis, "Two New Sources for Aelfric's *Catholic Homilies*" in *Journal of English and Germanic Philology*, XLI, 510-513.

7. Sigeric did not come to England, however, until 990; it is not likely, therefore, that this preface could be earlier than 990, and it is probable that it belongs to some time in the years 990 or 991; but see Sisam's studies mentioned at the end of note 6 above. For a further detail on the career of Sigeric, see Francis P. Magoun, "The Rome of Two Northern Pilgrims: Archbishop Sigeric of Canterbury and Abbot Nikolas of Munkathvera" in *Harvard Theological Review*, XXXIII, 267-289.

8. Supposedly the author of the *Chronicle of Aethelweard*; see VII, 6 and Chapter VII, note 74 above.

9. F. Dietrich, "Abt Aelfrik" in *Zeitschrift für die historische Theologie* (see note 6 above).

10. In the preface addressed to Sigeric (see note 7 above). The appropriate statement runs: ". . . . transtulimus hunc codicem ex libris Latinorum. . . . Nec ubique transtulimus verbum ex verbo, sed sensum ex senso, cavendo tamen diligentissime deceptivos errores, ne inveniremur aliqua haeresi seducti seu fallacia fuscati. Hos namque

auctores in hac explanatione sumus sequuti, videlicet Augustinum (Hipponensem), Hieronimum, Bedam, Gregorium, Smaragdum, et aliquando Haymonem."

11. But see Davis's article mentioned in note 6 above.

12. Gordon H. Gerould, "Abbot Aelfric's Rhythmic Prose" in *Modern Philology*, XXII, 353-366.

13. Abraham Wheloc, *Historiae Ecclesiasticae Gentis Anglorum Libri V a Venerabili Beda . . . Scripti* (Cambridge, 1643).

14. There are three general types of manuscript for these homilies. The first, represented by the Cambridge Manuscript (which goes to make up Thorpe's edition—see note 6 above), keeps the homilies of the first and second series apart and contains all prefaces; the second type, represented by Manuscript Corpus Christi College Cambridge 188, omits prefaces and tends to mix the first and second series; the third type gives the homilies in their proper chronological order according to the Church Calendar.

15. Also in Manuscript Corpus Christi College Cambridge 188. For Aethelwold, see note 1 above. For the other manuscripts of this work, see Miss White's monograph on Aelfric (note 2 above), 109-110.

16. This homily is in four extant manuscripts: (1) Cotton Vespasian D XIV in the British Museum; (2) Cotton Faustina A IX, in the same; (3) Cotton Vitellius C V, in the same; and (4) Corpus Christi College Cambridge 302. The only printed edition is that of B. Assmann (see note 6 above).

17. This is Wulfgeat of Ylmandun, a onetime favorite of King Ethelred the Unready, who was, however, stripped of his favor in 1006.

18. The manuscript of this piece in Bodleian Junius 99 gives the homily in full; it is partially preserved also in Manuscript Corpus Christi College Cambridge 201. There is a second homily, following in many of the manuscripts, which seems to be only an abridgement of the original; this homily is found in Manuscripts Bodleian NE F 4, 12; Bodleian Junius 23; Bodleian Junius 24; Cotton Tiberius C VI; and Trinity College Cambridge. The rather perplexing matter of the relationship of the first to the second of these manuscripts has been handled well by D. Zimmermann in *Die beiden Fassungen des dem Abt Aelfric zugeschriebenen angelsächsischen Traktate über die siebenfältigen Gaben des Heiligen Gastes* (Leipzig, 1888). He considers the first to be original with Aelfric; the second is a revision by the same man who arranged many of the homilies now ascribed to Wulfstan. See X, 1 and Chapter X, note 2 below.

Napier, for one, believed that the homily, *On the Sevenfold Gifts of the Spirit* was Wulfstan's; he prints it in his *Wulfstan* (Berlin,

1883); Jost (see note 6 above) is extremely skeptical of the authenticity of this homily as either Aelfric's or Wulfstan's.

19. Quoted from the opening of Aelfric's preface to the first series of *Catholic Homilies*.

20. First printed by William Somner in his *Dictionarium Saxonico-Latino-Anglicum* (London, 1659), Vol. II. The first volume contains the *Glossary*, noted in the present work a few lines below. J. Zupitza's edition, in his *Sammlung englischer Denkmäler in kritischen Ausgaben* (Berlin, 1880), is still extremely useful. Pieces of this work had previously been printed as unimportant bits of Anglo-Saxon antiquity. There seem to have been very many manuscripts of this work, and there is good reason to suppose that it was an extremely popular book of instruction. No less than fifteen manuscripts are still known, and at least the transcription of three others. These manuscripts are listed in Zupitza's edition just cited and in Miss White's book (see note 2 above), 121. About half the available manuscripts contain the *Glossary*.

21. Quoted from the second preface to the *Grammar*, written in Old English (the first is in Latin).

22. Aelfric's debt to Priscian is acknowledged in both prefaces. To quote from the second (in the vernacular): "I have endeavored to translate these extracts from Priscian to you, tender youths, in order that, when you have read through Donatus's eight parts in this little book, you may be able to appropriate the Latin and English languages for the sake of attainment in higher studies." Priscian, although he is undoubtedly the great authority on linguistic study for the Middle Ages as a whole, nevertheless owes much to Donatus, who came about a century and a half earlier (ca. 350). Donatus was the author of two works, an *Ars Grammatica* and an *Ars Minor*, the latter of which teaches the eight parts of speech and is one of the more elementary textbooks on grammar used during the Middle Ages.

23. See note 20 above.

24. These represent Donatus's eight divisions. See Lawrence K. Shook, *Aelfric's Latin Grammar: a study in Old English grammatical terminology* in *Harvard University Summaries of Theses* (Cambridge, Mass., 1940), 360-363.

25. This is found in two manuscripts: Cotton Tiberius A III and the St. John's College Oxford. It was first printed in Benjamin Thorpe, *Analecta Anglosaxonica* (London, 1868), 18-36, and has since had careful treatment in T. Wright, *Anglo-Saxon and Old English Vocabularies* (London, 1884), I, 89-101 and recently in W. H. Stevenson, *Early Scholastic Colloquies*, Volume XV of *Anecdota Oxoniensia, Medieval and Modern Series*. But by far the most up-to-date edition is G. N. Garmondsway's in the Methuen Library of Old

English (London, 1939). The piece is discussed further in the works of Dietrich (see note 9 above) and Miss White (see note 2 above). Miss White also gives a large part of the vernacular gloss in Modern English, as does George K. Anderson in G. B. Woods, H. A. Watt, and G. K. Anderson, *The Literature of England* (Chicago, 1936; 1947), I, 68-71. Its origins are studied particularly in J. Zupitza, "Die ursprüngliche Gestalt von Aelfrics Colloquium" in *Zeitschrift für deutsches Altertum*, XXXI, 32-45 and in E. Schröder, "Colloquium Aelfrici" in *Zeitschrift für deutsches Altertum*, XLI, 283-290.

26. The fully developed medieval debate, however, is not encountered in English medieval literature until the Middle English period proper. For that reason, any bibliographical suggestions at this point may be a trifle inappropriate. But the article by J. D. Bruce, "A Contribution to the Study of 'The Body and the Soul' Poems in English" in *Modern Language Notes*, V, 385-401; the introduction to F. Holthausen's edition of *Vices and Virtues*, volumes 89 and 159 of *Publications of the Early English Text Society, Original Series*; Hirzel's *Der Dialog, ein literarhistorischer Versuch* (Leipzig, 1895); Merrill's *The Dialogue in English Literature* (New Haven, 1911); and Walther's *Das Streitgedicht in der lateinischen Litteratur des Mittelalters* (Berlin, 1914)—are all helpful studies of this characteristically medieval type of literature.

27. *The Lives of the Saints* is the work of Aelfric most discussed by present-day scholars. There is only one good manuscript for the set; this is Manuscript Cotton Julius E VII in the British Museum, which was taken by W. W. Skeat for his authoritative edition, *Aelfric's Lives of the Saints*, volumes 76, 82, 94, and 114 of *Publications of the Early English Text Society, Original Series* (London, 1881-1900). Single biographical homilies—individual lives of the saints—are scattered here and there among the anthologies and readers of Old English literature. Specific treatments are those in Gordon H. Gerould, "Aelfric's Lives of St. Martin of Tours" in *Journal of English and Germanic Philology*, XXIV, 206-210; and especially in C. Grant Loomis, "Further Sources of Aelfric's Saints' Lives" in *Harvard Studies and Notes in Philology and Literature*, XIII, 1-8, together with Dorothy Bethurum, "The Form of Aelfric's *Lives of the Saints*" in *Studies in Philology*, XXIX, 515-533. Related to this subject are George R. Coffman, "A Note on Saints' Legends" in *Studies in Philology*, XXVIII, 580-586; C. Grant Loomis, "The Growth of the Saint Edmund Legend" in *Harvard Studies and Notes in Philology and Literature*, XIV, 83-113; Constance L. Rosenthal, *The 'Vitae Patrum' in Old and Middle English Literature* (Philadelphia, 1936); and A. A. Prins, "Some Remarks on Aelfric's *Lives of the Saints* and

his Translations from the Old Testament" in *Neophilologus*, XXV, 112-122. General treatments of the biographical elements are given in Benjamin R. Kurtz, "From St. Antony to St. Guthlac: a study in biography" in *University of California Publications in Modern Philology*, XII, ii, 104-146; and Donald A. Stauffer, *English Biography before 1700* (Cambridge, Mass., 1930). Special attention should be paid to Gordon H. Gerould, *Saints' Legends* (Boston, 1916) and to C. W. Jones, *Saints' Lives and Chronicles in Early England* (Ithaca, 1947).

28. See note 8 above.

29. Skeat's edition has been referred to in note 27 above.

30. Mentioned specifically by Miss White (see note 2 above), 130.

31. Mentioned specifically by Miss White (see note 2 above), 130.

32. Mentioned specifically by Miss White (see note 2 above), 129.

33. See Miss Rosenthal's monograph, cited in note 27 above.

34. Quite apart from the ingenuous nature of this remark, bespeaking an attitude far too common in the teaching of the Middle Ages—and later, it is well to note that Aelfric himself names as his source Ambrose, for the life of Saint Agnes; Terence, in the introduction to the life of Gallicanus; Marcellus, in the life of Petronilla; Jerome, in the life of the Four Evangelists; Bede, in the life of Aetheldred; and Landerth, in the life of Saint Swithin. No single collection of legends in Latin furnished him with material. His additions are of the usual kind—metrical, or at least alliterative, explanatory and homiletic increments.

35. See note 27 above.

36. The oldest separate printing of the *Interrogationes Sigewulfi* is in K. W. Bouterwek, *Screadunga* (Elberfeld, 1858), 17-23; it is the subject of George E. MacLean's monograph, "Aelfric's Anglo-Saxon Version of *Alcuini Interrogationes Sigewulfi Presbyteri in Genesin*" in *Anglia*, VI, 425-473 and VII, 1-50, also published separately (Halle, 1883). MacLean notes that in addition to its inclusion in Manuscript Cotton Julius E VII, along with *The Lives of the Saints*, the *Interrogationes Sigewulfi* appears in the following manuscripts: Corpus Christi College Cambridge 162; Corpus Christi College Cambridge 178; in a manuscript binding together the two preceding; Bodleian Junius 23; Bodleian Junius 24; Corpus Christi College Cambridge 303; and Bodleian Junius 104. MacLean's study is considered and discussed by A. Tessmann, *Aelfrics altenglische Bearbeitung der Interrogationes Sigewulfi Presbyteri* in *Genesis des Alcuin* (Berlin, 1891).

37. From Bede's *De Tempora Ratione*; see VII, 3 above and Chapter VII, note 39.

38. Actually five, if we count them in detail. They are (1) Cotton

Otho B X; (2) Bodleian Junius 23; (3) Bodleian Junius 24; (4) Corpus Christi College Cambridge S 6; and (5) Corpus Christi College Cambridge S 7. The two Bodleian Junius manuscripts are brought together in a transcript in Bodleian Junius 47. The early edition by Norman is entitled *The Anglo-Saxon Version of the Hexameron of St. Basil* (London, 1849). It was later published by Richard Morris in *Old English Homilies and Homiletic Treatises*, volumes 29 and 34 of *Publications of the Early English Text Society, Original Series* (London, 1867-1868); and recently has been edited by S. J. Crawford's *"Exameron anglice," or the English Hexameron* for Grein and Wülker's *Bibliothek der angelsächsischen Prosa*, x (Hamburg, 1921)—which contains an introduction, a complete collation of the manuscripts, a Modern English translation, and a comparative study of related passages from Aelfric's other works. Some consideration has been given the *Hexameron* in all of the works on Aelfric; see those mentioned in note 2 above. A short discussion of particulars is given in O. F. Emerson, "Aelfric's Hexameron" in *Archiv*, cxlv, 254-256.

39. Aelfric asserts this in that version of the *Catholic Homilies* represented by Manuscript Corpus Christi College Cambridge 188. He admits that he omitted it from his first edition (see Thorpe's version cited in note 6 above, ii, 446), "lest we fall into some error. The gospel of this day is very difficult for laymen to understand." The piece is given also in Manuscripts Corpus Christi College Cambridge S 17, Bodleian Junius 22 and Bodleian Junius 24—the last two, of course, at Oxford.

40. Appearing in the following manuscripts: Corpus Christi College Cambridge 188; Corpus Christi College Cambridge 178; Bodleian Junius 22; Bodleian Junius 24; Bodleian Library 343; and—virtually useless because of its condition—Cotton Vitellius D XVII. This homily should not be confused with *In Natale Unius Confessoris*, printed in Thorpe's edition (see note 6 above), ii, 548-562. It is dedicated to Aethelwold the Younger, Bishop of Winchester from 1007 to 1012.

41. G. Stephens, *Tvende Old-Engelske Digte mid Oversaettelger og Tillaeg* (Copenhagen, 1853), 15-21. The piece is found in Manuscripts Cotton Junius E VII and Cotton Vitellius D XVII. In both it appears in conjunction with the lives of St. Abdon and St. Sennes, but these two lives have never been attributed to Aelfric. It has, since the time of Stephens's edition, been included in all printed editions of *The Lives of the Saints* (see note 27 above).

42. First printed in Edward Thwaites, *Heptateuchus* (Oxford, 1698); the work contains also some of Aelfric's other Biblical commentaries and translations (see notes 43 and 49 below). In general, see C. W. M. Grein and R. Wülker, *Bibliothek der angelsächsischen*

Prosa, I (Cassel-Göttingen, 1872), which appears also under the title "Alfric de vetere et novo testamente" in volume III of the same series (Assmann's *Angelsächsische Homilien und Heiligenleben*; 1889); and in the works of Miss White (see note 2 above), Förster (see note 2 above), and Dietrich (see note 27 above) are discussions of all of Aelfric's works on Biblical material. To these should be added J. H. Ott, *Über die Quellen der Heiligenleben in Aelfrics Lives of the Saints* (Halle, 1892), for several of the saints' lives derived from the Bible.

The best modern edition of the *Heptateuch*, however, remains S. J. Crawford, *The Old English Version of the Heptateuch*, volume 160 of *Publications of the Early English Text Society, Original Series* (London, 1922). This contains also the treatise, *On the Old and New Testament* (see note 49 below), as well as Aelfric's preface to *Genesis* and a Vulgate text of the Heptateuch, and a very valuable bibliography (pp. 12-14). An important review of Crawford's edition is E. Ekwall's in *Anglia Beiblatt*, XXXV, 193-195.

43. *Job* was printed in Thorpe's edition of the *Homilies* (see note 6 above), I, 6; there was a fragment of an earlier text in William L'Isle, *Divers Ancient Monuments in the Saxon Tongue* (London, 1638)—reprinted by Crawford in his *The Old English Version of the Heptateuch* (see note 42 above). There are four manuscripts: Bodleian Laud E 381; Bodleian Library 343; Cambridge University Library; and Cotton Cleopatra B XIII; see the M. Förster edition in *Anglia*, XV, 473-477.

Esther was printed also in L'Isle's *Divers Ancient Monuments*, just cited, and is fully edited and discussed by B. Assmann, *Abt Aelfrics angelsächsische Bearbeitung des Buches Esther* (Halle, 1885).

In the main, the source-material and bibliography for *Job* and *Esther* both should be referred to notes 6 and 27 above for generalities concerning Aelfric's work with the scriptures, hagiology, and homiletics. But the reader should also bear in mind that both *Job* and *Esther* stand in direct relationship to the *Heptateuch*; therefore see note 42 above.

44. The best edition, with a full account of the manuscripts, is Bernhard Fehr, *Die Hirtenbriefe Aelfrics*, volume IX of Grein and Wülker's *Bibliothek der angelsächsischen Prosa* (Hamburg, 1914). The manuscripts are Boulogne-sur-Mer 63; Corpus Christi College Cambridge 265; Corpus Christi College Cambridge 201; Cotton Nero A I; Cambridge University Library; Cotton Tiberius A III; Corpus Christi College Cambridge 190; Bodleian Library 343; Cotton Vespasian D XIV; and Bodleian Junius 121. Of these, Manuscripts Corpus Christi College Cambridge 190 and Bodleian Junius 121 may be considered the chief manuscripts; and of these two,

Manuscript Corpus Christi College Cambridge 190 is probably the older: see G. K. Anderson, "Notes on the Language of Aelfric's English *Pastoral Letters* in Corpus Christi College Cambridge 190 and Bodleian Junius 121" in *Journal of English and Germanic Philology*, XL, 5-13. Supplementing Fehr's edition just mentioned is his article in *Englische Studien*, lii, 285-288. Fehr's edition contains a German translation, but there is no Modern English edition or translation. See the items cited in note 2 and note 9 above, particularly the works of Miss White and Dietrich; see also Assmann's text of the *Homilies* mentioned in note 6 above.

45. See the bibliographical items under note 1 above; also E. Breck, *A Fragment of Aelfric's Translation of Aethelwold's De Consuetudine Monachorum and its Relation to Other Manuscripts* (Leipzig, 1887); M. Bateson, "Rules for Monks and Secular Canons after the Revival under King Edgar" in *English Historical Review*, IX, 690-708; E. Feiler, *Das Benediktiner-Offizium: ein altenglisches Brevier aus dem elften Jahrhundert* (Heidelberg, 1901); also B. Fehr, "Das Benedictiner-Offizium und die Beziehungen zwischen Aelfric und Wulfstan" in *Englische Studien*, XLVI, 337-346.

46. See J. Zupitza, "Ein weiteres Bruchstück der Regularis Concordia in altenglischer Sprache" in *Archiv*, LXXXIV, 1-24; also W. S. Logeman, "De Consuetudine Monachorum" in *Anglia*, XIII, 365ff. and particularly XV, 20-40; and A. S. Napier, *The Old English Version of the Enlarged Rule of Chrodegang together with the Latin Original*, volume 150 of *Publications of the Early English Text Society, Original Series* (London, 1916). Extremely valuable on this subject is F. Tupper, "History and Texts of the Benedictine Reform of the Tenth Century" in *Modern Language Notes*, VIII, 344-367. The manuscript is Cotton Tiberius A III. Breck, in the study cited in note 45 above, tries to make out a case for Aelfric's authorship of the fragment of the *Concordia Regularis* found in Manuscript Cotton Tiberius A III. At least, he thinks, it is either a product of Aelfric's own pen or else of some one of his contemporaries or perhaps pupils. The qualifications in this statement tend to invalidate his study.

47. In Manuscript Bodleian Laud Miscellaneous 509; also in Manuscript Bodleian Junius 121, which contains the sermon on the text from *Matthew*, and in Manuscript Bodleian Junius 23.

48. It is believed that the *Homily to Wulfzeat* was composed before 1006, for in that year Wulfzeat was disgraced; see note 17 above.

49. See also the bibliographical references pertaining to the *Heptateuch*, *Job*, and *Esther* (see notes 42 and 43 above). The material was collected first by William L'Isle and appears in both his *A Saxon Treatise Concerning the Old and New Testament* (London, 1623) and his *Divers Ancient Monuments in the Saxon Tongue* (London,

1638). It has been printed in Grein and Wülker's *Bibliothek der angelsächsischen Prosa*, II (Cassel-Göttingen, 1877). Selections from it are given in R. K. Rask, *Angelsaksisk Sproglaere* (Stockholm, 1817) and in H. Sweet, *An Anglo-Saxon Reader* (Oxford, 1887; 1922). A complete text, and the best one, all things considered, is given in S. J. Crawford, *The Old English Version of the Heptateuch*, volume 160 of *Publications of the Early English Text Society, Original Series* (London, 1922), 15-75. See also the monograph by J. H. Ott, *Über die Quellen der Heiligenleben in Aelfrics Lives of the Saints* (Halle, 1892). Aside from the discussion in Crawford's edition just cited and in Miss White's book on Aelfric (see note 2 above), little attention has been paid this work.

50. This is dedicated to Bishop Kenulf of Winchester, who was ordained bishop and died in 1006, thus practically fixing the date of the composition. The part Aelfric played in this work, together with the text of Aelfric's *Life*, is presented by R. Stevenson in the appendix to the second volume of *Chronicon Monasterii de Abingdon*. The preface of Aelfric, and Wulfstan's version, is given by J. Mabillon in *Acta Sanctorum Benedictinorum* (Paris, 1835), v, 606.

51. See X, 3 and also Chapter X, note 1 below.

52. This work is found in two manuscripts: Corpus Christi College Cambridge 303, which is described by G. E. MacLean in *Anglia*, VI, 446-447; and Cotton Otho B X, which was severely damaged in the fire of 1731. It has been estimated that the whole piece consisted of some 520 lines, of which all but seventy have nevertheless been preserved.

53. This is, in my opinion, the definitive discussion: "Abt Aelfrics angelsächsische Homilie über das Buch Judith" in *Anglia*, x, 76-104. The matter is considered again, however, by A. S. Cook in his edition of the poem *Judith* (see IV, 5 and Chapter IV, note 42 above).

54. See her study (note 2 above), 196-198.

55. A. Reum, "De Temporibus, ein echtes Werk des Abtes Aelfric" in *Anglia*, x, 457-498; there is a summary of this in Miss White's book (see note 2 above), 188-192. There are at least seven manuscripts, all noted by Reum. But the better edition is that by H. Henel in volume 213 of *Publications of the Early English Text Society, Original Series* (London, 1942).

56. Four manuscripts are known, and part of a fifth: (1) Cotton Faustina A IX; (2) Cotton Vitellius C V; (3) Cotton Vespasian D XIV; (4) Corpus Christi College Cambridge 302. The only full edition is that by B. Assmann in Volume III of Grein and Wülker's *Bibliothek der angelsächsischen Prosa* (see note 6 above). We know nothing of importance about Sigeferth; it is consequently difficult to date this piece, but the year usually suggested is 1005.

57. Printed by Benjamin Thorpe in *The Homilies of the Anglo-Saxon Church* (see note 6 above), II, 604-609.

58. See, however, note 18 above.

59. In Manuscript Bodleian Library Hatton 100, transcribed into Manuscript Bodleian Junius 68. The standard edition is still H. W. Norman, *The Anglo-Saxon Version of the Hexameron of St. Paul . . . and the Anglo-Saxon Remains of St. Basil's Admonitio ad Filium Spiritualem* (London, 1848).

60. A few miscellaneous bibliographical items should be noted here briefly. A comprehensive study of Aelfric's doctrine is implicit in H. O. Halverson, "Doctrinal Terms in Aelfric's Homilies," Volume V, No. 1 of *University of Iowa Studies* (Iowa City, 1932); Kenneth Sisam, "Mss. Bodley 340 and 342: Aelfric's *Catholic Homilies*" (see note 6 above); A. E. H. Swaen, "Aelfric's *Prefatio Genesis Anglice*" in *Englische Studien*, LXVII, 318 (see note 42 above); C. E. Wright, "Two Aelfric Fragments" in *Medium Aevum*, VII, 50-55; Alinda E. Montgomery, "Devotion to the Blessed Virgin Mary in English Life and Literature before 1300" in *Summaries of Doctoral Dissertations, Northwestern University*, V, 20-24 (Evanston, 1937); and P. Meissner, "Studien zum Wortschatz Aelfrics" in *Archiv*, CLXV, 11-19; CLXVI, 30-39; and CLXVI, 205-215.

There has survived also a list of what may be the names of Aelfric's bondsmen or *festermen*. According to Anglo-Saxon canon law, each priest must have twelve *festermen* before he could be ordained. The list may be interesting enough as a biographical detail, but the full implications of such a list cannot well be realized with our present relative ignorance; and besides, there is little doubt that we are dealing here with Aelfric of York rather than with Aelfric of Eynsham. At any rate, there is no apparent relationship between these bondsmen and Aelfric's literary products. See E. Björkman, "Die 'Festermen' des Aelfric" in *Festschrift für Lorenz Morsbach* (Halle, 1931), 1-19; and W. H. Stevenson, "Yorkshire Surveys and Other Eleventh Century Documents in the York Gospels" in *English Historical Review*, XXVII, 1-25. There is some further discussion in H. Lindkvist, "Some Notes on Elfric's Festermen" in *Anglia Beiblatt*, XXXIII, 130-144.

X · Wulfstan's Works and other Homiletic Prose

1. WULFSTAN

AELFRIC's contemporary and a figure of importance in the earlier part of the eleventh century is given more to didactic, inspirational homily than was Aelfric himself. Wulfstan,[1] at least as far as his most famous work is concerned, towers as a prophet in the days of the Danish conquest. Little is known of his life beyond the record of his professional career. He was Bishop of London in 1001, later Bishop of Worcester, and then Archbishop of York from 1002 to 1023. It is supposed that he died in that last year.

There are four manuscripts which contain writings definitely assignable to Wulfstan, and a pastoral letter from Wulfstan which indicates that he was accustomed to write. The old guess by Wanley[2] that he was the author of more than fifty sermons is now rejected; some of these pieces seem to be by Aelfric. The whole question of the authorship of the many apparently anonymous homilies coming down from this period is at best extremely difficult. A conservative judgment would credit Wulfstan with fifteen surviving homilies and perhaps nine others as possibilities. There is no mention of Wulfstan's name in any of the homilies ascribed to him, but the superscription *Sermones Lupi Episcopi*[3] heads the manuscript which contains the four sermons indisputably accepted as Wulfstan's own. The Latin *lupus* was used occasionally in the period to translate English names having the element -*wolf*- (an extremely common element in Anglo-Saxon personal names); and Wulfstan of London, Worcester, and York is the only one in those years whose name, occupation, diocese, and see fit the conditions.

There is some eloquence in the *First Homily*, the *De Fide*

Catholica, and in the *Sermo ad Populum*. The most moving, however, and certainly the most impressive of Wulfstan's known utterances is the fiery address to the English, known in Manuscript Bodleian Junius 99 as the *Sermo Lupi ad Anglos quando Dani maxime persecuti sunt eos quod fuit anno millesimo XIIII ab incarnatione domini nostri Jesu Christi.*[4] At the time this sermon was delivered, Ethelred the Unready had fled to Normandy, and Swein was harrying England just prior to his acknowledgment as king of the country. Thus the sermon must have been composed very early in the year 1014, for Swein died in February. The homily opens on the note

> Hora novissima
> Tempora pessima
> Sunt; vigilemus.[5]

Englishmen have been to blame for the ravages wrought by the Danes; they must turn back to God, who has been thus chastising them for their iniquities. And these iniquities have been grave, in no way more apparent than in the decline of faith, the slackness of churchmen in fulfilling their religious duties, the betrayal of the English king by those who should have supported him. Indeed, betrayal has known no limits; fathers have betrayed sons, and sons mothers, and one brother another; and ever the longer the worse! A strange kind of rhapsodic refrain punctuates the homily from time to time. Violence of all kinds has raged: oath-breaking, murder, mockery, and lust. So now,

> In God's name let us do as we needs must, let us protect ourselves, as we very well can, lest we be all ruined together! Let us ... bow to the right and in some measure at least abandon wrong ... love God and follow God's law ... as well as we vowed when we were baptized; and let us set in order our words and works and cleanse our inmost thoughts; and ... let us think oft of the great Judgment to which we must all come, and shield ourselves from the welling flame of Hell-torture, and earn for ourselves fame and joy, which God has prepared for those who do His will in the world.

Whatever the judgment that scholarship may be able to lay down concerning the other homilies of Wulfstan, there can be no cavilling about the work for which he well deserves to be remembered.

Wulfstan obviously occupied a more exalted position in the Church than Aelfric.[6] But he was not averse to following stylistically in the footsteps of his subordinate; there is in his work the same fondness for alliteration, for the coupling of synonyms, for the metrical beat that will be discovered in Aelfric's most characteristic writings. There is in Wulfstan, however, a greater tendency to the repetition of catch-phrases, almost in the nature of refrains—as evidenced by the "let him know, who will ponder it" or "let him understand, who will" or the "do more, if he can" phrases in his famous *Sermo ad Anglos*. There is a certain jerkiness and trochaic push of phrase which gives the impression that Wulfstan was an aggressive and polemic preacher, and assuredly he was more the demagogue where Aelfric was not. For Aelfric, quite apart from his greater range and versatility, seems to be more poised, more intellectual—an excellent blend of the rhetorician and the ecclesiast; Wulfstan is far more the emotional orator and man of the moment. But he was alive to the dangerous times and the critical issues of his day; and certain enthusiasts may well insist that Wulfstan did Anglo-Saxon prose an incalculable service by preserving it with effective power in a time of national disaster.[7]

2. THE BLICKLING AND VERCELLI HOMILIES

THE story of the spiritual prose of the Old English period is not complete, however, with the recognition of the presence of Aelfric and Wulfstan and the men and forces which made them write. It is true, of course, that the efforts of Dunstan and Aethelwold reaped ample rewards in the writings of these two distinguished men. There were evidently lesser lights, however, and some few of them survive through their works, their names having been forgotten. The presence of an Ael-

frician and a Wulfstanian cycle of spiritual literature can perhaps be postulated; maybe, on the other hand, it is enough to
say that Benedictinism in England had become vocal during
the late tenth and early eleventh century.

For example, a collection of nineteen homilies of unknown
authorship was brought to light and published by Morris between 1874 and 1880.[8] Since they existed in only one manuscript, in the possession of the Marquis of Lothian at Blickling Hall in Norfolkshire, they have been known ever since
as the *Blickling Homilies*.[9] In the very first of these is a reference which fixes the date of 971, but whether this is the date
of the actual composition or the date at which the homilies were
transcribed from some collection of previous years is dubious.
As a whole, the collection bears every sign of being a compilation from many sources. It is generally agreed, however, that
the homilies are the product of the spiritual education and
reforms of Dunstan, Aethelwold, and others. The sources of
the sermons are, of course, scriptural, although to a rather unusual extent they draw upon the Apocrypha. The themes are
nearly always related to the idea of atonement against the
imminent Day of Judgment, for there was a widespread tradition—the millennial tradition—that God would judge the
world in the year 1000.

Some of the *Blickling Homilies*, like Aelfric's *Catholic
Homilies*, are occasional pieces. Thus there is a sermon for
Shrove Sunday, the First Sunday in Lent, the Third Sunday
in Lent, the Fifth Sunday in Lent, Palm Sunday, Easter Sunday, Holy Thursday, Whitsunday, Michaelmas, and Martinmas. Two treat of important stages in the Christian mysteries,
the Annunciation and the Assumption of the Holy Virgin.
One allegorizes the figure of Christ—Christ the Golden Blossom. Three are virtually saints' lives: the Birth of John the
Baptist, the story of Peter and Paul, and the Life of Saint
Andrew, which parallels the Cynewulfian *Andreas* (IV, 5).
One is a monitory sermon, *The End of the World is Near*.
Still another is too incomplete to warrant a safe guess as to
the text upon which it is based. Five of them are fragmentary.

Except for the subject of Judgment Day, the homilies as they
stand are characteristic as to topic and general treatment. But
they evidently antedate the first collection of Aelfric's *Catholic Homilies* by at least twenty years; they are more casual
in structure, more inclined to ramble, less averse to introduc-
ing legend and popular moralizing in a rather surprising way;
and, as Earle puts it,[10] "they are plainly . . . of the age . . .
when the line was very dimly drawn between canonical and
uncanonical." They are vigorous pieces, done with perhaps
greater attention to rhetoric than is commonly observed; but
they are not given to the alliterative and metrical style as are
the homilies of Aelfric or Wulfstan. And yet such a passage
as the following, from the best known of the *Blickling Homilies* ("The End of the World is Near") is reminiscent of the
gnomic passages from such poems as *The Wanderer* or *Beowulf* itself:[11]

> Nor let any man here in this worldly kingdom be in thought
> too rash, nor in body too strong, nor in enmity too ready, nor
> in strife too bold, nor of deceits too full, nor of wickedness too
> fond, nor of wrongs too subtle, nor of artifice too skilled. Nor
> need any man suppose that his body can or may improve the
> burden of sin in the grave; but there in the mold he will rot;
> and he will await doom when the Almighty God wishes to
> bring about the end of the world, and draws his flaming sword
> and shears through this world, and pierces the body, and
> cleaves this universe; and the dead will stand up; then will
> the body be made clear as glass, and naught that is wrong will
> be hidden.[12]

Mention of the *Blickling Homilies* is a reminder that *The
Vercelli Book* contains a prose miscellany, which is itself a
large contribution to the body of Old English homiletic
works. *The Vercelli Book* has already come under discussion
as a repository of some of the Old Christian epic poems, such
as *Andreas*. Apparently of a date near the year 1000, this
manuscript represents a compilation by some unknown scribe
of a mass of material in both prose and poetry with a predominantly religious atmosphere. Its presence in the Cathedral at

Vercelli, Italy, is still unaccounted for in satisfactory fashion; and the explanation that it was taken to Italy by Cardinal Guala, papal legate in England during the early years of the thirteenth century, is attractive but unconvincing. The general assumption now is that it was composed in England and may have arrived in Italy only after a devious path among clerical scholars, a path which is unfortunately altogether dark.[13]

The assemblage of homilies in this manuscript begins with one on the Passion of Christ, His burial and His sojourn in Hell, ending with the admonition that we all must give manifold thanks to the Lord for His suffering, which He endured for the redemption of man. A second homily describes the Last Judgment, when blood and fire will drench human beings—a day which we must prepare for by love and yearning for the bliss of God and the glory of the heavens. Homily number three makes clear the qualities which the true Christ demands—the first is Belief; the second is Hope; and the third is True Love—stating the nature of heavenly largess:

> There are three kinds of alms—one is bodily, that is, that one should give to the destitute those goods which he can; the second is spiritual, that he should forgive those who sin against him; and the third is, that one should busy oneself with the sinner and bring the erring one to right.[14]

Next comes a discourse on penance under the imminent shadow of the Last Judgment; and there are echoes here of a dialogue between the soul and the body—one of two or three notable illustrations of this most popular form of Christian instruction.[15] The fifth homily has for its topic the birth of Christ and is written under the heading: "For Midwinter; *Ostende Nobis, Domine!*" In substance it is not original, nor is it striking in style. The two poems, *Andreas* (IV, 5) and *The Fates of the Apostles* (IV, 4) intervene; and then the sixth homily—almost a continuation of the fifth—on the wonders of Christ's birth and the flight into Egypt. Nothing will illustrate better the helter-skelter order of the pieces in

The Vercelli Book, nor its structurally variegated nature, than the manner in which the fifth and sixth homilies, virtually a unit, are broken apart by two narrative poems. The seventh homily, on the other hand, departs from the holy life and becomes a sternly monitory piece on the topics of extravagance and gluttony, while counselling moderation at all times. Related to the seventh in tone and purpose is the eighth homily in the list, a return to the matter of the Last Judgment and the torments of Hell, emphasized this time in order to enjoin a careful shunning of sins, most of which are suggested perhaps by the two attacked in the seventh homily—extravagance and gluttony. And to put Man even more on his guard, the ninth homily treats of sudden death and its terrors, a theme familiar to anyone who has read much of medieval didactic literature. Equally familiar is the theme of *sic transit gloria mundi*, to which the tenth homily is devoted; we have seen this theme, couched almost in these very words, in *The Wanderer* (V, 1); but in this homily it gives off a heavily ecclesiastical aroma, with but little of the grandeur of the poetic piece. Yet if this world and all its joys are only transitory, the churchman can prepare the way out of this quicksand of doubt and instability. Three homilies—the eleventh, twelfth, and thirteenth—intended for Rogation tide, discuss the three special days when by fasting and prayer the Christian can fortify himself for the journey forth. These are "holy days, hallowing and curing our souls; and it behooves us to observe them well with fasting and with praying and with the worship of relics." Without referring to any particular day but rather "to such time as man will," the fourteenth homily reminds the listener that "we need not live among devils or among sinful men in eternal punishments and eternal damnation, but we must go rejoicing among the angels and all the saints of God into the heavenly land and afterwards enjoy bliss for ever and ever." This theme of damnation keeps returning; the fifteenth homily, entitled *Another Homily on the Day of Judgment*, begins with the observation that Saint Thomas asked our Lord when the coming of Antichrist should be; and our

Lord replied that it would be on the ultimate day. The threatening homily is then well launched. The pieces following, however, are less grim and more occasional. The sixteenth is a homily on Epiphany; the seventeenth on the feast-day of the purification of Mary. The eighteenth, on the festival of Saint Martin, appears to be a complete version of the homily found in only fragmentary form among the *Blickling Homilies*.[16] We arrive then at a break in the steady stream of sermonizing in prose, although the purpose of the following pieces is homiletic enough. *The Soul and the Body* has already been described (V, 4);[17] so has *The Dream of the Rood* (IV, 5). The *Homiletic Fragment I*, sandwiched between the two poems just named, is a dreary series of didactic verses, forty-seven in number, on the hypocrisy of men, with "honey in the mouth" and "a venomous tail behind"; "like bees they sting," though they give forth a "honey-taste" in their promises. And so the world wags; let us try to do better. There remain then in *The Vercelli Book* five prose pieces, after the fourth of which is *Elene* (IV, 4). The nineteenth homily calls upon men to turn to God, who wrought the heavens and the earth and all creatures. The twentieth deals with mortal sin; its beginning resembles very closely that of the eleventh. The twenty-first is in theme and general message almost the same as the nineteenth. The twenty-second, on the other hand, is less crabbed in thought and more hopeful in tone; it has for its subject the Christian virtues, according to Saint Isidorus. The twenty-third and last prose inclusion is a life of Saint Guthlac. Since there is another prose life of the saint in Manuscript Vespasian D XXI,[18] we are accustomed to refer to this twenty-third homily as the *Vercelli Guthlac*. Both this and the Vespasian version are prose adaptations into English of the Latin *Vita Guthlaci* by the monk Felix of Croyland.[19] Some have thought the Vespasian version to be by Aelfric;[20] it might at least be construed as Aelfrician. The story in both accounts parallels the narrative of the *Guthlac* poems (IV, 5), except that the prose versions are somewhat fragmentary, particularly that in the Vespasian manuscript.

As has been remarked, these prose homilies of *The Vercelli Book* give a curious impression of haphazardness in their arrangement, although it is fully apparent that this haphazardness is not so marked in the order of the prose as in the order of the poetic pieces. In fact, it would be not too difficult to follow the process going on in the mind of the scribe or scribes who compiled the manuscript. Perhaps any such theorizing on the subject, however, would be after the fact, mere rationalizing, and surely not very important for the moment. The numbering of the homilies in the preceding paragraph is simply according to the order of the pieces in *The Vercelli Book* and has no reference to the arbitrary numbering done by the scribe. Thus homilies six, seven, eight, nine, ten, and eleven of the numbering above are designated by the scribe as one, two, three, four, five, and six respectively; none of the other seventeen homilies is numbered. Nor does the numbering of the scribe convince one that he was thinking of the six numbered homilies as constituting any group by themselves. They have no more connection one with another than any six other homilies chosen out of the twenty-three.

3. MISCELLANEOUS HOMILETIC MATERIAL

THE present account of the homiletic prose of anonymous authorship written during the Old English period must close with a consideration of a large number of miscellaneous individual pieces which defy strict classification by theme or by structure. (1) an Aelfrician homily on the Third Sunday in Quadragesima, found in Manuscript Cotton Faustina A IX,[21] and, according to Wanley, in at least seven other manuscripts,[22] reminds the reader especially of those sermons among Aelfric's *Catholic Homilies* which treat of particular festivals. (2) There is a brief homily on the Finding of the Cross.[23] (3) A life of Saint Swithin, in a fragment, is associated with Aelfric, who has a homily on this particular saint, but the piece mentioned here is probably later than Aelfric himself.[24] (4) We have likewise a life of Saint Neet,[25] either by Aelfric or by a product of his influence. (5) There is a comparable life of Saint Mary of Egypt,[26] (6) a life of Saint Margaret,[27] and (7) a life of Saint Veronica.[28] Two pieces, (8) and (9), very much alike in theme, are Jerome's Account of *Malchus* in Manuscript Cotton Otho C I[29] and the *Mambres Magicus*[30] in Manuscript Cotton Tiberius B V, which is a warning against Hell by the soul of the late Jamnes or Mambres.[31]

4. BIBLICAL TRANSLATIONS

IN THE course of any discussion of Old English Christian didactic prose, the question of Biblical translation is bound to arise. In the main, such translations of the scriptures as took place during the Old English period fall into two categories: those that were interlinear translations, or glosses; and those that follow a more or less independent vernacular style. Since all of these translations were made from the Latin Vulgate, and since the authority of any Biblical text was in those days nothing short of overwhelming, the influence of Latin word-order, syntax, and vocabulary is exceedingly strong, so that even the "independent" translations are often less indigenous than most Old English prose. Those portions of the scriptures which were considered most suitable for a native version were the Gospels and the Book of *Psalms*, with some attention to the Pseudo-Gospel of Nicodemus.

Let us consider first the interlinear glosses. Incomparably the finest example of these is the famous *Lindisfarne Gospels*,[32] a superb example of the art of the medieval scribe. The Latin original dates from about the year 700 and was written by Eadfrith, Bishop of Lindisfarne. In the latter part of the tenth century, the manuscript was transferred to Chester-le-Street, near Durham; and there an interlinear gloss in the rather rare literary dialect of Northumbrian was added by Aldred, a churchman of Durham. Aldred's part in the insertion, however, seems actually to have begun in the Gospel of John (Chapter v, verse 10); the earlier Gospels were probably glossed under his direction. As will be obvious from the

foregoing, the *Lindisfarne Gospels* is invaluable for the linguist, but it represents also one of the two earliest pieces of
extant translation of the Gospels into the English language,
if the word-by-word rendering of Latin into English can be
called translation. The other early specimen is the *Rushworth
Gospels*,[33] so called because the manuscript in which it was
preserved was, at the time of its first historical appearance, in
the possession of a clerk of the House of Commons in the
Long Parliament by the name of Rushworth. The Latin text,
differing very slightly from that of the *Lindisfarne Gospels*,
was written a little later than the Lindisfarne Latin text. The
interlinear glosses of the *Rushworth Gospels* are by two men:
the first portion, into the second chapter of *Mark*, is the work
of Farman of Harewood,[34] and is written in North Mercian;
the second portion, in what Lindelöf[35] has called South Northumbrian, is the work of Owun, a churchman of the same general locality as Farman, though probably a Northumbrian by
birth.

Another important piece of interlinear translation is the
Durham Ritual-Book,[36] a tenth-century gloss to a Latin
prayer-book which contains some material from the Psalter
as well. And obviously the *Vespasian Psalter*, in Cotton Vespasian A I,[37] is a notable piece of its kind. It consists of the
Latin text of *Psalms* and thirteen hymns, known generally as
the *Vespasian Hymns*, to which has been added an interlinear
gloss of the early ninth century, one of the most valuable of
existing texts in Old Mercian. The first Psalm is missing from
the collection; otherwise the translation is complete. The
Hymns are very much in the manner of the Psalmist, even to
the echo of phrase and the cadence of verse, and their titles
are sufficient to illustrate their topics: "The Psalm that David
Wrote When He Fought with Goliath"; "A Song for the
Year of Need"; "A Song of the Exodus"; "A Song of Abac-
cus (Habakkuk) the Prophet"; "A Song of Life"; "A Song
of Isaiah the Prophet"; "A Song of Ezekiel the Prophet";
"A Hymn of Three Boys (Ananias, Azarias, and Misahel)";
"A Song of Zecariah the Priest"; "A Song of St. Mary";

"A Hymn to the Morning"; "A Vesper Hymn"; "A Hymn for Lord's Days."

On the other hand, there are the freer translations, which can more properly be called translations than can the interlinear glosses. There is one prose version of the Gospels, known usually as *The West Saxon Gospels*.[38] It exists in six manuscripts; and one, the Corpus Christi College Cambridge 140, attributes the composition of the whole to Aelfric. But while *The West Saxon Gospels* can be dated with confidence between 1000 and 1025, it can hardly be by Aelfric, since he himself, with all his copious allusions to his own work, does not describe anything quite approximating these *Gospels*. As we have it, this work represents the first surviving translation of a Biblical text of appreciable length in English literature. There is every indication that Bede did a translation of the Gospel of John, but it has not come down to the present day. The question whether one or more scribes performed the original translation of *The West Saxon Gospels* keeps recurring, but the answer is far away, if not downright impossible to find, and for practical purposes it can be assumed that one translator was responsible; although if this is true, then it was a translator who showed somewhat shifting stylistic traits as he progressed through the work. Perhaps nothing more need be said of this translation; it is in no sense comparable as literature to the Wyclif translations of the fourteenth century or the excellent performances of the sixteenth. It is only the beginning of an important branch of Christian teaching; it is earnest, sincere, straightforward, and pedestrian, and it shows a willingness to speak out in vernacular speech which is not too grossly inclined to fall back upon its Latin original. In other words, it is, considering the time and the environment, authentic English writing.

5. CHRISTIAN LEGEND AND PRECEPT

ONE cannot fail to be impressed by the hardiness of Christian legend among the anonymous writers of religious literature in

England before the Norman Conquest. The legends concerning the Cross—the growth of the wood and the fate of the
Cross after the Crucifixion—are epitomized in *The Dream
of the Rood* (IV, 5). Aelfric, moreover, has a homily on the
subject, and the story appears even more extensively in English literature of the Middle English period.[39]

Such spurious histories are well exemplified by *The Gospel
of Nicodemus*.[40] There are two manuscripts of this work in
Old English: Cambridge University Wanley 152 and Cotton
Vitellius A XV, the Beowulf Manuscript. The original *Gospel of Nicodemus* is an apocryphal scripture of about the third
century, divisible into two parts. The first part, the Prote-
vangel of James, treats of the Annunciation and pre-natal
existence of Christ; it has been aptly referred to as a parody
on the birth of John the Baptist. The second part is much
more important. It is known as The Acts of Pilate, and is a
detailed account of the trial of Jesus, His sentence and death,
and His descent into Hell. Not only does this second portion
act as a source for the various accounts of the so-called Harrowing of Hell Legend (V, 5), but it also refers us to the
legend of Joseph of Arimathea, and thus lays the foundation
for the story of the Holy Grail, which is itself a most important cycle in the medieval European literature of Christian
legendry.

Finally, there are the prose versions of the *Benedictine
Rule*. Six known manuscripts survive, all from the early eleventh century or later.[41] In view of the importance of Aethelwold (IX, 1) in the reform of this Rule, the composition of
the English version is ascribed to him, and the date 961 has
been set tentatively for the work. Subjoined to the Cotton
Claudius D III version is a code of regulations for the nuns
at Winteney, a sort of ancestor of the celebrated *Ancren Riwle*
of Middle English times.[42] It should be remarked that there
are also two manuscripts containing a *Benedictine Office*, of
approximately the same date, the relation of which to the
Benedictine Rule is obvious.[43]

Taken as a whole, the foregoing long catalogue of homiletic and scriptural writings does not offer a very attractive vista to the average reader. That these writings stand for sincerity, zeal, and unquestioned devotion to God on the part of their authors cannot be gainsaid. But the heaviness of thought and frequently of style are hard to bear; the overseriousness and deadly lack of humanity are equally forbidding. Still, we owe these pieces a large debt. They show us something, as nothing else could, of the aims, accomplishments, and mentality of the more enlightened ecclesiastical figures of the period.[44] Moreover, something of the discipline, the rigor, and the steadfastness of the churchman will transmit themselves to even the most unsympathetic reader through the pages of the *Benedictine Rule;* something, too, of the problems which beset him who spent his life in a monastery—the care of the estate, the nursing of the sick, the fight against idleness, sloth, and malice; a great deal of the imminence of God's judgment and awareness of the Millennial, as given in "The Signs of Doom" from *The Blickling Homilies,* for example. Consider for the moment how valuable are Aelfric's *Colloquy on the Occupations* and portions of his homilies or the sermons of Wulfstan for their vignettes of the secular life of the times as well as the ecclesiastical, where we have some opportunity to see how the Anglo-Saxon lived, what he ate and drank, how he was clothed, what his occupations might be. And as it was in Aelfric and Wulfstan, the greatest of these preachers, so was it in less degree among their unknown followers and imitators.[45]

NOTES TO CHAPTER TEN

1. The figure of Wulfstan has been engaging present-day research students of Old English literature for some time recently, and a definitive study of the man and his works is to be expected in the not too distant future. In the meantime some sketchy accounts of Wulfstan must suffice. There is the biography nearest to him in time, the *Vita Wulfstani* by William of Malmesbury, edited by Reginald R. Darlington for the Royal Historical Society (1928). This work is translated

into Modern English by J. F. H. Peile, *William of Malmesbury's Life of St. Wulstan, Bishop of Worcester* (Oxford, 1935). A somewhat fulsome biography published by the Society for the Propagation of Christian Knowledge is John W. Lamb, *Saint Wulstan, Prelate and Patriot* (London, 1933). See also Dorothy Whitelock, "A Note on the Career of Wulfstan the Homilist" in *English Historical Review*, LII, 460-465.

The older standard work on the writings of Wulfstan and the general problems connected with his compositions is A. S. Napier, *Wulfstan: Sammlung der ihm zugeschriebenem Homilien nebst Untersuchungen über ihre Echtheit* (Berlin, 1883); and an excellent reference-work dealing with the homilies is R. Becher, *Wulfstans Homilien* (Leipzig, 1910). See also the following highly important studies: A. S. Napier, *Über die Werke des altenglisches Erzbischofe Wulfstan* (Weimar, 1882); J. P. Kinard, *A Study of Wulfstan's Homilies: their style and sources* (Baltimore, 1897); W. Keller, "Die litterarischen Bestrebungen von Worcester in angelsächsischer Zeit" in *Quellen und Forschungen*, LXXXIV (Strassburg, 1900); K. Jost, "Wulfstan und die angelsächsische Chronik" in *Anglia*, XLVII, 105-123; F. Liebermann, "Zu Wulfstans Homilien" in *Archiv*, cli, 81; and again Karl Jost, "Einige Wulfstantexte und ihre Quellen" in *Anglia*, LXI, 265-315. An ingenious and illuminating article is E. Einenkel's arrangement of Wulfstan's best known homily in metrical form, "Der Sermo Lupi ad Anglos, ein Gedicht" in *Anglia*, VII, 200-203. Somewhat off the main road but still germane are R. Priebsch, "The Chief Sources of Some Anglo-Saxon Homilies" in *Otia Merseiana*, I, 129-147 (Liverpool, 1899) and "Quelle und Abfassungszeit der Sonntage Epistel in der irischen 'Cain Domnaig' " in *Modern Language Review*, II, 138-154, although the latter has little to do with Wulfstan.

Individual homilies have appeared in the anthologies and readers of Anglo-Saxon literature, but the *Sermon to the English People* is by all odds the most frequently reprinted.

A recent study, enlightening for the knowledge it affords of Wulfstan's methods as an author, is Dorothy Bethurum, "Archbishop Wulfstan's Commonplace Book" in *Publications of the Modern Language Association*, LVII, 916-929.

2. Humphrey Wanley, *Antiquae Literaturae Septentrionalis Liber Alter . . . Catalogus*, etc. (Oxford, 1705), 140ff.

3. The only other contemporary churchman of importance at this time who had a -*wulf*- in his name is Athulfus, Bishop of Hereford from 998 to 1002. Almost nothing, however, is known about Athulfus, and we understand even less about any incursions made by the Danes into Hereford during the years of Athulfus's incumbency, so that the

famous *Sermon to the English People* would have little point if it came from the then Bishop of Hereford. Besides, much is known of York at this date, and we know that Archbishop Wulfstan wrote some pastoral letters which in style tally pretty well with such of his homilies as have been generally accepted as his.

4. The manuscripts are enumerated in Napier's work (see note 1 above); there is an excellent recent edition by Dorothy Whitelock, *Sermo Lupi ad Anglos* (London, 1939).

5. The opening lines of the famous medieval hymn and vision-lyric dealing with the New Jerusalem, *Hora Novissima*, by Bernard of Morlaix, monk of Cluny (ca. 1145).

6. As long ago as 1855, Dietrich observed (in his "Abt Aelfrik" in *Zeitschrift für historische Theologie* (1855), IV, 544ff. and (1856), II, 220ff.): "Unbedenklich ist er der bedeutende Prediger und Volksschriftsteller nach Aelfrik zu nennen." The nearly hundred years between Dietrich and the present day have done nothing to disturb this judgment.

7. Such a view is implicit in the present-day enthusiasm for research in the Old English homily, one of the few fields of Old English literature not hitherto tramped flat by the horde of scholars.

8. See note 9 below.

9. The earliest complete edition is that of R. Morris, *The Blickling Homilies of the Tenth Century*, volumes 58, 63, and 73 of *Publications of the Early English Text Society, Original Series* (London, 1874-1880). A full bibliography of the studies in the sources of the homilies is M. Förster, "Altenglische Predigtquellen: I. Pseudo-Augustin und die 7. Blickling Homily" in *Archiv*, CXVI, 301-307 and CXXVII, 246-252. Individual homilies are discussed in the following: M. Förster, "Zu den Blickling Homilies" in *Archiv*, XCI, 179-206— which considers eight homilies; H. G. Fiedler, "The Source of the First Blickling Homily" in *Modern Language Quarterly*, VI, 122-124; A. S. Napier, "Notes on the Blickling Homilies; I. St. Martin" in *Modern Philology*, I, 303-308—which discusses the eighteenth; G. Grau, *Quellen und Verwandtschaften der älteren germanischen Darstellungen des jüngsten Gerichtes* in *Studien zur englischen Philologie* (Halle, 1908), XXXI, 192ff.; and Rudolph Willard, "On Blickling Homily XIII: 'The Assumption of the Virgin'" in *Review of English Studies*, XII, 12-17 (see also XIV, 1-19) and "An Old English *Magnificat*" in *University of Texas . . . Studies in English* (Austin, 1940), 5-28—which deals with Homily 13 in part.

10. J. Earle in *Anglo-Saxon Literature* (London, 1884), 213-215.

11. For a remarkable parallel between the description of Grendel's abode in *Beowulf* (see III, 3 above) and a passage from the seventeenth *Blickling Homily* (the Vision of Paul), see W. W. Lawrence

in *Publications of the Modern Language Association,* xxvii, 208-245; G. Sarrazin, in *Englische Studien,* xlii, 4ff.; and particularly Carleton F. Brown, *"Beowulf* and the *Blickling Homilies* and Some Textual Notes" in *Publications of the Modern Language Association,* liii, 905-916. The earlier scholars believed that *Beowulf* and the *Blickling Homilies* both drew upon some common source; Brown, however, goes so far as to suggest that the *Blickling Homily* passage is influenced directly by that in *Beowulf.*

12. This homily, number 10 in Morris's edition (see note 9 above), is found on pp. 106-107 of that book, with parallel Old English and Modern English texts. The passage quoted here is approximately half way through the homily.

13. See Chapter III and note 9 above. In addition to the publication of these homilies in Richard P. Wülker, *Codex Vercellensis* (Leipzig, 1894), there are isolated printings of separate homilies. It is well to remember, however, that Krapp's edition (see Chapter III, note 9 above) is confined to the poetry of *The Vercelli Book.* The full edition of all the homilies in this codex is still to be accomplished. In M. Förster, "Der Vercelli-Codex CXVII nebst Abdruck einiger altenglischer Homilien der Handschrift" in *Festschrift für Lorenz Morsbach* (Halle, 1913), published also as volume 1 of *Studien zur englischen Philologie,* there is published the text of Homilies 2, 6, 9, 15, and 22. R. P. Wülker, "Ueber das Vercellibuch" in *Anglia,* v, 451ff., gives Homily 13 and fragments of many others. A. S. Napier, in *Wulfstan* (Berlin, 1883), gives Homilies 2 and 10, under the impression that they are both by Wulfstan. A. O. Belfour, in *Twelfth Century Homilies in Manuscript Bodley 343,* volume 137 of *Publications of the Early English Text Society, Original Series* (London, 1909), 40-48, gives Homily 3. Rudolph Willard, in "Vercelli Homily VIII and the *Christ"* in *Publications of the Modern Language Association,* xlii, 314-330, gives Homily 8. There is exhaustive discussion of these homilies in the incidental material of all the foregoing studies; see also, however, R. Priebsch, "The Chief Sources of Some Anglo-Saxon Homilies" in *Otia Merseiana,* i, 129-147 (Liverpool, 1899) as well as the appropriate pages of G. Grau, *Quellen und Verwandtschaften der älteren germanischen Darstellungen des jüngsten Gerichtes,* Volume xxxi of *Studien zur englischen Philologie* (Halle, 1908).

In the meantime, M. Förster has made a beginning of the complete edition of these homilies in *Die Vercelli-Homilien, I* in Grein and Wülker, *Bibliothek der angelsächsischen Prosa,* xii (Hamburg, 1932). There are some pertinent notes by G. B. Schlutter, "Some Remarks on Max Förster's Print of Some Old English Homilies Contained in Vercelli Codex CXVII" in *Neophilologus,* xv, 264-270.

Related to the subject, though not directly, is Rudolph Willard, "Two Apocrypha in Old English Homilies," volume XXX of *Beiträge zur englischen Philologie* (Leipzig, 1935).

14. At the close of Folio 16 A of the manuscript; see Belfour's edition (note 13 above).

15. See V, 4 and Chapter V, note 20 above. The poem, as pointed out in that place, appears also in *The Exeter Book*. There is reason to assume a prose homily as the source of the poem; Thorpe so assumed in his edition of *The Exeter Book* (*Codex Exoniensis*; London, 1842), p. 525. The Vercelli *Soul and Body* Fragment, however, is not near this homily in the manuscript, for it does not appear until Folio 101 B. No direct source for the poems has actually been found. But Louise Dudley, "An Early Homily on the Body and Soul Theme" in *Journal of English and Germanic Philology*, VIII, 225ff. and *The Egyptian Elements in the Legend of the Body and Soul* (Baltimore, 1911), 91ff. discusses a vision-homily (also in Benjamin Thorpe's *Ancient Laws and Institutes of England*; London, 1849, 446ff. and in A. S. Napier's *Wulfstan*; Berlin, 1883, 140-141) which yields an interesting key. Rudolph Willard has added to the discussion of the matter two unpublished homilies—Homilies 2-4 of Manuscript Bodleian Junius 85 and Homily 50 of Manuscript Cambridge University Library, I i, 1.33; see his "The Address of the Soul to the Body" in *Publications of the Modern Language Association*, L, 957-983.

16. See note 9 above.

17. See note 15 above.

18. The prose life of Saint Guthlac just referred to (in Manuscript Vespasian D XXI) has been treated thoroughly by P. Gonser, "Das angelsächsische Prosa-Leben des heiligen Guthlacs" in *Anglistische Forschungen*, XXVII (Heidelberg, 1909). For the resemblance to the Vercelli Guthlac, see Max Förster, "Der Vercelli-Codex CXVII nebst Abdruck einiger altenglischer Homilien der Handschrift" in *Festschrift für Lorenz Morsbach*, volume L of *Studien zur englischen Philologie* (Halle, 1913), 85. There is an older edition with English translation by C. W. Goodwin, *The Anglo-Saxon Version of the Life of St. Guthlac* (London, 1848), but Gonser's edition is preferable in every way; even better is the treatment in C. W. Jones, *Saints' Lives and Chronicles in Early England* (Ithaca, 1947).

19. See VII, 6 and Chapter VII, note 73 above.

20. This ascription was made early in the eighteenth century by Humphrey Wanley. There are certain stylistic reminders of Aelfric's work, but the language of the Vespasian *Guthlac* is definitely older than Aelfric's time. See Caroline L. White, *Aelfric: a new study of his life and writings* (New Haven, 1898), volume II of *Yale Studies in English*, 134-135.

21. First printed in L. C. Müller, *Collectanea Anglo-Saxonica* (Copenhagen, 1835) and then by G. Stephens in *Tvende Old-Engelske Digte* (Copenhagen, 1853).

22. Mentioned in H. Wanley, *Antiquae Literaturae Septentrionalis Liber . . . Catalogus* (Oxford, 1705), 31, 123, 127, 133, 161, and 209.

23. In R. Morris, *Legends of the Holy Rood*, volume 46 of *Publications of the Early English Text Society, Original Series* (London, 1871), and A. S. Napier, *History of the Holy Rood-Tree*, volume 103 of *Publications of the Early English Text Society, Original Series* (London, 1894).

24. This piece is preserved as a fragment at Gloucester and was published by J. Earle in *Gloucester Fragments*, 1 (London, 1861), and Skeat in *Aelfric's Lives of the Saints*, volume 76 of *Publications of the Early English Text Society, Original Series* (London, 1881), 440-470. There is a brief discussion by H. Morley in *English Writers* (London, 1888), 11 and a more cogent one by Caroline L. White in her *Aelfric* (New Haven, 1898), volume 11 of *Yale Studies in English*, 37-40 and 128-129. Aelfric's homily on Swithin in *Lives of the Saints* is based upon this *Life of Swithin* ascribed to a certain Lan(d)ferth; but the question whether the Gloucester fragment is Landferth's *Life*, or whether this life came before or after Aelfric's homily, remains unanswered. Aelfric, however, lived for some time studying in Winchester and so would be thoroughly familiar with the legends about Saint Swithin. See J. H. Ott, *Ueber die Quellen der Heiligenleben in Aelfrics Lives of the Saints* (Chapter IX, note 42 above) and Gordon H. Gerould, "Aelfric's Legend of St. Swithin" in *Anglia*, XXXII, 347-357.

25. Often spelled *Neot*. The life is found complete in Manuscript Cotton Vespasian D XXI. See M. Förster, "Der Inhalt der altenglischen Handschriftes Vespasianus D XXI" in *Englische Studien*, LIV, 46-68—for bibliography only. The first printing of the life of St. Neet is G. C. Gorham, *The History and Antiquities of Eynesbury and St. Neot's in the County of Cornwall* (London, 1824), 11, 256-261—see also pp. xcvii-cii in the supplement. It is also in O. Cockayne, *The Shrine* (London, 1864-1869), 12-17. Both of these editions have Modern English translations. There is an excellent text by R. Wülker, "Ein angelsächsisches Leben des Neot" in *Anglia*, III, 104-114. The best discussion is probably that by Wülker; but see also W. H. Stevenson, *Asser's Life of King Alfred, together with the Annals of St. Neot's Erroneously Ascribed to Asser* (Oxford, 1904). The tendency is for most of these scholars to assign the life to Aelfric.

26. Printed by J. Earle in *Gloucester Fragments* (see note 24 above), 11 (London, 1861), and by Skeat in his edition of Aelfric's

Lives of the Saints, volume 94 of *Publications of the Early English Text Society, Original Series* (see note 24 above), 2-53, with discussion by both editors. There has been no great amount of attention bestowed upon this piece, and little to stand in the way of its being Aelfric's, although Skeat is unwilling to admit it in so many words.

27. In Manuscripts Cotton Tiberius A III, Cotton Otho B I, and Corpus Christi College Cambridge S 17. The best text is that edited by B. Assmann in Grein and Wülker's *Bibliothek der angelsächsischen Prosa*, III (Cassel-Göttingen, 1889), 170-180. It is also published in an earlier edition by O. Cockayne in *Narratiunculae Anglice Conscriptae* (London, 1861). For a special discussion of the Legend of Saint Margaret, see F. Vogt, "Über die Margaretenlegenden" in *Paul und Braune's Beiträge*, I, 263-267.

28. In Manuscripts Cambridge University Library; Corpus Christi College Cambridge D 5—only in part; and (the key manuscript) Bodleian Junius 74. It was first published in L. C. Müller, *Collectanea Anglo-Saxonica* (Copenhagen, 1835) and again by C. W. Goodwin, *The Anglo-Saxon Legends of St. Andrew and St. Veronica* (London, 1851). In Manuscript Bodleian Junius 74 is the section, supplementary to the Veronica Legend, known as the *Nathanis Judaei Legatio*; this Goodwin prints in his edition just cited. Again, M. Förster, "Der Inhalt der altenglischen Handschrift Vespasianus D XIV" in *Englische Studien*, LIV, 53-54, is most valuable for its bibliographical material. The text of this life is included also in B. Assmann, *Angelsächsische Homilien und Heiligenleben* in Grein and Wülker's *Bibliothek der angelsächsischen Prosa*, III (Cassel-Göttingen, 1889) and in R. D. N. Warner, *Early English Homilies from ... Vespasian D XIV*, volume 152 of *Publications of the Early English Text Society, Original Series* (London, 1917)—which is especially important because it contains also the *Nathanis Judaei Legatio*.

29. Printed first by O. Cockayne in *The Shrine* (London, 1864-1869), 35-44; later in B. Assmann, *Angelsächsische Homilien und Heiligenleben* in Grein and Wülker's *Bibliothek der angelsächsischen Prosa*, III (Cassel-Göttingen, 1889); and again in W. H. Hulme, "Malchus" in *Journal of English and Germanic Philology*, I, 431-441. There is some discussion by Assmann and a little by Hulme, but see further F. Holthausen, "Quellenstudien zu englischen Denkmälern: I. zum altenglischen Leben des heiligen Malchus" in *Englische Studien*, XLVI, 177-186.

30. In O. Cockayne, *Narratiunculae Anglice Conscriptae* (London, 1861), 50; also in M. R. James, "A Fragment of the Penitence of Jamnes and Mambres" in *Journal of Theological Studies*, II, 572-577, and M. Förster, "Das lateinisch-altenglische Fragment der Apokryphe von Jamnes und Mambres" in *Archiv*, CVIII, 15-28.

31. While it is impossible to discuss in a work of this scope all the saints' lives and homilies which might be of interest, the majority have been at least touched upon. See Chapter VIII, note 27 above, and especially Charles W. Jones, *Saints' Lives and Chronicles in Early England* (Ithaca, 1947), as well as the following:

A. THE LIFE OF ST. ANDREW (THE PROSE "ANDREAS"): See IV, 5 and Chapter IV, note 43 above. This appears to be an Old English saint's life based on the Latin *Life* (see Chapter VIII, note 44 above), which underlies the poem *Andreas*. It is found in Manuscript Corpus Christi College Cambridge 198 and has been edited by C. W. Goodwin, *The Anglo-Saxon Legends of St. Andrew and St. Veronica* (London, 1851); by R. Morris in *The Blickling Homilies of the Tenth Century*, volumes 58, 63, and 73 of *Publications of the Early English Text Society, Original Series* (London, 1874-1880), 228-249—because the introductory portion of this saint's life is in the Blickling Homily collection; and by J. W. Bright, *An Anglo-Saxon Reader* (New York, 1891; 1935), 113-128, which gives a good text. The subject-matter is treated exhaustively by J. Lipsius, *Die Apokryphen, Apostelgeschichten, und Apostellegenden* (Brunswick, 1883-1900).

B. THE LIFE OF ST. CHAD: The text, with good discussion is in A. S. Napier, "Ein altenglisches Leben des heiligen Chad" in *Anglia*, X, 131-156.

C. THE LIFE OF ST. CHRISTOPHER: The text, badly burned, is in the Beowulf Manuscript, Cotton Vitellius A XV. It is printed by G. Herzfeld, "Bruchstück einer altenglischen Legende" in *Englische Studien*, XIII, 142-145; by E. Einenkel, with the Latin original, in "Das altenglische Christoforous-Fragment" in *Anglia*, XVII, 110-122; and by Stanley Rypins, *Three Old English Prose Texts*, volume 161 of *Publications of the Early English Text Society, Original Series*. The text in Rypins's edition is the best; the discussion by Herzfeld is probably the most useful of the three.

D. DIALOGUE-FRAGMENTS: These are treated best in A. S. Napier, "Altenglische Kleinigkeiten" in *Anglia*, XI, 1-10. They seem to be answers to questions of a catechistic nature, and are entirely on Biblical and moral subjects—Adam, Sarah, and Noah; the Virgin Mary; evil deeds; Noah's Ark; St. Peter's in Rome; robbers; the Temple of Solomon. A little unemphatic on the Old English field, but interested greatly in the Middle English representatives, is M. Förster, "Two Notes on Old English Dialogue Literature" in the *Furnivall Miscellany* (Oxford, 1901), 86-106. There is a fine bibliography on the whole subject in M. Förster, "Beiträge zur mittelalterlichen Volkskunde" in *Archiv*, CXXI, 30-46.

E. MISCELLANEOUS EXCERPTS HAVING TO DO WITH ECCLESIAS-

TICAL MATTERS: Here are a few items bearing upon Church laws, canons, disciplines, real-estate holdings, which belong more to a survey of ecclesiastical history—institutional and economic—than to a study of medieval literature; nevertheless they throw indirect light upon many aspects of medieval life—W. Berbner, *Untersuchungen zu dem altenglischen Scriftboc* (Bonn, 1907); Benjamin Thorpe, *Ancient Laws and Institutes of England* (London, 1840); F. Kluge, "Fragment eines angelsächsischen Briefes" in *Englische Studien*, VIII, 62-63; F. Kluge, "Indicia Monasterialia" in *Internationale Zeitschrift für allgemeine Sprachwissenschaft*, II, 118-129 (see additional comments by W. S. Logeman in *Englische Studien*, XII, 305-307); F. Roeder, *Der altenglische Regius Psalter*, volume XVIII of *Studien zur englischen Philologie* (Halle, 1904), XII; A. S. Napier, "Two Old English Fragments" in *Modern Language Notes*, XII, 105-111 and 111-114; W. H. Stevenson, "Yorkshire Surveys and Other Eleventh Century Documents in the York Gospels" in *English Historical Review*, XXVII, 1-25; R. Brotanek, *Texte und Untersuchungen zur altenglischen Literatur- und Kirchengeschichte* (Halle, 1913), 27-28; M. Förster, "Die altenglischen Texte der Pariser Nationalbibliothek" in *Arnold Schröer: zum siebzigsten Geburtstag* (volume LXII of *Englische Studien*), 113-131; D. C. Douglas, "Fragments of an Anglo-Saxon Survey from Bury St. Edmunds" in *English Historical Review*, XLIII, 376-383; M. Weinbaum, "Ags. Survey von Bury St. Edmonds" in *Archiv*, CLVII, 77-78; M. Bateson, "The Supposed Latin Penitential of Ecgbert and the Missing Work of Halitgar of Cambrai" in *English Historical Review*, IX, 320-325; F. Liebermann, "Wulfstan und Cnut" in *Archiv*, CIII, 47-54—which disproves Wulfstan's authorship of the *Institutes of Polity*; H. Böhmer, *Kirche und Staat in England und in der Normandie im elften und zwölften Jahrhundert* (Leipzig, 1899); F. Liebermann, "Angelsächsischer Protest gegen den Cölibat" in *Archiv*, CIX, 376; B. Fehr, *Die Hirtenbriefe Aelfrics in altenglischer und lateinischer Fassung* in Grein and Wülker's *Bibliothek der angelsächsischen Prosa*, IX (Hamburg, 1914) especially pp. lxxxiii-cxxvi; F. Hervey, *The History of King Eadmund the Martyr and of the Early Years of his Abbey* (New York, 1929).

F. THE "ELUCIDARIUM": See also section (D) of this note above. The fragment is printed in J. Zupitza and J. Schipper, *Alt- und mittelenglisches Übungsbuch* (Vienna, 1928). Discussions are given in M. Förster, "Two Notes on English Dialogue-Literature" in the *Furnivall Miscellany* (Oxford, 1901), 86-106 and in a brief article in *Archiv*, CXVI, 312-314; and especially in F. Schmitt, *Die mittelenglische Version des Elucidarium des Honorius Augustodunensis* (Würzburg, 1909). This piece, a dialogue on the Christian virtues and the attainment thereof, written by a French cleric in the year

1092, is actually pretty much outside the scope of the present work.

G. THE FIFTEEN SIGNS BEFORE JUDGMENT DAY: This theme, an important element in eschatological and millennial literature, is also better known in its Middle English versions. It is to be found in B. Assmann, "Vorzeichen des jüngsten Gerichts" in *Anglia*, XI, 369-371; in G. Grau, *Quellen und Verwandtschaften der älteren germanischen Darstellungen des jüngsten Gerichtes*, volume XXXI of *Studien zur englischen Philologie* (Halle, 1908), 261-280; and by R. D. N. Warner in *Early English Homilies from . . . Vespasian D XIV*, volume 152 of *Publications of the Early English Text Society, Original Series*, 82-91. There is discussion in all of the foregoing, and an extended treatment by G. Nölle, "Die Legende von den fünfzehn Zeichen vor dem jüngsten Gerichte" in *Paul und Braune's Beiträge*, VI, 413-476.

H. ROYAL LEGENDS OF KENT: See in particular F. Liebermann, *Die Heiligen Englands* (Hannover, 1889) and W. de G. Birch, *Liber Vitae: register and martyrology of New Minster and Hyde Abbey* (London, 1892).

I. MISCELLANEOUS LETTERS: These are scattered about in date, but most of them are from the tenth and eleventh centuries. See the most complete edition: J. M. Kemble, *Codex Diplomaticus Aevi Saxonici* (London, 1839-1848), especially vol. III, p. 327; and a varied group of such letters in A. W. Haddan and W. Stubbs, *Councils and Ecclesiastical Documents Relating to Great Britain and Ireland* (Oxford, 1869-1878). Individual letters are treated in the following: F. Kluge, "Fragment eines angelsächsischen Briefes" in *Englische Studien*, VIII, 62-63; W. de G. Birch, *Liber Vitae: register and martyrology, etc.* (London, 1892), 96-100; H. Brotanek, *Texte und Untersuchungen zur altenglischen Literatur- und Kirchengeschichte* (Halle, 1913), 135-149; M. Konrath, "Eine altenglische Vision von jenseits" in *Archiv*, CXXXIX, 30-46; K. Sisam, "An Old English Translation of a Letter from Wynfrith to Eadburga" in *Modern Language Review*, XVIII, 253-272.

J. DEFENSOR's "LIBER SCINTILLARUM": In the early eighth century this collection of sayings from the Church Fathers and the scriptures was written down by one Defensor on the Continent. In the tenth century there was composed an interlinear translation of this into Old English. The only edition is that by E. W. Rhodes, *Defensor's Liber Scintillarum, with an Interlinear Anglo-Saxon Version*, volume 93 of *Publications of the Early English Text Society, Original Series* (London, 1889). There is here a minimum of discussion. The work, obviously didactic, is long and extremely dull, utterly belying its title; its general nature is similar to that of the

" 'Scribal Preference' in the Old English Gloss to the Lindisfarne Gospels" in *Modern Language Notes*, XLVIII, 519-521 and—most helpful for its implications concerning textual scholarship in general— "A Theory of Emendations" in *Speculum*, IX, 179-183. See also F. C. Burkitt, "Kells, Durrow, and Lindisfarne" in *Antiquity*, IX, 33-37; M. K. Mincoff, "Zur Altersfrage der Lindisfarner Glosse" in *Archiv*, CLXXIII, 31-43; and once more A. S. C. Ross, "Prologomena to an Editor of the Old English Gloss to the Lindisfarne Gospels" in *Journal of English and Germanic Philology*, XLII, 309-321.

33. See note 32 above. The best edition is that by Skeat.

34. For this scribe, see Robert J. Menner, "Farman Vindicatus" in *Anglia*, LVIII, 1-27; for Aldred, see N. R. Ker, "Aldred the Scribe" in *Essays and Studies*, XXVIII, 7-12.

35. U. Lindelöf, *Die südnordhumbrische Mundart des zehnten Jahrhunderts*, volume X of *Bonner Beiträge zur Anglistik* (Bonn, 1908), particularly section 6.

36. The old edition of this work is that of J. Stevenson, *Rituale Ecclesiae Dunelmensis*, volume X of *Publications of the Surtees Society* (London, 1840). A new edition has appeared in volume CXL of *Publications of the Surtees Society* (London, 1927) under the title, *Rituale Ecclesiae Dunelmensis: the Durham Collectar*, edited by A. H. Thompson with prefatory note and text by U. Lindelöf. Previously Lindelöf had done a collation, "A New Collation of the Gloss of the Durham Ritual" in *Modern Language Review*, XVIII, 273-280. There are good but brief discussions of the work in B. Fehr, "Altenglische Ritualtexte für Krankenbesuch, heilige Ölung, und Begräbnis" in *Festgabe für Felix Liebermann* (Halle, 1921), particularly pp. 20-67; and in J. Lingard, *The History and Antiquities of the Anglo-Saxon Church* (London, 1845; 1858), II, 359ff. A more detailed discussion is that of F. Liebermann, "Das Rituale Dunelmensis" in *Archiv*, CIV, 122ff. Lindelöf, who was a true enthusiast at the time of the revised edition of the Surtees Society (1927), published an account, "Die neue Ausgabe des Rituale Ecclesiae Dunelmensis und die Sprache der Glosse" in *Anglia Beiblatt*, XXXIX, 145-151.

37. The *Vespasian Psalter*, however, is but one of several, which would include the *Cambridge Psalter*, the *Lindisfarne Psalter*, the *Sarum Psalter*, the *Canterbury Psalter*, the *Regius Psalter*, the *West Saxon* or *Paris Psalter* (see V, 8 above), the *Arundel Psalter*, the *Junius Psalter*, the *Lambeth Psalter*, and the *Bosworth Psalter*. The best general accounts of these various psalters are those in J. D. Bruce, *The Anglo-Saxon Version of the Book of Psalms* (Baltimore, 1894) and in K. Wildhagen, *Studien zum Psalterium Romanum in England und zu seinen Glossierungen* (Halle, 1913). But individual works on

the separate Psalters are many and are rather important in the history of the scholarship of English Biblical translations.

The *Vespasian Psalter* is printed by H. Sweet in *The Oldest English Texts*, volume 83 of *Publications of the Early English Text Society, Original Series* (London, 1885). For other texts, there are the following: (1) the *Cambridge Psalter*—see K. Wildhagen, *Der Cambridge-Psalter* in Grein and Wülker's *Bibliothek der angelsächsischen Prosa*, VII (Hamburg, 1910); (2) the *Lindisfarne Psalter*—see J. Stevenson, *Anglo-Saxon and Early English Psalters*, I, which is volume XVI of *Publications of the Surtees Society* (London, 1843); (3) the *Sarum Psalter*—see J. Stevenson's work just cited, II, which comprises volume XIX of *Publications of the Surtees Society* (London, 1847); (4) the *Canterbury Psalter*—see F. Harsley, *Eadwine's Canterbury Psalter*, volume 92 of *Publications of the Early English Text Society, Original Series* (London, 1889); (5) the *Regius Psalter*—see F. Roeder, *Der altenglische Regius-Psalter*, volume XVIII of *Studien zur englischen Philologie* (Halle, 1904); (6) the *Junius Psalter*—see E. Brenner, "Der altenglische Junius-Psalter" in *Anglistische Forschungen*, XXIII (Heidelberg, 1908); (7) the *Lambeth Psalter*—see U. Lindelöf, "Der Lambeth-Psalter" in *Acta Societatis Scientiae Fenniae*, XXXV, no. 1, and XLIII, no. 3; (8) the *Bosworth Psalter*—see U. Lindelöf, "Die altenglischen Glossen im Bosworth Psalter" in *Mémoires de la Société Néo-Philologique de Helsingfors*, V, 138-231; (9) the *Arundel Psalter*—see G. Oess, "Der altenglische Arundelpsalter" in *Anglistische Forschungen*, XXX (Heidelberg, 1909).

The transcriptions by Stevenson and Sweet of the *Vespasian Psalter* are examined critically by Sherman Kuhn, "The Gloss to the *Vespasian Psalter*: another collation" in *Journal of English and Germanic Philology*, XL, 344-347; a further recent study attributes the gloss to a Mercian scribe of about 930; see Sherman Kuhn, "The *Vespasian Psalter* and the Old English Charter Hands" in *Speculum*, XVIII, 458-483.

The discussions of the above-mentioned Psalters are implicit in the introductions to all the editions mentioned above, and for further references one should consult V, 8 and Chapter V, note 62 above, as well as the following: K. Wildhagen, *Über die in Eadwine's Canterbury Psalter enthaltene altenglische Psalter-interlinear-version* (Halle, 1903); U. Lindelöf, *Studien zu altenglischen Psalterglossen*, volume XIII of *Bonner Beiträge zur Anglistik* (Bonn, 1914); K. Wildhagen, *Der Psalter des Eadwine von Canterbury*, volume XIII of *Studien zur englischen Philologie* (Halle, 1905); G. Oess, *Untersuchungen zum altenglischen Arundelpsalter* (Heidelberg, 1910); O. Heinzel, *Kritische Entstehungsgeschichte des angelsächsischen Interlinear-psalters*, volume 151 of *Palaestra* (Leipzig, 1926); and H. Klappenbach, *Zu altenglischer Interlinearversionen von Prosaparaphrasen lateinischer Hymnen* (Leipzig, 1930).

38. The six manuscripts of *The West Saxon Gospels* surviving are Corpus Christi College Cambridge 160; Cambridge University Library I i.2.11 of about 1050; Bodleian Library 441 of nearly the same time; Cotton Otho C I; Bodleian Hatton 38, from the first part of the eleventh century; and British Museum Royal I, A. xvi, from about the middle of the eleventh century. Unless otherwise stated, the remainder of the manuscripts are from the early years of the eleventh century. The standard edition is that by W. W. Skeat, *The Holy Gospels in Anglo-Saxon, Northumbrian, and Old Mercian Versions, Synoptically Arranged* (see note 32 above). Less valuable only because it is of less comprehensive scope is J. W. Bright, *The Gospels in West Saxon* (Boston, 1904-1906). In addition to these excellent texts there are the following indispensable reference-works: A. Drake, *The Authorship of the West Saxon Gospels* (New York, 1894); R. Handke, *Über das Verhältnis der westsächsischen Evangelienübersetzung zum lateinischen Original* (Halle, 1896); L. M. Harris, *Studies in the Anglo-Saxon Version of the Gospels* (Baltimore, 1891); H. Glunz, *Die lateinische Vorlage der westsächsischen Evangelienversion in seinem Verhältnis zur irisch-angelsächsischen Kultur des Frühmittelalters* (Leipzig, 1928), and especially his *History of the Vulgate in England from Alcuin to Roger Bacon* (Cambridge-New York, 1933).

39. See R. Morris, *Legends of the Holy Rood*, volume 46 of *Publications of the Early English Text Society, Original Series* (London, 1871); A. S. Napier, *The History of the Holy Rood-Tree*, volume 103 of *Publications of the Early English Text Society, Original Series* (London, 1894); and W. W. Skeat, *Aelfric's Lives of the Saints*, volumes 76, 82, 94, and 114 of *Publications of the Early English Text Society, Original Series* (London, 1881-1900). For some idea of the prevalence of this legend in Middle English literature, see J. E. Wells, *A Manual of the Writings in Middle English* (New Haven, 1916-1935), 316-319, with full bibliography on pp. 812-813 of the original edition and at the appropriate places in the supplements.

40. There are two versions, in the Cambridge University Library manuscript and in the Beowulf Manuscript. Furthermore, a transcript was made by the seventeenth-century scholar Junius from Manuscript Bodleian Junius 74, which seems to be based on both of the surviving manuscripts just mentioned. There is an excerpt of *The Gospel of Nicodemus* in Manuscript Cotton Vespasian D XIV, from the eleventh century. The best edition is clearly that of S. J. Crawford,

The Gospel of Nicodemus (Edinburgh, 1927); the first in time was that by H. Thwaites in his *Heptateuchus* (Oxford, 1698). Another good one is that by W. H. Hulme, "The Old English Version of the Gospel of Nicodemus" in *Publications of the Modern Language Association*, XIII, 457-541, with a supplementary article of great value, "The Old English Gospel of Nicodemus" in *Modern Philology*, I, 579-614. Two bibliographical guides are M. Förster, "Der Inhalt der altenglischen Handschrift Vespasianus D XIV" in *Englische Studien*, LIV, 46-68 and "Zum altenglischen Nicodemus-Evangelium" in *Archiv*, CVII, 311-321. R. D. N. Warner, *Early English Homilies from . . . Vespasian D XIV*, volume 152 of *Publications of the Early English Text Society, Original Series* (London, 1917), also prints a text of the Vespasian excerpt (pp. 77-88). For a full discussion of the origin of this Pseudo-Gospel, see the thorough, although badly dated, treatment in R. Wülker, *Das Evangelium Nicodemi in der abendländischen Litteratur* (Paderborn, 1872).

For an interesting sidelight on other adventitious material in Old English didactic and religious prose, see Rudolph Willard, *Two Apocrypha in Old English Homilies*, volume XXX of *Beiträge zur englischen Philologie* (Leipzig, 1935).

41. See Chapter IX, note 1 above. The six manuscripts are Corpus Christi College Cambridge 178, Corpus Christi College Cambridge 198, Cotton Titus A IV, Cotton Faustina A X, Wells Cathedral, and Cotton Claudius D III. The best edition is A. Schröer, *Die angelsächsischen Prosabearbeitungen der Benediktinerregel* in Grein and Wülker's *Bibliothek der angelsächsischen Prosa*, II (Cassel-Göttingen, 1885); then comes H. Logeman, *The Rule of St. Benet*, volume 90 of *Publications of the Early English Text Society, Original Series* (London, 1888); also A. Schröer, *Die Winteney-Version der Regula S. Benedicti* (Halle, 1888). For general discussion there are E. Sievers, *Die angelsächsische Benediktinerregel* (Tübingen, 1887); A. Schröer, "Die angelsächsischen Prosabearbeitungen der Benedictinerregel" in *Englische Studien*, XIV, 241-253; and D. Blair, *The Rule of St. Benedict* (Fort Augustus, 1906). A translation is given in E. Thomson, *Godcunde Lar and Theowdom* (London, 1875).

42. See the reference to Schröer's treatment of the Winteney Version mentioned in note 41 above.

43. There are two manuscripts: Bodleian Junius 121 and Corpus Christi College Cambridge S 18. The edition is that of E. Feiler, *Das Benediktiner-Offizium* (Heidelberg, 1901); an earlier edition is in E. Thomson, *Godcunde Lar and Theowdom* (London, 1875), which has been completely superseded. Further discussion is offered by B. Fehr, "Das Benedictiner-Offizium und die Beziehungen zwischen Aelfric und Wulfstan" in *Englische Studien*, XLVI, 337-346.

44. Some miscellaneous items of interest to the special reader in this field are: J. B. L. Tolhurst, "An Examination of Two Anglo-Saxon Manuscripts of the Winchester School: the Missal of Robert of Jumièges and the Benedictional of St. Ethelwold" in *Archaeologia*, LXXXIII, 27-44; H. T. Silverstein, "The Vision of Leofric and Gregory's Dialogues" in *Review of English Studies*, IX, 186-188; H. Henel, "Altenglischer Mönchenaberglaube" in *Englische Studien*, LXIX, 329-349; Ivor Atkins, "The Church of Worcester from the Eighth to the Twelfth Century" in *Antiquaries' Journal*, XVII, 371-391; and G. R. Stephens and W. D. Stephens, "Cuthman: a neglected saint" in *Speculum*, XIII, 448-453.

45. See note 44 preceding.

XI · Secular Didactic Writing in Old English Prose

▬▬◀━

WHAT, it may be asked, did the teacher in Old English prose convey to his pupil, if it was not a message primarily religious? The answer is likely to be, very little indeed. But it is possible to be moralistic without being dogmatic. It seems only proper to distinguish in a brief note between these two kinds of prose composition, just as it was possible in much greater degree to distinguish between religious and secular Anglo-Saxon didactic poetry.

In fact, there are some prose pieces which merely repeat in prose form what has already been considered under the head of Old English didactic verse. Thus there is a prose version of the *Dialogues of Solomon and Saturn* (V, 8), which needs no further attention here beyond the statement that it represents a perennial kind of instruction-piece; as late as the fifteenth century one can see this prose discussion reincarnated in *Questiones bitwene the Maister of Oxinfort and his Scoler*.[1] *Hadrian and Ritheus*[2] is a similar work. It also comes from some time in the eleventh century. Hadrian, the Roman emperor, came to have, whether deservedly or not, the reputation of a philosopher and a sophist second only to that of his successor Marcus Aurelius. Ritheus has been variously identified as Pittheus, a Greek enigmatist, or Epictetus, with the probabilities favoring the latter identification.[3] With the possible exception of the *Dialogues of Solomon and Saturn*, however, the most notable example of the literature of this kind in the Old English prose library is the collection, in English translation, of the Latin maxims known as the *Distichs of Cato* (*Disticha de Moribus ad Filium*) by an unknown author.[4]

The original of this work, one of the most often quoted in all medieval literature, was written down in the third or fourth century. The English translation, which is not a translation of all of the Distichs but only of those which appealed especially to the Anglo-Saxon scribe, was once attributed to Aelfric, chiefly because in one of the three manuscripts containing this work[5]—the Anglo-Saxon *Distichs* being preserved in only three—the translation follows a portion of Aelfric's *Grammar* (IX, 2). While this fact scarcely proves that Aelfric was the author, it makes not impossible the theory that Aelfric's influence was at work; there is no particular reason, however, in respect to either style or language why even this theory should be maintained. It is known, for example, that Alcuin was familiar with these Distichs, although the Old English version cannot possibly be by him. Rather they should be thought of as another instance of the careful compiling by enthusiastic churchmen and teachers of such worldly wisdom as could be found in their academic and spiritual traditions, and the making accessible of that wisdom to their native English flocks. There are one hundred and forty-four of these Distichs in the Latin original, grouped rather unevenly into four sections. The Anglo-Saxon translator seems to have run through the entire lot and culled out sixty-eight; apparently he made a review of the Latin material and squeezed out eight more, making a total of seventy-six for his English collection, or a little more than one half of the original.

It would be thoroughly impracticable to attempt in the present survey any close analysis of the contents of these Distichs. They belong to the proverb-literature of the ages, and were it not for the prose form of this Old English version, they might well have been discussed along with such works as *The Proverbs of Alfred* (VIII, 3). Moreover, these Distichs do not form any consecutive pattern of thought, certainly not in the sense that the Biblical Book of *Proverbs* offers such a pattern. They cover almost every conceivable kind of moral precept, but the more common themes, on which are played innumerable variations, are the following:[6]

> When praised, thou of thyself the judge must be;
> Accept no praise not spoken truthfully.
>
> [1, 14]

If to thy sons thou canst not riches give,
Then teach them trades that they may safely live.

[I, 28]

Ask not if gods there be above the earth;
For earth care thou, who art of mortal birth.

[II, 2]

(Observe the strong Lucretian tone of the foregoing Distich.)

Nor praise nor blame thyself. Fools thus have erred,
When by vain hope of glory they were stirred.

[II, 16]

Guard well thy health with special care and skill;
Thyself and not the seasons blame when ill.

[II, 30]

From others' actions seek to find the clue
To what thou best mayst shun and best mayst do.

[III, 13]

When to poor judgment thou dost failure owe,
Say not that Fortune's blind, for 'tis not so.

[IV, 3]

If through thy life thou wouldst a good name save,
Be not to pleasure base an abject slave.

[IV, 17]

Who silent is and melancholy, shun;
Perchance the quiet rivers too deep run.

[IV, 31]

Secure thy chance when first it be at hand,
Lest that once scorned thou dost in vain demand.

[IV, 45]

The numbering of these Distichs quoted here is that of the
Latin original, with reference to Book and Distich. Of course
any such quotations are but sampling; yet it should be clear
that these Distichs represent a fund of practical worldly wisdom, with more than a trace of classical paganism. Still, the
Old English churchman does not hesitate to use these pagan
traces as he sees fit for the inculcation of Christian morality,
and so he has done here, we know, because *The Distichs of
Cato* seems to have been a work included in the curriculum for

the upbringing of the young. The Middle English period knew Dionysius Cato well, and even Chaucer's Pertelote could cite him to her pompous spouse Chauntecler.

NOTES TO CHAPTER ELEVEN

1. See V, 8 and Chapter V, note 52 above. The piece was first printed in Benjamin Thorpe, *Analecta Anglosaxonica* (London, 1868), II, 110-115, and again, with fuller discussion, in J. Kemble, *The Dialogues of Salomon and Saturnus* (London, 1848). Kemble was of the opinion that a large part of the work is missing; but this view is not maintained by subsequent authorities. The Middle English *Questiones bitwene the Maister of Oxinfort and his Scoler* has been edited by Harley in *Englische Studien*, VIII, 284ff. In this dialogue, the scholar learns, from his conversation with the master, about God's position at the first creation, about God's first speech, about the origin of the world "Heaven"; he learns a workable definition of God, about the ingredients which went to make up Adam, about the etymology of the name of Adam, of his age and size when first created, about God's favorite flowers, and other wonders of Creation.

2. Or *Adrian and Ritheus*. This is found in Manuscript Cotton Julius A II, with a fragment in Manuscript Bodleian Junius 61. There is an early edition by Thomas Wright in *Altdeutschen Blättern*, II, 189-193 (1838), but the first detailed study is that by J. Kemble in *The Dialogues of Salomon and Saturnus* (London, 1848), 198-207. The material of Kemble was touched up and freshened by M. Förster, "Zu Adrian und Ritheus" in *Englische Studien*, XXIII, 431-436.

3. Kemble (see note 2 above) is the one who has discussed this point most comprehensively.

4. This survives in three Old English manuscripts: Trinity College Cambridge R.q.17; Cotton Julius A II; and Cotton Vespasian D XIV. It was first published in L. C. Müller, *Collectanea Anglo-Saxonica* (Copenhagen, 1835) and later, with discussion, by J. Kemble in *The Dialogues of Salomon and Saturnus* (London, 1848), 258-269. Still later it was given a much more substantial treatment in Julius Nehab, *Der altenglische Cato* (Berlin, 1879). The textual matter was further amplified by R. D. N. Warner, *Early English Homilies from . . . Vespasian D XIV*, volume 152 of *Publications of the Early English Text Society, Original Series* (London, 1917) and by E. Sievers, *Metrische Studien*, IV (Leipzig, 1919), 601-615. The

best discussion of the work as a whole, however, remains Nehab's, although a review of Nehab's study by G. Schleich in *Anglia*, III, 383-396 is an almost necessary supplement, and, of course, there is always the introduction by Warner.

5. In the Trinity College Cambridge manuscript (see note 4 above).

6. See the text by Warner in *Publications of the Early English Text Society, Original Series* (see note 4 above).

XII · Prose Fiction of the Old English Period

As WE advance into the eleventh century, after the Benedictine Reform has left its mark upon the didactic literature of the age and after the heroic epic and elegiac poems have themselves become something in the nature of antiques, there comes into view a little group of pieces which give promise of things to come. In a sense these works may be considered foreign importations, but their presence in England suggests that story-telling for its own sake was returning, not this time from the lips of a *scop* nor yet from the pen of a doctrinaire churchman, but rather from a narrator with a lighter touch, one who either had traveled in foreign lands or had come somehow into contact with legends of other times and other places. No longer is he speaking in alliterative verse of the deeds of Germanic chieftains; he is recounting in prose the adventures of an outlander in a country remote and strange. In short, we have reached the point of transition from the older form of fiction in Old English literature to the beginnings of the romance, which was to develop fully within the Middle English period. How plentiful these prose narratives may have been at the time of the Norman Conquest or a little before, there is no way of telling, for only three works have been left to indicate the growing cosmopolitanism of story-telling at the close of the Old English period.

The first of these works is *Apollonius of Tyre*.[1] From the great mass of legendary narrative material gathered together over many centuries and finally appearing in English during the fourteenth or fifteenth century, the *Gesta Romanorum*,[2] one story in Latin (Chapter 153 of the later collection) was translated by some unknown Old English scribe between the years 1030 and 1060. There is only one extant manuscript—

Corpus Christi College Cambridge 201³—and the story is told only in part.

Apollonius, Prince of Tyre, incurs the enmity of Antiochus, King of Antioch, and is forced to leave his native land and flee to Tarsus. Thénce he departs to seek another haven of safety; his ship is wrecked, and he is left the only survivor. He is washed ashore naked and meets a fisherman, who clothes him and directs him to the city of Pentapolis. Here he meets the king, Arcestrates, at the bath and obtains from him an invitation to a royal banquet. Although he has been regally clothed for the occasion, he sits in dejection at the festivities. The king's daughter, however, raises Apollonius out of his melancholy, although not without difficulty. In the course of the banquet, Apollonius impresses all with his playing on the harp. The king's daughter rewards him with treasure, and he is given a dwelling, because the maiden's heart has turned to love for him. She arranges that Apollonius shall be her teacher. Three suitors for the daughter's hand present themselves, but the maiden prefers Apollonius, "and as soon as he perceived that he was loved, his countenance grew all red." Events are about to shape themselves into a romantic conclusion.

At this point the Old English version breaks off until just before the end of the story, where the tale is resumed; but the intervening narrative can be filled in from the Latin original. Apollonius marries the king's daughter and soon afterwards hears that his old enemy Antiochus is dead and that he is eligible for the kingship of Antioch. He sets out with his wife for Antioch. On the way, the lady gives birth to a daughter and seemingly dies. She is cast overboard in a chest and floats to Ephesus, where she is found and revived, adopted by the man who found her, and finally dedicated to the service of Diana. Apollonius meanwhile rears his daughter Tharsia and leaves her with his friend Stranguillio and Stranguillio's wife to be instructed. Stranguillio's wife becomes jealous of the girl and hires a false steward to kill her. The girl is rescued at the last moment by pirates and is carried off to Mytilene, where she is sold as a slave, and after much hardship she finally comes to rest in the protection of Athenagora, the local potentate. After fourteen years, Apollonius returns to Tarsus and hears that his daughter is dead. In great distress he leaves the city but is driven by a storm to Mytilene, where he discovers Tharsia. He marries her to Athenagora and takes the young couple with him, bound for Tarsus. He is warned in a dream, however, that he should go to Ephesus; when he does so, he is reunited with his wife. The story then proceeds to its happy conclusion; Apollonius punishes Stranguillio and his wife for their double-dealing, and, returning to Tarsus, lives in happiness to an old age.

Nothing, indeed, is needed beyond the mere outlining of this story to illustrate the difference between the prose romance and the old heroic epic. Here are high adventure, shipwrecks, pirates, traitors, dreams of omen, separation and reunion, and above all love. There are also a few happy little human touches which would have been either beyond the powers or beneath the dignity of the *scop*. Can anyone imagine Beowulf as falling in love, let alone blushing when that love was revealed to him? Quite properly the incidents in *Apollonius of Tyre* must be referred to the late Greek romances,[4] from which, to judge by names and locales, the story ultimately derives. We can therefore remember Odysseus cast upon the beach in the presence of Nausicaa; we can look ahead to the dozens of medieval romances and ballads involving a male Cinderella, a false steward, a jealous wife, a lady adrift on the waters, until, with a special twist given to the story in Gower's *Confessio Amantis*,[5] it emerges with something approaching immortal shape into Shakespeare's *Pericles*.[6]

On the other hand, *The Letter of Alexander to Aristotle*[7] introduces us to one of the great cycles of medieval romance, the Legend of Alexander. As we should expect of the career of one of the great heroes of antiquity, one of the Nine Worthies of the World, the life of Alexander the Great and the story of his conquests developed into a large mass of saga mixed with historical fact. A Greek account, the *Pseudo-*

Kallisthenes,[8] is the fountain-head of all the medieval stories concerning Alexander, representing as it does the peak of popular imagination as it dealt with the great warrior. This compilation was translated into Latin not later than 340 by Julius Valerius, and a Latin epitome of the whole was written sometime in the ninth century.[9] In this same century was composed a Latin *Letter of Alexander to Aristotle* and five more epistles between the two great men. About a hundred years later came the fuller, more up-to-date *Historia Alexandri Magni, Regis Macedoniae, de Proeliis* by the Archpresbyter Leo.[10]

It is apparent that the ninth century Latin *Letters of Alexander to Aristotle* was known to some Old English cleric or clerics, who translated the work into the vernacular, where it came to be included as an item within the Beowulf Manuscript.[11] The Old English epistle opens with the customary greeting. Alexander has reached India and wishes to tell Aristotle of the many remarkable things he has seen in that wonderful country. He tells of creatures of wondrous hues. He had conquered Darius of Persia in May; and in July he arrived in India and defeated Porus, with his countless multitudes of men and elephants which amazed Alexander, but not more than did the trees with golden branches and leaves or the palaces built of precious stones. Seldom has he seen anything as cheap and vulgar as mere silver. Never has he seen such fertility as in the land of Caspia, which has been his most recent conquest. He refers again to the astonishing dendrology of the entire region, in particular to the fleece-bearing trees in close proximity to burning deserts. At one time he and his men were all dying of thirst, when Severus, his thane, found a little water in a hollow rock and gallantly offered it to the king. For this he was rewarded. Then ensues a series of adventures in which the Greeks are hard pressed by hunger and thirst and savage foes in mysterious meres, and by scorpions before moonrise, horned serpents of variegated colors, lions, tigers, and strange beasts "which the Indians call *dentes tyrannum*," climaxed by the appearance of "Indian mice in the size and likeness of foxes." Alexander, however, has triumphed over all obstacles and has come to the land of the Medes and Persians, where he is fighting many bloody fights. Porus wishes to treat with him, and a meeting is appointed, where "I mocked him with my answers and told him that he was much too old—so old that he could not be warmed except by fire and flame. Then he was very glad, rejoicing at my answers and words, because I had told him that he was much too old." The arrogant Alexander does not cut a very attractive figure in the epistle. Porus, willy-nilly, becomes his friend.

The adventures of Alexander continue for many pages; he meets more animals of amazing physical attributes and formidable names, which the Old English scribe makes no attempt to translate. The conqueror is astonished to find both blizzards and volcanoes in immediate juxtaposition. There comes the surprising adventure of the mysterious-speaking trees, one of which prophesies Alexander's death. He is much downcast to hear this and wishes, as he has said repeatedly in the epistle, that he were at home in Macedonia with his mother and sisters.

> These things I write, my dear master, that you first of all may rejoice in the piety of my life. . . . I have rewarded other earthly kings as an example that they may know more readily that my power and glory are greater than those of any other kings who ever were in the world.

The naïveté, the crude boastfulness of the older epic hero are still here, it is true, but the astonishing and absurdly fantastic details which bespeak a tropical imagination in the narrative are something else. The high priest three hundred years old, ten feet high, who exhibited to Alexander the prophesying tree, is in a sense symbolic of the whole story.

It is, then, the marvels of the Orient which *The Letter of Alexander to Aristotle* obviously celebrates. And another translation from a similar Latin original, *The Wonders of the East*,[12] rounds out the group of pieces showing this Oriental or Levantine influence. *The Wonders of the East* belongs to the middle of the eleventh century, just as the preceding piece does, and probably owes its origin to the same scholarly interest of the time in the exotic. Only it is generally inferior in material and style to *The Letter of Alexander to Aristotle*, the substance of which it often imitates. There are two surviving manuscripts—Cotton Tiberius B V and Cotton Vitellius A XV (the Beowulf Manuscript). Of these two, the Tiberius manuscript is more nearly complete, so far as can be judged, since neither is of full length. Nor is either version a close translation of the Latin original; and there is, indeed, some question whether the Latin text usually associated with the piece actually is the original.[13] Evidently, however, the author of *The Wonders of the East* was acquainted with the Legend of Alexander, particularly that part of the legend treated in *The Letter of Alexander to Aristotle*, and he seems to have felt entirely free to draw upon other sources, notably Herodotus and Pliny, although it would be foolish to mention here all the possible places where he could have found stories about wonderful plants and animals.[14]

Both manuscripts of *The Wonders of the East* are predominantly West Saxon. As to the content of the work, it is largely a heaping-up, if not a compilation, of fabulous statements of considerable unreliability, a kind of unnatural natural history which we have seen before in the cases of the *Physiologus* (IV, 5) and *The Phoenix* (IV, 5). Unlike *The Letter of Alexander to Aristotle, The Wonders of the East* is told in the third person. Eight-foot animals with the eyes of valkyries, two-headed serpents, horned asses, monstrous dog-like creatures with horses' manes and boars' tusks and fiery breaths, and hairy-heeled men—these constitute the gallery of wonders. The women are even more hairy than the men—phenomenally so. The list of prodigies becomes wearisome in the extreme. As for the flora, we have already seen their like in *The Letter of Alexander to Aristotle*. It is obvious that when Othello told Desdemona of his wondrous adventures among the anthropophagi and other remarkable peoples, he was only giving some extra literary dignity to an age-old theme. The chief point of interest here, however, is the sharp contrast be-

tween the gold-bearing trees which Alexander saw and the
English oak and ash and all that they suggest.

NOTES TO CHAPTER TWELVE

1. A bibliography and a brief account of this work is that in R.
Wülker, *Grundriss zur Geschichte der angelsächsischen Litteratur*
(Leipzig, 1885), 504; an even better running account is that in A.
S. Cook and C. B. Tinker, *Select Translations from Old English
Prose* (Boston, 1908), 207 and in the *Cambridge History of English
Literature*, I, 496. The oldest edition, which gives also a literal Mod-
ern English translation, is that in B. Thorpe, *The Anglo-Saxon Version of the Story of Apollonius of Tyre* (London, 1834); a better
one, without translation, is J. Zupitza, "Die altenglische Bearbeitung
der Erzählung von Apollonius von Tyrus" in *Archiv*, XCVII, 17-34.
Various selected portions are given in the earlier readers and anthologies; the most extensive of such selections are in A. S. Cook, *A First
Book in Old English* (Boston, 1894), 164-188 and in Samuel Moore
and Thomas A. Knott, *The Elements of Old English* (Ann Arbor,
1919; 1940), 58, 64, 67, 73, 78, 82, 86, 90, 94, 98, 106. Discussions as to the sources and origins of the story are in J. Zupitza,
"Welcher Text liegt der altenglischen Bearbeitung von Apollonius
von Tyrus zu Grunde?" in *Romanische Forschungen*, III, 269-279;
E. Klebs, *Die Erzählung von Apollonius aus Tyrus* (Berlin, 1899);
R. Märkisch, *Die altengische Bearbeitung der Erzählung von Apollonius von Tyrus*, volume VI of *Palaestra* (Berlin, 1899); O. F. Emerson, "The Old English Apollonius of Tyre" in *Modern Language
Notes*, XXXVIII, 269-272; C. O. Chapman, "Beowulf and Apollonius
of Tyre" in *Modern Language Notes*, XLVI, 439-443; and Philip H.
Goepp, "The Narrative Material of Apollonius of Tyre" in *English
Literary History*, V, 150-172.

2. Probably the best edition of the *Gesta Romanorum* is that by S.
T. H. Herrtage, volume 33 of *Publications of the Early English Text
Society, Original Series* (London, 1879). There is an older edition
by Hermann Oesterley (Berlin, 1872).

3. More than half of the manuscript is missing, if we are to judge
by what there is in No. 153 of the *Gesta Romanorum*. The Anglo-
Saxon version follows the usual method of Old English translators of
Latin texts, made famous by Alfred in the Preface to his translation of
Gregory's *Pastoral Care*, in that the translation is done sometimes
word for word and sometimes as a mere paraphrase.

4. See W. H. Schofield, *English Literature from the Norman Conquest to Chaucer* (London-New York, 1906), 305; B. Ten Brink, *Early English Literature*, translated by H. M. Kennedy (London, 1883), vol. I, 114 and 169-171; and the bibliography in H. O. Taylor, *The Classical Heritage of the Middle Ages* (New York, 1911), 361. An early and very thorough treatment is A. Rohde, *Der griechische Roman* (Leipzig, 1875). For the medieval romances of this type in Middle English, see particularly Laura H. Hibbard (Loomis), *Medieval Romance in England* (Oxford, 1924), 164-173 and 184-194.

5. Book VIII, 271ff. in the Oxford edition by G. C. Macaulay (Oxford, 1901). Macaulay also has an edition in volumes 81 and 82 of *Publications of the Early English Text Society, Original Series* (London, 1900-1901).

6. For the relation of these two versions of the story, see A. H. Smyth, *Shakespeare's Pericles and Apollonius of Tyre* (Philadelphia, 1898).

7. Two early editions are those in O. Cockayne, *Narratiunculae Anglice Conscriptae* (London, 1861), 1-33, with collation by A. Holder in *Anglia*, I, 506-512; and in W. M. Baskerville, "Epistola Alexandri ad Aristotelem" in *Anglia*, IV, 139-167. The standard present-day edition, however, is Stanley Rypins, *Three Old English Prose Texts in MS. Cotton Vitellius A XV*, volume 161 of *Publications of the Early English Text Society, Original Series* (London, 1924), at the base of which lies his article in *Modern Language Notes*, XXXVIII, 216-220. A supplementary bibliography and brief discussion is found in F. Pfister, "Auf den Spuren Alexanders des Grossen in der älteren englischen Litteratur" in *Germanisch-Romanische Monatsschrift*, XVI, 81-86.

8. This dates from about the year 200; see note 10 below.

9. See note 10 below.

10. For the growth of the Legend of Alexander in Western Europe during the Middle Ages, the best single treatment, which comprises also an edition of two Middle English fragments on the Life of Alexander, is Francis P. Magoun, *The Gests of King Alexander of Macedon* (Cambridge, Mass., 1929). But it is also instructive to check the legendary accounts of Alexander's career with what the sober historians have been able to ascertain; see, therefore, E. A. W. Budge, *History of Alexander the Great* (Cambridge, 1889) and *The Life and Exploits of Alexander the Great* (London, 1896); E. I. Robson, *Alexander the Great: a biographical study* (London, 1929); P. Meyer, *Alexandre le Grand dans la littérature française du moyen âge* (Paris, 1896); and C. A. Robinson, *Alexander the Great* (New York, 1947). A good summary of the Legend, with exhaustive bib-

liography, is given in J. E. Wells, *A Manual of Writings in Middle English* (New Haven, 1916; 1935), 98ff. and 778ff. A special matter in the Legend is discussed by M. M. Lascelles in "Alexander and the Earthly Paradise in Mediaeval English Writings" in *Medium Aevum*, v, 31-46, 79-104, and 173-188.

11. Manuscript Cotton Vitellius A XV.

12. Published in O. Cockayne, *Narratiunculae Anglice Conscriptae* (London, 1861), 33-39; in F. Knappe, *Das angelsächsische Prosastück "Die Wunder des Ostens"* (Berlin, 1906); and in Stanley Rypins, *Three Old English Prose Texts in Ms. Cotton Vitellius A XV*, volume 161 of *Publications of the Early English Text Society, Original Series* (London, 1924). The discussion of the piece is carried out adequately in the introductory pages of the above works; of these Rypins's edition is preferred. See also Max Förster, "Zur altenglischen Mirabilien-Version" in *Archiv*, cxvii, 367-370.

13. The Latin text is in Manuscript Cotton Tiberius B V rather than in the Beowulf Manuscript.

14. See Chapter IV, notes 53 and 54 above. Many of these stories should be classed as folklore; for details see Stith Thompson, *Motif-Index of Folk-Literature*, volumes xix through xxiii of *Indiana University Studies* (Bloomington, 1936).

XIII · Scientific Writings in the Old English Period

THE Anglo-Saxon scholar, when not dogmatic or missionary, was still not necessarily the wild believer in extreme fantasy that a reading of the preceding chapter might imply. On the contrary, enough has survived from what may be called the scientific writing of the period to make clear that the Anglo-Saxon scholar could be eminently practical. As early as the year 500 or thereabouts, Gildas, if it was indeed he, had composed a sermon and hymn combined which called into illustration the various parts of the body, often anatomized into obscure and far-fetched terms. This is the *Lorica Hymn* (See Chapter XI; especially note 31 κ above), which is a curiously isolated forerunner of the Renaissance conceit but which is apparently a not inconsiderable unit in the relatively untouched field of early Celtic literary and popular traditions.

Yet even in this scientific and quasi-scientific literature one must make generous allowance for the incredible as well as the superstitious. We have seen how the Old English *Charms* (V, 7) presented in fragmentary form a picture of early beliefs in folklore, even when they were mixed with Christian exhortation. For example, there is Byrhtferth's (or Bridferth's) *Handbook*, or *Enchiridion*.[1] The author was apparently a monk at Thorney, Cambridgeshire, and later at Ramsay, on the Isle of Man. He was the writer of a life of Saint Dunstan[2] and of a *Commentary* on the scientific works of Bede,[3] in particular of the *De Temporum Ratione* and the *De Natura Rerum*, as well as on the *De Indignitatione* and the *De Ratione Unciarum*, which have been ascribed to Bede.[4] Byrhtferth seems to have been a man of obscure life but evidently one of great activity and versatility. We should suppose that one of his assets was that he received some training abroad. He appears to have flourished in the 980's, and all the evidence suggests that he was the most celebrated mathematician in England during his lifetime.

The *Handbook*, found complete in Manuscript Ashmole 328, and in fragmentary condition in three other manuscripts,[5] begins with a full account of the "rime-craft" or arithmetic of the western world. It is based for the greater part upon astronomical concepts—when we come to the definition of a circle, we find that it is expressed in terms of celestial circles. There follow complete directions for astronomical findings, as well as a description of the months and the making of a calendar. The multiplication-table appears in a crude form resembling alliterative verse, no doubt as an aid to memory. Following the section on astronomy, however, comes a short account of the alphabets and of the parts of speech. Another part deals with the kinds of poetry and the forms of verse. The religious element in Bridferth's background emerges in his little treatise on Easter and the partaking of the Lamb. The religious combined with the humanistic reveals itself in the enumeration of the Greeks, Romans, and Hebrews and in the comparative judgments handed down concerning Homer and Virgil on the one hand and the sayings of Isaiah on the other. The work ends on a homiletic note, with some counsel to young clerics, a few matters of doctrines and legend, such as the allusion to the binding of Satan for a thousand years, and some reflective remarks on the Seven Deadly Sins and the Four Cardinal Virtues. The piece is in English for the most part, although there are many scraps of Latin and a few interlinear glosses. It cannot be said to have the coherence necessary to make a good textbook on mathematics, but it contains a surprising amount of lore, and it is difficult enough to appreciate how much miscellaneous information of a strictly worldly kind was at the command of an Anglo-Saxon scholar.

After all is considered, however, the Bridferth *Handbook* is the only piece left from the period which belongs in the realm of mathematics, and the substance of the compilation would hardly oblige a modern mathematician to pay it much attention. With the *Herbarium Apuleii*[6] the matter is somewhat different, for medical science, from the standpoint of therapeutics, has a queer way of repeating itself. The full title of this work is *Herbarium Apuleii Platonici; quod accepit ab Escolapio et Chirono Centauro Magizro Achillis.* Its best modern edition is still that published in Cockayne's *Anglo-Saxon Leechdoms, Wortcunning, and Star-Craft of Early England.*[7] The herbal survives in as many as four manuscripts.[8] As the full title indicates, it was believed to have been the Latin work of Apuleius in the second century—a writer better known as a story-teller and romancer than as a medical man.[9] Some investigators have felt, however, that the Old English versions which we possess are more clearly obligated to Dioscorides, the Greek authority on *materia medica,* who flourished in the first century. Neither ascription is really necessary, because the material presented is the accretion or syncretism of centuries of popular as well as professional lore.[10] But the original of the Old English *Herbarium Apuleii* was in Latin, and, while it is undoubtedly a composite of several works in the field and covers a long period in the course of its development, it was the medical Bible of Anglo-Saxon and Middle English physicians. The contents, to anyone interested in the story of the efforts of mankind to cure bodily ills, is nothing less than fascinating. No brief summary can do it justice. The sophisticated citizen of the twentieth century may be fain to smile at the ingenuousness of the prescriptions, at least until he remembers the mote in his own eye. Yet even in all tolerance one can but wonder at the herb *callitrichos,* or water-wort:

> If swellings annoy maidens, take this wort . . . pound it apart, lay it to the sore; it healeth it. If a man's hair fall off, take this same wort, pound it in oil, smear the hair therewith; it soon becometh fast.[11]

The quality of the therapeutic technique is indicated well by the following disquisition on the wood-thistle; it combines, as will be seen, an empirical kind of scientific description of the locale and function of the plant with an obvious astrological supplement:

This wort, which is called *carduus silvaticus*, and by another name wood- or wild-thistle, is gotten in meadows and along ways. For sore of the maw or stomach, take so tender and so green the upper part of the head of this same wort which we named *carduus silvaticus*, administer it in sweetened vinegar; it relieves the soreness.

In order that they may dread no ill gaincomers, take this same wort *carduus silvaticus* in early morning, when first the sun ascendeth; and let that be when the moon is in Capricorn, and keep it. As long as thou bearest it with thee, nothing will come against thee.[12]

There is, in fact, a strong tendency to set up these drugs optimistically as universal panaceas. So of lithewort:

This wort, which is named *hostriago*, and by another name lithewort, is produced about burial-places and on barrows, and on walls of houses which stand against downs.

For all things which are generated on a man by way of disease, take this wort, which we call *hostriago*, and pound it; then lay it to the sore. All the things, as we said before, which are generated upon man's body to loathe, it thoroughly will heal.[13]

The continuation of the *Herbarium*, once again derived largely from Dioscorides, is slightly more exact and more practical than the earlier portion and given much less to folk-lore and astrology than to immediate physical effects. Thus:

Colocynth. This wort, which is named *colocynthis agria*, that is, *cucurbita agrestis*, wild gourd, which is also named *frigilla*, just as another gourd spreadeth abroad its stems upon the earth, and it hath leaves like the cucumber, and deeply cut, and it hath a spherical fruit and bitter, which is to be gathered at the time when it is turning its greenness to fallow.

For stirring of the inwards, take the inward neshness, or soft part of this fruit, without the kernels, by weight of two pennies; give it, pounded in mild beer broth(?) to be drunk; it stirreth the inwards.[14]

In short, altogether recognizable as a prescription.

It is probable that the Old English *Herbarium* belongs

somewhere in the first half of the eleventh century. Of approximately the same period, and immediately associated with it in the manuscripts, is the *Medicina de Quadrupedibus*.[15] This rather baffling work begins with the following observation: "It is said that Idpartus, King of Egypt, was called by Octavian the Emperor, his friend. He taught health in these words, speaking thus . . ." Cockayne[16] believes Idpartus to be a fictitious person, "a stalking-horse for a bookmaker." The work, however, is ascribed as a whole to Sextus Placitus the Platonic or the Papyrian, whoever he may have been. Cockayne remarks sardonically that "if the small wit invented Idpartus, why not also Sextus Placitus?" We know nothing about Sextus. But it is evident that the Latin original of the *Medicina de Quadrupedibus* is not so long as the Old English version, whence the certain conclusion that the version in the vernacular represents an accrual, from probably Germanic sources, of fresh pharmaceutics.

As a matter of fact, the *Medicina de Quadrupedibus* strikes the reader as far more committed to folklore than to practical medicine. The uses of the various parts of a badger's anatomy, for instance, are many and spectacular; the hart is likewise a most useful animal. A complete illustration of the range of medicinal values is afforded by the fox. Gynecological ailments can be cured by the application of a salve made from foxes' limbs and fat; the same ointment is good for both a headache and an earache. For pains in the spleen, one should boil a fox's lung or liver in hot ash. The testicles of a fox, in hot broth, will cure warts. The same will cure a hydrocele. Sore jaws will be relieved by an emulsion of powdered foxes' muscles; a fox's tail is an aphrodisiac when hung upon a human being's arm. A bath made from the boiling of the entire carcass of a fox will cure rheumatism; a fox's gall-bladder will cure either earache or dimness of the eyes. Hares, scorpions, and he-goats similarly contribute their shares to the amelioration of health. For what is believed to be leprosy, goats' urine mingled with honey and salt is the lotion indicated. Ivory, or "elephant-bone," powdered and mingled with honey, is the accepted beauty-wash.

He who wishes, however, to get a picture far more complete than that offered by the better known works of the Old English period of the everyday business of living, breeding, and dying, should read from the first page to the last the *Leech-Book*[17] found in Manuscripts London Harleian 55 and London Regulus 12 D XVII. The authoritative edition is that by Cockayne in the second volume of his *Leechdoms*.[18] This work originated probably during the later tenth century. It consists of (a) a treatise on medicine and (b) a conglomeration of prescriptions and recipes, better organized than most such collections, or, as Cockayne puts it, "more monkish in character." As to its source, it is derived from one or two of the Greek authorities on medicine, such as Paulus of Aegina and Alexander of Tralles and Philagrios. The manuscripts are occasionally marred by that form of "secret writing" or code-symbols with which idle minds amuse themselves. Fortunately, these marks are mostly in the margins and so do not affect greatly the sense of the text. The treatise on medicine, which goes to make up the first part of the *Leech-Book*, is in two sections; at the end comes a colophon mentioning Bald and Child. Child is presumably the scribe, and Bald the owner, of the book and therefore probably the leech who used the book. This is conjectural, however, and certainly immaterial.

Space and the demands of proportion forbid any extended discussion of the contents of the *Leech-Book*. In the main it is to be noted that the treatise on medicine is organized not from the standpoint of individual drugs or animals—in other words, the *materia medica*—but from the standpoint of the ailment to be treated. It is astonishingly varied in the range of its materials; virtually all the important flora of England may be called upon in the making of the prescription, and the compounding is attended by a minimum of prayers and exorcizations. So in the case of this particular remedy for the "dry disease," which is a wasting disease of vague nature, probably tuberculosis:

Oxa taught this leechdom: take wallwort, and cloffing, and kneeholn, and life everlasting, and cammock, and white hellebore, in the proportion of nine to one, brownwort, bishopwort, and atterlothe, and red nettle, and red hove, and wormwood, and yarrow, and horehound, and pellitory, and pennyroyal; put all these worts into foreign ale, and then let the man drink for nine days and let blood. For the "dry" pain, make into a drink alexanders, sedum, wormwood, two kneeholns, sage, savine, carrot, lovage, feverfew, marche, costmary, garlic, ashthroat, betony, bishopwort, work them up into double-brewed ale, sweeten with honey, drink for nine mornings no other liquid; drink afterwards a strong potion, and let blood. Oxa taught this leechdom. Against "dry" rot; put into foreign ale the nether part of kneeholn, tow, matricaria, and brownwort, of all equal quantities; boil down to one third part, and let him drink while he may require it; and where the disease has settled, follow him up ever with the cupping-glass till the place be made whole.[19]

And occasionally we find mention of no specific herb as a remedy, but merely a dietary regimen, perhaps not too sensible, judged by the strict standards of twentieth-century medicine, yet justifiable at least for its psychological impact:

Of the bellies of children, and of overfilling, and if their food do not well digest, and if sweat come from them, and stink foully. When a man perceives that, then shall not a bit of a single piece of solid food be offered them, but various drinks, that the newness of the drinks be good for them. If one eats food over measure, this case one tends the more easily, as one the sooner brings about that he spew, and be empty; if one tends him when troubled with the evil humor arising from overeating, then come on him various diseases: breast pain, neck disease, disease in the jowl, scurf of the head, purulence in the neck, boils not easy to cure, and the like of those. If for these they may not sleep, then shall one give them hot water to drink; it will still the mucus within, and will cleanse the belly. Let them employ the bath moderately, and take meat and take drink mingled with water.[20]

How much closer such a prescription brings us to the realization that the Anglo-Saxons were as other men than do all the pages of their Christian prose and poetry together! It is difficult to imagine Beowulf as afflicted with a toothache or a boil or indigestion; by a process of perverse extension, it is difficult enough to conceive of the Anglo-Saxons as sitting down to a meal and suffering from overindulgence. Such has been the effect of too narrow a list of works in Old English literature to be read and studied. For the soul of him whose knowledge of the literature of England before the Norman Conquest is based for the greater part upon *Beowulf* and a few homilies, the social historian can but shake his head and deplore. Yet even the specialist in primitive epic literature will note with satisfaction that the *Leech-Book* concludes with instructions on how to replace a man's intestines.

The collection of recipes and prescriptions, gathered together by Cockayne and published in the third volume of his *Saxon Leechdoms*,[21] is found in Manuscript Harleian 585 and is virtually a complete gathering of the miscellanea of plant folklore. The material is altogether similar to that contained in the *Herbaria*, the *Medicina de Quadrupedibus*, and the *Leech-Book*. They are often, however, nothing more nor less than charms, akin to those already mentioned (V, 7). And even in these prescriptions it is difficult to decide how much the ingredients are to be measured out from practical, rule-of-thumb experience or from the residuum of popular superstition. Observe the hit-and-miss nature of the dosage in the following:

> Work a spew-drink thus: boil a cucumber in water, let it boil long, then strain a half-bowl, rub down a hundred libcorns into the drink.
> Work another out of beer and out of forty libcorns, put in seventeen peppercorns if thou wilt.
> A spew-drink: put into beer or wine, fennel, let it stand one night, administer it to be drunk. Work a salve for head-pain and for joint-pain and for eye-pain and for a wen and for the dry-rot disease; take helenium and radish, wormwood and bishopwort, cropleek, garlic and *radix cava*, of all equal quan-

tities, pound them, boil them in butter and celandine and red nettle; put them into a brazen vessel; leave it therein till it be turned color; strain through a cloth, smear the head with it; and the limbs where it is sore. For side-pain: betony, bishopwort, helenium, radish, dock, that namely which will swim, marrubium, groundsel, cropleek, garlic, rue, hindheal, lupin, horehound, seethe these in butter, smear the sides therewith; it will be well with the man.[22]

Occasionally we find verse in these recipes, and then we are likely to step back centuries into primitivism:

> And thou, waybroad, mother of worts,
> Open from the east and mighty within;
> Over thee carts creaked, over thee queens rode,
> Over thee brides bridalled, over thee bulls breathed,
> All these thou withstoodst and with stound stayedst
> As thou withstoodst venom and vile things
> And all the loathly ones that rove through the land.[23]

Nine such herbs are thus described in obscure language, in which Woden and the Christian God seem to walk side by side, and in which the seeming religious inconsistency is merely symbolic of the loose bonds in which Christianity before the Norman Conquest held the English people:

> Now these nine worts avail against nine exiles from glory, that is, devils; against nine venoms, and nine flying evil things, against the red venom, against the stinking venom, against the white venom, against the yellow venom, against the green venom, against pale livid venom, against watchet venom, against the brown venom, against the purple venom, against worm-blister, against water blister, against thorn blister, against thistle blister, against ice blister, against poison blister, if any ill come flying from the east, or any come from the north, or any from the west; over the human race Christ stood over men. I alone knew Him beaming, and the nine adders behold Him. All weeds now give way to worts. Seas may dissolve, all salt water, when I blow this venom from thee.[24]

Or again,

> In case meat turn sour, take earth-gall, dry it to dust, shed

it into ale or into whatever thou wilt drink, it shall be well with thee. In case a man is not able to sleep, take henbane seed and juice of garden mint, shake them up together, and smear the head therewith; it will be well with it.

When first thou art told that thy cattle are lost, then say thou before thou say anything else:

"Bethlehem hight the borough
In which Christ was begotten;
It is far-famed throughout all the earth;
So may this deed before men be known
Through the holy rood of Christ. AMEN!"

Then say thy prayers thrice to the east, and say thrice, "May the Cross of Christ bring me back my beasts from the east," then pray thrice to the west, and say thrice, "May the Cross of Christ bring me back my beasts from the west," then pray thrice to the south, and say thrice, "May the Cross of Christ bring me back my beasts from the south," then pray thrice to the north, and say thrice, "May the Cross of Christ bring me back my beasts from the north. It was lost and is found. The Jews hung up Christ; they did the worst of deeds; they hid what they could not hide; so may this deed in no wise be hidden, through the holy Rood of Christ. AMEN!"[25]

The *Peri Didaxeon*, or *Schools of Medicine*,[26] found in Manuscript Harleian 6258, belongs to the same category of literature as the preceding works; it is, however, what might be called a textbook on medicine, at least in part. The beginning, indeed, is a succinct statement of the conception of medicine which ruled all thought during the Middle Ages:

Here beginneth the book *Peri Didaxeon*, that is, the setting forth for how many years leechcraft was hidden; and the learned leeches sagaciously investigated the ascertaining of it. The earliest was Apollo, and his son Aesculapius or Asklepios; and Asklepios was uncle of Hippocrates; these four [*sic*] invented earliest the building up of leechcraft. About fifteen hundred years after the flood of Noah, in the days of Artaxerxes, who was king of the Persians, they lighted up the light of the leechcraft. We know that Apollo first invented *methodiken*, that is, the irons, when one healeth men with knives, and

Aesculapius *empeiriken*, that is, the leechening of leechcraft, and Asklepios *logiken*, that is, the observance of the law, and the cupping-glass, and Hippocrates *theoriken*, that is, observation of sicknesses. Then Plato and Aristotle, the very learned philosophers, followed after these the aforesaid leeches, and they said, that in the human body there are four humors, inasmuch as the rainbow is also composed thus, that is the humors in the head, and the blood in the breast, and the raw bile in the inwards, and the black bile within the gall. And each one of them rules for three months, that is, from the fifteenth of December to the twenty-fifth of March they say that the humor in the head is dominant. And from the twenty-fifth of March to the twenty-fifth of June the blood in the breast is dominant; from the twenty-fifth of June to the twenty-fifth of September the raw bile in the inwards is dominant—hence these days are called *kunades*, that is, the *dies caniculares*, or dog-days, so that of them are forty-five days, and in those days no leech can rightly give aid to any sick man. And in the fourth division is from the twenty-fifth of September to the fifteenth of December, that the black bile in the gall is dominant. This is distinguished according to the four cardinal points of the heavens, and of the earth, and of the air, and of the deep. Then, as the Lord pleased, man was brought about. This needs searching and order.[27]

There follows a series of recipes for various diseases, with particular reference to Hippocrates. Some of the remedies are heroic even among a list of heroic remedies:

Ad gingevas, as the Greeks call them, that is, in our language, the flesh that waxes about the teeth and makes the teeth wag and disturbs them; take a leek, cut up and pound it, and wring the ooze from it, one spoon full, and vinegar one spoon full, and of honey three spoons full, and make it boil thrice. Then take it as hot as the man can bear it, and let him keep a part in his mouth till it be got cool, then again another part likewise, then a third part likewise.[28]

Or

For acidity, that is, the hot water which shooteth up out of the breast, and at whiles out of the maw. Let him drink five handfuls of salt water, and again take seed of wormwood, and boil it in water and mingle it with wine, and let the man drink it; also, take three or five peppercorns, and let him eat them. Again, take one pennyweight of betony and boil in water, and give him to drink fasting. Again, take rue and pound it, and then lay it in vinegar, and give it him fasting to drink. Again, take seed of lovage, a handful, and let him eat it.[29]

As a supplement to all this medicinal lore there are various scattered pieces of scientific import. Most of them have been collected by Cockayne in his above-mentioned work. Such matters as the following are of interest—the determination of the sex of a foetus; the formation of a foetus; a table of lunar periods and their relation to the prognosis of a man's illness; the interpretation of dreams, much too detailed and elaborate for discussion here,[30] as they fall in the various lunar months; and a very extensive glossary of dream-interpretations attributed to the prophet Daniel,[31] which envisages almost any conceivable dream. What is generally annoying about these treatises, to be sure, is their total lack of order or method or design; anyone, having dreamt of a certain thing, would have to plow through the entire treatise to find the interpretation of the particular matter about which he had dreamed. The chances are, however, that he would eventually find it or something very like it.[32]

There should be noted also the presence of scattered leechdoms, called very appropriately by Cockayne "fly-leaf" leechdoms, found in margins and fly-leaves of various manuscripts, and adding nothing of importance to the type as it has been already illustrated. So also of many scattered charms, notably those beginning with the "Matthew-Mark-Luke-John" formula.

Lexicography can scarcely be considered as one of the arts or sciences practiced by the Anglo-Saxons, but there are a few word-lists from the Old English period which have been of great value to the early students of the language.[33] The *Epinal Glosses* and the *Erfurt Glosses* date from not later than 700;

the *Leyden Glosses* are probably from the same approximate time, although the dating of this particular piece has long been a troublesome problem. The *Cambridge*, or *Corpus*, *Glosses* are definitely eighth-century. These are all southern Mercian in dialect although with frequent Kentish and West Saxon admixtures.[34] The *Brussels* and *Boulogne Glosses*[35] are of similar nature and date. The so-called *Bede Glosses* and *Lorica Glosses*[36] come along about a century later—at least from the first half of the ninth century. The *Bede Glosses* are Kentish, while the *Lorica Glosses* are Mercian. That these glosses were being written toward the end of the Old English period, and that they were therefore not intended as interesting antiquities and nothing else, is shown by the presence close to the year 1000 of the *Royal Glosses*[37] in Mercian and the *Vespasian* Glosses[38] in Kentish. The *Lindisfarne* and *Rushworth* interlinear glosses of the Gospels have already been mentioned, as have *The Durham Ritual-Book* and *The Vespasian Psalter*. The Continental lodging-places of some of these glosses are significant of the traveling of scribes during the period, and the usual implication arises that there were many more such early ancestors of the dictionary than have actually survived.

The schemes in all these glosses are virtually the same. There is a list of Latin words, generally "hard words," or the names of plants, animals, and other things. Sometimes the list is more learned than at other times. Following the Latin word is its Old English equivalent, sometimes a close translation, at other times—especially when the Latin word is unfamiliar—a mere approximation. In some instances no English word can be found to serve, and so the Latin word is Anglicized. In all the glosses the words are arranged alphabetically except in the case of the *Leyden Glosses*, where the grouping is topical, with some attention to alphabetical order within a given group. There is no attempt at definition, etymology, or further illustrations; there are two parallel lists in which the Latin word is coupled with its English translation, and that is all. In the alphabetical order only is there any sign of a systematic method. But this is the ninth century or thereabouts which we are discussing, not the nineteenth or the twentieth.

NOTES TO CHAPTER THIRTEEN

1. The best edition is that of S. J. Crawford, *Byrhtferth's Manual*, volume 177 of *Publications of the Early English Text Society, Original Series* (London, 1929); there is also an older one by F. Kluge, "Angelsächsische Excerpte aus Byrhtferths Handboc oder Enchiridion" in *Anglia*, VIII, 298-337. But even Crawford's edition should be read with one eye on the supplementary comments and corrections by Heinrich Henel, "Notes on Byrhtferth's Manual" in *Journal of English and Germanic Philology*, XLI, 427-433; see further Henel's "Byrhtferth's *Preface*: the Epilogue of his *Manual?*" in *Speculum*, XVIII, 288-302.

An excellent earlier discussion is that of K. M. Classen, *Über das Leben und die Schriften Byrhtferths, eines angelsächsischen Gelehrten und Schriftstellers um das Jahr 1000* (Dresden, 1896). A noteworthy bibliography is found in Charles and Dorothea Singer, "An Unrecognized Anglo-Saxon Medical Text" in *Annals of Medical History*, III, No. 2, 136-149—also printed separately (New York, 1921). Further discussion of Byrhtferth with general bibliographical information is G. F. Forsey, "Byrhtferth's *Preface*" in *Speculum*, III, 505-522. Details and excerpts from Byrhtferth's work are treated in S. J. Crawford, "Byrhtferth of Ramsey and the Anonymous Life of St. Oswald" in *Speculum Religionis* (London, 1929); H. Henel, "Ein Bruchstück aus Byrhtferths Handbuch" in *Anglia*, LXI, 122-125; and Charles W. Jones, "The Byrhtferth Glosses" in *Medium Aevum*, VII, 81-97.

2. This is published in Thomas Wright, *Biographia Britannica Literaria* (London, 1842), I, 476-478.

3. See note 1 above, also Thomas Wright, *Biographia Britannica Literaria* (see note 2 above), I, 474ff.

4. See VII, 3 above as well as Chapter VII, notes 37, 38, and 39 above.

5. Manuscripts Corpus Christi College Cambridge S 13; Cotton Vitellius E XVIII; and Cotton Galba A II. But see the introduction to Crawford's definitive edition (note 1 above).

6. First printed in O. Cockayne, *Leechdoms, Wort-Cunning, and Star-Craft of Early England* (London, 1864-1866), although it had

been discussed earlier in Thomas Wright, *Biographia Britannica Literaria* (London, 1842), I, 95-104. See also H. Berberich, "Das Herbarium Apuleii nach einer frühmittelenglischen Fassung" in *Anglistische Forschungen*, v, 7-64 (Heidelberg, 1902)—published separately as a dissertation (Heidelberg, 1900); J. F. Payne, *English Medicine in the Anglo-Saxon Times* (Oxford, 1904), particularly pp. 62-92—a most valuable study; and Charles Singer, *From Magic to Science: Essays on the Scientific Twilight* (New York, 1928), 168-198.

The general relationship of plants and meteorology in early English times is touched upon in Eugene S. McCartney, "The Plant Almanac and Weather Bureau" in *Classical Weekly*, XVII, 105-108. Two recent discussions with printed text of the favorite manuscript—Cotton Vitellius C III—are A. J. G. Hilbelink, *Cotton MS. Vitellius C III of the Herbarium Apuleii* (Amsterdam, 1931) and George A. Flom, "On the Old English Herbal of Apuleius, Vitellius C III" in *Journal of English and Germanic Philology*, XL, 29-37.

Whoever brings out an up-to-date edition of Cockayne's massive text would be doing the literature of the Old English period a great service.

7. See the final paragraph of note 6 preceding. This work is still one of the great works of its kind; it is full to the point of being compendious. In the matter of the *Herbarium*, the material is divided by Cockayne thus: vol. I, 1-69—*Herbarium*; vol. I, 71-249—*Herbarium Apuleii*; vol. I, 251-325—*Herbarium from Dioscorides*—for which see note 10 below. All Latin texts are translated into English.

8. The earliest and best, as observed in note 6 above, is Manuscript Cotton Vitellius C III (ca. 1025); the others are Bodleian Hatton 76, Harleian 585, and Bodleian Junius 58.

9. Lucius Apuleius was born at Madaura, Numidia, about 125. His best known work is without question *The Golden Ass*, a collection of stories on the Greek "romance" model of the times. The most famous of these is the tale of Cupid and Psyche. But Apuleius had influence in many other types of plot-situation, particularly in the field of farcical narrative and adventure. In addition to *The Golden Ass*, he was responsible for *Florida*, an anthology of pithy but empty platitudes; *Apologia*, a prime source of his biography; and *On the God of Socrates*, a pleasant exposition of the Platonic doctrine of beneficent "daemons" or spirits.

10. A valuable article discounting these ascriptions to Apuleius and Dioscorides themselves is that of Charles Singer in *Journal of Hellenic Studies*, vol. 47 (1927).

11. O. Cockayne, *Leechdoms, Wort-Cunning, and Star-Craft of Early England* (London, 1864-1866), I, 152-153.

12. Cockayne (see note 11 above), I, 224-225.

13. Cockayne (see note 11 above), I, 124-125.

14. Cockayne (see note 11 above), I, 324-325.

15. Printed in Cockayne (see note 11 above), I, 326-373; see also J. Delcourt, "Medicina de Quadrupedibus" in *Anglistische Forschungen*, XL (Heidelberg, 1914).

16. Cockayne (see note 11 above), I, lxxxix.

17. Printed in Cockayne (see note 11 above), II, 2-364; also in G. Leonhardi, *Kleinere angelsächsische Denkmäler*, in Grein and Wülker's *Bibliothek der angelsächsischen Prosa*, VI (Hamburg, 1905). Discussions will be found also in the works of Payne and Singer (see note 6 above).

18. But see the important preface by Cockayne (note 11 above); also Singer's article mentioned in note 10 above.

19. Cockayne (see note 11 above), 120-121.

20. Cockayne (see note 11 above), II, 240-241.

21. Cockayne (see note 11 above), III, 2-80; published also by Leonhardi (see note 17 above), 122-155. The piece is known also as the *Lacnunga*.

22. Cockayne (see note 11 above), III, 20-21.

23. Cockayne (see note 11 above), III, 32-33.

24. Cockayne (see note 11 above), III, 36-37; see also F. P. Magoun, "On Some Survivals of Pagan Belief in Anglo-Saxon England" in *Harvard Theological Review*, XL, 33-46.

25. Cockayne (see note 11 above), III, 60-61.

26. Published in Cockayne (see note 11 above), III, 82-145; also in H. Löweneck, *Peri Didaxeon, eine Sammlung von Rezepten in englischer Sprache aus dem 11/12 Jahrhundert* (Erlanger, 1896). These editions give complete introductions, but see also the works of Payne and Singer (note 6 above).

27. Cockayne (see note 11 above), III, 83-85.

28. Cockayne (see note 11 above), III, 102-103.

29. Cockayne (see note 11 above), III, 128-129.

30. This is printed in Cockayne (see note 11 above), III, 171ff.; see also Max Förster, "Die altenglische Traumlunare" in *Englische Studien*, LX, 58-93.

31. Cockayne (see note 11 above), III, 199-215.

32. In order to follow through the multitudinous examples of scientific, quasi-scientific, superstitional, folkloristic writings surviving from the Old English period, the following list is recommended. At the head stands the superb work of Lynn Thorndike, *A History of Magic and Experimental Science during the First Thirteen Centuries of Our Era* (New York, 1923 ff.). In addition:

A. GENERAL TREATMENTS: Charles Singer, "Early English Magic

and Medicine" in *Proceedings of the British Academy* (London, 1924), IX, 341-374; Charles H. Haskins, *Studies in the History of Mediaeval Science* (London, 1924); and H. Henel, "Altenglischer Mönchsaberglaube" in *Englische Studien*, LXIX, 329-349.

B. LEECHDOMS: F. Liebermann, "Angelsächsische Arzneikunde im 12. Jahrhundert fortlebend" in *Archiv*, CXLVII, 92-93; F. Liebermann, "Speiseverbote der Angelsachsen" in *Archiv*, CLXVII, 250; David Riesman, *The Story of Medicine in the Middle Ages* (New York, 1935)—an excellent performance; Pearl Kibre, "Hippocratic Writings in the Middle Ages" in *Bulletin of the History of Medicine*, XVIII, 371-412; and Erika von Ehrhardt-Siebold, "The Hellebore in Angle-Saxon Pharmacy" in *Englische Studien*, LXXI, 161-170.

C. PLANTS, HERBARIA, AND WEATHER (see note 6 above).

D. ASTROLOGY, ASTRONOMY, AND TIME: Arthur R. Green, "Anglo-Saxon Sundials" in *Antiquaries' Journal*, VIII, 489-516; Max Förster, "Die altenglischen Verzeichnisse von Glücks- und Unglückstagen" in the *Klaeber Miscellany* (Minneapolis, 1929), 258-277; H. Henel, "Planetenglaube in Aelfrics Zeit" in *Anglia*, LVIII, 292-317.

E. LAPIDARIES AND THE LORE OF PRECIOUS STONES: Joan Evans and Mary S. Serjeantson, *English Mediaeval Lapidaries*, volume 190 of *Publications of the Early English Text Society, Original Series* (London, 1933); R. Von Fleischhacker, "Ein altenglischer Lapidar" in *Zeitschrift für deutsches Altertum*, XXXIV, 229-235; R. M. Garrett, "Precious Stones in Old English Literature," volume XLVII of *Münchener Beiträge zur romanischen und englischen Philologie* (Munich, 1909); Joan Evans, *Magical Jewels of the Middle Ages and Renaissance, Particularly in England* (Oxford, 1922).

F. GENERAL MAGIC: G. Storms, *Anglo-Saxon Magic* (The Hague, 1948).

G. GENERAL PROGNOSTICS (in addition to Cockayne—see note 11 in Chapter III above—and the foregoing items in note 32): R. T. Hampson, *Medii Aevi Kalendarium: or dates, charters, and customs of the Middle Ages* (London, 1841); O. Cockayne, *Narratiunculae Anglice Conscriptae* (London, 1861), 49ff.; E. Sievers, "Bedeutung der Buchstaben" in *Zeitschrift für deutsches Altertum*, XXI, 189-190; W. de G. Birch, "Edition of Divination Alphabet" in *Transactions of the Royal Society of Literature*, second series, XI, 508 (London, 1878); B. Assmann, "Eine Regel über den Donner" in *Anglia*, X, 185; B. Assmann, "Prophezeiung aus dem 1. Januar für das Jahr" in *Anglia*, XI, 369; M. Förster, "Der Inhalt der altenglischen Handschrift Vespasianus D XIV" in *Englische Studien*, LIV, 46-68—particularly p. 52; A. S. Napier, "Altenglische Kleinigkeiten" in *Anglia*, XI, 1-10; G. Hellman, *Denkmäler mittelalterlicher Meteorologie*

(Berlin, 1904); A. Dieterich, "A. B. C. -Denkmäler" in *Rheinische Museum für Philologie*, N.F. 56, 77-105; M. Förster, "Die Klein-literatur des Aberglaubens im altenglischen" in *Archiv*, CX, 346-358; M. Förster, "Beiträge zur mittelalterlichen Volkskunde" in *Archiv*, CXX, 43-52 and 296-305—also CXXI, 30-46; CXXV, 39-71; CXXVIII, 55-71 and 285-308; CXXXIV, 264-293; M. Förster, "Die Weltzeit-alter bei den Angelsachsen" in the *Luick Festschrift* (Marburg, 1925), 183-203.

33. The general subject of the glosses is discussed fully in Alois Brandl, *Angelsächsische Literatur*, published as part of Paul's *Grund-riss der germanischen Philologie* (3rd ed., Strassburg, 1911) and separately (Strassburg, 1908); cf. p. 1055 in particular. See also A. G. Kennedy, *A Bibliography of Writings on the English Language from the Beginnings to the End of 1922* (Cambridge-New Haven, 1922), 128-129.

Particularly valuable, however, is the recent collection by Herbert D. Meritt, *Old English Glosses* (Modern Language Association General Series, XVI) (New York, 1945).

34. W. M. Lindsay, *The Corpus, Epinal, Erfurt, and Leiden Glosses* (London, 1921). But see Meritt (note 33 above) and Sherman M. Kuhn, "The Dialect of the Corpus Glossary" in *Publi-cations of the Modern Language Association*, LIV, 1-19—which denies any dialectal admixture, pointing out that the differences in dialect are due to chronological changes in the Old Mercian itself.

35. The *Brussels Glosses* are printed by F. J. Mone in *Quellen und Forschungen zur Geschichte der teutschen Literatur und Sprache* (Aachen-Leipzig, 1830) and by Benjamin Thorpe in Appendix B to *Mr. Cooper's Report* (London, 1836). The *Boulogne Glosses* are published by A. Holder in *Germania*, XXIII, 385ff.; also in the works of Mone and Thorpe just mentioned. See, however, Meritt (note 33 above).

36. The *Bede* and *Lorica Glosses* are printed in Henry Sweet, *The Oldest English Texts*, volume 83 of *Publications of the Early English Text Society, Original Series* (London, 1885). See Meritt (note 33 above).

37. See note 38 below.

38. There are some other glossarial fragments, and it is hardly necessary in a work of this scope to attempt to fix the bibliography of each of these. The reader is referred to the bibliographical lists fur-nished by A. G. Kennedy in his *Bibliography of Writings on the Eng-lish Language* (see note 33 above), 128-129 and to Herbert Meritt's work cited in the same note. A good example of these minor glosses is discussed by Meritt in "Old English Sedulus Glosses" in *American Journal of Philology*, LVII, 140-150. See also Charles W. Jones, "The

Byrhtferth Glosses" in *Medium Aevum*, VII, 81-97. The article by J. T. Muckle, "Greek Words Translated Directly into Latin before 1350" in *Mediaeval Studies*, IV, 33-42, gives some interesting information about the learned vocabulary which suggested to Anglo-Saxon scholars the desirability of such glosses as those described in the text above. Similar in its nature to the minor glosses is the material presented in O. S. Anderson Arngart, *Old English Material in the Leningrad Manuscript of Bede's Ecclesiastical History* (Lund, 1941).

XIV · Retrospect

As the centuries followed one after another, the Norman Conquest faded slowly away, like the great rock seen by the mariner which, as he passes beyond, melts gradually into the horizon. Epic literature became medieval romance, the reflection of a different age. Church literature increased in prestige and in stature over an ever-widening empire. All of the important types of Old English literature continued into the Middle English period; they put on new dress, however, to suit new surroundings, and soon this new dress transmuted each of the old types into what seemed to be a new form. And, of course, with the advent of the medieval drama and of the popular ballad there were unquestionably new forms. More and more Old English literature came to be neglected as the bygone expression of a conquered people written in a plebeian tongue; and by the time English had been reestablished as a language of social standing, *Beowulf* and what it represents had been immured in libraries and cloisters. Only in such a phenomenon as the alliterative revival in West Midland verse of the fourteenth century is there any particular evidence that anyone was even remembering what English writers had once created.

The upheavals of the Renaissance brought about a change in this unfortunate state of affairs. The Renaissance humanist had a definite antiquarian interest, although this interest was directed chiefly toward the Greek and Latin classics. With the Reformation in England, however, the curiosity of the humanist was mingled with a characteristic desire to justify Protestantism, as well as the sovereignty of the Crown. The pioneer works of Archbishop Parker and his fellow-antiquarians, John Joscelin, Laurence Nowell, and William Lambard, in the 1560's and 1570's, to say nothing of the earlier scratchings of John Leland in the 1530's—all are actuated in large measure

by the desire to find in ancient English writings some authority
for or defense of the establishment of an authentic English
Church and independent State. In the seventeenth century,
too, men sought once more, in the glamor of antiquity, for a
defense of their political and religious views. It has been disturbing to the altruistic and indefatigable scholars of the nineteenth and twentieth centuries to observe the relatively selfish
and even base motives which prompted the renaissance of
studies in Old English literature and the Old English language, but one can hardly be squeamish much longer about
human motives, which have often produced the most magnificent results regardless. To all diggers and delvers, bibliophiles
and sycophants, from Leland in the sixteenth century to
Wanley, Elstob, Thwaites, and Hickes in the early eighteenth
century, many thanks and much praise. Without their efforts
we should be even more ignorant today about Anglo-Saxon
civilization before the Norman Conquest than we actually are.[1]

What have we collected and what can be done with our
achievement?

In the first place, we should review briefly what is available
in Old English literature for reading, study, delight, and—
horribile dictu—profit. The term "Old English literature"
(or "Anglo-Saxon literature") should cover all written remains, surviving as well as conjectural, composed in England
from the time of the coming of the Angles and Saxons
through, let us say, the first generation after the Battle of
Hastings; more specifically, it should include everything from
the runic literature—nearly all of which has been lost—to the
entries in *The Anglo-Saxon Chronicle* dating from about the
time of the death of William the Conqueror, though hard-
and-fast dates, in determining the boundaries between Old
and Middle English, are both futile and meaningless. This
literature, as we have traced it, comprises a miscellaneous
narrative type exemplified in the various kinds of epic poetry;
a reflective sort of lyric, or "elegiac" verse; didactic poetry in
many forms; a few personal poems; a large *corpus* of monitory
prose, consisting of saints' lives, expositions of theological

matters, homilies, and instructive dialogues; several translations from foreign writings, including some Biblical translations and paraphrases; some works on grammar, geography, astronomy, and mixed natural lore; a large amount of medical and pharmaceutical material; and the usual stones and pebbles of early literature, such as glosses, inscriptions on monuments, and runes. In other words, nearly every kind of recognizable literary type is somehow represented. The most striking exceptions are the drama and the novel, however this latter type is to be defined. The liturgical plays of medieval drama, it is true, probably had their beginnings in the last century or two of the Old English period. The general fiction of the age, however, which did duty for the novel and the short story, is discoverable in the epics, or as incidents or illustrations in the didactic literature, although the first manifestations of the exotic romance popular in the later Middle Ages are discernible late in the Anglo-Saxon period. While most of the work is written in the vernacular, a great deal of it is nevertheless in Latin, and the Anglo-Latin element must always be considered in any discussion of Old English literature as a whole.

So much for what has survived. But what else was there? It is altogether probable that at least as much Old English literature has perished as has survived. To put it in another way, what we have now to go by very likely represents no more than half of what was actually written. Indeed, the ratio of the amount of lost literature to that which has come down to us is probably much higher than the ratio of one to one.[2] Speculations about the unknown are obviously nothing more than intellectual entertainment. It can scarcely be overemphasized, however, that our knowledge of Old English literature is necessarily incomplete, that it can probably never be much greater than it now is, and that we are in no position to offer more than generalities about what we actually hold in our possession. Nor have we any right, therefore, to pass judgment upon the total accomplishment of the Anglo-Saxon writers in this period, since that total accomplishment is no longer accessible. The combination of the paucity of original manuscripts, the high frequency of illiteracy over a stretch of centuries, the depredations of time, and the malice of men make too formidable a coalition against the dissemination of the whole truth.

Yet we are entirely justified in making a provisional appraisal of what has actually survived from the Old English period. The generalities which have been uttered about this literature, here and elsewhere, are no doubt familiar enough; but they should be dwelt upon, because they have not been sufficiently emphasized in the past and because they are fundamental in any approach to Old English literature. Unhappily, this literature has lost caste in the minds of many through the fact that the study of Old English has become, particularly in the United States, a linguistic study instead of being what it should be—a means to an end, and that end the net contribution of the Angle, the Saxon, and the Jute to English civilization before the Norman Conquest and later. Now there is no denying the importance of the Old English language in the history of the English language as a whole; its rock-bottom foundation to the vast structure of Modern English has been consistently underestimated. Nor is there any denying the hazard of language which must be surmounted and mastered before there can be a true perception of the possibilities of Old English literature, even though there are many good translations of most of the items in our list. But, as we all should know by this time, translation is at best only a half-measure, *faute de mieux*, and translations of Early English are particularly inadequate. We owe it to the Anglo-Saxon writer to learn in first-hand fashion what there is to learn about his medium of language. Once that language has been brought under control, however, we are under an equal obligation to extend our range of knowledge concerning his literature.

For most of us who took a course in Old English at an American college, there was a semester's wrestling with a grammatical system and a vocabulary extremely unfamiliar to us unless we had had previous experience with a Germanic language. We whetted the poor knives of our intellects on selections from Alfred or the Alfredian *Bede* or Aelfric or the writers of elegiac verse and anonymous homilies, all taken in small doses; and altogether too often we were misled—with or without the full knowledge and consent of the instructor— into complacent amusement by the sight and sound of such naïve syntactic and stylistic prodigies as the thirteen-fold negative in the account of Orpheus and Eurydice, or such artless misconceptions of a situation as the Alfredian version of the enchantment of Ulysses by Circe. The uncouth sounds so foreign to the ear of a Modern English speaker afforded another source of tolerant and condescending though no doubt innocent merriment. And then came *Beowulf* (which had probably already been read in translation), with its complexities of background and its difficulties of poetic vocabulary and stylistic cruxes, all of which kept us too busy to realize that there were other pieces of Old English poetry fully as rewarding as *Beowulf* and a good deal less familiar. The British, never so hypnotized as the Americans by the monster of German nineteenth-century scholarship, have generally done better by their earliest literature. Fortunately the teachers of Old English in the United States have begun to turn their faces slowly toward the light.

Fortunately, too, Old English literature is significant enough to lend itself to appreciation from most of the common present-day approaches to literature. Perhaps even the economic determinist can make something of the Anglo-Saxon law-codes and charters,[3] of the power of the Church over its subjects, and possibly of the wars between the Geats and the Swedes, although he might be hard put to it to explain Grendel. There the folklorist and the anthropologist step in. Even —God forbid!—the psychoanalytic approach could explain and emphasize the fatalism of the Old English epic warrior, his willing reception of Christianity, and the suppression of sex in terms of extrovertent physical activity, in which Old English literature delights—a suppression which, however, can lead to moody introspection, whence the elegiac verse. The specialist on the history of ideas has before him here the solid basis of medieval Christian theology, the maritime tradition, the pagan survivals. And assuredly the critic of poetry can have his day in praise of the occasional bursts of magnificent power in the lines of many Old English poems or in the simple, ingenuous, yet compelling prose of Bede, though here I should insist that the critic has less business than ever to attempt to apply strict objective standards. For Old English literature is essentially romantic and abhors pseudo-scientific measurements. As for the sociologist, he has perhaps the finest opportunity of all to deal with the varieties of this literature, because there is little in this literature which does not somehow proclaim aloud its environment, and in its massive, incoherent, repetitious way delineate in outlines now vague, now sharp, the features of life in England before the Norman Conquest.

Which of these many possible interpretations of this literature an individual may wish to accept is strictly his own privilege. The essential fact remains that Old English literature both can and should be studied in different ways; it has the materials and it has the potentialities. The general student of English literature, however, has scarcely been aware of them. All of us at one time or another have read, in or out of translation, the impressive account of the funeral of Scyld Scefing in *Beowulf*, the resounding lines heralding the approach of Grendel, the Biblical echoes in Hrothgar's homily on pride, the lament of the last treasure-guardian; and we have surveyed the epic ruin and decay portrayed in the closing sections of that poem. But we can find many of these very achievements in the Caedmonian and Cynewulfian poems; indeed, it would be silly to attempt to enumerate here all of the many passages in Old English poetry and prose which have the power to linger in the memory.

Moreover, it is the manner in which such passages from Old English literature fall into their places in the unending tradition of English letters which affords the thoughtful reader one of his deepest fascinations. Certain lines from the Caedmonian poems remind one, however remotely, of Milton. A passage from *Guthlac B* savors of the pre-Raphaelite.

The Dream of the Rood is in certain lines worthy of Richard Rolle or William Blake or others of the mystic brotherhood. Nothing is farther from the truth than the idea that the Anglo-Saxon was not moved by nature; his reactions to its external manifestations at least were immediate, if sometimes limited and perverse. We know that the Anglo-Saxon was always aware of the sea, to which *The Seafarer* is an imperishable tribute. He realized also that "summer's lease hath all too short a date." This mood, deepening into the conviction that all things must pass—whether material things, as in *The Wanderer*, or human problems, as in *Deor's Lament*—makes for the somberness in Old English literature which all have noted. While most have heard, however, of the grimness of this literature, as we find it overwhelmingly in its pagan elements, few remember that the Christian teacher emphasizes a more hopeful future and can become eloquent on the subject. And so the resonant lines of *Doomsday*, promising peace and joy in the world to come, may reveal to us by implication a great deal about the Anglo-Saxon's fears and terrors by night and by noonday, but they reveal to us also that he could wait in expectation of a life of blissful tranquillity.

A first glance at Old English prose suggests inevitably paths which do not appear attractive. This prose is fundamentally an instrument of the teacher and the preacher. It was possible, to be sure, for the Anglo-Saxon to comment on life without being doctrinaire and theological. The *Gnomic Verses*, the *Riddles*, the dialogues, the *Distichs of Cato*, and the *Proverbs of Alfred* are clear examples. The Alfredian translations, particularly those of Boethius, Bede, and Orosius, can be termed informative and not merely monitory or hortatory literature. The long cataloguing of sermonistic writings from the pens of Aelfric, Wulfstan, and nameless churchmen such as those who composed the *Blickling Homilies* is not an inviting task, and this statement is made with the full realization that these particular pieces of Old English literature are the special bait to lure the scholar of the present day.

On the other hand, there is always the late Oriental prose

fiction and the scientific prose to console us. We could wish here, however, for more system. But it is just as well left unsystematic—we can then realize that the mind of the Anglo-Saxon is not yet the mind of his fellow-countryman in the Renaissance, to say nothing of times still to come. The Anglo-Saxon from the age before the coming of William the Conqueror is still groping, still hampered by the past even in the practical aspects of living. Nothing shows better the grip which generations gone by still hold on the Anglo-Saxon than the authority-acknowledging formulas, "it is said" or "they say," which preface so much of his informative writing, or the fulsome tributes to ancient masters which sprinkle the didactic texts. As contributions to human knowledge, therefore, the learned writing of the Anglo-Saxon is, to the twentieth century, virtually negligible. As indices of his culture, however, they are at least as valuable as his more ambitious and more artistic literary performances; in most respects they are even more vital. The leechdoms, recipes, and star-lore, of the people as they are and consequently obscure to a regrettable degree, form nevertheless a colorful recurring strand in the English literary tapestry, as any reader of Drayton or Spenser or Herrick or Hardy must duly recognize. Does the Beowulfian tradition return any more insistently or earthily or pungently?

In fact, it is quite evident that the immediate future of scholarly investigations in this Old English terrain will be devoted to the widening of our knowledge of such hitherto neglected areas of the field as the prose homily, the folkloristic remains, the gnomic poetry, the scientific and the pseudo-scientific collections of popular wisdom. We have tramped the fields of Old English poetry almost flat. Here lies, on the other hand, the nearly forgotten prose, endowed with great possibilities for the social historian and for the literary historian who realizes that there is more to literature than poetry. Many scholars, in fact, are at present engaged upon the difficult and thankless task of classifying, evaluating, and indexing the prose homilies. Much still remains to be done in this field of Old English vernacular prose, however; it remains for the future to see what will be accomplished. But there is little doubt that our chief desideratum in Old English literature looms large at this very point in the road.

Whatever posterity decides to do about this corner of English literature cultivated a thousand years ago, one thing is still certain, and that is that Old English literature needs no apology. It is not difficult to be condescending, even contemptuous, in our judgment of it. In some measure this judgment will depend upon what the individual reader may be seeking. Old English literature is the expression of a people which has not yet found itself. Most of us would agree on that. It therefore presents none of the far-reaching problems of modern industrial and mechanical life. It is Church-ridden. It ignores women to what seems to us an intolerable degree. Its structure is all too often weak; it repeats itself; its subject-matter is limited; it lacks sensuousness and brilliance; it has little esthetic appeal. So much for its liabilities. But consider closely its origins. One has no right to expect the impossible. This literature, with all its deficiencies, has a fierce masculinity, a stern moral fiber ingrained on simple but rigorous ethical principles, and a stout-hearted pessimism tinged at least upon the surface with Christian hope. Virility, sturdiness, and insight—this is the trinity from which all abiding literature must spring. For the rest, Old English literature has rude and direct power, a muffled kind of romantic eloquence, and a naïve but instinctive ability to put its hand upon eternal truths. To him who would try to seek out these virtues at all times, we may paraphrase *Bede's Death-Song* and observe that he is no wiser than he should be.

NOTES TO CHAPTER FOURTEEN

1. Rosamund Tuve, "Ancients, Moderns, and Saxons" in *Journal of English Literary History* (ELH), VI, 165-190; and Margaret

Ashdown, "Elizabeth Elstob, the Learned Saxonist" in *Modern Language Review*, xx, 125-146.

2. All types of literature may be represented in this body of lost writings. The kind of material which we are likely to look for and which we even know something about, although there are no tangible remains, is best discussed in the following: R. W. Chambers, "The Lost Literature of Mediaeval England" in *Library*, 4th series, v, 293-321; Robin Flower, "Laurence Nowell and a Recovered Anglo-Saxon Poem" in *British Museum Quarterly*, viii, 130-132—which illustrates the case of an occasional piece that may turn up from time to time; R. M. Wilson, "Lost Literature in Old and Middle English" in *Leeds Studies in English and Kindred Languages*, ii, 14-37; and R. M. Wilson, "More Lost Literature in Old and Middle English" in *Leeds Studies in English and Kindred Languages*, v, 1-49 and vi, 30-49.

3. References to the Anglo-Saxon *Law-Codes* have been given already under Chapter VIII, note 6 above. There is an extensive literature treating the Anglo-Saxon *Charters*. The text of these charters is given in the following: J. M. Kemble, *Codex diplomaticus aevi saxonici* (London, 1839-1848)—still the most ambitious collection of these documents; B. Thorpe, *Diplomatarium anglicum aevi saxonici* (London, 1865); H. Sweet, *The Oldest English Texts*, volume 83 of *Publications of the Early English Text Society, Original Series* (London, 1885)—for charters antedating 900; W. de G. Birch, *Cartularium Saxonicum* (London, 1885-1893)—not more extensive than Kemble's collection but with more up-to-date apparatus; J. Earle, *A Hand-Book to the Land Charters, and Other Saxonic Documents* (Oxford, 1888); A. S. Napier and W. H. Stevenson, *The Crawford Collection of Early Charters and Documents Now in the Bodleian Library* (Oxford, 1895); and F. E. Harmer, *Select English Historical Documents of the Sixth and Tenth Centuries* (Cambridge, 1914).

Studies and discussions of these texts are also plentiful, particularly J. K. Wallenberg, "Studies in Old Kentish Charters" in *Studia Neophilologica*, i (Uppsala, 1928); M. Förster, "Die Freilassungsurkunden des Bodwin-Evangeliars" in *A Grammatical Miscellany Offered to Otto Jespersen on his Seventieth Birthday* (Copenhagen-London, 1930), 77-79; E. Ekwall, "On Some Old English Charters" in *Festschrift für Karl Luick* (Marburg, 1925) 152-157; J. B. Grundy, "Index to Hampshire Charters and Place-names" in *Archaeological Journal*, lxxxv, 188-196; J. B. Grundy, "The Saxon Land-Charters of Hampshire" in *Archaeological Journal*, lxxxiv, 160-340; J. B. Grundy, "The Saxon Charters of Somerset" in *Somerset Archaeological and Natural History Society Publications*, lxxv, 65-96; Julia

Keays-Young, "The Eadmund-Aelfric Charters" in *Review of English Studies*, VI, 271-283; Helen M. Cam and O. G. S. Crawford, "The 'Hoga' of Cutteslowe" in *Antiquity*, IX, 96-98; and F. E. Harmer, "Anglo-Saxon Charters and the Historian" in *John Rylands Library Bulletin*, XXII, 339-367—an extremely valuable article.

The best and fullest treatments of wills and testaments of this period is Dorothy Whitelock, *Anglo-Saxon Wills* (Cambridge, 1930).

Index